ECSTASY AND THE DEMON

ECSTASY
AND THE DEMON

FEMINISM AND
NATIONALISM IN THE
DANCES OF MARY WIGMAN

Susan A. Manning

University of California Press
Berkeley · Los Angeles · London

University of California Press
Berkeley and Los Angeles, California

University of California Press, Ltd.
London, England

© 1993 by
The Regents of the University of California

Library of Congress Cataloging-in-Publication Data

Manning, Susan.
   Ecstasy and the demon : feminism and nationalism in the
dances of Mary Wigman / Susan A. Manning.
      p.   cm.
   Includes bibliographical references and index.
   ISBN 0-520-08193-5
   1. Wigman, Mary, 1886–1973.   2. Dancers—
Germany—Biography.   3. Choreographers—Germany—
Biography.   4. Modern dance—Social aspects—
Germany—History.   5. Modern dance—Political
aspects—Germany—History.   6. Feminist
theory.   I. Title.
GV1785.W5M36   1993
792.8′028′092—dc20   92-32232
[B]   CIP

Printed in the United States of America
9   8   7   6   5   4   3   2   1

For BGM and KRM

Contents

Illustrations

Preface

In this book I move from the discipline of dance studies into an interdisciplinary space bounded by ongoing dialogues on the history of the body and the sexual and national politics of artistic modernism. My purpose is twofold: to introduce dance scholars to methods of ideological critique and to introduce scholars from other fields to dance studies as a potential partner in cross-disciplinary inquiry.

When I began my research, my intent simply was to recover the dances of Mary Wigman, a performer and choreographer whose name had survived as an innovator of modern dance but whose works had led a shadowy existence between legend and oblivion. But as I pursued my research, it became clear that more than Wigman's dances demanded recovery and that to account for what I had found required revising the story of twentieth-century dance and culture. It was at this point that I determined to address a broader readership than just dance scholars, for Mary Wigman's career seemed to have implications for cross-disciplinary conversations that I could not fathom alone. My intent is to engage nonspecialists along with dance scholars in continuing the inquiries initiated here.

As soon as I entered the Mary Wigman Archive at the Academy of Arts in West Berlin, it became clear why the secondary literature glossed over the specifics of her choreographic career. For the sheaves of programs bearing the imprimatur of the National Socialist Cultural Ministry belied the common notion that her career had been curtailed under the Third Reich. It became evident that before Wigman's death in 1973 most commentators had echoed her postwar memoirs, which claimed that the Nazis had branded her a "degenerate artist." Quite simply, she seemed too innovative a dancer and choreographer for commentators to doubt her story.

Fortunately for me, I was not the first scholar to plumb the archive she had bequeathed to the Academy of Arts. Hedwig Müller already had begun researching a biography, and in 1986 she published *Mary Wigman: Leben und Werk der grossen Tänzerin*, the first study to reveal the complexity of the choreographer's relationship with National Socialism. Writing with utmost tact, Müller demonstrates how Wigman's memoirs, although not wholly false, clearly distorted her situation under the Third Reich. For even though after 1936 she fell out of favor with Joseph Goebbels, Hitler's cultural minister, she retained her status as the figurehead of German dance. In contrast to other artists labeled "degenerate," neither her life nor her livelihood was ever endangered. Müller explains Wigman's entanglement with fascism as a result of opportunism, heartfelt patriotism, a love affair with a highly placed Nazi official, and a desire to pursue her artistic vision at whatever cost.

That Hedwig Müller had written Wigman's biography freed me to write a narrative of her choreographic career. Yet as I pieced together the surviving evidence of her works, it became clear that the movement of *Ausdruckstanz* (dance of expression), as German modern dance was called, also deserved recovery and demanded reconsideration. For not only Wigman but also many of her colleagues collaborated with the National Socialists. In the other arts, most of the leading practitioners before 1933 either emigrated or withdrew into an "inner emigration" after 1933, but in *Ausdruckstanz* many of the leaders before 1933 later struck up an alliance with the National Socialists. And yet during the twenties Wigman and her colleagues were widely considered as innovative in their field as Kurt Weill and Bertolt Brecht were considered in theirs, to name only two of the legendary (and legion) artists who established their early reputations during the Weimar years. In fact, many of the interdisciplinary surveys of the arts during the Weimar era—from Peter Gay's *Weimar Culture* (1968) to John Willett's *Art and Politics in the Weimar Period* (1978) to Stephanie Barron's *"Degenerate Art": The Fate of the Avant-Garde in Nazi Germany* (1991)—leave out modern dance altogether. It is not difficult to understand why, given that *Ausdruckstanz* undermines the master-narrative of a sharp break between Weimar and Nazi culture.

Until recently, the chronicles of American modern dance also left out the preexistent tradition of *Ausdruckstanz*. In the early thirties Wigman undertook three tours of the United States and created such a sensation that her impresario, Sol Hurok, subsidized the founding of a New York branch of the Mary Wigman School, later renamed the Hanya Holm Studio. However, as American modern dance came into its own over the subsequent decade, its chroniclers constructed an artistic heritage based on native sources. Mythologizing the Americanness of American modern dance, the postwar annals nearly erased the precedent of the German dancer and her colleagues.

My research has led me to question the historiography not only of Weimar culture and American modern dance but also of dance modernism. In the standard literature, twentieth-century choreographers vie to realize the modernist ideal of dance reduced to its essential medium, "the configuration of motion in space," in the words of André Levinson. But to position Wigman in a parade of modernists advancing the formal values of pure dance does not answer the question of why she and so many of her colleagues collaborated with National Socialism. Nor does it answer the question of why American modern dancers became entangled in nationalist agendas certainly less destructive than those of their German counterparts but equally worthy of examination.

Presenting an alternative to the parade-of-modernists approach to dance history, I locate Wigman's dances at a convergence between feminism and nationalism. This is where my argument may become hard to take, for just as surely as Wigman's dances can be interpreted in nationalist terms, so can they be interpreted in feminist terms. In the most basic sense, I call her dances feminist because they subverted the eroticization of the female performer, and nationalist because they projected an essentialized national identity, a mystical aura of Germanness. Under the Third Reich, these dimensions of her practice became complicated in ways that paradoxically supported and undermined fascist aesthetics.

Also troubling is the relevance of my definitions of feminism and nationalism to the works of American modern dancers. Like Wigman's dances, the dances of Isadora Duncan and Martha Graham challenged the voyeurism of the male spectator and staged their own and their female spectators' desires for self-authorship. And just as Wigman danced the Germanic Soul, so Duncan and Graham danced the American Self. Although my focus remains on Wigman, my argument brings in Duncan as a counterexample and as a reminder that the German dancer cannot be assessed separately from her American counterparts and that early modern dance as a whole deserves closer scrutiny.

In writing this book, I faced the problem of how to integrate my reconstructions of Wigman's dances with the several inquiries provoked by my research. For my considerations of *Ausdruckstanz*, American modern dance, and dance modernism threatened to generate book-length studies of their own. To contain the inquiry, I have surrounded my reconstructions with three frames. Thus the opening pursues a critique of the standard literature on twentieth-century dance and suggests an alternate approach that reads early modern dance in ideological terms. Then follows, intercut with my reconstructions, a history of *Ausdruckstanz* that attempts to answer the question of why so many modern dancers collaborated with the National Socialists. At the end comes a revisionary look at American modern dance in the thirties.

The decision to broaden my readership posed another problem: how to address readers from a variety of disciplines—theater, literature, history, art history, feminist theory—while citing, building on, and quarreling with a dance history bibliography that many of my intended readers may not have realized existed in the first place. It seemed the only way around this dilemma was to ask my readers to meet me halfway. For I alone cannot write Mary Wigman's story into the myriad cross-disciplinary inquiries that resonate with, but remain unaware of, the complexities of her situation as an artist and woman in twentieth-century Germany.

Acknowledgments

For sharing their memories of Mary Wigman with me, I thank Walter Sorell, Jean Weidt, Hanya Holm, Lilian Espenak, Tina Flade, Truda Kaschmann, Fé Alf, Louise Kloepper, Erika Thimey, Pola Nirenska, Lotte Goslar, Shirlee Dodge, Margrit Bassow, Isa Partsch-Bergsohn, Til Thiele, Helmut Gottschild, Gerhard Bohner, and Susanne Linke. Collectively, they portrayed the larger-than-life quality of their mentor and associate. That their portrait becomes subsumed by my inquiry reflects not on their powers of eloquence but rather on the necessity of my desire to write Wigman's story from a point of view other than discipleship. For supporting my efforts to do so, I owe a special debt to her niece and executor, Marlies Wiegmann Heinemann.

For assisting my labors and travels in Germany, I thank Dirk Scheper and Hannelore Erlekamm at the Academy of Arts in West Berlin, Kurt Peters and especially Frank-Manuel Peter at the Deutsches Tanzarchiv Köln, the late Kurt Petermann at the former Akademie der Künste der DDR, Gunhild Oberzaucher-Schüller at the Institut für Musiktheater in Bayreuth, and the staffs of the Deutsches Theatermuseum in Munich and the Bundesfilmarchiv in Koblenz. My scholarly indebtedness to Hedwig Müller is evident from my text; my appreciation of her friendship I acknowledge here.

The network of dance scholars has supported this project since its inception. Selma Jeanne Cohen, Deborah Jowitt, and Marcia Siegel each managed to wade through my dissertation and find a book submerged within its prose. Lynn Garafola, Susan Foster, Mark Franko, and Cynthia Novack commented on earlier and later drafts, and their specific criticisms all have found their way into the final version. Ann Daly offered a productive critique of my first attempt to borrow terminology from feminist theory, and Heidi Gilpin provided an encouraging reading as the end approached.

Marion Kant, Anna Markard, Selma Odom, and Valerie Preston-Dunlop all generously answered queries regarding their areas of expertise.

This book began as a dissertation advised by Martin Meisel, Professor of English and Comparative Literature at Columbia University. In innumerable ways, his presence sustained me in an academic milieu that seemed indifferent to my endeavors. His faith allowed me to find a voice with which to counter the institutional voice so aptly summarized by one prominent member of the faculty: "Writing about dance? In an English department!"

The English department at Northwestern University, where the boundaries of literary studies are permeable in many directions, has proven a wonderfully congenial home for a maverick dance and theater scholar. Thanks to Joe Roach and Susan Lee, the Department of Theatre and Program in Dance has become a second home. Many colleagues from several departments have read and commented on the manuscript. For helping me find my way to a diversity of readers, I thank Chris Herbert, Martin Mueller, Paul Breslin, Jules Law, Sharon Achinstein, Helen Deutsch, Wendy Wall, and Julia Stern (English); Joe Roach (now at New York University), Lynne Blom, Sandra Richards, and especially Tracy Davis (Theatre); Johannes Birringer (Performance Studies); Michael Leja and Karl Werckmeister (Art History); Rainer Rumold (German); Carolyn Dean (now at Brown University), Peter Hayes, and Laura Hein (History). Friends outside the academy—Melissa Benson, Karin Miller-Lewis, Isa Van Eeghen—have contributed their insights as well.

Funding for this project has come from the German Academic Exchange Service, the Lane Cooper Foundation, the Whiting Foundation, and the Mellon Foundation. At Northwestern the Center for Interdisciplinary Research in the Arts and the Office for Sponsored Research provided crucial support at the final moment. For helping me negotiate the endless end, I thank two superb research assistants, Ulrike Weber and John Paluch. And without the first-rate child care and housekeeping skills of Felicia Azor, this book could not have been written in the first place.

This book is dedicated to my parents, Kent Roger Manning and Barbara Groenke Manning, each of whom contributed to its making in a distinct way. For it was my father's German-Jewish roots that in one sense prompted the inquiry, and it was my mother's example that encouraged me to pursue what at first seemed a very private passion.

Yet my greatest thanks are reserved for my husband, Doug Doetsch, who has enabled me beyond measure.

Introduction

Long before I had read feminist theory, it was clear to me that early modern dance comprised a feminist practice. Pioneered by women, early modern dance rejected the codified movement vocabulary of ballet, and this move undermined the representational system associated with the nineteenth-century ballerina. Fashioning idiosyncratic movement styles, early modern dancers defied the sexual division of labor that had defined choreography as a male task and performance as a female task. Borrowing techniques from physical culture and popular entertainment and relying on improvisation as a fundamental working method, early modern dancers eschewed the virtuosity and opera-house spectacle that had framed the ballerina as sylph or swan.

Now that I have read feminist theory, I would say that nineteenth-century ballet provided a textbook demonstration of the male gaze and that early modern dance introduced the possibility of female spectatorship. For the choreographic conventions of nineteenth-century ballet positioned the male spectator as a voyeur, leaving the female spectator only with the desire to be desired. In contrast, the choreographic conventions of early modern dance foreclosed the spectatorial position of the voyeur, granting the female spectator the agency to desire.[1]

Long before I had encountered the term "ideological critique," it was clear to me that early modern dance comprised a nationalist practice as well as a feminist practice. For in opposition to the internationalized vocabulary of ballet, early modern dancers fashioned representational frames that spectators read as intrinsically German or American. But it was Benedict Anderson's definition of nationalism as an "imagined community" that helped me understand how danced projections of Germanness or Americanness could articulate imagined connections between individual bodies and the collective body of the nation.[2]

1

Borrowing the concepts of female spectatorship and the "imagined community," I position early modern dance at a convergence between feminism and nationalism. However, the convergence is not as simple as my preliminary definition suggests. For within the practice of early modern dance, reinventions of the male gaze coexisted with its subversion, and claims of universality coexisted with reliance on essentialized national identities. Moreover, the dramatization of feminism and nationalism in the cultural practice of early modern dance happened in specific historical contexts, and these contexts inflected the convergence in varying ways. In this book I offer a case study of how feminism and nationalism collided in the works of one early modern dancer, Mary Wigman.

In agreement with other commentators, I define Wigman's choreographic modernism in terms of her project to make dance an autonomous language, a project abbreviated by the term "absolute dance." I disagree with other commentators, however, in not seeing her choreographic project as fixed over time. Rather, my reconstructions of selected works from the teens through the fifties argue that her modernism significantly shifted over the course of her career in response to changing working conditions and sociopolitical contexts.

Mary Wigman made her choreographic debut in 1914, and over the next five decades she created more than two hundred dances. From Monte Verita, an artists' colony in the Swiss Alps where she spent the years of World War I; to Dresden, where she based her school and touring company in the twenties and thirties; to Leipzig, where she taught and choreographed through the period of Soviet occupation; to West Berlin, where she premiered her last work in 1961, just months after the building of the Berlin Wall: Mary Wigman changed the venue and focus of her work in dramatic ways over the course of her long career. In my narrative, her responses to diverse working situations determine the shifts in her stagings of absolute dance.

As I will argue, her dances from 1914 through the late twenties established a mode of modernism that can be read as feminist *and* nationalist. Around 1930 her choreographic career entered a period of crisis and transition, and once the National Socialists came to power in 1933, her modernist mode subtly transmuted under the sway of fascist aesthetics. Strikingly, her dances created under the Third Reich not only supported the new status quo but also functioned resistively by recalling and revising the feminist and nationalist dimensions of her Weimar works. Ironically enough, exactly those dimensions disappeared in her postwar dances, ironically because the dances created after 1945 attempted to recover the modernist mode of her dances created before 1933.

From the teens through the mid-twenties, Wigman's solos challenged the eroticization of the female performer and the voyeurism of the male spectator. At the same time, her solos projected a mystical aura of Germanness. Thus I read her solos as both feminist and nationalist. During this same period, her all-female dance group dramatized a utopia that reconciled the choreographer's authority with her dancers' autonomy. Like her solos, her group dances can be read in both feminist and nationalist terms. For the utopia dramatized by her ensemble allowed female spectators to imagine a cultural space where their needs for affiliation and self-realization did not conflict and allowed German spectators of either gender to imagine a cultural space where the competing visions of the left and the right did not conflict.

In 1928 financial difficulties forced Wigman to disband her all-female ensemble. As she refocused her energies on solo choreography and experimented with alternative formats for group choreography, her representational strategies shifted in ways that anticipated, but did not determine, the reconfiguration of her practice under the Third Reich. What did determine her choreographic transition to fascism was the availability of subsidy from Goebbels's Cultural Ministry. In works commissioned for National Socialist dance festivals in 1934 and 1935, she consolidated a format for group choreography that substituted a representation of the *Volksgemeinschaft* (folk,—i.e., Aryan—community) for the earlier community of women dancers.

Wigman's embrace of a fascist aesthetic culminated with her contribution to the opening-night spectacle for the 1936 Berlin Olympic Games. *Olympic Youth* explicitly celebrated Olympic symbolism and implicitly glorified the presence of the Führer, who reviewed the spectacle from the stands. The utopian reconciliation of authority and autonomy evident in earlier works gave way to the dystopian counterpoint between the leader and the mass. It is this shift—and Wigman's choreographic realization of the *Führerprinzip* (leadership principle)—that I term fascist.

After 1936, Wigman became aware of a dissonance between her

vision of German dance and the program of the Cultural Ministry. Denied direct subsidy and thus unable to pursue group projects, she choreographed and toured solos under the rubric "The Most Beautiful Dances." These solos outwardly conformed to Goebbels's redefinition of dance as the display of "beautiful women's bodies."[3] At the same time, her new solos inwardly mused on the role of the individual artist within the *Volksgemeinschaft*. Thus Wigman's choreographic strategies shifted in ways that can be read as both fascist *and* resistive. Her late solos not only celebrated the Germanic but also opposed her vision of the Germanic to the National Socialist conception of the nation. Moreover, her late solos not only assented to Goebbels's redefinition of dancer as Woman but also dramatized Woman as an implicit comment on the masculinist ethos of the Third Reich.

Wigman retired from the stage in 1942, and over the next two decades she staged only group works. As a ballet boom engulfed the German stage, her group dances aspired to an internationalized modernism, which rigidified her staging of gender. Attempting to recall the modernism of her Weimar dances, her late group dances bracketed her career under the Third Reich. Like her memoirs, her postwar dances functioned as a denial of her collaboration with National Socialism.

To tell this story about Wigman's dances is to challenge the common periodization of German cultural history. Quite simply, the pattern of Wigman's career does not fit the master-narratives of a transition from expressionism to the "new objectivity" in the mid-twenties, the persecution of the avant-garde after 1933, or the de-Nazification of the arts after 1945. This is not to say that the careers of all other German artists do follow these master-narratives but rather that Wigman's career exposes the insufficiencies of the common periodization with particular clarity. Her career and the history of German modern dance also point up the limitations of approaches to interdisciplinary study that privilege a paradigm derived from one art, apply it blankly to other arts, and leave out arts that do not fit the paradigm. For this as well as other reasons, *Ausdruckstanz* is left out again and again in surveys of Weimar culture. Explicitly calling for the inclusion of dance history within cultural history, I implicitly argue for an interdisciplinary approach that attends to divergences as well as convergences between the arts.

In a paradigm derived from art history and often applied to theater, Weimar modernism divides between a pre-1924 period of expressionism and a post-1924 period of the "new objectivity" (*Neue Sachlichkeit*) or Epic Theater.[4] Contrary to this division, Wigman's dances bore a family resemblance to expressionism from the early twenties at least through the early thirties and, arguably, through the remainder of her choreographic career. Indeed, her career provides a case study for the seemingly antithetical arguments over the politics of expressionism that engaged German émigrés during the thirties. Had contenders in the "expressionist debate" turned their attention to dance, Georg Lukács could well have cited her works commissioned by the National Socialists as proof of the expressionist coloring of fascist culture, at least through the mid-thirties. And Ernst Bloch could well have appropriated her oeuvre as counterevidence for his contention that the decentering effects of expressionism work against any status quo.[5]

Wigman's career also counters the master-narrative of a sharp break between Weimar and Nazi culture. Among the more recent recitations of this narrative was the 1991 exhibition "'Degenerate Art,'" which featured a reconstruction of the 1937 exhibition in Munich bearing the same title. The museum show left the impression that under the Third Reich nearly the entirety of the Weimar avant-garde was censored or silenced. Although the catalog noted the gestures of support for National Socialism made by Emil Nolde, Ernst Barlach, Erich Heckel, and Mies van der Rohe,[6] the arrangement of the show suggested that just as the Nazis had banned the paintings by modern masters now regrouped on the museum walls so too had they labeled the Weimar film, literature, and music on display as "degenerate." Significantly, the multimedia show excluded Weimar dance. Had *Ausdruckstanz* been included, then the counternarrative of collaboration between modern artists and National Socialists noted in the catalog would have intruded more overtly into the exhibition hall. For Wigman was not alone in striking up an alliance with the fascist regime. Many of her colleagues did as well, and only recently have dancers and scholars begun to acknowledge this fact.

The facts include these: not only did Mary Wigman participate in the 1934 and 1935 German Dance Festivals organized by Goebbels's Cultural Ministry but so too did Rudolf Laban, Yvonne

Georgi, Gret Palucca, Harald Kreutzberg, Dorothee Günther, Maja Lex, Valeria Kratina, Herta Feist, Lizzie Maudrik, Helga Swedlund, Jens Keith, Lotte Wernicke, and Lola Rogge—all dancers and choreographers who had established reputations during the Weimar period. In contrast to the other arts, where the majority of leading artists before 1933 either emigrated or withdrew into an "inner emigration," only a minority of the leading choreographers before 1933 emigrated—notably Kurt Jooss, Jean Weidt, Valeska Gert, and Rudolf Laban, after he had fallen from Goebbels's grace. As much continuity as discontinuity marked the passage of *Ausdruckstanz* from Weimar to the Third Reich.

Finally, Wigman's career and the history of *Ausdruckstanz* challenge a common perception that 1945 marked nearly as decisive a break in the German arts as 1933. According to a paradigm derived from dramatic production, after the fall of the Third Reich the performing arts had to start from "point zero," *Stunde Null.* On 1 September 1944 the Cultural Ministry officially closed all theaters. Once production activity resumed after the war, first in an occupied Germany and then in a divided Germany, the theater drew its leadership from the ranks and the example of artists who had been exiled. Most influential of all was Bertolt Brecht. Building on the precedent of exile theater, the postwar theater distanced itself from National Socialism.[7]

Once again, were dance history integrated into cultural history, a paradigm predicated on dramatic production necessarily would undergo revision. For just as German dance experienced more continuity than did the other arts over the decisive rupture of 1933, so too did dance evidence more continuity than did other spheres of cultural life over the rupture of 1945. The only other art form experiencing a comparable passage was film, and few film historians have gone as far as Horst Koegler, a leading German dance critic, when he writes: "It is not without amazement that we note how uninterrupted was the passage of German dance from dictatorship to democracy. After 1945 German dance was dominated essentially by the same personalities who had brought it to a certain prominence before 1945."[8] As evidence for the continuity of leadership, Koegler cites Mary Wigman, Gret Palucca, Harald Kreutzberg, Tatjana Gsovsky, Helga Swedlund, Jens Keith, Alexander von Swaine, Lisa Czobel, and Dore Hoyer.

Why does German dance follow a trajectory so divergent from the common periodization of German cultural history? What can explain the alliance of so many German modern dancers with the fascist regime? And what can account for the continuity of leadership in dance "from dictatorship to democracy"? I would suggest that at least a partial explanation lies in the particular way that German dance worked out the relations between modernism, the avant-garde, and mass culture. And so, to provide a context for my reconstructions of Wigman's dances, I sketch a history of German dance that attends precisely to those relations.

My history is not comprehensive. That is, it focuses on *Ausdruckstanz*, the movement led by Wigman and Laban and practiced by their many followers in Germany. I do not take up the question of *Ausdruckstanz* as it developed in other Central European cultural centers, nor do I survey the full range of Weimar dance—from ballet reform efforts within the opera house to Oskar Schlemmer's dance and theater experiments at the Bauhaus to the revue dancing popularized by the Tiller Girls to the choreographed crowds in Max Reinhardt's productions and in films such as Fritz Lang's *Metropolis*. My focus on *Ausdruckstanz* defines the movement precisely as its practitioners did—as a loose alliance of dancers who worked outside preexistent institutions and created their own networks around private studios and concert performances.

So defined, *Ausdruckstanz* blurs the distinction between modernism and the historical avant-garde posited by Peter Bürger in his *Theory of the Avant-Garde* (1984).[9] According to Bürger, modernists focused on creating an autonomous and self-reflexive art, in contrast to the avant-gardists, who focused on breaking down the barriers between art and life. However apt a characterization of visual art during the period, Bürger's distinction simply does not hold for *Ausdruckstanz*. For Wigman, Laban, and their many followers endeavored to conceptualize dance as an autonomous language *and* to reintegrate the dancer's experience of movement into everyday life. Although Wigman was more commonly associated with the modernist project of conceptualizing dance as an autonomous language (absolute dance) and Laban with the avant-gardist or populist project of reintegrating dance into everyday life, I argue that both worked along a continuum between the two projects and that this continuum defined *Ausdruckstanz*.

This defining continuum involved a paradoxical relationship to mass culture that further blurs Bürger's distinction between modernism's antagonistic stance toward mass culture and the historical avant-garde's desire to reconnect with mass culture. For German modern dancers clearly differentiated dance as art from dance as exercise, yet at the same time they envisioned dance as a new form of physical culture. It was the resolution of this paradoxical relationship to mass culture under the Third Reich that accounts for the relatively unbroken continuity of German dance over the years 1933 and 1945.

During the twenties, *Ausdruckstanz* drew its patronage from amateur students devoted to *Tanz-Gymnastik* (dance gymnastics), as popular in Germany then as aerobics were in the United States during the eighties. This popularity meant that both the modernist and avant-gardist projects of *Ausdruckstanz* were tied to the mass cultural interest in physical culture and sport. Indeed, the improvisational methods of *Ausdruckstanz* blurred the distinction between professional and amateur dance, for concert dancers deployed the same methods as amateur devotees of *Tanz-Gymnastik*. Amateur students not only flocked to the private studios opened by Wigman, Laban, and their followers but also provided a ready audience for the dancers and dance groups that toured from city to city.

By the late twenties, however, the provocative tensions underlying Weimar dance threatened to come undone. As an oversupply of trained dancers encountered an undersupply of new students, dancers began to look elsewhere for patronage and came up with radically different sources. Some dancers managed to find positions in opera houses, which meant that they had to modify the improvisational techniques of *Ausdruckstanz* and acquire ballet training. This solution negated the avant-gardist project of breaking down the barriers between art and life. Other dancers applied to churches, political parties, and labor unions to offer their services as instructors in organized leisure activities, which often meant that they had to de-emphasize the artistic and develop the gymnastic components of *Tanz-Gymnastik*. This solution negated the modernist project of framing dance as an autonomous language. The onset of economic depression only reinforced the economic straits of many dancers and intensified their search for new forms of patronage.

When the National Socialists came to power in 1933, they supplied the new institutional support, in effect substituting the patronage of the state for the patronage of amateur students. As they did for the country as a whole, the National Socialists put the dancers back to work—in the opera house, in mass spectacles, in physical education programs, and in leisure organizations. Responsibility for reorganizing German dance was divided between Goebbels's Cultural Ministry, which credentialed professional dancers, and Alfred Rosenberg's Fighting League for German Culture, which oversaw a massive physical education program. Significantly, this bureaucratic compartmentalization, and the resulting segregation of stage dance from physical culture, unraveled the paradoxes that had defined Weimar dance. In effect, National Socialist patronage and policy rigidified the modernist project of *Ausdruckstanz* while supplanting the avant-gardist project with a compulsory physical education program.

The resolution to the crisis of Weimar dance effected by National Socialism remained in place during the postwar period. Or, more accurately, dance in the Federal Republic and in the Democratic Republic worked out the implications of National Socialist policy and practice in different ways. In both East and West Germany dance remained centered in the opera house, where its modernist project was redefined more in terms of ballet than in terms of *Ausdruckstanz*. *Ausdruckstanz* persisted in both Germanies, however, in the West as a marginalized practice through the fifties and sixties that resurfaced in a movement called *Tanztheater* (dance theater) and in the East as an officially sanctioned component of a stylistic fusion with ballet that also went by the name of *Tanztheater*. My narrative of German dance ends with the event of reunification and speculates on the future of dance after the fall of the Berlin Wall.

As a coda to my argument, I turn to Wigman's reception in the United States and challenge the way dance critics have constructed the Americanness of modern dance. In most of the literature, a consensus adopted by choreographers associated with the Bennington Festival from 1934 to 1939—Martha Graham, Doris Humphrey and Charles Weidman, and Hanya Holm—defines the movement of American modern dance. This consensus privileges codified movement vocabularies over improvisation, and formal experimentation and innovation over social engagement. However, in tracing the reception of Wigman in the United States and the career of her most well known disciple, Hanya Holm, I have realized the extent to which advocacy of the Bennington consensus has obscured a contest among American modern dancers in the early thirties, before the future direction of the movement had consolidated.

In that contest, leftist dancers associated with the journal *New Theatre* proposed an alternative vision of modern dance to that advocated by the dancers associated with Bennington. In the vision articulated in the pages of *New Theatre,* the professionalization of modern dance was less crucial than its politicization. The leftist dancers turned to the Popular Front, unions, German-Jewish leisure organizations, and the Federal Dance Project for support. But none of these potential patrons proved long-lived, and by the late thirties the politically engaged dancers either came to terms with the patronage system consolidated by the Bennington choreographers—the college dance department and the New York studio system—or stopped working. To recover the contest between the Bennington choreographers and the leftist dancers is to recover as well the short-lived controversy over Wigman's fascism that flared in the pages of *New Theatre* before it ceased publication in 1937.

In writing Wigman's choreographic career and the history of *Ausdruckstanz* into German cultural history and revising the chronicle of American modern dance, I introduce methods not usually found in dance studies. These methods can be grouped under the rubric "ideological critique," a general term for approaches that understand art as a social production rather than as a set of transcendent values. In other disciplines within the humanities, ideological critique has become the new establishment. But in dance studies, aesthetic appreciation still reigns as the dominant paradigm, creating an asymmetry between disciplines that reflects the elusive nature of dance texts. For until recently, the issue for dance studies has been not to revise the canon but rather to envision a canon in the first place.[10]

My interest in ideological critique arises partly from intellectual predilections and partly from practical considerations. With the exception of the surviving film clips of Wigman dancing, the archival fragments synthesized in my reconstructions do not allow for sustained movement description, a methodology that has supported the disciplinary development of dance studies. Unable to pursue extended movement analysis, I had to find alternative methods for analyzing and interpreting Wigman's dances. For my purposes, Raymond Williams's call for a "sociology of culture," the concepts of the male gaze and female spectatorship as developed by feminist theory, and Benedict Anderson's definition of nationalism as an "imagined community" proved useful.[11]

However, although I have borrowed terms from feminist theory and cultural studies, my argument remains grounded in the well-established method of performance reconstruction. Piecing together the archival fragments of Wigman's dances, I work much like a traditional dance historian—collating the surviving evidence of film clips, choreographic notes, photographs, programs, reviews, and interviews with former students and members of her company. But when it comes to interpreting the evidence, I work more like a literary critic than like a traditional dance historian.

Following the broad outlines of reader-response criticism and performance approaches to dramatic scripts, I construct Wigman's dances as structures for the interaction of performer and spectator. In my constructions, context becomes a constitutive element of text, as I imagine the shifting expectations of Wigman's audiences from the teens through the fifties. From this I imagine the varying ways her choreography positioned the spectator over time. In so doing I cannot separate my own responses to the evidence from my imagination of her audiences' reactions. Leafing through reams of photographs, comparing film clips, I see how Wigman's defiance of the male gaze in the twenties gave way to an acceptance of the gaze in the thirties. Reviewers' comments from the thirties about the new "femininity" apparent in her works support my perceptions. Similarly, piecing together her group dances from the twenties and thirties, I see a shift in her staging of an "imagined community," from a utopian reconciliation of authority and autonomy to a dystopian counterpoint between the leader and the mass. Again, reviewers' comments inform and confirm my readings. In the end, my theorization of the spectator in Wigman's dances plays between her contemporaries' recorded responses and my own.

This play potentially conflates the gaze of the contemporary spectator as conceived in the singular, the gaze of the spectator as gendered and as nationalized, and the retrospective gaze of the historian. To avoid this slippage, I have made explicit the differences between these spectatorial positions. The differences are most evident in my reconstructions of Wigman's dances from 1930 to 1942, which reveal the choreographer's own retrospective view denying collaboration with the National Socialists contradicting the spectatorial positions glimpsed through other sources.

To colleagues in other fields, this working method may appear risky, if not precarious. As one scholar of Victorian literature exclaimed, "It's as if all I had to go on were seven reviews in literary journals and not the volume of poetry Tennyson published! Doesn't that render the enterprise of dance research futile?" His question rendered me speechless.

In retrospect, I can provide two rejoinders. The first challenges the presumed stability of the New Critical text. Has not poststructural theory suggested the ultimate instability and variability of all texts? From this perspective, dance in particular and performance in general mark one end of a continuum along which all textual modes are to some degree unstable. Indeed, although dance studies always remained marginal within the New Critical academy, the discipline has the potential to become more central within the poststructural academy.

My second rejoinder defends the method of performance reconstruction. The simple fact is that the dance scholar never has the luxury of starting from a New Critical text, from a text that appears complete and self-sufficient. The dance scholar has no choice except to pursue the elusive and uncertain text of performance. An event bound in space and time, a performance can be read only through its traces—on the page, in memory, on film, in the archive. Each of these traces marks, indeed distorts, the event of performance, and so the scholar pursues what remains elusive as if moving through an endless series of distorting reflections.[12] But this pursuit leaves its own sort of illumination, and that illumination is what the scholar records, in effect penning a journal of the process of inquiry.

The dancer or scholar committed to recovering dance texts may proceed in one of two ways. Or, more accurately, the reconstructor may favor one of the opposing ends of a single continuum. At one end of the continuum, the researcher posits a coherent, originating text—for instance, the opening-night performance—and affirms that although one cannot recover that text fully, a close approximation is possible. This was the procedure followed by Millicent Hodson in her brilliant reconstruction of Nijinsky's *Le sacre du printemps* for the Joffrey Ballet (1987), based on visual evidence and choreographic notations in the musical score.[13] At the other end of the continuum, the dancer or scholar emphasizes that reconstruction necessarily involves interpretation and highlights the fact and process of that interpretation. Susanne Linke followed this procedure in her powerful reconstruction, based on a film record, of Dore Hoyer's *Affectos Humanos* (1987). Unlike Hoyer, who followed the convention of offstage costume changes, Linke put on and changed costumes in full view of the audience, as if to underscore the disjunction between her own stage persona and her assumed persona. (Like Linke, Hoyer was a student of Mary Wigman, and the performances of *Affectos Humanos* on film and on stage have inflected my imagining of Wigman's dancing.)[14]

My study tends more toward the end of the continuum represented by Linke than toward the end represented by Hodson, for I remain aware of how my interpretive stance has shaped my inquiry. One of the challenges (and frustrations) of dance scholarship is that the reader often has no independent access to the texts under discussion and must rely on the author's descriptions. In an effort to counteract this effect, I have attempted to reconstruct Wigman's dances with a certain transparency so that the reader has access to my evidence and can interpose alternative readings. I also have attempted to write multiple perspectives into my reconstructions, differentiating my retrospective view as a historian from the contemporary voices of Wigman herself, her critics, and her disciples. Nonetheless, the reconstructions remain my own constructions. Another scholar could return to the archives with a different set of agendas and recover a quite different, though no more plausible, account of Wigman's career.[15]

Together with this introduction, the next chapter lays the groundwork for my reconsideration of Wigman's career. Titled "Ideology and Absolute Dance," that first chapter challenges the formalist historiography of dance modernism and initiates an ideological critique through a highly selective rereading of the practice of Western theater dance prior to Wigman's choreographic debut in 1914. Chapter two, "*Gestalt im Raum*," then begins the narrative of Wigman's career, focusing on her works created on Monte Verita, an artists' colony in the Swiss Alps where she spent the years of the First World War in voluntary exile. Chapter three, "Mask and *Gemeinschaft*," considers her major group dances and selected solos from the twenties, once she had returned to Germany and become a leading representative of *Ausdruckstanz*. Her choreographic transition from the twenties to the thirties makes up chapter four, "From Modernism to Fascism," and chapter five, "Body Politic," dramatizes the complexities of her changing choreographic response to fascism.

The final two chapters then examine her legacy in Germany and the United States. In one sense, the last two chapters circle back to the first chapter, for in considering Wigman's influence and reception, chapters six and seven contextualize the opening review of the literature. Chapter six, "From *Ausdruckstanz* to *Tanztheater*," traces the continuities and discontinuities between the old and the new German modern dance and enters the debate among German critics over the relation of *Ausdruckstanz* to National Socialism. Chapter seven, "Mary Wigman and American Dance," follows Wigman's impact within the arena of American dance at mid-century and recovers the contest between the Bennington choreographers and the leftist dancers that informed her reception. The last chapter circles back to the first chapter in another way as well, for it resumes a discussion initiated in the opening chapter on how critics and dancers constructed and mythologized the Americanness of modern dance.

1

Ideology and Absolute Dance

On 11 February 1914 Mary Wigman made her choreographic debut in Munich. Twenty-seven years old, she had begun her formal
dance training three and a half years earlier at Emile Jaques-
Dalcroze's institute at Hellerau. Since the previous summer she had
apprenticed herself to Rudolf Laban, and it was now on a program
at the Laban School that she made her debut. She premiered two
solos, *Witch Dance I* and *Lento*, neither set to music. Photographs
suggest that Wigman cast the two dances in contrasting modes. In
Lento (fig. 1) the camera captures her in repose, her body curved
in a languid serpentine and costumed in a torso-hugging sheath;
in *Witch Dance I* (fig. 2) the camera captures her in the midst of
action, her body hurtling through the air and costumed in a billow-
ing cape. It is as if the dancer first becomes the visual equivalent to
the musical quality of "lento" and then becomes the kinetic embodiment of the quality of the demonic.

The one extant review, by Rudolf von Delius, provides no further descriptive details. In fact, Delius mentions neither solo by
name, and yet his assessment of Wigman sets the terms for her
critical celebration as an exponent of absolute dance. In his account,
Wigman's dancing culminates a process set in motion by Isadora
Duncan and realizes the modernist ideal of an art that refers solely
to its own medium and condition. This achievement involves a
double breakthrough: first, freeing dance from its dependence on
the accompaniment of music and, second, freeing dance from its
reliance on the referent of costume. Delius writes:

> The inner logic with which the new dance approaches its goal is as-
> tounding. Fifteen years ago Isadora Duncan set the program: free,
> natural movement after the model of the Greeks. . . . Then Mary
> Wiegmann from Hannover arrives onstage. [Not until 1918 did the
> dancer change the spelling of her last name.] And immediately we
> feel: the chain of development reaches its peak in her dancing. . . .

Fig. 1.   Mary Wigman in *Lento,* a solo included in her 1914 debut concert (courtesy of the Mary Wigman Archive)

The breakthrough to the elemental finally is achieved. Everything historical falls away as totally uninteresting. The person again stands alone in opposition to primal forces. . . . Finally dance becomes entirely self-sufficient, the pure art of bodily movement. . . . Dance has become a sovereign art. When it requires music, then it will command music, but only to serve its own purposes. The same goes for costume. . . . The costume no longer presents itself as an external get-up or as trimmings that one can change at will, but rather the

Fig. 2. Mary Wigman in the first version of *Witch Dance*, a solo included in her 1914 debut concert (courtesy of the Mary Wigman Archive)

costume becomes a part of the body-soul like eyes and hair. . . .There is no longer anything witty, interesting, virtuosic, or refined. No conformity, no masquerade, no theatrics.[1]

Strikingly, the Wigman literature since 1914 has deviated little from the broad outlines of Delius's analysis. Critics largely have agreed that Wigman's formal innovations focused the spectator's attention on what the choreographer defined as the essence of dance. Thus she choreographed dances to silence or to percussive accompaniment (although at times her solos were accompanied by piano scores from the classical, romantic, and modern repertory), highlighted the spatial dimension of movement, and rejected the referents of narrative and character as deployed in nineteenth-century ballet. In the Wigman literature, these are the formal innovations that have defined her choreographic modernism, her performance of absolute dance.

Despite this critical agreement, however, Wigman has occupied a contested place in the literature on twentieth-century dance. This is so because dance writers have functioned as critical advocates, and they all claim for their favored choreographer or choreographic school the most complete realization of absolute dance. In other words, critical disagreement has centered not on the modernist project of conceptualizing dance as an autonomous language but rather on which choreographer or choreographic school has come closest to realizing the ideal of self-reflexivity.

In this chapter, I first survey the Wigman literature in order to demonstrate how her seemingly contested place within dance modernism remains within the parameters of a historiography predicated on the teleology of absolute dance. I then initiate a break from the literature of absolute dance by rereading Wigman's 1914 choreographic debut in ideological terms.

THE MASTER-NARRATIVE OF
ABSOLUTE DANCE

In the historiography of twentieth-century dance, Mary Wigman figures as a fulfillment of the Zeitgeist, as a point of contention, as a footnote and an absence, and as a point of departure. German critics in the twenties hailed her as an embodiment of the spirit of the times, coining the term absolute dance to distinguish her achievement from that of her predecessors. In the thirties American critics debated her significance and divided into two camps: one faction commended her methods, the opposing faction castigated her influence. By the sixties and seventies, Wigman had nearly disappeared from the annals of twentieth-century dance. In the eighties she reappeared, as German critics celebrated her example as a point of departure for the new German dance theater (*Tanztheater*).

Yet however varied these positionings of Wigman appear, all are informed by a Greenbergian account of modernism.[2] In this account, twentieth-century dance traces a progressive evolution, breaking from the pictorialism integral to eighteenth- and nineteenth-century theater dance and then reenacting this break in successive approaches toward the ever-receding horizon of absolute dance. In the eighteenth and nineteenth centuries Western theater dance adhered to a mimetic ideal, aspiring to be "a living picture of the passions, manners, customs of all nations of the globe," in the words of Jean Georges Noverre (1760), the leading theoretician of the pictorial ballet.[3] In the early twentieth century the mimetic model gave way to an ideal of self-reflexivity, dance "devoted . . . to those characteristics which belong exclusively to dancing," "the configuration of motion in space," in the words of André Levinson (1925), a leading theoretician of dance modernism.[4]

From the first decades of the century until the present, critics have defined dance modernism as the break from pictorialism and have valued choreographers insofar as they interpret the ideal of self-reflexivity more rigorously than did their predecessors. However, although critics have agreed on the formal standard for assessing twentieth-century choreographers, they have disagreed on which choreographers measure up to the standard. Was it Isadora Duncan or Vaslav Nijinsky who rejected more decisively the codified vocabulary and narrative conventions of pictorial ballet? Was it Mary Wigman or Martha Graham who departed more profoundly from Duncan's and Nijinsky's reliance on music? Was it George Balanchine or Merce Cunningham who more cleanly divorced motion from emotion?

What critics have disputed is the genealogy of dance modernism. While celebrating modernism's formal break from pictorialism, they have constructed divergent genealogies, divided along generic lines, that is, ballet versus modern dance, as well as along national lines, such as German or European versus American dance. These genealogies serve as vehicles for critical advocacy, for as critics read dance modernism as a progressive evolution, they champion whichever choreographer or choreographic school they position at the endpoint of the succession. It is these divergent agendas of critical advocacy that explain the disparate positionings of Wigman within the historiography of twentieth-century dance.[5]

The German critic Fritz Böhme first grafted an account of Wigman's formal breakthrough to absolute dance onto a national and generic genealogy, the genealogy of German modern dance. In his book *Tanzkunst* (1926), Böhme traces how Wigman and her colleague Rudolf Laban achieved the ideal of absolute dance by presupposing and surpassing the achievements of German gymnastic reformers and dance soloists at the turn of the century. Although gymnastic reformers such as Emile Jaques-Dalcroze had systematized the movement discoveries of dance soloists such as the Wiesenthal sisters, the practice of both reformers and soloists remained tied to individual personalities and to music. Choreographing dances to silence, Wigman and Laban shifted attention away from the temporal dimension and toward the spatial and dynamic dimensions of movement. Recovering the connection between ecstasy and movement, Wigman and Laban shifted attention away from the personality of the dancer and toward the suprapersonal energies of the dance. These innovations achieved the ideal of absolute dance, dance "that speaks through movement alone."[6]

Premising his argument on a Hegelian view of history, Böhme constructs a German genealogy for the *Ausdruckstanz* practiced by Wigman and Laban. In Böhme's view, "every era has its necessary form," and *Ausdruckstanz* constituted the "necessary form" of the Weimar years, an embodiment of a new experience of life, a sense of a spiritual center amidst apparent flux and uncertainty.[7] In Böhme's genealogy, the form of *Ausdruckstanz* realized an "idea" (*Geist*) implicit in the philosophy of Novalis and Nietzsche, the idea of unity between the body and the spirit. However, not until the twenties were the conditions right for the realization of this idea, conditions prepared by the thinking of Freud, who uncovered the connection between the body and the unconscious, and Ludwig Klages, who proclaimed the intellect the antagonist of the soul. In other words, German philosophy prepared the way for the new dance form.[8]

This Hegelian notion of idea preceding art allowed Böhme to discount the possible influence of late nineteenth- and early twentieth-century ballet on the development of *Ausdruckstanz*. He mentions the "Russian ballet" from Petipa to Diaghilev only in passing, dismissing the Russian repertory as "graceful and technically-accomplished trifles with banal content."[9] He does suggest that after Noverre ballet entered a period of decline and that *Ausdruckstanz*, not the Russian ballet, reinvigorated Noverre's spirit of reform.

Writing as an American advocate of modern dance in the thirties, John Martin simplified and recast Böhme's formal analysis of Wigman's achievement.[10] Echoing the German critic, Martin considered the choreographer's concretization of space essential to her innovation of absolute dance. In his 1939 volume, *Introduction to the Dance*, he explains:

> For Wigman . . . space assumed definite entity, almost as a tangible presence in every manifestation of movement. . . . The dancer . . . is no longer an ego in a vacuum . . . but an epitome of the individual in his universe. He is continuously engaging the forces within him with those forces which press upon him from without, sometimes yielding to them, sometimes opposing them, but ever aware of them, and finding his identity only in this dynamic process.
>
> . . . With Wigman the dance stands for the first time fully revealed in its own stature; it is not storytelling or pantomime or moving sculpture or design in space or acrobatic virtuosity or musical illustration, but dance alone, an autonomous art exemplifying fully the ideals of modernism in its attainment of abstraction and in its utilization of the resources of its materials efficiently and with authority.[11]

Focusing solely on Wigman's concretization of space, Martin overlooks both her collaboration with Laban and the innovation Böhme considered of equal importance to the rediscovery of space, the rediscovery of ecstasy. This narrowed focus allows Martin to truncate the German genealogy implicit in *Tanzkunst* and to install Wigman within an American genealogy of modern dance, positioning her as the transitional figure between two generations of American modern dancers, the generations of Isadora Duncan and Martha Graham. From the American critic's point of view, the German choreographer's concretization of space enabled her to transcend the "subjectivity" of Duncan's improvisational methods and establish the "objectification of form" as the point of departure for Graham and her contemporaries.[12]

Unlike Böhme, Martin felt compelled to counter the claims of the Russian ballet to the achievement of absolute dance. Although the critic acknowledges that Nijinsky's *Le sacre du printemps* made "a definite step in the direction of absolute dance form" and that "functional modernism" was within the reach of Diaghilev's Ballets Russes, he denies Nijinsky and the Ballets Russes the breakthrough to absolute dance, stating:

> [In the twenties, ballet] welcomed painting as painting and music as music, but never so much as thought of the possibility of dance as dance. As a result, no structural basis for building the ballet in its own terms as an autonomous medium was evolved, and alone among the arts it failed to attain the new levels of freedom and integrity of form made possible by the principles of modernism.[13]

Making such assertions, Martin refuted the claims made for Nijinsky and the Ballets Russes by his critical antagonist Lincoln Kirstein—apologist for ballet, patron of George Balanchine, and avowed foe of Mary Wigman.

Kirstein's and Martin's conflicting views of Wigman originated in their conflicting prescriptions for the Americanization of European theater dance. While Martin believed that American dance should adopt the form of modern dance and thus celebrated Wigman, Kirstein believed that American dance should adopt the form of ballet and thus celebrated Nijinsky, denigrating Wigman's claim to absolute dance. Although the ballet apologist acknowledges that Wigman "doubtless invented a new type of gesture," he considers her achievement "self-indulgent" for it derived from "the idiosyncrasies of its creator" rather than from the *danse d'école*.[14] In his *Dance: A Short History of Classic Theatrical Dancing* (1935), he sneers: "But Mary Wigman, in spite of her energy, or perhaps on account of its blind drive, always remained Mary Wigman, the German blue-stocking with a female virginal egotism which could not be masked by soul-immersion in Nietzsche, dim readings of the Bhagavad Gita or in her half-controlled self-hypnotized projections of grief, passion, ecstasy, or boredom."[15]

Disputing Böhme and Martin's claim that Wigman realized the ideal of absolute dance, Kirstein reassigns this achievement to Nijinsky. "Before Nijinsky," he declares, "no one, neither Fokine, Duncan nor Noverre, had conceived of movement simply as movement."[16] Further, although Nijinsky had "reaffirmed the classic *danse d'école* by annihilating it," George Balanchine "employed [the classic idiom] with . . . a masterly extension of allusion, fact and phrasing."[17] In other words, Nijinsky's break with tradition made possible Balanchine's return to tradition. And it is this referentiality that makes ballet superior to modern dance. Thus Kirstein's history functions as critical apology for the choreography of George Balanchine and for the Americanization of the Russian ballet.

The debate between Martin and Kirstein that raged through the thirties ended in a draw during the forties and fifties, as both modern dance and ballet became established as American art forms and attained international recognition. Thereafter the standard literature effected a compromise and featured two complementary accounts of dance modernism, the account of American modern dance from Isadora Duncan to Martha Graham to Merce Cunningham and Judson Church, and the account of modern ballet from Vaslav Nijinsky to George Balanchine. Just as Clement Greenberg saw the center of modernism shift from the School of Paris to the New York School, so the descendants of Martin and Kirstein pictured American dance at mid-century as the legacy and fulfillment of European innovations earlier in the century. In the complementary accounts of dance modernism penned by postwar American critics, Mary Wigman is no longer a point of contention but appears only as a footnote, if at all.

In a 1967 essay titled "The New American Modern Dance," Jill Johnston updated John Martin's chronicle of American modern dance, narrating the history of modern dance as a continuing series of "upheavals . . . paralleling the revolutions in the other arts."[18] Echoing Martin, she notes how Martha Graham and her colleagues had reacted against Isadora Duncan and, extending the dialectic, notes how Merce Cunningham and his peers had reacted against the generation of Graham. The choreographers associated with Judson Church then consolidated the innovations of Cunningham, and "the new American modern dance at last assumed the dimensions of a full-fledged movement."[19]

According to Johnston, not until Cunningham appeared did modern dance catch up with the evolution of visual art traced by Clement Greenberg, for "neither Graham nor the social realists so fashionable in the thirties had anything in common with the great structural and esthetic upheavals that had been going on in France since the turn of the century."[20] It was Cunningham who, like Jackson Pollock, realized the implications of "the music of Satie, the poetry of Apollinaire, the plays of Jarry" and "expressed the radical shift in emphasis from the rational, securely focused, unitary concept of composition to the fragmentation and juxtaposition of elements with no essential beginning or ending, no transitional continuity, no focal climaxes and no dramatic resolutions."[21] The choreographers associated with Judson Church then extended the progression of American modern dance by exploring the implications of Cunningham's innovations.

In Johnston's account, Cunningham and Judson Church become heirs to the School of Paris, thereby dispossessing all other potential heirs. Thus the choreographers engaged by Diaghilev's Ballets Russes, notably George Balanchine, expounded a "deceptive" modernism, effecting "a revolution more in the style of movement than in the choreography."[22] In passing, Johnston cites Mary Wigman as a member of the generation, including Martha Graham and Doris Humphrey, that initiated "the first intensive explorations of formal design in space and movement."[23] But Johnston supplies no further details on the German choreographer, who becomes a footnote within the development of American modern dance.

In a 1973 essay titled "Balanchine's Formalism," David Michael Levin, a professional philosopher, countered Johnston's claims. Building on Kirstein's polemic, Levin argues that the modernist dialectic outlined by Greenberg more closely matches the evolution of twentieth-century ballet than the evolution of modern dance, contending that Balanchine "came to understand, more profoundly perhaps than anyone before him, the possibility of abstracting the pure classical syntax of the mobile human body as the defining condition, or essence of the ballet art."[24] Although Levin considers alternate modes of modernism characteristic of Martha Graham and Merce Cunningham, he rejects them as too "theatrical," too dependent on gesture, decor, and props. Thus only Balanchine's corpus fulfills the modernist dictum outlined by Greenberg, the "revelation" of "essence."[25] In Levin's account, even the ballet choreographers celebrated by Kirstein, notably Fokine and Nijinsky, do not come close to Balanchine's achievement. Not surprisingly, Mary Wigman warrants no mention.[26]

Despite Johnston's and Levin's vehement partisanship, most critics in the sixties and seventies held to a historiography of compromise. Whether they favored modern dance or ballet, they agreed that choreographers working in America, namely Balanchine and Cunningham, had realized the ideal of self-reflexivity more completely than had their predecessors. In a 1961 essay titled "Avant-Garde Choreography," Selma Jeanne Cohen inaugurated the era of compromise by pointing out that Cunningham and Balanchine "share the conviction that the proper subject of dance is dancing."[27] Over the next two decades most critics came to agree with Cohen, and by the eighties it had become a critical commonplace that the pure dance aesthetic of Balanchine and Cunningham provided the signature style of American dance. Indeed, it became a critical commonplace that the modernist project of conceptualizing dance as an autonomous language had reached its culmination in postwar America.

In the sixties and seventies the postwar aesthetic of American dance exerted a strong influence on West German dance. While ballet companies vied to stage the Balanchine repertory, modern dance studios vied to offer instruction in Graham and Cunningham technique. Reacting in part against what was perceived as the domination of American formalism, younger choreographers created the movement of *Tanztheater*. Inspired by the example of Mary Wigman and other survivors of *Ausdruckstanz,* these younger choreographers saw themselves reviving a German dance tradition that had been interrupted first by the suppression of "decadent art" during the Nazi era and then by the importation of American culture during the Adenauer era. In the historiography of *Tanztheater,* Wigman became a point of departure.

The writings of Norbert Servos, a critic and choreographer, exemplify this revival of interest in Wigman. Introducing his monograph on Pina Bausch, the most prominent exponent of *Tanztheater,* he positions the new German dance as both a divergence from and a continuation of *Ausdruckstanz.* Although Bausch reestablishes contact "with this almost forgotten revolutionary tradition" of Wigman and her contemporaries, she does so "without its ecce homo pathos, without its universal fatalism."[28] Thus she approaches a goal toward which "*Ausdruckstanz* had probably always aspired but had failed to achieve: releasing dance from the constraints of literature, relieving it of its fairytale illusions and leading it towards reality."[29] In so doing, Bausch does not reduce dance to a mode "that speaks through movement alone" (to quote Böhme's definition of absolute dance), a mode that Servos associates with American formalism. Rather, she evolves a mode of dance-theater based on a reinterpretation of the *Gestus* posited by Brecht's Epic Theater. In contrast to Brecht, who used the *Gestus* to "support or contrast a literary statement," Bausch isolates the *Gestus* from literary reference. Thus, "the body is no longer a means to an end. It has itself become the subject of the performance."[30] According to Servos, this reduction of dance to the narrative of the body reinvigorates the project of Wigman and *Ausdruckstanz*, the "emancipation" of the body from the constraints of industrialized society, the constraints encoded in ballet. *Ausdruckstanz* and *Tanztheater* dramatize the "unfulfilled desires" the body experiences in modern life.[31]

Drawing on the thinking of Ernst Bloch and Norbert Elias, Servos recalls Böhme's references to the writings of German philosophers. Just as Böhme wrote a German genealogy for *Ausdruckstanz*, so Servos writes a German genealogy for *Tanztheater*. In so doing, Servos inverts the progressive logic of the standard Greenbergian account. The story of German modern dance becomes a story not of breakthroughs but of breakdowns, the false classicisms of the Nazi and Adenauer eras. In reviving and transforming *Ausdruckstanz*, *Tanztheater* reconnects to the tradition of German modern dance before it was derailed by fascism and Americanization. Servos places Wigman at that point of reconnection.

Hedwig Müller's biography echoes Servos's genealogy by noting that just months before Wigman's death Pina Bausch took up her new position as resident choreographer at the Municipal Theater in Wuppertal.[32] The implication is clear: Pina Bausch began where Mary Wigman left off. Like Servos, Müller does not abandon, but rather reinterprets, the rhetoric of absolute dance. In her account, Wigman holds onto an unchanging ideal of absolute dance while struggling to survive through the changing times of Weimar, Nazi, and postwar Germany. Thus Müller's biography both celebrates and contextualizes "the great dancer," integrating the teleological narrative of dance modernism that has framed discussions of Wigman since Rudolf von Delius with a historicized account of the compromises the choreographer made under the Third Reich.

From Rudolf von Delius to Hedwig Müller, the Wigman literature has iterated her achievement of absolute dance, an iteration that has served varying agendas of critical advocacy. In breaking from the agenda of critical advocacy, I set aside the teleological narrative of dance modernism in order to pursue an ideological critique of Wigman's dances.

REWRITING THE HISTORY
OF MODERN DANCE

"Feminism" and "nationalism" are awkward terms to apply to dance. First, because both are catch-all phrases encompassing a wide range of historical and cultural conditions. So to apply the two terms to dance requires specifying exactly which "feminism(s)" and "nationalism(s)" are at issue. Second, even when the terms are so specified, it is important to avoid reducing dance to an ism. As often observed, if dancers could say what they were dancing in words, they would not need to dance. Indeed, the radical difference between verbal expression and dance expression underlies much of the rhetoric on absolute dance. I do not deny this radical difference, but rather look for ways to conceptualize dance as a site of ideological contest, that is, as a cultural space where "the categories and judgments that connect our utterances and practices to dominant structures and powers" (to quote Joseph Roach's definition of ideology) undergo dispute and transformation.[33] Thus, when I say that Wigman's choreographic debut in 1914 marked a point of ideological complication in the practice of early modern dance, I do not mean that her first publicly performed works reflected contemporary notions of "feminism" and "nationalism." Rather I mean to say that her dance practice both countered and continued the "categories and judgments" of "dominant structures and powers."

To make this argument, I read the practice of early modern dance in relation to the practice of nineteenth-century ballet. In my reading, the production and reception of nineteenth-century ballet provides a textbook demonstration of what contemporary feminists have theorized as the male gaze. That is, nineteenth-century ballet represented women as if seen from the perspective of the male voyeur, so that even female spectators took on the perspective that scripts women as objects of desire. In defying the conventions of ballet, early modern dancers challenged the male gaze and introduced possibilities for female self-authorship and female spectatorship. Appropriating the privilege previously reserved for the (usually male) ballet master, the (usually female) early modern dancer scripted her own performance. In so doing, she appeared to script the experience of many women in the audience. For her mode of female self-authorship and female spectatorship relied upon her universalizing and essentializing of female experience. In different ways, Isadora Duncan, Mary Wigman, and Martha Graham all danced Woman. Contemporary theorists would label this strategy "cultural feminism," for it assumed that all women share similar experiences and attitudes *as women,* irrespective of their differences in race, class, sexual orientation, or nationality.

National differences did figure in the performances of early modern dancers, however, and they inflected their stagings of cultural feminism with the accents of nationalism. For Isadora Duncan and Martha Graham danced not only Woman, but also the American Self. And Mary Wigman danced the Germanic Soul. In other words, just as early modern dancers essentialized gender, so they essentialized national identity. Benedict Anderson's definition of nationalism as an "imagined community" clarifies how such essentialized notions of identity contribute to the articulation of nationality. As Anderson points out, nationalism involves "an imagined political community"—"*imagined* because the members of even the smallest nation will never know most of their fellow-members, meet them, or even hear of them, yet in the minds of each lives the image of their communion."[34] Differently stated, nationalism involves imagined connections between the individual body and the collective body, and the practice of early modern dance became a vehicle for such imagining.

On the simplest level, it is the conjunction of female self-authorship and spectatorship with the essentializing of gender and national identity that positions early modern dance at the convergence between feminism and nationalism. But this convergence becomes complicated in several ways. First, not only did different choreographers realize the convergence differently but also each choreographer realized the convergence differently over time. Second, early modern dance contained universalizing elements that worked against and stood in tension with gender and nationality. The primary universalizing element was what John Martin termed "metakinesis," what dancers now refer to as kinesthesia—the ability of one body to sense another body and to reexperience physically sensations projected by that other body. Although all dance involves kinesthesia, early modern dance intensified its effect. Indeed, John Martin argued that early modern dance took kinesthesia as its starting point and that in this way kinesthesia displaced the codified vocabulary of ballet.[35]

In rejecting the ballet vocabulary, early modern dancers gave up its transnational legibility, transnational in the sense that audiences across Europe and North America were familiar with the ballet vocabulary and could decode its conventions. Without recourse to this internationalized vocabulary, early modern dancers had to fashion alternate referents for their idiosyncratic movement styles. In other words, they had to find new ways to connect their individual bodies to the collective body of the audience. One way was to heighten and thus to essentialize the attributes the dancer shared or possibly shared with the spectator—body consciousness, gender, nationality. To deploy all three referents resulted in paradox or contradiction, for the projection of kinesthesia countered the performance of Woman or National Type. In consequence, early modern dancers either performed the paradox or attempted to resolve the contradiction by dramatizing the relationship of the individual body to the collective body. Thus their solos layered the referents of kinesthesia, Woman, and National Type, and their group works focused on the counterpoint between the individual and the group. In this way their group works staged utopian (and dystopian) visions of Community.

Early modern dance had a sociology as well as a semiology, and its social basis rested on the patronage of amateur students. A craze among amateurs for dance instruction quite literally supported the emergence of the practice. According to the bourgeois morals of the nineteenth century, "respectable ladies" practiced social dancing, but only "women of ill repute" took up stage dancing.[36] But by the end of the century this distinction between professional and amateur dancing had broken down, as middle-class women took up modes of amateur performance—Delsartism and aesthetic gymnastics—also practiced by professional dancers.[37] Flocking to the private dance studios opened by early modern dancers, amateur students also provided a ready audience for their performances. That many more women than men studied the new art of movement, and that the trend was more popular in Germany and the United States than elsewhere, also informs the feminism and nationalism of the practice.

To illustrate these generalizations, I now turn to readings, that is, to my reconstructions, of specific works: first *Giselle*, as emblematic of nineteenth-century ballet, and then Isadora Duncan's dancing, as emblematic of early modern dance before Mary Wigman made her 1914 choreographic debut. Finally, I reread the evidence of her debut as prelude to my subsequent account of her career.

Premiered at the Paris Opera in 1841, *Giselle* became a hallmark of the Romantic repertory. Within a decade of its premiere, productions were mounted in London, Berlin, Milan, Saint Petersburg, and New York. In the mid-1880s Marius Petipa, ballet master at the Maryinsky Theater in Saint Petersburg, revised the ballet, and modern productions are descendants of this version. My reconstruction of *Giselle* is based on the broad outlines of the choreography as it has survived in the repertory and is recorded on film and video, corrected by the libretto and scenario penned by Théophile Gautier at the time the work premiered.[38] As I will argue, the male gaze became a constitutive element of the ballet, overdetermined structurally and institutionally.

Divided into two acts, the ballet tells the story of a peasant girl, Giselle, who has fallen in love with an aristocrat in disguise, Prince Albrecht. Near the end of the first act, set in Giselle's village, her spurned peasant lover, Hilarion, reveals Albrecht's ruse. Overwhelmed with despair, Giselle goes mad and dies in grief. Whether she intentionally or accidentally wounds herself with Albrecht's sword, or dances herself to death, remains ambiguous in the original documentation and in the subsequent production history of the ballet. Also ambiguous is the final tableau. According to the libretto, Giselle dies in her mother's arms. According to the scenario, she is comforted at the end by Bathilde, Albrecht's aristocratic fiancée, whose unexpected arrival on the scene had confirmed his true identity.

In the second act Giselle reappears in the realm of the Wilis, the ghosts of maidens who died from unconsummated love and now take revenge on any man who enters their nocturnal realm. Himself crazed with despair, Albrecht follows Giselle beyond the grave, and although threatened by the shades, he remains unharmed. After a final duet, the two part forever. The details of the ending also differ in the libretto and scenario, although in both Bathilde reappears, a plot twist that has disappeared in subsequent versions. According to the scenario, at the end Bathilde returns in order to "forgive" and "comfort" Albrecht.[39]

As recounted in the libretto and scenario, the narrative of the ballet suggests two spectatorial positions, the perspective of Albrecht (or Gautier) and the perspective of the Wilis. From the perspective of the Wilis, Albrecht's betrayal of Giselle is clear, and they desire revenge. In the original version, the Wilis dance Hilarion to death and then seek out Albrecht. Albrecht is saved, however, partly through the fortuitous break of day and partly through Giselle's ambiguous intervention. Divided between her identities "as a woman and as a wili," she attempts to protect Albrecht by directing him to hold onto the cross marking her grave, while at the same time she threatens him by dancing so seductively that he dares to leave the protection of the cross. As the scenario describes the action:

> Myrtha [Queen of the Wilis] resorts to a diabolically feminine ruse. She commands Giselle, who as her subject cannot disobey, to execute the most alluring and graceful poses. At first Giselle dances timidly and with reluctance, but she then finds herself carried away by her instinct both as a woman and as a wili, and she lightly springs forward and dances with such sensuous grace and such overpowering fascination that the heedless Albrecht leaves the protection of the cross and goes towards her with arms outstretched and eyes shining with desire and love. The fatal delirium takes hold of him, he pirouettes, jumps, and follows Giselle in her most daring bound. In the grip of this frenzy, he is consumed with the secret desire to die with his mistress and follow his "beloved shade" to the grave.[40]

In a classic enactment of male sexual anxiety, Albrecht experiences his desire for Giselle as potentially life threatening.

Within the narrative, Albrecht clearly is to blame for what befalls him and Giselle. As the scenario notes at the moment when Albrecht's true identity is revealed: "Loys [Albrecht's alias] is nothing but an imposter, a seducer who has been deceiving the trusting Giselle. . . . Loys, or rather Duke Albrecht of Silesia, excuses himself as best he can, replying that after all not much harm has been done."[41] Despite the scenario's acknowledgment of Albrecht's callousness, however, the spectator in the theater never turns against Albrecht and, indeed, identifies with his despair and sense of loss. Moreover, the spectator conflates Albrecht's with Giselle's loss, and laments their separation rather than the asymmetry between her loss of reason and life and his loss of her through his own duplicity. In other words, although the narrative of *Giselle* hints at the possibility of female spectatorship, its choreographic structure subverts this narrative potential and reaffirms the spectatorial position of the male protagonist.

The choreography substitutes the single perspective of Albrecht for the dual perspective of the narrative (Albrecht/the Wilis) by setting a succession of duets for the protagonists. In the first act, Giselle and Albrecht perform a pantomime of the lovers' game of plucking petals from a daisy while reciting "I love you, I love you not."[42] In the second act, the two again dance together, substituting expressive virtuosity for pantomime. Their dancing plays on the dramatic potential of the two performers moving together and apart, with Albrecht trailing Giselle and only momentarily connecting with her, as described in the extended passage quoted above.[43] The spectator in the theater follows the formal momentum of the action and reads Giselle's and Albrecht's coming together as a positive value, their going apart as a negative value, whatever the narrative frame. The performance suggests a mutual infatuation, not a duplicitous seduction.

Within the narrative, the Wilis' desire for revenge intrudes an awareness of Albrecht's betrayal. It is a tantalizing possibility that women in the 1841 audience might have identified with the narrative perspective of the Wilis and not with the perspective of Albrecht (or Gautier). Might women in the audience have identified with the Wilis' angry revenge against Hilarion rather than with Albrecht's longing for Giselle? At least in contemporary productions, the Wilis are staged as an animate background against which Albrecht enacts his desire for Giselle, and the libretto and scenario suggest that this was also the case in 1841. In my own encounter with the work, to experience a performance wickedly undermines the potential of my narrative identification with the Wilis. However aware I remain of Albrecht's responsibility for Giselle's demise, I cannot help but desire their union. It is as if the performance of the work substitutes the male gaze for the possibility of female spectatorship glimpsed in the narrative.

Although my reading of *Giselle* is based partly on my own theater-going in the late twentieth century, it also takes into account the conditions of production and reception in 1841. For just as the onstage action placed the spectator in the position of a voyeur, so too did the offstage operations of the Paris Opera. In 1831, ten years before the premiere of *Giselle*, the Opera was leased to a private entrepreneur, Louis Veron, who boosted attendance by opening the Foyer de la Danse, the performers' green room, to subscribers. There members of the Jockey Club could flirt and strike up liaisons with their favorite dancers. Although the star system also introduced by Veron insulated ballerinas such as Carlotta Grisi from the necessity of attaching themselves to wealthy men, the subsistence wages paid to members of the corps de ballet rendered them vulnerable to such attachments.[44] As in the action of *Giselle*, the Foyer de la Danse allowed upper-class men to pursue liaisons with lower-class women, with the approbation of their upper-class mates. Indeed, *Giselle* can be read as a legitimation of the prostitution sanctioned by the Paris Opera, and the Foyer de la Danse as the literalization of the male gaze embodied in the structure of the ballet.[45] As Gautier once summarized his aesthetics:

> An actress [or dancer] is like a statue or a picture that is offered for your inspection, and it is permissible to criticize her without any scruples of conscience, to reproach her for being ugly just as a painter might be rebuked for faulty drawing (any question of pity for physical defects is out of place here), and to praise her for her charms with the same calm detachment shown by a sculptor standing before a marble statue.[46]

Just as the male gaze constitutive of Romantic ballet was overdetermined, so too was the female spectatorship constitutive of early modern dance. Over the course of the nineteenth century the relations between amateur and professional dancing changed, and this change shaped the spectatorship of the practice expounded by Isadora Duncan and her peers. At the time *Giselle* premiered, amateur and professional dancing were segregated: "respectable women" attended waltzes; "disrespectable women" pursued stage careers as professional ballerinas. But toward the end of the century, the boundary separating professional and amateur dance blurred, as middle-class women took up forms of physical culture that resembled dance and the new female soloists turned to modes of amateur performance.[47] Middle-class female spectators who had practiced physical culture could identify—socially and kinesthetically—with the early modern dancer in a way that bourgeois women during the Romantic era could not identify with the ballerina. At the same time, early modern dancers had to fashion representational strategies that addressed the female spectators' identification with their performance.

Although arguably the most renowned proponent of early modern dance, Isadora Duncan was not alone. Dance historians have chronicled the activities of many other female soloists in the decade before the First World War—Loie Fuller, Ruth St. Denis, Grete Wiesenthal, Maud Allan, Clotilde von Derp, Gertrud Leistikov, Sent M'ahesa, Valentine de St.-Point. Nonetheless, successive generations have taken Isadora as exemplary of her era, and so I view her here. My reconstructions are based on the stage tradition of Duncan dancing as passed from student to student and recorded on video and film, supplemented by the evidence of drawings and photographs and on the writings of the dancer herself, her spectators, and her critics.[48] In my reading, Duncan introduced possibilities for female spectatorship that could not have been realized by nineteenth-century ballet, albeit possibilities marked by the assumptions of cultural feminism, the universalizing and essentializing of female experience.

Isadora's dancing rejected the frames of narrative, spectacle, and virtuosity that had enclosed the Romantic ballerina. Most often she danced alone on a bare stage, surrounded by dark curtains, costumed in a gauzy robe or tunic, accompanied by a single piano or an entire orchestra. Transforming techniques borrowed from physical culture, she evolved a vocabulary based on simple steps such as runs, leaps, and skips. As Deborah Jowitt has demonstrated, Duncan adapted the waltz rhythms from social dances, the statue posing taught by disciples of Delsarte, and the jumps taught in *Turnverein,* schools for gymnastics founded by German immigrants to the United States.[49] (It has been documented that Isadora attended a *Turnverein* in her native Oakland.)[50]

Watching Duncan dancing, spectators could imagine themselves doing the same moves, and, indeed, many of her female spectators did try to do the same moves. Imitators of Duncan taught and performed across the United States and Europe. Yet the paradox of her style was that although everyone could imagine themselves doing her moves, no one could perform her dances like she could, including the students she had trained herself. The singularity of Isadora's charismatic presence opposed the commonality of her movement vocabulary.

This stylistic paradox accompanied a structural paradox that juxtaposed gender-specific or nationality-specific referents with abstract or universalized referents. Consider the example of *Ave Maria* (c. 1914), as reconstructed from photographs and written accounts.[51] Set to Schubert, the dance was choreographed the year after Duncan's two children had drowned, a fact well publicized. Visualizing the design of Schubert's music, the dance externalized the grief the soloist felt at the death of her own children. Choreographed the year World War I broke out, the dance also generalized the condition of a generation of mothers threatened with the premature deaths of their sons. Duncan's experience potentially became the experience of all women, and all women potentially became the lamenting mother, the Virgin Mary suggested by the title. Thus the solo conflated the representational strategies of autobiography and archetype. Dancing her own experience, Duncan seemingly danced the experience of all women.[52]

Yet the gender-specific portrayal of the mother in *Ave Maria* stood in tension with Duncan's projection of a powerful kinesthesia. Visualizing the qualities and rhythms of Schubert's score, her dancing projected the kinesthetic response to loss, whether experienced by a man or a woman. A spectator described the dance: "A gesture reaching toward the earth and then lifted upward recurred again and again. . . . Unutterable agony and suffering were there—but always that hopeful, loving, upward gesture."[53] A photograph by Arnold Genthe (fig. 3) presumably captures this "upward gesture." As seen through the camera lens, Duncan raises her arms over her

Fig. 3. Isadora Duncan in *Ave Maria,* a solo choreographed around the same time that Mary Wigman made her debut (courtesy of the Dance Collection, New York Public Library for the Performing Arts, Astor, Lenox and Tilden Foundations)

head, lifts her upper chest, and tilts her face upward, while her lower torso and legs remain weighted to the ground. Her posture simultaneously animates the downward pull of gravity and the upward struggle against gravity, representing the emotion of grief with an ambiguous twist. Does Duncan's persona experience a moment of release from sorrow, an awareness of perhaps a divine presence that affirms life? Or does her persona resurface only momentarily from the depths of grief, like a drowning person gulping air before a final descent? In either case, her broad stance and bared upper chest make her appear vulnerable and open, as if inviting the spectator, whether male or female, to share her experience.

How did spectators of *Ave Maria* reconcile its representation of Mother with its kinesthetic representation of loss? Quite simply, they saw no contradiction but rather a continuum between the kinesthesia of Duncan's performance and the gender of her person. In the writing of female spectators and male critics alike, kinesthesia, the speech of the body, became a female-identified trait. Margherita Duncan, the dancer's sister-in-law and the spectator quoted earlier, interpreted the "upward gesture" in *Ave Maria* as suggestive of "the love that nurtures children, that brings the whole race out of the bosom of earth up into the arms of God."[54] In relation to other works, Margherita wrote about how Isadora's musical visualization seemed to reflect her own subjective responses:

> The first time I ever saw Isadora Duncan . . . dancing . . . I experienced what I can only describe as an identification of myself with her. It seemed as if I were dancing up there myself. This was not an intellectual process, a critical perception that she was supremely right in every movement she made; just a sense that in watching her I found release for my own impulses of expression; the emotions aroused in me by the music saw themselves translated into visibility.[55]

Echoing Margherita, other female spectators also described Duncan as if she were their mirror. As Mabel Dodge Luhan commented: "It seemed to me I recognized what she did in the dance, and that it was like my own daily, nightly return to the Source."[56]

Male critics concurred with female spectators in conceptualizing Duncan and her dancing as quintessentially female. As Sheldon Cheney wrote: "Through it all one should remember the intense feminine nature beyond the artist-creator, the essential womanliness, the torrential but tender mother-love in her."[57] And as Hans Fischer noted: "[Duncan] has discovered a language in which women can express themselves as perfectly as men can express themselves in the other arts."[58] These comments by male critics betray the extent to which Duncan's cultural feminism allowed for the reinvention of the male gaze. Although the male critic no longer positioned himself as voyeur, or at least not as readily as Gautier had earlier, he took up a new position as intellectual apologist, putting into words what the female dancer could express only through movement. This new function for the male critic reiterated the old division between male rationality and female physicality. Celebrating the speech of the body, Duncan became ensnared by the mind-body duality she attempted to undo.[59]

Not that she was at a loss for words. On the contrary, Duncan wrote at length about her dancing, and two essays in particular, "The Dance of the Future" (1903) and "I See America Dancing" (1927), reveal how her essentializing of gender was of a piece with her essentializing of national identity. In the earlier essay, she sketches her educational philosophy, which she realized the following year when she opened a school in Berlin. She notes:

> In this school I shall not teach the children to imitate my movements, but to make their own. . . . An intelligent child must be astonished to find that in the ballet school it is taught movements contrary to all those movements which it would make of its own accord.
>   This may seem a question of little importance, a question of differing opinions on the ballet and the new dance. But it is a great question. It is not only a question of true art, it is a question of race, of the development of the female sex to beauty and health, of the return to the original strength and to natural movements of woman's body. It is a question of the development of perfect mothers and the birth of healthy and beautiful children. The dancing school of the future is to develop and to show the ideal form of woman.[60]

Here Duncan clearly connects her essentializing of gender to the program of eugenics. Echoing the rhetoric of the physical culture movement at the turn of the century, she defends the liberation of women's bodies in terms of "race improvement."[61]

Her 1927 essay, "I See America Dancing," elaborates the racial categories of her thinking. As in the 1903 essay, she opposes her vision of "the dance of the future" to European ballet. But in a new departure, she also opposes her vision to jazz dancing, the popular fox-trots and Charlestons of the time. Duncan writes:

> It seems to me monstrous for anyone to believe that the Jazz rhythm expresses America. Jazz rhythm expresses the South African savage. America's music will be something different. It has yet to be written. . . . Long-legged strong boys and girls will dance to this music—not the tottering, ape-like convulsions of the Charleston, but a striking upward tremendous mounting, powerful mounting above the pyramids of Egypt, beyond the parthenon of Greece, an expression of Beauty and Strength such as no civilization has ever known. . . . And this dance will have nothing in it either of the servile coquetry of the ballet or the sensual convulsion of the South African negro.[62]

Positioning her dance as neither ballet nor jazz, Duncan locates its sources in the Irish jigs danced by her pioneer grandmother, modified by an admixture of "native" traditions. She writes:

> I remember . . . my grandmother . . . [dancing] Irish jigs; only I fancy that into these Irish jigs had crept some of the heroic spirit of the Pioneer and the battles with the Redskins—probably some of the gestures of the Redskins themselves, and, again, a bit of Yankee Doodle when Grandfather Colonel . . . came marching home from the Civil War. All this Grandmother danced in the Irish jig; and I learnt it from her, and put into it my own aspiration of Young America, and finally my great spiritual revelation of life from the lines of Walt Whitman. And that is the origin of the so-called Greek dance with which I have flooded the world.[63]

In describing her dance, Duncan envisions an Anglocentrism that encompasses traces of the "Redskins," though not of the "African savage." Her essentialized Woman becomes an essentialized American.

To what extent did spectators read this image of America in her dancing, an image that from a contemporary perspective must be termed racist? That some spectators read her as a quintessential American is clear from their accounts. But what is less clear is whether spectators read her dancing in the racial categories she proposed. This is how Max Eastman composed Duncan's identity: "America fighting the battle against Americanism—that was Isadora. . . . If America triumphs over itself—over its cheap greed and prudery, its intellectual and moral cowardice, its prudent and prurient hypocrisy—if America triumphs over that, Isadora will be sculptured in bronze at the gate of the Temple of Man [*sic*] in the new day that will dawn."[64]

Duncan most probably would not have disagreed with Eastman, for she too opposed what she saw as the puritanism and materialism of American life. But I wonder if Eastman, and other spectators who constructed Duncan as quintessentially American, did not see their own imagining of America in her dancing. If so, then her dancing functioned to imagine connections between the individual body and the collective body, that is, to articulate nationalism.

Thus far my ideological critique has been quite rudimentary. I associate *Giselle* (and by implication the internationalized practice of nineteenth-century ballet) with the male gaze, and Isadora Duncan (and by implication the practice of early modern dance) with female spectatorship and the "imagined community" of nationalism. Such broad strokes surely miss the complexities that ensued when the nineteenth-century ballerina turned choreographer—as did Therese Elssler, Lucile Grahn, and Katti Lanner—and when distinct national schools of ballet developed in Denmark, Italy, and Russia to challenge the preeminence of the French school. Not to mention the complexities that ensued when men took up the practice of early modern dance—as did Alexander Sakharoff and Ted Shawn—and when proponents of the genre performed across Europe and North America to acclaim that resounded from country to country. A further complication occurred in 1909, at the height of Isadora's career, when Diaghilev's Ballets Russes premiered in Paris, reforming ballet in ways that paralleled the precepts of early modern dance as well as revolutionizing spectatorship and the images of the male and female dancer.

Such exceptions and examples point toward a thoroughgoing revision of Western theater dance, a project that I cannot undertake in this book, for obvious reasons. However, I do intend to move toward a large-scale reexamination of Western theater dance by offering a small-scale critique of Wigman's dances. For the purposes of this limited revisionism, the broad strokes of my analysis of nineteenth-century ballet and early modern dance do seem justified, for they enable the more subtle analysis that follows. This book is like a map undergoing revision, with some territories as yet only roughly indicated, but with one territory—that bounded by Wigman's career—already shaded and contoured.

With this qualification, I now turn to my rereading of Mary Wigman's choreographic debut. My rereading turns on a comparison of images, the photographs of Duncan's *Ave Maria* (c. 1914) and Wigman's *Witch Dance I* (*Hexentanz*), also choreographed in 1914. In my interpretation, Wigman took as a given the female spectatorship established by the Duncanesque dancer and challenged the universalizing of female experience implicit in that spectatorship. At the same time, Wigman disrupted the way the Duncanesque dancer imagined the relation between the individual body and the collective body.[65] Yet Wigman's works had paradoxical effects, for although on one level her performances undermined the dramatization of Woman and National Type, on another level her performances reconfigured spectators' essentialized notions of female identity and national identity.

Consider the photographs of *Ave Maria* (fig. 3) and *Witch Dance I* (fig. 4) and note the difference in costuming.[66] Duncan wears a long, loose dress gathered at the waist that identifies her as "feminine" and that simultaneously conceals and reveals the contours of her female body. Like everyday dress, her costume distinguishes the body from the surrounding space, despite the soft focus of Arnold Genthe's camera. In contrast, Wigman wears a costume—a close-fitting cap and a length of cloth attached at neck, wrists, and thighs—that makes no reference to female dress beyond the dance. Delius noted the novelty of this conception: "The costume no longer presents itself as an external get-up or as trimmings that one can change at will, but rather the costume becomes a part of the body-soul like eyes and hair."[67] In a sense, the costume functions to mask the body, to blur its female contours, its human contours. This costume-as-mask integrates the space of the body with the space of the environment, for the viewer no longer can perceive a clear boundary separating the body from the surrounding space. The costume-as-mask frames the dancer not as a persona but as a dynamic configuration of energy in space.

Witch Dance I anticipated the paradigmatic mode of Wigman's solo choreography during the teens and twenties, a period that saw her creation of more than a hundred solos.[68] These solos decisively rejected the mode of solo choreography practiced by the Duncanesque dancer, discarding the strategies of autobiography, archetype, and musical visualization and fashioning a strategy I have termed the *Gestalt im Raum* (configuration of energy in space).[69]

Fig. 4. Mary Wigman in the first version of *Witch Dance* (1914), a solo that exemplifies her use of the costume-as-mask (courtesy of the Mary Wigman Archive)

The principle of the mask was central to this strategy. At times Wigman used actual facial masks, but more often her costume or her facial expression, or both, functioned like masks. And in another sense her dancing became a metaphoric mask, for she did not dramatize her autobiography onstage but rather staged her self-transformation into an other. She conceptualized her body as a medium and her dancing as a channel for subconscious drives and supernatural forces, for ecstatic and demonic energies, for the abstract designs of time, space, and motion. Critic after critic wrote about how she seemed to make the space move, animating suprapersonal forces beyond her physical self, focusing attention not on the dancer but on the dance. This is what no film could capture, what critics such as John Martin struggled to put into words, and what generations of students have struggled to vivify in their own dancing.

In my viewing experience, Susanne Linke's re-creation of Dore Hoyer's *Affectos Humanos* has realized the principle of the *Gestalt im Raum*. Her performances have shown me that the spectator never entirely loses sight of the woman dancing, as I had surmised previously from the photographs and reviews of Wigman. Rather the spectator senses a palpable tension between the charismatic presence of the performer and the performer's attempt to mask herself, to transcend herself, to release and realize the spatial and dynamic form of the dance. Indeed, Linke's performance takes its power from this palpable tension, which finds a structural analogue in the dramatic situation of one dancer (herself) attempting to take on the identity of another dancer (Hoyer). Inferring from Linke's performance, I have some sense of what contemporary critics meant when they noted the paradox of Wigman's simultaneous presence and absence onstage.

A clear technical explanation of Wigman's heightened spatial sense is difficult to find. The best English-language source is *Elements of the Free Dance* (1930) by Elizabeth Selden. Her primer outlines the technical innovations associated with Wigman and Laban: centering the body within the torso and acknowledging weight and mass rather than centering the body along the spine and emphasizing lightness (as in ballet); emphasizing "dynamic rhythm" (as opposed to the "linear rhythm" of ballet), defined as "*the arc of inner tension* that connects the beginning with the end of a motion"; [70]

and deploying "action-modes" (as opposed to ballet steps) such as folding-unfolding, rising-falling, pressing-pulling, bending-reaching, rotating and twisting, undulating and heaving, swinging, swaying, vibrating, and shaking. Selden's account squares with the reminiscences of former students at the Wigman School, which I present in chapter three.

At this point in history, it is possible to "know" Wigman's *Technik* only through the teaching and performing of her disciples, and none profess to "know" the secret of the choreographer's own masterful performances of her principles. In general, I have followed Susan Foster's lead in *Reading Dancing* and conceptualized dance practice as a set of representational strategies, and in this sense I deploy the term *Gestalt im Raum* as shorthand for Wigman's framing of the dancing body in performance.

The *Gestalt im Raum* repositioned the spectator, for the female spectator no longer could see herself easily mirrored in Wigman's dancing, and the male critic no longer could define Wigman as Woman. Or, more accurately, spectators were forced to redefine their conceptions of Woman and National Type if they were to ascribe an essentialized gender and national identity to the performing body. Dancing, Wigman seemed more like a dynamic force than like a persona with recognizable traits. Nonetheless, spectators remained aware that she was a woman and of German nationality. Watching Wigman dancing, spectators did not know whether to reinterpret their essentialized notions or abandon such notions altogether.

In one sense, Wigman's repositioning of the spectator worked negatively rather than positively, rendering the spectator's attempts at interpretation problematic, challenging the categories (Woman, Dancer, Space, German) the spectator brought to the performance. But in forcing spectators to give up familiar categories, Wigman's dancing invited their projection of unfamiliar categories. If the dancer appears neither "feminine" nor "masculine," as an early critic asserted, then how does one conceptualize personhood outside the (heterosexist) duality of gender? If the soloist actually dances with the "invisible partner" of space, as Wigman once wrote, then how does one conceptualize the suprapersonal force she animates? As a godhead, the demonic, the Freudian subconscious, the ecstatic, the Germanic?

Just as Rudolf von Delius initiated the commentary on Wigman's realization of absolute dance, so he initiated the commentary on her realization of essential Germanness. He wrote: "For the first time the wild, Germanic unity of feeling has found its dance form. There is no longer anything witty, interesting, virtuosic, or refined. No conformity, no masquerade, no theatrics."[71] In refusing to dance overtly in national character, Wigman appeared covertly to define Germanness as an intensity of feeling that bordered on the ecstatic and the demonic. Thus her danced vision of national identity echoed the rhetoric of German Romanticism. Similarly, in refusing to dance overtly as Woman, she appeared to covertly redefine Woman as an exemplar of self-transcendence. Again her dancing echoed established cultural images, including that of the Romantic ballerina. Yet her solos from the twenties cannot be reduced to either side of the paradox: her dancing body did *and* did not essentialize national identity, did *and* did not essentialize female identity.

In one of the subtle shifts that characterized her choreographic career, Wigman reversed her rejection of Duncanesque representational strategies during the mid-thirties. The nearly twenty solos premiered between 1937 and 1942 de-emphasized the principle of the *Gestalt im Raum* and embraced strategies the choreographer earlier had discarded—autobiography, archetype, musical visualization. Now spectators could define Wigman as Woman and Germanic in a way that they could not before. In the context of the Third Reich, this shift can be read as the choreographer's accommodation with fascist aesthetics, which required an identification with the *Volk* and a clear distinction between "masculinity" and "femininity." This shift also can be read as the choreographer's search for a position from which to comment on fascist aesthetics, for her late solos mused on the role of the individual, the artist, and the woman in the *Volksgemeinschaft*. Wigman's deployment of Duncanesque strategies had an ambivalent effect, staging both an accommodation with and a limited resistance to fascist aesthetics.

What is startling about Wigman's career is the fine line separating her Weimar dances from her dances created under the Third Reich. From one perspective, the form her other critics have termed "absolute dance" and I have termed *Gestalt im Raum* did persist through her choreographic career, providing a signature style that has placed her among the ranks of dance modernists. But from another perspective, her formal signature underwent significant transmutation over time, so although the principles of absolute dance remained visible, a succession of ideological significances emerged. These ideological significances did not adhere in the formal transmutations alone. Or, more accurately, the formal transmutations involved changing contexts and cannot be read apart from these contexts—Wigman's immediate working environments and the changing structures for dance patronage in twentieth-century Germany. Ideology, form, and context interact in complex ways, and it is their interaction that the remainder of my study follows through Wigman's career.

2

Gestalt im Raum

At issue in this chapter is how Mary Wigman evolved her signature style, which other critics have termed "absolute dance" and I have termed *Gestalt im Raum*. According to Rudolf von Delius and his successors, the choreographer's 1914 debut marked an advance determined by the progressive logic of modernism. Yet, as I will argue, the evidence of Wigman's early dances suggests that her choreographic practice evolved over a period of several years, however prescient *Witch Dance I* appears in retrospect. From 1914 to 1919 her dances emerged in a complex counterpoint to the choreography of her contemporaries—not only Isadora Duncan but also Emile Jaques-Dalcroze, Rudolf Laban, and the dancers associated with the Dadaist Cabaret Voltaire. Although she rejected Duncan's and Dalcroze's working method of musical visualization, Wigman maintained her female predecessor's focus on solo choreography and on choreography for a small group of her students. At the same time, she adopted the working method that Dalcroze shared with Laban—improvisation based on movement analysis. Yet she rejected the festival format for group choreography so central to the work of Dalcroze and Laban. And although her use of the mask paralleled the practice of the Dadaist dancers, she conceptualized the principle of the mask in an unprecedented fashion.

The formation of Wigman's choreographic practice cannot be separated from the milieus in which she worked, first as a student at Hellerau from 1910 to 1912 and then as a bohemian artist on Monte Verita from 1913 to 1919. Hellerau and Monte Verita were cultural spaces committed to life reform in a newly industrialized society. In both milieus Wigman encountered visions of cultural renewal that became another sort of influence on her work, an influence that her work partly embraced, partly rejected, and ultimately reinterpreted.

The dancer's personal biography also cannot be overlooked in tracing the formation of her practice. In 1918 Wigman suffered a breakdown and withdrew from active performing. When she resumed her public career in 1919, the elements of her mature style had coalesced. It was at this point that she changed the spelling of her name from Wiegmann to Wigman. In retrospect, her breakdown marks the divide between her years of imitation and experimentation and her period of wide public recognition.

The choreographer's disparate memoirs, published for the most part after 1945, never directly admit her breakdown. In fact, her memoirs fashion a narrative that often has been retold in the dance literature, a narrative that emphasizes her dissatisfaction with Dalcroze's belief in the necessary integration of music and movement and the liberation of her encounter with Laban's dictum of "dance without music." Perhaps not surprisingly, the artistic autobiography implicit in her memoirs accords with the genealogy of *Ausdruckstanz* constructed by Fritz Böhme and other German critics during the twenties, a genealogy that insists upon a sharp break between Dalcroze's method of eurhythmics and the practice that Wigman and Laban evolved in collaboration on Monte Verita.

In my retelling of the early years of Wigman's career, the choreographer borrowed more from Dalcroze's method than she later realized and experienced more discontent when working with Laban than she publicly admitted. My account at times reads between the lines of her memoirs. It also draws upon Hedwig Müller's biography, the research of other scholars who have investigated Hellerau and Monte Verita, and my reconstructions of Wigman's early dances. As my reconstructions will demonstrate, her early dances traced a different relation to her male mentors than that sketched in her memoirs.

The following discussion divides into four sections. In the first part I briefly chronicle the dancer's childhood and adolescence and in the second part narrate her experiences at Hellerau and on Monte Verita. The third part then examines the evidence for her early solos and suggests how the improvisational working methods of Dalcroze and Laban enabled her to reject Duncanesque dancing and to conceptualize the *Gestalt im Raum*. This section culminates with a reconstruction of the solo cycle *Ecstatic Dances*, which vivifies how Wigman consolidated her distinctive practice between the years 1917 and 1919.

The fourth part then focuses on the development of her group works, which reversed the relation to her teachers and predecessors implied by her solos. For her group dances rejected the large-scale festival format favored by Dalcroze and Laban and adopted a mode that recalled Duncan's practice of choreographing for a small group of her students. In so doing, Wigman achieved what almost always had eluded Duncan, that is, composing roles for her dancers that did *not* reduce them to pale imitations of herself. As her group choreography evolved, she reinterpreted the utopian impulse of the festival productions staged by Dalcroze and Laban, substituting a community of women for their communities of Mankind. Although Wigman did not fully realize this vision until the twenties, her group choreography through the teens suggested possibilities pursued later.

WIGMAN'S EARLY LIFE, 1886–1910

In 1886 Mary Wiegmann was born into an enterprising family clan in Hannover, the eldest daughter of one of three brothers who together had built a successful business. The late nineteenth century was a period of rapid industrialization in Germany, commonly referred to as the *Gründerzeit* (era of founders), when men like the Wiegmann brothers could prosper from selling sewing machines and bicycles and in one generation move from the working class to the bourgeoisie. Mary's mother, Amalie, helped out in the family business, located behind the family home. She was widowed young: Mary, her eldest child to survive infancy, was nine; her son Heinrich six; and her youngest child, Elisabeth, not yet two. In 1898 Amalie married her husband's twin brother and business partner. And so a few months before her twelfth birthday, Mary's uncle became her stepfather.[1]

The family's upward mobility required that Mary's younger brother Heinrich attend a Gymnasium in preparation for university study and entry into the professions. However, when the director of the private *höhere Töchterschule* (higher girls' school) that Mary and Elisabeth attended suggested that Mary enroll in the first girls' Gymnasium to open in Hannover, her mother and stepfather rejected the idea. They feared lest their daughter become a bluestocking, even though Mary, intellectually curious and an avid reader, welcomed the prospect. Had she attended the Gymnasium and continued her education further, she might have counted among the first generation of German women educated at German universities, an elite that numbered just over four thousand by 1914.[2]

Rather than attend Gymnasium, Mary was sent to study languages abroad, at boarding schools in England and Switzerland. At age sixteen she returned home and passed her time—as she had since childhood—reading, writing poetry, pursuing her interests in music and theater. While still in school, she had written and staged plays for family get-togethers and directed her friends in games of "living statues." From the age of six or seven, she had studied piano, and later took up voice lessons. Considering her pupil especially talented, the singing teacher recommended professional training. Mary responded enthusiastically to the idea, although her parents once again vetoed the suggestion.[3]

Her parents did, however, encourage her to attend *Tanzstunden*, lessons in comportment and social dance intended as preparation for a young lady's debut in society. From her parents' point of view, there was no question but that their daughter's future required a suitable marriage, and they never entertained the idea that she might work for a living instead. From Mary's point of view, learning to dance afforded her great pleasure, especially dancing the waltz.[4] She had experienced similar pleasure when a boarding-school friend taught her skirt-dancing, an experience that she viewed in retrospect as her first contact with the tangible entity of space. Her memoirs recall her experience of "becoming entangled and disentangled by the enveloping skirts, enormous skirts."[5] But during her boarding-school days Mary had no idea that such movement experiences could form the basis for an expressive language.

After finishing her schooling, Mary spent seven years at home, struggling to reconcile her parents'—and the larger society's—expectations that she become a wife and mother with her own sense of wanting more from life. Although she became engaged twice, neither engagement resulted in marriage. Her memoirs recall her despair at this time: "I cried, I begged, and asked my creator to bring me clarity. I didn't know what I should do, I had to break away, I didn't want to continue any longer, I could not. The entire bourgeois life collapsed on top of me, you might say."[6]

While still living at home, Mary saw a performance by the Wiesenthal sisters. Grete Wiesenthal, just a year older than Mary and
the leading member of the troupe, had studied ballet since childhood at the Vienna Court Opera, where she had joined the corps
de ballet in 1901. But within a few years, dissatisfied with the opportunities offered by the Court Ballet and inspired by the dancing
of Isadora Duncan, she began to choreograph her own dances. In
1907 she left the Vienna Court Ballet, and the following year she
began to tour independently, accompanied by her sisters Else and
Berta. Mary, aged twenty-one, saw the Wiesenthals in 1908 on their
first independent tour.[7]

The sisters' performances highlighted Grete's revisionings of
the Viennese waltz. Her choreography transformed the popular
nineteenth-century social dance into a form for a woman alone or
with intimates of her own sex. The expressiveness of Grete's hands
while performing *The Blue Danube Waltz* particularly impressed
Mary. Her memoirs recount:

> *The Blue Danube Waltz* deeply impressed me. . . . For the first time in
> my life I saw that hands can be more than hands, that hands can
> become buds and flowers that can bloom before one's eyes. . . . And
> when the moment came when I finally broke away from the bour-
> geois family circle, I remembered Wiesenthal's hands. And I said: I
> would like to do something similar. With God's help I would like to
> do something that keeps the body in motion, something that sets the
> body in motion.[8]

During the same year that she saw the Wiesenthals, Mary also
saw a demonstration by Emile Jaques-Dalcroze and his students.
Around the turn of the century, Dalcroze, a professor of harmony
at the Music Conservatory in Geneva, had developed a method
for relating music and movement, called "eurhythmics." Originally
conceived as an educational tool for heightening musical sensitivity
through movement improvisation, eurhythmics became a source
for choreographic experimentation as well. Wigman's memoirs recount her experience of being "impressed" by "the bodily action
that I saw on the stage" as "a pair of young girls in picture-book
beautiful Greek costumes [demonstrated] Weber's Invitation to the
Dance."[9] Once again she responded to the power of the articulate
body in space.

The 1908 performances by the Wiesenthal sisters and by Dal-

croze and his students directed Mary away from her avocations of
music and theater and toward the vocation of dance. When she
heard that Dalcroze planned to open an institute at Hellerau, near
Dresden, she managed to secure the necessary funds to enroll and
left the family circle in Hannover. Having rejected the role of bourgeois wife and mother, she was determined to prove herself an
independent woman and an artist. In 1910, at age twenty-three,
she began her training as a dancer.[10]

HELLERAU AND MONTE VERITA,
1910–1919

Hellerau, a planned community and the first garden city in Germany, was the vision of the Deutsche Werkbund, an organization
dedicated to the reform of industrialized life. The community, located in a picturesque landscape outside Dresden, centered around
a factory organized according to the craft ideal and homes for
workers set amidst abundant open space. Just as construction began on the project, the leaders of the Werkbund saw a demonstration of eurhythmics. Convinced that Dalcroze's method offered a
perfect complement to their utopian vision, the Werkbund leadership invited Dalcroze to establish an institute at Hellerau, and he
agreed to leave his professorship in Geneva. Sharing his sponsors'
utopian vision, he wrote: "I want to raise rhythm to the status of a
social institution and prepare the way for a new style . . . which will
become the product of the soul of all inhabitants."[11]

Dalcroze's institute modeled an alternative to the stratified system of higher education in Germany. It was coeducational at a time
when German universities had just begun to admit women as ma-
triculated students, and it offered classes open to all members of the
community—workers, their wives, and their children—at a time
when continuing education and community outreach were still
novel concepts. The pedagogical approach of eurhythmics paralleled the ideals of progressive education: learning by doing rather
than learning by rote and experiencing the arts as a means for
developing the whole person. As the prospectus for the institute
stated, "The aim of the entire method is to build an entirely harmonious person, his understanding and his character together."[12]

Contrary to the masculine pronoun in the prospectus, the first professional class, of which Wigman was a member, enrolled six times more women than men. Wigman's classmates numbered more than a hundred, among whom were others who would go on to make a reputation in dance: Rudolf Bode, Gertrud Falke, Valeria Kratina.[13] The professional curriculum offered classes in rhythmic gymnastics; solfège, and voice and ear training; piano improvisation; dance and gymnastics; and anatomy. Dalcroze's classes in rhythmic gymnastics adopted improvisation as a primary teaching strategy. Selma Odom describes typical class exercises:

> Students might begin by walking around the room, following the teacher's [piano improvisations,] responding directly to the beat and to changes in speed and dynamics. . . . They might also be asked to react quickly, starting and stopping, or responding to changes in tempo, moving perhaps twice as fast or twice as slow, following the musical cues. Another fundamental practice was the "stepping" of rhythmic patterns. . . . [The teacher] would play, and after listening carefully, the students would immediately repeat what they heard in movement, matching their steps to the duration and sequence of notes they perceived. Sometimes they would "echo" the pattern, moving in silence, immediately following the example played, or they would move in canon, making one pattern while listening to the music for the next one. . . .
>
> The work to develop the sense of measure, or bartime, was formed by enlarging the basic arm motions of conducting. . . . Experienced students could beat regular bartime with their arms while simultaneously stepping rhythms of great complexity. . . .
>
> [Dalcroze] developed literally hundreds of exercises to help students feel the infinite variety of what could be achieved through shaping the flow and energy of breathing. Other concepts were also used to encourage the sense of phrasing, such as contrasting muscular force (light or heavy movements), using a real or imaginary weight or resistance (stretching an elastic), or simply taking turns moving with a partner or in groups (alternating voices, movement versus stillness).
>
> Exercises such as stepping rhythms, beating bartime, or abdominal breathing with sudden contraction could all be done in a more or less straight-forward, neutral manner ("realizations") or with stylized or emotional variations ("expressive realizations"). The work with expression led to "plastique animée"—choreography, really— of more complex forms such as inventions, fugues, and rondos. Here the movement would fuse stepped rhythms with almost any

sort of expressive body attitude and gesture appropriate to the music. Sometimes students even created what was called "plastic counterpoint," or realizations independent of, but related to, the music.[14]

At Hellerau, Wigman acquired the fundamental working method that she would deploy through the remainder of her career—improvisation based on conceptual principles. She learned how to manipulate movement by improvisationally varying its formal qualities. Unlike the first generation of early modern dancers, such as Isadora Duncan, who had to find their own methods for transforming extratheatrical movement techniques into theatrical disciplines, Wigman inherited a system for doing so. In this system, movement became not only a "subjective" response to music but also an "objective" visualization of musical qualities. Although Wigman later rejected Dalcroze's assumed interdependence of music and movement, she retained the working method of structured improvisation.

According to her memoirs, Hellerau enabled her to embark on a choreographic career, albeit in private, and at the same time frustrated her desire to dance without music. She acknowledged that "there I found that dancing was my way of expressing myself artistically." Nonetheless, she noted that "I didn't think too much of the Dalcroze Institute, but I did as I was told and then I danced for myself in my room at night."[15]

In the drama of Wigman's memoirs, her ambivalence toward Hellerau set up her experience of liberation on Monte Verità. Termed the "origins of the counterculture" by historian Martin Green, Monte Verità was an artists' colony in the Swiss Alps where Wigman spent the years of the First World War in voluntary exile with Rudolf Laban and his circle of dancers. She remembered her encounter with Laban as both freeing and disciplining her artistic energies, and her contact with the countercultural milieu of Monte Verità as a passionate release from the bourgeois mores of her upbringing. However, her memoirs gloss over the ambivalence she felt toward Laban after the war, once both had returned to Germany and become rivals for the leadership of German dance. And her memoirs only hint at her experience on Monte Verità as the only one of Laban's close female associates *not* erotically entangled with her mentor.

As Wigman tells the story, she had promised Dalcroze that she would direct an eurhythmics institute planned for Berlin. While waiting for the Berlin school to open, however, she decided to take a summer course from Laban on Monte Verita. (She had heard about the choreographer from Emil Nolde, to whom she had been introduced by a roommate in Dresden, and from Suzanne Perrottet, Dalcroze's assistant who had quit Hellerau in order to work with Laban.)[16] Halfway through the summer course, Wigman received the final contract for her teaching position in Berlin, but by then the prospect no longer seemed interesting, and she sent back the contract unsigned.[17] In retrospect she wrote, "To me it was meant to be a short summer course, and it turned into a life's direction."[18] She followed Laban to Munich in winter 1913–1914 and returned with him to Monte Verita the following summer, where the two remained in voluntary exile after war broke out in August 1914.

At both the Laban School in Munich, founded in 1912, and at the school's summer home on Monte Verita, which became its permanent home during the war years, the curriculum was based on the rubric of *Tanz-Ton-Wort* (dance-sound-word). As a school prospectus defined the curriculum:

> The gymnastic, musical, and pantomimic dance; the meter, dynamic, rhythm, melody, and harmony of music and speech; the risk, choice, remembrance, linking, and articulation of ideas: these are the developmental means that together determine the totality of man's activity. . . . The mastery of these expressive means will enable the student to disseminate and to enjoy the noble joy of life in artistic form.[19]

Like Dalcroze, Laban relied on improvisation as his fundamental working method. But during this period Laban's method was not as systematic as eurhythmics, and the limits placed on improvisation were less restrictive. Significantly, movement did not necessarily require the accompaniment of music but could be performed to the accompaniment of speech, percussive sound, or silence. Laban's challenge to the eurhythmic interdependence of music and movement accorded with Wigman's own proclivities, and she remembered:

> We danced with music and without it. We danced to the rhythms of poetry, and sometimes Laban made us move to words, phrases, little poems we had to invent ourselves. . . .

Laban had the extraordinary quality of setting you free artistically, enabling you to find your own roots, and thus stabilized, to discover your own potentialities, to develop your own technique and your individual style of dancing.

He had built up and devised his gymnastic system [based on the natural organic movement of the human body and the principles of tension and relaxation.] Otherwise, however, there were as yet no limits, no theoretical lines drawn, no strict laws to be followed. What years later was to become his dance theory . . . was at that time still a free country, a wilderness, an exciting and fascinating hunting ground where discoveries were made day after day.[20]

Working with Laban, Wigman was not compelled to dance to music, as she had been at Hellerau. The open-ended improvisations he set allowed her to release and to intensify the expressive range of her movement. At the same time as his method freed her, it disciplined her more rigorously than had eurhythmics. On Monte Verita, Wigman became the instrument for Laban's movement research, for it was during this period that he generated the insights later systematized in his movement notation and theory of spatial harmony. Wigman's memoirs recall:

During those months Laban started to work intensely on his dance notation. . . . His gymnastic system . . . was the first result of his research. His swing scales, by then properly defined, were the basis for his "Theory of Harmony of Movement." . . .

The first of these scales consisted of five different swinging movements leading in a spiral line from downward to upward. The organic combination of their spatial directions and their natural three-dimensional qualities led to a perfect harmony. The different movements not only flowed effortlessly from one to the other, they seemed to be born of each other. . . .

It also was hard work for me! Every movement had to be done over and over again until it was controlled and could be analyzed, transposed, and transformed into an adequate symbol. . . .

I believe the foundations of my career as a dancer as well as a dance pedagogue were laid in those few weeks.[21]

The freedom and the discipline she experienced on Monte Verita enabled Wigman to refine the working method she had first encountered at Hellerau—structured improvisation based on the manipulation of the spatial, temporal, and dynamic dimensions of movement.

The milieu of Monte Verita encouraged risk taking, in art and

in lifestyle. Founded in 1900 by Ida Hofmann and Henri Oedenkoven, the colony near Ascona originated as a commune for disaf-
fected young people who desired an alternative to the lifestyle of
the urban bourgeoisie. Over time it became a gathering place for
rebels of many kinds from the *Bildungsbürgertum* (educated bourgeoisie), among them artists and writers—Hermann Hesse, Else
Lasker-Schüler, Marianne Werefkin, Alexey Jawlensky; political
anarchists—Peter Kropotkin, Erich Mühsam, Gusto Gräser; mys-
tics and psychoanalysts—Otto Gross, Theodor Reuss; Dadaists—
Hugo Ball, Emmy Hennings, Tristan Tzara.[22] While Hellerau attempted to reform the existing structure of industrialized society,
Monte Verita provided an alternative to that structure.

Challenging the mores of the urban bourgeoisie, Asconans also
challenged the role of middle-class women in industrialized society.
Over the period from 1902 to 1915 Ida Hofmann, cofounder of
Monte Verita, published a series of pamphlets on the women's question. Her writings attacked civil and church marriages, advocating
instead cohabitation, "marriage of conscience." She believed that
women's freedom and equality with men depended not on paid
employment—"the mournful and unnatural necessity of bread-
winning"—but on a life lived close to nature—the practices of
vegetarianism and nature cure.[23] In fact, Monte Verita served as a
nature cure resort, and one of the dancers' few sources of income
came from the "natural" physical therapy they performed on pa-
tients at the area's numerous health spas.[24]

Hofmann's doctrine of free love was put into practice on Monte
Verita. Among the marriages of conscience were her own with
Henri Oedenkoven and Marianne Werefkin's with Alexey Jawlensky. With the exception of Wigman, the women involved with Laban also lived out Hofmann's credo. When he arrived on Monte
Verita, Laban was married to Maja Lederer, a singer, who bore him
five children. While still living with her, he also took up with Suzanne Perrottet, who bore him a son, and with Dussia Bereska, who
bore him at least one other child. Laban organized his women as a
sort of "freemasonic" lodge of women, called "Libertas und Frater-
nitas." He took responsibility for none of his children, leaving the
duties of parenting to their mothers.[25]

Wigman's memoirs hint at Laban's erotic relations with many of
his students and colleagues. She recounts her first teaching assign-

ment, when Laban had fallen ill and asked her to take over his classes:

> I had never done any pedagogic work previously, except perhaps one or two sessions when there was an emergency. Those females who subjected themselves to the hardship and training of physical and rhythmic movement did not do so for the love of the dance, but for Laban's sake, and they had only contempt for me. I had to fight for each step and each inch of floor space. However, when after many weeks Laban returned to work, I was able to present him with his dancing harem completely intact.[26]

In this passage, Wigman's substitute teaching sustained Laban's students until the master teacher—and his erotic aura—could return. In another passage, Wigman indicates that her substitute teaching enabled Laban to pursue his "flirtations" during class hours. She writes: "We had gymnastics in the early morning, personally conducted by Laban. On occasion he would wink at me and sneak off with a vaguely uttered excuse. Then I had to take over the class. I knew that the 'boss' would be in the office flirting with the beautiful Italian secretary—only to relax and escape from the sight of his enthusiastic but by no means always attractive dance pupils."[27] In both passages, Wigman's shyly mocking tone distances her from the erotic aura of her mentor.

According to her memoirs, she stayed with Laban "until I felt that I had had enough technical training."[28] As the choreographer narrates the events of 1918:

> Then I went into solitude, into a retreat in Switzerland, and I knew very well what I wanted.
> It was a religious community in which I had chosen to work. There was a nunnery nearby. . . .
> That was a terrible and wonderful year. I was ill and in need, but an ideal spurred and guided me, and I worked each day as long as there was light to see. I created dances which to me seemed expressive of the joys, the sorrows, the conflicts of mankind, and finally I felt ready to come out of my nunlike solitude and dance for others.[29]

According to Hedwig Müller, Wigman's "retreat" was to a sanatorium after she had suffered a breakdown. Her biographer presents her breakdown as the result of an overdetermined sequence of events: first the choreographer's decision to leave the Laban School and open her own studio, then the death of her stepfather and her brother's return from the war as an amputee, and finally an "unhappy love affair" that demanded a definitive choice between "profession or marriage." Müller comments: "In principle the decision was already made, but the current situation brought it once again into question. Caught between desire and social norms, Mary Wigman broke down."[30] Strikingly, each event in the overdetermined sequence narrated by Müller involved the loss of a male intimate or authority figure—her father's twin, the brother of her childhood, a last potential spouse, and her male mentor. At the same time as she experienced estrangement from men, she turned to a woman friend and colleague for support. Berthe Trümpy was one of the dancer's first students, and she later accompanied her on her first German tour and subsidized the founding of the Wigman School in Dresden. Although Wigman later had several long-term affairs with men, she built her career from this point around mostly female associates. In other words, her breakdown marked a period of transition during which she turned away from the enabling authority of her male mentor and embraced the enabling atmosphere of female collegiality. Not only her professional biography but also her oeuvre suggests this shift, for as I will argue in the following chapter, the trajectory of Wigman's career after 1918 challenged the (heterosexist) duality of gender and staged a utopian vision of female community.

SOLOS, 1914–1919

That Wigman adopted the improvisational working methods of Dalcroze and Laban is clear, because her later writing, as well as the reminiscences of former students and members of her company, attests to her reliance on structured improvisation. But what is less clear is how this working method enabled her technical realization of the *Gestalt im Raum*. Perhaps a dancer trained by Wigman or by one of her students could attempt to recover her transformation of Dalcroze's and Laban's methods in the studio. But I cannot recover her practice in this way and so am left with only archival fragments. Given that Wigman had yet to achieve wide public recognition during the teens, the evidence that survives of her early concerts is scanty, especially when compared with the piles of photographs, programs, and reviews that document her career during the twenties and thirties.

Nonetheless, the surviving evidence does allow me to draw two interrelated conclusions. First, that not until 1919 did Wigman arrive at the sort of solo program that established her reputation in the early twenties. That program typically arranged her solos so that "lighter" dances framed "darker" dances. Her first appearance in a large public theater, on 18 June 1917 at Zurich's Pfauen Theater, anticipated this arrangement. The concert opened with *Prelude VIII* and *Aria*, both set to Bach. Two cycles formed the centerpiece of the concert: the first, given the overall title *Ghostly Dances*, comprised *Mexican Song of Magic, Satan's Pleasure*, and Saint-Saëns's *Dance of Death*; the second cycle, given the overall title *Dreams*, was set to music composed by Laban and comprised *The Stillness, Dark Rhythms*, and *Egyptian Song*. The concert closed with Liszt's *Devil's Waltz*.[31]

However, not until Wigman resumed her public career in February 1919, following her breakdown, did the program arrangement anticipated by the Pfauen Theater concert become formalized. Through the early and mid-twenties, her solo concerts typically opened and closed with dances, often set to preexistent piano scores, that emphasized the abstract qualities of motion. In contrast, the dances thus framed, often set to an original percussive score or to silence, emphasized the suprapersonal forces seemingly animated by her dancing. Both kinds of solos relied upon the principle of the *Gestalt im Raum*, although the "lighter" and "darker" solos marked opposing endpoints of a continuum from the intoxication of dance to demonic and ecstatic possession.

My second conclusion is that as this program arrangement took shape, the vestiges of representational framing that had characterized Wigman's dances before 1918 gave way. It seems that the alternation of "lighter" and "darker" solos supplanted the loosely representational pretexts evident in Wigman's earlier concerts. Consider the example of a concert, titled "The Self in Rhythm and Space" ("Der Mensch in Rhythmus und Raum"), that she presented during February 1916 in several informal venues: the titles of her dances suggest either the pictorialization of literature and visual art (*Thus Spake Zarathustra, The Plastic Arts*) or musical visualization (*Valse triste*, set to Sibelius; *Zingara*, to Chaminade; and *Fairy Tale*, to Raff). The descriptive evidence that survives suggests that spectators both interpreted the dances in accord with the representational pretexts offered by their titles *and* perceived a nonrepresentational quality that could not be accounted for in representational terms. Rudolf Lämmel remembered *The Plastic Arts* as "an interesting attempt to represent painting, sculpture, and graphics in dance terms."[32] The one extant review, authored by "H. B." (Hans Brandenburg?) in the *Berner Tagblatt*, concurred with Lämmel as to the illustrative quality of *The Plastic Arts*. In contrast, H. B. found a quite inexplicable quality in *Thus Spake Zarathustra*: "One watches with pleasure and interest the beautiful flow of movements that have nothing measured, nothing studied or drilled about them. Everything comes from personal inspiration and instinctive expression of will and opinion."[33] Given the dense quality of Nietzsche's text, it is not surprising that Wigman's "pictorialization" seemed beyond verbal description.

"The Self in Rhythm and Space" comprised Wigman's major solo program between her 1914 debut at the Laban School and her 1917 concert at the Pfauen Theater. In April 1916, two months after presenting "The Self in Rhythm and Space," she saw a performance by Isadora Duncan, which she found "horrible."[34] Although she had reacted against Duncanesque dancing since her choreographic debut, it is interesting to speculate on whether seeing Duncan herself made a difference as she prepared her program for the Pfauen Theater, a program that anticipated her prototypical concert during the early twenties. If Duncan's performance did have an influence, it was both positive and negative. Unlike "The Self in Rhythm and Space," the Pfauen Theater program emphasized dances set to classical compositions (Bach, Liszt) and in this way perhaps took Duncan's practice as a model. Also unlike the 1916 concert, the Pfauen Theater program de-emphasized pictorializations of literary and visual motifs, at least judging from the titles and the extant reviews, and in this way perhaps took Duncan's practice as a negative example. One reviewer commented: "What we admire about Fräulein Wiegmann's performance is her powerful expressivity, supported by her most thorough physical training and directed by her strong imagination. What we miss in her accomplishments is sunniness, happiness, and joy in beauty."[35] Was it the experience of seeing Isadora that reinforced Wigman's desire to reject "sunniness" in favor of "expressive power," to reject "The Self in . . . Space" in favor of the *Gestalt im Raum?* As Rudolf Lämmel remembered the Pfauen Theater concert: "Courageous attempts. Renunciation of costume, make-up, lighting. In short, paying no attention to and negating all the theatrical resources brought to the stage."[36]

Lämmel was one of the critics who, along with Fritz Böhme, constructed a genealogy for absolute dance that positioned Wigman as its endpoint and culmination. Hence Lämmel's retrospective view posits a linear progression in her early career. The evidence of her early concerts suggests otherwise, however, for after her Pfauen Theater program her choreographic practice did not advance further toward the ideal of absolute dance but rather retreated toward the representational framing of her performance. Her next solo concert, titled *Ecstatic Dances* (*Ekstatische Tänze*), premiered on 10 November 1917 at the Laban School in Zurich. Deeply influenced by a conference on the occult held earlier that year on Monte Verita, the concert was subtitled "a first evening of ritual performance art" ("*Erster Abend ritueller Vortragskunst*"). A poetic and detailed description by Berthe Trümpy documents this concert and evidences its clear representational framing.[37]

It is illuminating to compare Trümpy's "scenario" with the reviews of the solo cycle in its revised form, prepared by Wigman for her 1919 touring program. In contrast to Trümpy, who interprets the 1917 version as a series of impersonations, the reviewers of the 1919 version comment on the way the dancer subverted the projection of a coherent persona. As reconstructed from these accounts, the two versions demonstrate Wigman's decisive move away from representational framing after 1918.

The first version of *Ecstatic Dances* provides the representational pretext of varied modes of religious ecstasy. The titles of the six solos—*The Nun* (*Die Nonne*), *The Dancer of Our Lady* (*Der Tänzer unsrer lieben Frau*), *Idolatry* (*Götzendienst*), *Sacrifice* (*Opfer*), *The Dervish* (*Der Derwisch*), *Temple Dance* (*Tempeltanz*)—establish a sequence of impersonations. Changing costumes between solos, employing props, Wigman presents her self-transformations as a succession of characters. Strikingly, she takes on recognizably feminine and masculine personae as well as personae that blur the distinction between masculinity and femininity. Nonetheless, the representational context for the work supports the spectator's assignment of gender, judging from the evidence of Trümpy's scenario, which varies the personal pronoun from "he" to "she" to "it" in tracing the choreographer's changing personae.[38]

Trümpy's scenario reads the gender of Wigman's personae from her spatial attitudes: a passive attitude toward space signals a feminine persona, an active attitude a masculine persona, and the integration of passive and active attitudes suggests the blurring of femininity and masculinity. The difference between passive and active attitudes toward space can be demonstrated through variations on a simple walk: a dancer can exhibit an active attitude by propelling herself energetically forward, or a passive attitude by allowing herself to be pulled forward as if by external forces. Judging from oral history, in her later teaching Wigman set endless variations for her students on the difference between active and passive orientations toward space. However, whether in 1917 she intended *Ecstatic Dances* to associate gender differences with active and passive attitudes toward space, or whether Trümpy independently constructed the correspondence, remains an open question.

As visualized by Trümpy's scenario, Wigman appears in a gray frock and red robe for the opening dance, *The Nun*. Wax candles and incense mark the studio space, curtained in black, as a place for religious devotion. The choreographer's deathly white face reminds Trümpy of a medieval ecstatic: "She raises her arms with difficulty; her pain-twisted hands fall, protecting her chest and lap—everything becomes ice-cold, the cold that emanates from the snow-blown face kills, kills everything—somewhere a convulsion arises in her poor body—repose, repose, rigid ice-cold repose— her hands soar like gentle ornaments on a Gothic volute."[39] Her rigid stillness, the stasis of action, reveals a passive attitude toward space. In Trümpy's reading, this passive attitude toward space supports Wigman's impersonation of a female religious.

In *The Dancer of Our Lady* the choreographer transforms herself into a (male) acrobat showing off tricks for the Virgin Mother. An image of the Virgin hangs on the wall, in front of which Wigman performs: "The good dancer stands on his head—looks about him —somewhat surprised—how remarkable everything appears—he stands again seriously on one leg and shows the Virgin Mother how well he can do it."[40] Wigman's self-confident locomotion projects an active attitude toward space, and in Trümpy's reading this active attitude supports her impersonation of a male devotee.

In the following *Idolatry,* Wigman's worship takes on a more primitive and asexual form. She appears in a straw cape and cap, her mouth smeared with red, an apparition from the "primeval forest," turning and turning until collapsing, her energy spent:

> Suddenly the space draped with black disappeared—a being crouches in the middle of the primeval forest shaded an evil poison green; the being pale as straw with a blood-smeared mouth; the cap on top of his head has a dark hole; one sees into the vicious, empty head—the head rattles, rattles, meanly—he will devour the moon, uh, the poison-yellow moon; snakes will crawl out of his stomach, poison-yellow, red, green; insects whir in his head, horrifically venomous. Vampire—the straw cloak slides hissing over the modern primeval forested bog, uh, the evil mud creatures sch, schsch-uh, the big drum—bumm—silence—bumm—the great spirit, greater than the mad priest of the primeval forest, catches him in a circle; he must spin, always spin, until he collapses in the furious swamp and darkness.[41]

At first referred to by Trümpy as "it," later as "he," Wigman at first actively shapes the space, but by the end, spinning and collapsing, passively gives way to space. Thus her dancing subverts the association set up in the opening two solos between femininity and a passive attitude toward space and between masculinity and an active attitude toward space, blurring the distinction of gender.

For *Sacrifice* Trümpy's account returns to the feminine pronoun used when describing *The Nun.* As before, Wigman's feminine persona dictates a passive attitude toward space:

> A priestess—she wants to give her sweet, beautiful body to a distant and alien godhead. At first she searches for gestures shyly and gently. A trembling wave of motion runs through her, then again, more passionately. The shells of her hands solemnly float upwards. She bends her body low—how moving is the thin line of her back! How proudly humble! Each movement gently, offering itself with unbounded devotion.[42]

The masculine pronoun returns in Trümpy's account of *The Dervish.* Dressed in red pants and a green cap and sporting a beard, Wigman begins sitting, making hand gestures as if carrying out a ritual procedure. Then the figure, referred to as "he," slowly begins circling, ultimately returning to "his" ritual gestures but unable to fully execute them, as if the circling had unbalanced "his" focus:

> There he sits with stiffly bent knees. . . . He raises his hands, lays them on his back; he completes the prescribed gestures of the ritual almost indifferently. He rises slowly—Now terror appears in his steel-blue eyes, gazing from over his woolly beard; with deep steps he plunges into a circle; suddenly terrified, he reels into a wall—Oh, now the eternity in him has burst open, like a wound; he feels the horror of infinity; the magical spell grips him; he wants to flee from himself; again repose—Again he attempts the ritual gestures, but never again will they become familiar and calming; the deep wound of eternity tears him apart, destroys him.[43]

Like the figure in *Idolatry,* the dervish first adopts an active attitude toward space but then withdraws and assumes a passive attitude toward space. Unlike the figure in *Idolatry,* however, the dervish's mingling of spatial attitudes does not blur his gender identity.

Trümpy describes the final *Temple Dance* with a feminine pronoun. Wigman appears in a red filmy gown, softly gesturing, finally sinking to the ground. A distant gong sounds, closing the series of transformations: "Now everything is in the process of being extinguished—tall wax candles, the woman floating in a delicate red veil, her heavy dark hair barely held by a shimmering band. A gesture of her wonderful hands gently dies away; a diagonal through the dark space ends with a dreamlike sinking to the floor—stillness—from the distance the sounding of a temple gong."[44] Sinking and stillness epitomize a passive attitude toward space. Hence the cycle ends with a reassertion of feminine identity.

As reconstructed from reviews, the revised version of *Ecstatic Dances,* premiered in 1919, does away with the representational pretext and gendered personae of the version described by Trümpy. Wigman eliminates the two solos Trümpy identified as male impersonations—*The Dancer of Our Lady* and *The Dervish.* She adds a new solo titled *Prayer (Gebet),* roughly based on *The Nun.*[45] In the revised version, *Prayer* introduces *Sacrifice* ("a priestess . . . each movement gently offers itself with unbounded devotion"), *Idolatry* ("a being crouches in the middle of the primeval forest"), and *Temple Dance* ("now everything is extinguished"). Included on the choreographer's 1919 touring program, the revised cycle allowed for flexible

Fig. 5. Mary Wigman in *Idolatry,* part of the solo cycle *Ecstatic Dances* as revised for her first solo tour in 1919 (courtesy of the Mary Wigman Archive)

programming of her repertory. As became her common practice, not all the solos in the cycle necessarily appeared on the same program or in a fixed order. One program lists *Temple Dance* and *Idolatry*, another *Sacrifice* and *Idolatry*. Whether all four solos were presented together or one pair was singled out, the cycle displayed the dialectic between "lighter" and "darker" solos that came to characterize the arrangement of Wigman's concerts as a whole.

The revised version of *Ecstatic Dances* no longer suggested a series of impersonations but rather a continuing transformation of ecstatic states. Confronting the changing *Gestalt* of the dancer, spectators grappled with its seeming lack of fixed gender, neither consistently feminine, masculine, nor androgynous. One reviewer notes: "Mary Wigman's work begins where charm leaves off—generally understandable, direct, and primarily sensual charm. She doesn't want to work with feminine means; she is impersonal and objective."[46] Another reviewer comments, "Some have characterized Wigman's art as masculine. 'Impersonal' is more apt."[47] The reviewers' characterizations of Wigman's solo choreography as neither "feminine" nor "masculine" but rather "impersonal" point toward her realization of the *Gestalt im Raum*.

Among the four solos that constitute *Ecstatic Dances*, the surviving evidence for *Idolatry* most vividly demonstrates the principle of the *Gestalt im Raum*. A photograph (fig. 5) shows Wigman "[spinning], always [spinning]," as Trümpy noted. The camera freezes her twirling, her face hidden between a long, stiff ruffle of straw hanging around her neck and a close-fitting cap over her hair. A dark bodysuit covers her legs and feet and her arms to the wrists. Her hands flail out from the mass of spinning straw, the only reminders of bare human flesh. As in *Witch Dance I,* her costume functions like a mask. The onstage apparition eclipses the dancer's offstage persona. As a critic comments, "The artist entered wearing a grotesque mask, disguising herself in order to appear undisguised."[48]

In spring 1919 Wigman appeared in Davos, Zurich, Arosa, Saint Gallen, and Winterthur. Her program included *Ecstatic Dances* in addition to other newly choreographed cycles: *Dance Songs (Tanzlieder)*, usually placed first on the program; *Dances of Night (Tänze der Nacht)*, often excerpted, along with solos from *Ecstatic Dances,* and placed in the center of the program; and *Hungarian Dances (Ungarische Tänze)*, usually placed last on the program and set to

Brahms. This was the program that the choreographer took on her
first German tour in fall 1919. Accompanied by Berthe Trümpy
and partially subsidized by her mother, who had become reconciled to her daughter's dance career, Wigman performed in
Munich, Berlin, Nuremberg, Hannover, Bremen, Hamburg, and
Dresden.[49] In retrospect, Fritz Böhme described the Berlin premiere of *Idolatry* as the originating moment of absolute dance:

> For that time it was a rather vehement and impulsive dance, which
> accelerated to a breath-taking tempo and then ended with a sudden
> collapse. . . . In that solo the question of the relation between music
> and dance was newly solved: music as sound, an ascending yet sub-
> servient dynamic means for underscoring the sequence of move-
> ment. . . . Movement was no longer a moving picture or moving
> sculpture. . . . Dance without music was born.[50]

For once, I do not dispute Böhme's assessment, for my research
concurs with his genealogy in viewing the 1919 version of *Ecstatic
Dances* as the crystallization of Wigman's choreographic practice.
Over a period of five years, from her choreographic debut in 1914
to her first German tour in 1919, the dancer consolidated the
practice that Böhme labels absolute dance and I term the *Gestalt
im Raum*.

Other scholars have examined the formation of a complementary mode of absolute dance on Monte Verita at the Dadaist Cabaret Voltaire. Annabelle Melzer, Naima Prevots, and Harold Segel
all have pointed out parallels between Wigman's dancing and Dadaist dances—the use of the mask, the dissociation of music and movement, the primacy of the dance idea. Indeed, as all three scholars
argue, such parallels were not unlikely, given that members of Laban's circle—Suzanne Perrottet, Claire Walther, Sophie Taeuber—
regularly performed at the Cabaret Voltaire. On 29 March 1917,
according to Hugo Ball's diary, Wigman attended a performance
that featured Sophie Taeuber's "abstract dance" titled "Song of the
Flying Fish and the Sea Horses" and Claire Walther's "expressionist
dances." A month later, on 28 April 1917, Ball's diary again noted
Wigman's presence at a performance that featured Suzanne Perrottet dancing to piano and violin compositions by herself, Laban,
and Arnold Schönberg.[51] Annabelle Melzer proclaims "the meeting
between the Laban-Wigman dancers and the dada performers . . .
one of the most interesting liaisons in the history of avant-garde
performance."[52] Melzer continues:

By 1917, a stable working relationship is evident between the Laban-Wigman dancers and the Dada Gallery performers. All dance events at the Gallery were performed by dancers of the Laban-Wigman school and whether choreographed by one of the dancers or by Ball or another of the dadas, a semblance of stylistic unity, an agreement on medium and method seems apparent. Barefoot bodies, in draped cloth or athletic costumes, often masked, moved in group or solo dances to the beat of a gong, a drum or to the sound of silence. The costumes were neither meant to reveal nor conceal, only to add to the effect of the dance idea by whatever texture, color or line seemed best, and to allow the dancer the greatest liberty of movement. Costume, scenery, "music," were all subordinated to the "idea" of the dance. Simple, essential gestures spoke a new vocabulary of movement while experimental creations in time furthered the development of a new temporal rhythm in the dance. Designs in time and space would now arouse an audience by sheer power of aesthetic form.[53]

In this passage, Melzer conflates the innovations of Laban and Wigman and further conflates their "shared" aesthetic with the aesthetic of Dadaist dance. To be sure, it is difficult to distinguish the rhetoric voiced by Hugo Ball—"the dance has become an end in itself"—from the program of absolute dance articulated by Laban, Wigman, and their critics.[54] Visual evidence, however, does provide a basis for discriminating between Dadaist performance, Wigman's dancing, and Laban's choreographic works. Like many other theater reformers and performance artists of the time, the Dadaists, Wigman, and Laban were interested in the use and principle of the mask. But they each deployed the mask in a different way.[55]

Judging from a photograph titled *Mathematician* (fig. 6), Laban's use of the mask is perhaps the most conventional. For the mask seems to fall into the category Susan Smith labels satiric in her survey of *Masks in Modern Drama*—a type of masking found throughout performance history that early twentieth-century theater reformers and modern dramatists borrowed and transformed. As Smith defines the satiric mask:

> A mask is usually thought of as a shield or disguise protecting the identity of the masker. A satiric mask, however, exposes the masker. At once comic and sinister, the distorted mask stresses the wearer's ridiculous behavior as it suggests the grossness and depravity of which he is capable. The satiric mask isolates a characteristic, distorts or enlarges it, and freezes it permanently. The masker, unaware that

Fig. 6.   Rudolf Laban in *Mathematician*, a solo that uses a satiric mask
(courtesy of the Laban Centre)

he is being exposed and ridiculed, struts before the audience, fool-
ishly displaying his guilt.[56]

Titling his figure *Mathematician*, Laban reverses the social evalua-
tion of the rational thinker. Wearing elongated fingernails and a
rectangular head mask decorated with narrow triangular forms

that echo his threatening hand gear, Laban's mathematician becomes a dracula. His mask projects and defines a particular character type—cerebral yet threatening.[57]

In contrast, a photograph of Sophie Taeuber in an "abstract
dance" (fig. 7) shows a mask that falls into none of the types cate-
gorized by Susan Smith. This was the work that occasioned Hugo
Ball's much-quoted remark:

> A gong beat is enough to stimulate the dancer's body to make the
> most fantastic movements. The dance has become an end in itself.
> The nervous system exhausts all the vibrations of the sound, and
> perhaps all the hidden emotion of the gong beater too, and turns
> them into an image. Here, in this special case, a poetic sequence of
> sounds [composed by Ball] was enough to make each of the indi-
> vidual word particles produce the strangest visible effect on the
> hundred-jointed body of the dancer.[58]

Designed by Taeuber's husband, Hans Arp, her "costume" and
"mask" form a single unified body construction, unlike Laban's costume and mask, which remained clearly distinct. Her unified body
construction in effect masks the entire body. This body mask erases
the human contours of the performer, substituting its geometrical
forms for the particular form of the performer's individual body.
The head becomes an elongated rectangular volume, the arms cy-
lindrical forms, the body an elliptical volume. The body mask functioned like a puppet, the performer like a puppeteer. Significantly,
whatever the gender of the puppeteer, the puppet bespoke no gender. The body mask dematerialized—and desexualized—the body
so completely that it theoretically became possible for either a male
or female dancer to perform the dance without changing its effect.
This type of masking recalled Loie Fuller's performances in 1890s
Paris and anticipated Oskar Schlemmer's theater experiments at
the Bauhaus.

In comparison with Laban and Taeuber as well as with Fuller
and Schlemmer, the singularity of Wigman's conception of the
mask becomes apparent. What is striking about *Witch Dance I* and
Idolatry is that the dancer wears no facial mask. Rather her costume
serves as a sort of mask—again a type not included in Susan Smith's
survey. Her costume-as-mask rendered her neither a character
type nor a puppeteer. Rather the "subjectivity" of her performing
persona always shadowed the "objectivity" of her *Gestalt*. Her dancing played on the tension between the gendered performer and

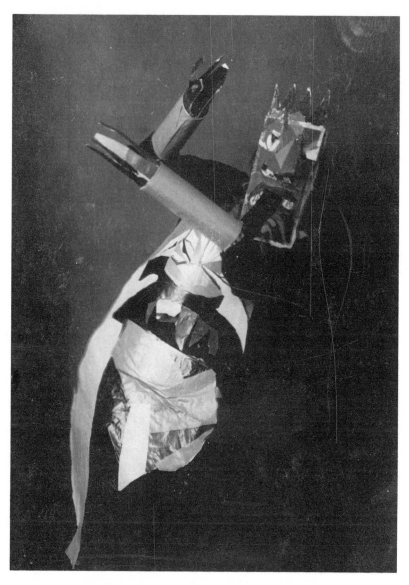

Fig. 7. Sophie Taeuber in an "abstract dance" presented at the Dadaist Cabaret Voltaire in 1917 (courtesy of the Fondation Arp)

the genderless *Gestalt*. As far as I can determine, this use of the costume-as-mask was without precedent in European performance at the time.

GROUP DANCES, 1914–1919

During the teens, Mary Wigman had more experience as a performer in group works staged by others than as a choreographer of her own ensemble dances. At Hellerau she took the role of a fury in Dalcroze's and Adolphe Appia's festival production of Gluck's *Orpheus and Eurydice*. In Munich she participated in carnival celebrations organized by Laban in winter 1914. And on Monte Verita she participated in several more of Laban's group dances, including the festival production of *Sun Festival* that celebrated the gathering of occultists in summer 1917.[59] *Sun Festival* marked Wigman's last appearance in a group work that she did not choreograph herself.

As was true of her solo choreography, the year 1918 marked a divide in the development of her group choreography, a divide between a period of participation and experimentation and a period of consolidation of her distinctive mode of group choreography. Since this consolidation did not take place until after Wigman had returned to Germany, founded her own school, and trained her own dancers, I reserve its discussion until the subsequent chapter. To bring this chapter to a close, I will reconstruct festival productions by Dalcroze and Laban in which Wigman appeared, plus two of her early group dances for which scenarios survive, *The Queen* (c. 1916) and *Dance of Death* (c. 1917). My reconstructions demonstrate that although Wigman's solos borrowed subject matter from her mentors' festival productions, her early group dances decisively rejected the large-scale format of festival.

The idea of festival, like the idea of the mask, excited the interest of theater reformers in the early twentieth century. Festival productions were often staged for one-time occasions, as was true at Hellerau and Monte Verita. But even when produced in repertory, as was the case for Max Reinhardt's 1910 stagings of *Oedipus Rex* and the *Oresteia*, festival productions challenged the conventions of the bourgeois theater, most especially its separation of spectators and performers. In attempting to break down the barrier erected by the proscenium arch, festival productions typically integrated amateur and professional performers and focused attention on the group rather than on the individual. From the teens through the twenties, Wigman's group choreography eschewed the festival format. Then in *Totenmal* (1930) and again in *Olympic Youth* (1936), she departed from her earlier practice and embraced the festival format in a changed context that radically altered the ideological import of the form deployed by Dalcroze and Laban.

Hellerau not only introduced Wigman to the working methods of improvisation and formal analysis that she would make her own but also involved her in a production seminal to the history of Western theater, the staging of Gluck's *Orpheus and Eurydice* undertaken in collaboration by Dalcroze and Adolphe Appia. The production summarized the theatrical reforms initiated by Dalcroze and Appia and traced a continuity between these theatrical reforms and the social reforms envisaged at Hellerau. To Wigman, one of the members of the chorus, *Orpheus* suggested possible subject matter as well as a potential model for her own group choreography. Over the next two decades, her solos borrowed subject matter from *Orpheus*, even though her group dances rejected the festival format.

A first version of *Orpheus* premiered during a festival in summer 1912, a final version the following summer. Five thousand visitors from all over Europe attended the 1913 production, including many theater artists interested in Dalcroze's and Appia's theatrical reforms—George Bernard Shaw and Harley Granville-Barker from England; Max Reinhardt and Leopold Jessner from Germany; Serge Wolkonski, Serge Diaghilev, and Konstantin Stanislavsky from Russia; Paul Claudel from France.[60] Students at Hellerau, including Wigman, who took the role of a fury in the 1912 production, made up the vast majority of the performers, supplemented by two professionals engaged to perform the singing roles of Orpheus and Eurydice.[61]

The production took place in a theater specially designed by Appia. Essentially a large, open, rectangular hall, the space could accommodate about two hundred and fifty performers and about five hundred spectators. Neither a proscenium arch nor a raised stage nor an orchestra pit separated the performers and spectators, who occupied a continuous space. Appia outfitted the space with a movable set of steps, which echoed the bleacher-type seating for the spectators, and with a system of diffused lighting, which arrayed literally thousands of lights behind translucent linen panels covering the walls and ceiling of the hall. As Alexander von Salzmann, the chief technician, commented, "instead of a lighted space, we have a light-producing space."[62] Spectators too remarked on the integration of space and light, performer and setting, made possible by Appia's design.

As reconstructed by Richard Beacham, the Dalcroze and Appia *Orpheus* altered the "happy ending" scripted by Gluck's librettist Calzabigi. In Gluck's version, Amor reappears at the end and restores Eurydice to life. In contrast, at the close of the Hellerau version the mourners returned and reprised the opening funeral dirge for Eurydice. That Dalcroze and Appia decided to omit Amor's return and repeat the opening instead reinforced other production decisions. Throughout, the staging de-emphasized Orpheus's relationship to Amor and Eurydice while emphasizing Orpheus's interactions with the mass of mourners, furies, and blessed spirits. This shift of attention away from the interplay of individual characters and toward the relation of the individual to the mass underlay the changed ending: Orpheus and Eurydice disappear, leaving the chorus in control of the stage. Moreover, the structural circularity disrupted the narrative momentum and underscored the theatricality of the preceding action, the integration of light, space, music, and motion.[63]

Integrating the performers and spectators within a single continuous space, Appia's novel theater design intended to involve the spectator in the production. Since the theater enclosed approximately twice the number of spectators as performers, the spectators sensed their own presence as an integral component of the event. And just as the audience constituted a self-aware collectivity, so too did the performers onstage—literally, student members of the Hellerau community and, figuratively, members of a chorus.

The integration of spectator and performer found an analogue in the integration of formal elements: actor and chorus, music and movement, space and light. Further, the integration of formal elements became an analogue for the social reforms envisioned by the

founders of Hellerau. Just as Dalcroze's and Appia's theater reforms centered around the spectator-as-participant, so the reforms
effected by the Deutsche Werkbund centered around the worker
as a participant in the labor process. Just as the staging of *Orpheus*
fused the media of music and movement, so the idea of Hellerau
attempted to unify work and leisure, industry and art, nature and
culture. Appearing as one of the furies in the 1912 production,
Wigman performed the utopian vision of cultural renewal Dalcroze and Appia shared with the founders of Hellerau. As Dalcroze
outlined this vision:

> Rhythm . . . is the basis of all art; it is also the basis of human
> society. . . . And once a society is properly trained, from school up-
> wards, it will itself feel the need for expressing its joys and sorrows
> in manifestations of collective art, like those of the Greeks of the best
> period. We shall then be offered well-organized festivals, which will
> express the popular aesthetic will, and where divers groups will per-
> form in the manner of individuals in a form at once metrical and
> individual. . . . What can be more gratifying than to interpret freely,
> and in an individual manner, the feelings that actuate us, and which
> form the whole essence of our personality—of externalising, without
> constraint, our sorrows and joys, our aspirations and desires—of al-
> lying eurhythmically our means of expression with those of oth-
> ers—to group, magnify, and give style to the emotions inspired by
> music and poetry? And this gratification is not of a passing, artificial,
> or abnormal order: it is an integral factor in the conditions of exis-
> tence and the progress of the individual. It cannot but contribute to
> the raising of the instincts of the race, and the permeation of the
> altruistic qualities necessary for the establishment of a healthy social
> order.[64]

Drawing students and spectators from across Europe, Dalcroze
considered festival a gesture of internationalism. When World War
I broke out in August 1914, Dalcroze was in Geneva and decided
not to return to Hellerau. When he later protested Germany's militarism, he was officially dismissed from his post.[65] However, it must
be remarked that a fine line separates the internationalism espoused by Dalcroze from the rhetoric of eugenics. When Dalcroze
wrote about "raising the instincts of the race," he presumably
meant "humankind." But later upholders of the festival ideal redefined the festive community in decidedly nationalist and racist
terms.

Like Dalcroze, Laban favored the festival format for his group choreography. But Laban did not depend on architectural reform of the theater to realize his vision. Rather, he staged festivals out of doors on Monte Verita, unifying spectators and performers through their shared experience of nature. This conception of festival reached its high point in *Sun Festival* (*Sonnenfest*), staged on 17–18 August 1917 as part of the Nonnational Congress, a conference on the occult. The conference was organized by Theodor Reuss, a Freemason of sorts and the founder of the Monte Verita branch of the Ordo Templi Orientis (OTO). The title of the congress underscored that participants gathered as initiates in a mystical community rather than as citizens of nations at war. As World War I entered its final phase, bohemians from France, Italy, and Germany attending the congress asserted their belief that spirituality exerted a greater force than nationality.[66] The design of *Sun Festival* alluded to the mystic beliefs of the OTO and, by extension, to the experience of exile on Monte Verita during the war years.

Along with other members of Laban's circle—Suzanne Perrottet, Ernst Mohr, Karl Weysel, Dussia Bereska—Mary Wigman led the dancing in the all-night performance.[67] *Sun Festival* was performed over a twelve-hour span from sunset to sunrise in three different outdoor locations. The first part, "Dance of the Setting Sun" ("Die sinkende Sonne"), took place in a mountain meadow near sunset. The audience watched the sun set over a distant lake as a recitation of verses from Otto Borngräber's "Song to the Setting Sun" alternated with simple group dances, which Laban termed *Reigen* (chain dances). His autobiography recalls the action:

> After a solemn *Reigen* round the fire, a speaker, accompanied by attendants, came up the slope. The moment when his head appeared over the edge of the bank was exactly timed so that the lower rim of the setting sun was just touching the horizon. Standing there he spoke the first lines of his poem to the setting sun. Drawing closer and walking towards the fire, he was encircled by a welcoming group of dancers. He then recited the second passage of the poem, with the sun by now half hidden below the horizon. During the farewell *Reigen* addressed to the sun, women and children came out of the rows of spectators and up to the fire-place to fan the flames. . . . Finally there was a poem to the twilight. It was accompanied by a solemn *Reigen* which in the end formed into a procession leading the spectators away from the meadow.[68]

The production resumed shortly before midnight. This second part, titled "Demons of the Night" ("Die Dämonen der Nacht"), did away with verse speaking and relied solely on aural, visual, and kinesthetic imagery, substituting firelight for sunlight. As at the end of the first part, spectators and participants formed a unison procession to mark the opening and closing of the section. The action was structured around the appearance of successive groups of "demons"—kobolds, masked dancers, witches and fiends, shadows. Laban's memoirs recount the progression:

> A group of dancers with drums, tom-toms and flutes assembled among the spectators, and torches and lanterns lighted up the way to a mountain peak where bizarrely-shaped rocks looked down on a circular meadow. Here five blazing fires were lit and a group of kobolds performed leaping dances around and through them.
>
> Then a group of masked dancers approached. The huge masks, made of twigs and grass, covered their whole bodies. Behind these diverse squatting, towering, angular and spiky shapes hid witches and fiends. Creeping up, they stripped off the disguises of the dancers in a wild scene and burned them. As a finale, around the dying glow of the embers, came the dance of the shadows. Then the torches of the attendants were rekindled and, with dancers in front and behind, the long train of spectators was led back to the starting-point.[69]

Presumably, the action of the witches and fiends removing and burning the masked disguises of the dancers possessed a mystical meaning known only to initiates of the OTO. Members of the order—so the action suggests—were required to set aside their everyday identities, their masks, and literally undergo a trial by fire to emerge as their true selves, their shadow selves obscured in the course of daily life.

The final section, "The Victorious Sun" ("Die siegende Sonne"), took place the following morning, as a group of dancers welcomed the rising sun. The action, more simplified than in the previous sections, relied solely on *Reigen* against the backdrop of the natural landscape: "A group of women dressed in loose cloaks of colored silks rushed up the hill. On the horizon the disc of the rising sun appeared and glowed through the dancers' garments. In a *Reigen* to the awakening day the night spook was dispelled by wave upon wave of people surging onwards, moving joyfully, as a symbol of the ever-returning day-star."[70] The configuration of dancers imitated the patterns of nature, which in turn mirrored the mystic spirit: the dancers' circling mirrored the endless cycle of day and night, the esoteric repetition of light and darkness. Performing *Sun Festival,* Laban's dancers enacted a ritual of spiritual renewal.

Three months later, Wigman premiered *Ecstatic Dances.* In that solo cycle her own performance seemed to compress and multiply the spiritual self-transformation implied by *Sun Festival.* Similarly, her earlier solo, *Witch Dance I,* can be seen as an abstraction of her role in Dalcroze and Appia's *Orpheus.* In the 1912 production she impersonated a fury; in the 1914 solo she embodied the quality of "witchness." Strikingly, it was Wigman's early solos, not her group dances, that borrowed subject matter from Dalcroze's and Laban's festival productions.

Rejecting the festival format, her early group dances turned to a small-group format. In focusing on small-scale works choreographed for her students and colleagues, Wigman's practice recalled the precedent of Isadora Duncan. Unlike Duncan, however, she choreographed group dances as well as solos from the very beginning of her career. Two months after her choreographic debut, on 28 April 1914, she reappeared on a program sponsored by the Laban School in Munich and premiered, in addition to four new solos, her first group dances—two duets for herself and Karl Weysel, titled *Dance for Two, I* and *II* (*Zweitanz, I* and *II*), and a trio for herself, Weysel, and P. Von Lendecke titled *Dance for Three* (*Dreitanz*). Little descriptive evidence survives.[71] Wigman's 1916 program titled "The Self in Rhythm and Space" included two duets for herself and Claire Walther—*Graphics,* the last section of *The Pictorial Arts,* and *Fairy Tale.* Again little descriptive evidence survives.[72] Her Pfauen Theater program in June 1917 also included one group dance, *Dance of Death* (*Totentanz*), for an undetermined, though presumably small, number of dancers. (Although a scenario survives, its relation to this 1917 concert is unclear.) Wigman's one large-group composition before 1918 was titled *The Queen* (*Die Königin*), for which the program and scenario do survive, albeit undated.

Judging from the two surviving scenarios in Wigman's hand, it is hard to say why her early group dances rejected the festival format. Was it because she could not command the required resources either in terms of matériel or personnel? Perhaps, but even when

Wigman had the necessary resources at her disposal during the twenties, she remained uninterested in the idea of festival, at least as interpreted by Dalcroze and Laban, until the end of the decade. Was it because she fashioned her group dances as an extension of her solo choreography? Her 1914 and 1916 concerts suggest that this might have been the case, but her composition of *The Queen* for an enlarged group argues against this hypothesis. Did she reject festival because she wanted to move away from representational pretexts for her performance? Again the evidence argues against this hypothesis, for the scenarios for *The Queen* and *Dance of Death* do present representational frames. These frames script gender in unconventional ways, however, and this interest, I would suggest, led Wigman to reject the immediate example of her predecessors. Both *Orpheus* and *Sun Festival* presented the conventional image of Woman as poetic muse (Eurydice, the women rushing up the hillside at dawn). Was it because she was determined to challenge such conventional images that Wigman rejected the festival format favored by her male mentors?

The Queen was subtitled a "dance pantomime." Premiered at the Laban School in Zurich, Suzanne Perrottet composed the music, Wigman appeared in the title role as the Queen, and other dancers in the Laban circle took on the various roles of the Magician (Ernst Mohr), the Magician's Apprentice (Olga Feldt), the Slave (Walther Kleiner), and the Queen's dancers (Claire Walther and Nina Macciachini). Students from the Laban School appeared, collectively, as the Demon. A scenario printed in the program describes the action:

> Once upon a time a queen lived in a beautiful castle with her retinue, including two female dancers and a small black prince, her prisoner. The three were her favorites, and she enjoyed playing with them. They watched as she danced out her longing, and together they danced dances of life and youth.
>
> A powerful magician lived right next to the queen's palace. He loved the queen and wanted to carry her off to his kingdom.
>
> One day he managed to conceal himself behind the curtains in the queen's chamber. From there he overheard the queen dancing with her three playmates. Secretly he cast a sleeping spell over the two female dancers and the small black slave so that he could use his time alone with the queen to tell her of his love. But she did not want to hear him and laughed at him. That made the magician angry, and

· together with his apprentice he beseeched his master, the great demon, to take revenge on the queen.

And so the great demon transformed the beautiful queen into an ugly monstrosity that no one could stand. The queen turned to her three playmates for sympathy, but in vain. They did not recognize her, and they were afraid of her. But the magician despaired over the transformation of the queen. He would have liked to make his beloved queen beautiful again, but he did not possess the requisite power. So he wandered about in despair.

But his small apprentice saw the suffering of his master and determined to help him. Secretly the apprentice went in search of the great demon, who lived in the valley of death. There he guarded the flowers of love. The apprentice found his way there and stole the curious flowers while the demon slept. He brought them to the queen, who sadly crouched at the door of her palace. She inhaled the scent of the flowers of love. All of a sudden her ugliness disappeared, and she stood there radiantly beautiful.

Then all came in joyous spirits and bowed before her. But she bowed before the magician and whispered her love to him.[73]

Wigman's scenario reads like a parody of nineteenth-century story ballet. Like Odette in *Swan Lake,* the Queen undergoes a transformation, but she is turned not into a beautiful swan but rather into "an ugly monstrosity." Like many a nineteenth-century ballet, the story ends with the coupling of a fairy-tale prince and princess. But in Wigman's scenario, the Queen does not desire the Magician, and the Magician alone does not possess the power to trick her into loving him. The typical narrative of a nineteenth-century ballet portrays the male protagonist torn between two visions of femininity—Albrecht torn between the peasant Giselle and the aristocratic Bathilde, Siegfried torn between the innocent Odette and the evil Odile. But Wigman's scenario turns this convention around, picturing a Queen whose fate is decided by the interaction between a Magician (played by a man) and the Great Demon (played by a group of students). The Queen desires neither, preferring instead a trio of playmates, both male and female. Wigman's parody of the narrative conventions of nineteenth-century ballet cannot be separated from her parody of the heterosexist coupling inscribed within that tradition.

The scenario for *Dance of Death* moves away from the parody of *The Queen.* Moreover, it moves away from the clear narrative that supported the parody. In so doing, the scenario suggests a stage work that extended an image over time rather than told a story. The scenario recounts the choreographer's vision:

> The night lies still and heavy over the earth. Black clouds hover everywhere, threatening and gloomy. Nowhere a light, nowhere a sound. The night is close, permeated by weighty dampness, like a presentiment of disaster. All of a sudden a groan arises from the agonizing atmosphere. Slowly and hesitantly the groan rings out of the darkness and swells to a single cry of anguish, of deathly distress. Then again it subsides into the immense silence.
>
> But it is as if the night has woken. A pale brightness pushes through the cloud masses. A moonbeam falls from somewhere and shines like dull silver over the wide plane and in its path meets something gray and formless and holds it fast, enveloping it with shimmering light until the form appears fully impregnated by the light. And suddenly a movement begins in the gray and formless thing. Slowly and stiffly the thing disengages itself from the floor and grows into a form of unnatural thinness. Like a gray column, it rises from the ground, huge and terrible. For a long time the form doesn't move. Its cloak hangs heavy and unfolded; a gray veil covers its head. An uncanny absence of being pervades the image seemingly born from the earth.
>
> Suddenly a convulsion seizes the figure, excruciating and sharp. Again the moaning permeates the stillness, more slowly than the first time and more ghastly. And it is as if the ground echoes the moaning. The sound breaks from the deep and disperses toward all sides. And an oscillation passes over the ground, a wave. Pushing and shoving from below, groaning and sighing from the abyss. And in a single cry of horrible agony everything sets loose. Forms creep over the ground, gray and barely distinguishable from the earth that had spit them out. A cruelly distorted life is everywhere in motion. And in the midst of all the commotion the huge gray form remains upright and rigid. The form towers over the swarming on the ground, its frightening rigidity more uncanny than before. And again a jolt passes through its body; a scream sounds, loud and shrill; the figure's arms move convulsively under the cloak. Two hands appear, gaunt and bony, and shake a rattle in a monotonous rhythm. The screaming sounds in short intervals; each time the entire ground seems to respond. The rhythm of the rattling becomes increasingly violent. The forms on the ground rise and sink, up and down, in a wild, fantastic dance.
>
> It is a frightful dance. Spindly, bony forms stretch upward to immense heights, crouch together in anticipation. Minute grotesque beings extend themselves in long chains on the floor, pushing and shoving one another in the passion of the dance.

A woman dances in a white gown. She has no face underneath her veil, yet eyes beam from under the veil, grayish and shallow. She hurls her upper torso into raging swings, crouches on the floor, and writhes upward in mad contortions. A dancing man approaches. He marks a smaller and smaller circle around her; he comes closer and closer with swaying steps, and reaches his long, bony arm toward the woman. The small beings, the grotesque ones, swarm around his feet and inhibit his walk. Other beings, women frightening in their gaunt nakedness, crash into him. They hang from him, drag him to the ground, then race over him.

Now only a wide, horrible confusion everywhere, an inextricable chaos of bodies. The rattling is smothered by the constantly swelling screaming of the dancing mass. Arms are catapulted upward, legs are raised in crazed contortions. Heads, ghostly and lifeless, are turned on thin, lean necks. Here and there the mass pushes, now and again it surges. Between times the screaming sounds louder and louder, faster and faster. A single body convulses out of the raging, dancing mass. Two, three forms race in wide leaps, crushing whatever writhes under their feet.

The large figure in the gray cloak remains unmoving in the midst of this mad dance. From time to time the figure jerks convulsively and groans and screams. But the gaunt hands swing the rattle no longer and hang limp and lifeless. Gradually the screams become fainter and less frequent, and the raging bodies of the dancing mass slow down their pushing and shoving. Again it seems as if the ground opens and sucks in what belongs to it. The dancing figures become fewer and fewer; one after the other they disappear, sinking into the grayness that gave them birth. The woman in the white dress with the phosphorus eyes still whirls about alone in the death-muted dance. Her spinning becomes slower, the outline of her form less distinct, until she too sinks away and disappears. Then it is entirely still. Once more the moaning sounds agonized and soft, slowly dying away in the dark.

And when the moon shines clear and full through the clouds, then the field is empty and abandoned. And in the spot where the large, gray form watched over the wild dance, solitary and towering, something gray and formless lies without moving. The moonlight glides calmly over the thing. The still night betrays nothing of the fantastic dance.[74]

The scenario pictures all the stage figures as *Gestalten*—anonymous, formless forms—until the point when the recognizably gendered man approaches the faceless woman. From that moment the formless forms also take on gender, as frighteningly emaciated and naked women. But once the women succeed in hindering the man's advance and the chaotic mass of their bodies subsides into stasis, they reassume the status of *Gestalten,* as at the beginning. In the scenario for *Dance of Death* gender becomes the last gesture of personhood, the final sign of animate life. Caught between life and death, the pictured figures are caught between the identity of gender and their transformation into *Gestalten,* the nonhuman and nongendered.

Just as the scenario for *The Queen* parodies the conventions of narrative ballet, including the convention of heterosexual romance, the scenario for *Dance of Death* subverts the convention of character and replaces characters with *Gestalten.* From one perspective, the vision implied by the scenario for *Dance of Death* anticipated Wigman's later group choreography in a way that the scenario for *The Queen* did not, for in most of her later group dances *Gestalten* came to replace characters and image to replace story. But from another perspective, the scenarios for *Dance of Death* and *The Queen* suggest a dialectic in Wigman's later group choreography that parallels the continuum between her "lighter" and "darker" solos, for some later works picked up on the narrative parody of *The Queen,* and others extended the buried half-narrative of *Dance of Death.* But from yet a third perspective, her later group dances moved in a direction that could not be foreseen on Monte Verità, for they evolved in response to the working conditions and resources she found upon her return to Germany after the war ended.

3

Mask and *Gemeinschaft*

The twenties were the great decade of Wigman's career. From 1920 to 1930 the choreographer created over seventy new solos and more than ten major group works. Beginning with a handful of students in 1920, she developed an ensemble that numbered twenty dancers by 1924. Contemporary critics hailed her achievement of what had eluded predecessors such as Isadora Duncan, that is, her successful transition from solo dancing to group choreography. As Hans Fischer remarked: "Wigman stands at once as the decidedly greatest and last solo dancer and as the first master of group dance."[1] The renown of the Wigman School followed the upward trajectory of the choreographer's reputation. Founded in 1920, the Dresden school quickly became a center for serious dance training, and the school produced many of the leading modern dancers of the day—Gret Palucca, Yvonne Georgi, Vera Skoronel, Margarethe Wallmann, Harald Kreutzberg, Max Terpis, Hanya Holm. And not only aspiring professionals but also devoted amateurs were drawn to the school.

During the twenties Wigman's name became associated with the artistic vanguard, and articles on her dancing appeared in a wide variety of journals devoted to contemporary art and culture, from *Die neue Schaubühne* and *Der Sturm* to *Der Querschnitt* and *Die Welt-bühne*. At the same time, Wigman's practice of *Tanz-Gymnastik*—her methods oriented for amateurs—was widely disseminated by her many students and became an integral part of the physical culture movement. A 1925 film, *Ways to Strength and Beauty* (*Wege zu Kraft und Schönheit*), surveyed the contemporary interest in physical culture, intercutting shots of Wigman's dancers with shots of marathon runners, boxers, and gymnasts.[2] During the Weimar period Wigman's practice existed on the cusp between physical culture and the artistic vanguard.

Not surprisingly, the archives swell with documentation of her career in the twenties: hundreds of photographs, programs, and reviews; dozens of articles from contemporary journals; even a few film clips. Oral history with students from this period and former members of her company add to the research sources. The abundance of surviving evidence allows for reconstruction of most of the major group works and solo cycles from the twenties. Among these I have chosen to reconstruct *The Seven Dances of Life* (1921), *Scenes from a Dance Drama* (1924), *Dance Fairy Tale* (1925), and *Dance of Death* (1926) in order to trace the formation of Wigman's characteristic mode of group choreography. In addition, I have reconstructed a 1926 solo titled *Witch Dance II*, which made explicit what had remained implicit in the identically titled solo from 1914. While Wigman's solos from the twenties extended her signature style established during the teens, her group dances after 1921 radically departed from her ensemble works composed on Monte Verità. That is, the 1914 *Witch Dance* anticipated the 1926 version in a way that the *Dance of Death* scenario composed on Monte Verità did not anticipate the 1926 work with the same title.

What made the difference in terms of her group choreography? I suggest that the difference lay in the working conditions at the Wigman School in Dresden. There the choreographer wielded a different sort of authority over her students and colleagues than had Laban on Monte Verità, an authority perhaps equally charismatic though not as erotically charged. The mostly female students at the Wigman School encountered a mostly female teaching staff. The students also encountered a more formalized curriculum than that on Monte Verità. And the better students had the opportunity to acquire extensive performing experience through their participation in the dance group. Students and dancers from the period remember the school and company as enabling milieus that allowed them to develop as artists. Moreover, the dancers' reminiscences acknowledge no overt conflict between their artistic self-realization and Wigman's charismatic authority.

In my account the utopian reconciliation of authority and autonomy evident in the day-to-day operations of the school and company found dramatization in the group works choreographed by Wigman. I term this utopian reconciliation *Gemeinschaft*, playing off the common distinction between *Gemeinschaft* and *Gesellschaft* in German social theory. As Ferdinand Tönnies and other social philosophers formulated the distinction at the end of the nineteenth century, earlier forms of social cohesion (*Gemeinschaft*) had given way to the fragmentation of modern society (*Gesellschaft*). In my reading, the practice of Wigman's group choreography modeled a *Gemeinschaft* that stood as an implicit alternative to the *Gesellschaft* of the larger society. In this way her group dances reinterpreted the visions of cultural renewal enacted at Hellerau and on Monte Verita.

Strikingly, the *Gemeinschaft* dramatized by Wigman's group dances included only women from 1923 to 1928. Although men studied at the Wigman School, no man ever joined the dance ensemble. Was this a deliberate decision on the choreographer's part, or the result of happenstance? A case can be made for happenstance, for many fewer men than women studied at the school, and the few men who did study there found ample professional opportunities other than graduation into the company.[3] Yet a case also can be made for intentionality, for Wigman had cast men in dance works on Monte Verita and would do so again later. Moreover, the dynamic between the leader and the group so central to her ensemble in the mid-twenties would have been significantly altered with mixed casting, as the dynamic did change in 1930 when the choreographer cast men in *Totenmal*.

The *Gemeinschaft* of Wigman's group dances extended the principle of the *Gestalt im Raum*. Just as the soloist transcended her "subjectivity" through the "objectivity" of her spatial awareness and deployment of the principle of the mask, so a member of the group transcended her individuality through participation in the ensemble. But the ensemble did not erase the dancer's autonomy any more than the principle of the mask erased the soloist's "subjectivity." Rather, the individuality of the dancer coexisted with her consciousness of the group, just as the "subjectivity" of the gendered performer coexisted with the "objectivity" of the nongendered *Gestalt*. As Wigman herself stated the relation between solo and group dance:

> The development of each dancer ought to be considered from a twofold viewpoint: On the one hand, perfecting the dance personality as an individual; and on the other hand, blending this individuality with an ensemble. Briefly and seen from an over-all viewpoint: Solo and Group Dance. These two orientations do not necessarily

have to exist in contrast to one another. Whether both can be har-
monized depends on the dancer's will and strength to attend to these
two tasks and to muster enough understanding that subordinating
his own personality to a multiform organism is not synonymous with
giving up his individuality.[4]

This chapter divides into three parts. In the first part I reconstruct Wigman's pedagogy and the milieu of the Dresden school,
drawing partly on oral history and partly on contemporary records
and archival documents. This section provides not only an account
of working conditions that underlay Wigman's dramatization of *Gemeinschaft* but also an account of the technical basis that underlay
the interrelated principles of *Gemeinschaft* and the *Gestalt im Raum*.
In the second part I trace the formation of Wigman's choreographic practice for her ensemble. In my telling, her first major
group work, *The Seven Dances of Life*, shows her moving away from
the erotic subject matter of *The Queen* and moving toward the all-
female ensemble of her later dances. Her practice then crystallized
in *Scenes from a Dance Drama* and found variation in *Dance Fairy Tale*
and *Dance of Death*. In the third part, I reconstruct *Witch Dance II*,
a solo that partially survives on film, providing the most concrete
evidence of her solo style during the mid-twenties.

Although my reconstruction of *Witch Dance II* to some extent
balances my discussion of Wigman's solos and group dances during
this period, my emphasis remains on her group choreography. My
focus is intended partly to correct the misperception in the standard English-language literature that the German dancer was a
brilliant soloist, albeit flawed group choreographer. In challenging
the English-language sources, I return to the view voiced by Wigman's German critics in the twenties: that her solo and group choreography were of equal significance and stature. Nonetheless, my
view radically departs from that of Fritz Böhme, Hans Fischer, and
their colleagues. From the perspective of Wigman's critical advocates, her group choreography marked an "advance" over the
practice of soloists such as Isadora Duncan. In other words, her
group dances furthered the ideals of absolute dance also promoted
by her solos. From my perspective, the *Gemeinschaft* of Wigman's
group dances countered and continued the principle of the *Gestalt
im Raum* familiar from her solos, creating an "imagined community" among women that reintroduced the female spectatorship

partially disrupted by her solos. This "imagined community" also allowed spectators of either gender to glimpse a body politic where the visions of the left and right did not conflict, as they most certainly did in the factionalized politics of the Weimar era. Thus my reconstructions resume the redefinition of feminism and nationalism in dance terms.

THE WIGMAN SCHOOL, 1920–1932

When Wigman, accompanied by Berthe Trümpy, embarked on a tour of German cities in fall 1919, she did not intend to repatriate. Rather, she intended to maintain Zurich as her home base, since she already had gathered a small circle of students there. And so, with another German tour planned for the following spring, she returned to the Swiss capital and applied for a permanent residence visa. However, the Swiss authorities had become tired of the many politically suspicious exiles who had sought shelter in Switzerland during the war years, and they consequently denied her application. Thus she returned to Germany in spring 1920, knowing that she must resettle but not knowing where.[5]

Indirectly, the Kapp Putsch made her decision for her. As the military marched on Berlin and officials of the newly formed Weimar Republic fled, a general strike paralyzed the country. Wigman, who happened to be in Dresden, could not leave the city, nor could other performers scheduled for guest appearances reach the city. She took advantage of the opportunity to perform night after night and soon was a well-known personality. Young dancers inspired by her performances sought her out. At first she gave private lessons in her hotel room, but then Trümpy decided that more space was needed and bought her a house that also could serve as a studio. Dresden became Wigman's home base.[6]

Informality marked the early years of the Wigman School, which opened in fall 1920. The living room of the house served as classroom and rehearsal studio. When Wigman was away on tour, Trümpy took over the teaching. Both their classes served as choreographic workshops for group dance. Their improvisational methods allowed students to contribute their movement inventions to Wigman's group projects, as well as enabling them to create their own dances. In summer 1922 the school sponsored the first of many programs devoted to student choreography. Many of the students who showed works were involved in rehearsals for Wigman's first dance group, which made its debut the following spring.[7] In most respects the dance school and the dance ensemble developed in tandem. In one important respect, however, their development diverged. Although men studied at the school, no man ever joined the dance group.

The debut of the dance group in spring 1923 coincided with a new phase in the development of the Wigman School. First, the staff underwent significant turnover. Trümpy left in 1924.[8] Following her departure, the bulk of day-to-day teaching fell to Elisabeth Wiegmann, Mary's sister, and to Hanya Holm, a leading member of the dance group. Around the same time, Will Goetze, Wigman's composer and accompanist, joined the staff as musical instructor. And Anni Hess joined the enterprise as office manager and house-keeper—Wigman's apartment was located on the school's premises—and remained as helpmate until the choreographer's death.[9]

Second, as the number of students increased exponentially, the school formalized its operations and curriculum. By 1926 the school had 360 students enrolled, several dozen of whom were full-time professional students, the remainder lay students from the community. The professional students pursued a set three-year curriculum that culminated in a certification examination.[10] Certification from the Wigman School carried great weight in the German dance world, convincing at least one set of parents to allow their daughter to attend.[11] Thus not only did the greater number of students necessitate a more formalized program, but the more formalized program drew a greater number of students, from across Germany and from abroad.

By the mid-twenties Wigman's endeavors supported fourteen employees at the school and an equal number of dancers in the dance group.[12] Like her entrepreneurial forefathers, she had built a small-scale family concern into a large-scale business venture. Proceeds from her solo tours and school tuition subsidized the dance group. (The dancers were not paid wages but only expenses, so most taught or received stipends from home to cover living costs.)[13] In addition, a friends' organization raised private monies to subsidize the operation. Wigman invested her capital well—her renown as a dancer and choreographer and her reputation as a pedagogue. She had become an independent woman indeed.

Improvisation formed the core of Wigman's method, underlying not only her pedagogy but also her theory and practice of composition. Dalcroze and Laban had provided the framework for her approach, which she inflected with her own inventions and inclinations. In retrospect, former students at the Wigman School note its de-emphasis on "technique" in favor of "ideas," "expression," and "creativity." But this is the perspective of dancers who continued their careers in a modern dance world that over time devalued improvisational facility while revaluing the acquisition of virtuosity. It seems clear that during the Weimar period Wigman *Technik* was highly valued. Students at the school acquired not a "technique" in the American sense, a codified movement vocabulary, but *Technik* in the German sense, a method for experiencing and structuring movement. This approach empowered them to teach and choreograph and enabled them to assimilate virtuosic skills learned later.[14]

The difference between "technique" and *Technik* accounts for what seem extraordinary career paths by contemporary standards: dancers who began their training in their late teens or even later and after a year or so of formal instruction embarked on professional careers as teachers or performers. This description fit Wigman herself, as well as many of her students. Tina Flade, a Dresden native, decided to become a dancer after seeing Wigman perform. But first she completed her *Abitur*, certifying successful completion of the Gymnasium, before enrolling in the Wigman School at age seventeen. After eight months of study she became a member of the dance group.[15] Lilian Espenak, Norwegian by birth, was in Dresden studying for her *Abitur* when she saw a concert presented by the Wigman School and decided to enroll. She never did complete Gymnasium. Rather, after a year and a half at the school she too joined the dance group.[16] That both Flade and Espenak were oriented toward the *Abitur* evidences the middle-class origins of most of the students at the school and members of the dance company.[17]

The middle-class girls who attended the Wigman School pursued a rigorous three-year curriculum that included instruction in music, pedagogy, and anatomy as well as "the entire spectrum of movement from technique [*Technik*] to expression [*Ausdruck*] to composition [*tänzerischer Gestaltung*]," as the brochure for the school announced.[18] Certification required students to present a concert of their own dances, both solos and group works, and to complete a written examination.[19] Pola Nirenska, a student at the school during the late twenties, remembers choosing the essay topic "Women in the Arts."[20]

Dance instruction divided between "technique classes" and "class lessons." Although technique classes emphasized the acquisition of technical skills and class lessons the acquisition of compositional skills, both were taught through improvisation. In technique class students would learn the *Schrittskalen* (locomotive scales), *Drehen* (spinning), *Kreisen* (circles), *Vibrato* (vibrations). In class lessons they would explore the interplay of space, time, and energy. Erika Thimey, a student at the school during the late twenties, recalls class lessons taught by Hanya Holm, "hundreds of them, each one different, based only on the awareness of space."[21] Louise Kloepper, also a student during the late twenties, notes that in technique class students would follow the teacher's lead, but in class lessons the group would watch each student's individual improvisation and offer comment and criticism.[22]

Laban's theory grounded much of the movement work at the Wigman School. Underlying the improvisations were movement oppositions systematized by Laban, such as tension/relaxation, rising/sinking, opening/closing, advancing/retreating, promoting stability/promoting mobility, giving into gravity/resisting gravity.[23] Wigman acknowledged her debt to Laban, even while opposing her "personal" and "practical" discoveries with his "theoretical" formulations. In 1923 she wrote:

> The connection between my school and the Laban school is rather close insofar as I teach the same principles as Laban. Yet my independent work over the last few years has developed my pedagogy in a more personal direction, which naturally gives the work a different coloring. The greatest difference between my school and Laban's lies in the approach, for I am incapable of working in a totally theoretical way, despite my passion for purely objective achievements. My pedagogy always arises from practice. Laban's space harmony can prove theoretically how the correspondences between tension and impulse systematically develop, alternate, complement one another, etc. What I find astonishing is how often my own practical discoveries accord with Laban's theory.[24]

Truda Kaschmann, a student of both Laban and Wigman in the mid-twenties, concurs with Wigman's self-assessment. She remembers Laban giving much more explanation than Wigman. "Perhaps he explained too much," she added.[25] Erika Thimey notes how the brevity of explanation at the Wigman School made students figure out the relation between theory and practice for themselves.[26]

Wigman's teaching adapted Laban's movement scales as loco-motive scales. In Laban's theory of space harmony, movement scales (set sequences of movement), demonstrated the correspon-dence between spatial directions and dynamic qualities, much as musical scales demonstrate harmonic relations. Thus Laban's move-ment scales associated dimensional movement in space (upward, downward, forward, backward, and sideward) with strong, bound, sustained, and direct movement qualities (to use the terms Laban later defined in his theory of Effort). Conversely, Laban's scales as-sociated diagonal movement in space with free, light, sudden, and indirect movement qualities. Practicing the scales, students would physically experience the association between spatial directions and dynamic qualities and come to understand, in Wigman's words, how "each direction is characterized by its own movement expression."[27]

Clearly modeled on Laban's movement scales, Wigman's loco-motive scales associated types of locomotion with spatial and dy-namic qualities.[28] The essential difference between the active and passive scales, according to Rudolf Bach, was a different attitude toward space: "forward motion active, space drawn into itself, space thrust aside, toward a goal. Backward motion passive, space allowed to stream away from itself, pushed back by space, having no goal."[29] Erika Thimey remembers practicing the scales and re-alizing how the active scale related to the inhalation of breath and muscular tension (*Anspannung*), and the passive scale to the exha-lation of breath and muscular relaxation (*Abspannung*).[30]

The technique called vibrations derived from Wigman's own choreography. In the early twenties she had ripped a muscle and as a result never again could jump as before. As an alternate mode of resisting gravity, she developed a vibrating action of the entire body, involving short and steady movement pulses.[31] According to Fé Alf, a student at the school during the late twenties, the impulses might remain localized in one body part or might carry the whole body into movement through space.[32]

Another technique derived from Wigman's choreography was spinning. *Monotony Whirl* (*Drehmonotonie*), premiered in 1926, presented a seemingly endless duration of turning in place. Wigman's spinning technique required that students learn, as she wrote, "to place [the] feet, to displace [the] hips, to regulate the posture of the torso in order to achieve the abstract form of rotation and to be able to bring these turns back into the sphere of their ecstatic experience."[33] Rudolf Bach once described a class focused on spinning during which students practiced seemingly endless variations on the technique: on the entire foot and on the toes; with the upper torso held upright, bent forward, and bent backward; with the arms leading freely or rigidly and with both arms rising and sinking; with jumps on two feet and hops on one foot; with shifts of the hips in different directions; with circles of the upper torso in opposition to the direction of turning. All these variations were also used while spinning and traveling forward or following a circular or spiral path through space.[34]

Yet another technique, called circles, involved rotations of the hips that could be given varied dynamic qualities or enlarged to provide the impetus to carry the dancer through space. Like spinning, the technique could be given nearly endless variations. Erika Thimey remembers, "We did a lot of curves with the hip. You can use the movement of the hip as an accent, for example; as soon as you put a certain tension in your body, it becomes rigid, which is a dynamic style. Or, you can use the hip movement as a curve, which of course becomes a swing, in a certain dynamic."[35] At the Wigman Centennial in 1986 Jutta Ludewig, a student of the choreographer during the mid-forties, demonstrated myriad variations on circling in space: without changing front, with changing front, locating the circle behind the body, in front of the body, leaning toward the center, leaning away from the center.

Advanced technique classes moved beyond the practice of the locomotive scales, vibrations, spinning, and circles and involved students in structured improvisations designed to explore the expressive potential of movement. In Rudolf Bach's account students would work alone as well as in pairs or in small groups. In one exercise they individually experienced the difference between moving as if pulled by an unknown force or as if motivated by a force partly within and partly without themselves. In another exercise they would work with partners, meeting and separating in different ways—pacing toward one another and turning around a central point before continuing on in the same direction, or running toward one another, grabbing each other's arms and whirling together before flying apart. The dancers also worked in a large group, forming two lines through which one dancer moved as if in a dream or as if pulled toward a vision. Or a small group would join the single dancer, like guards leading a prisoner toward execution. Or the group forced the dancer back through the channel, as if blocking her approach to their treasure.[36] Many of these exercises had analogues in Wigman's group choreography.

Building on the exploration of expressive movement in advanced technique classes, class lessons emphasized students' own creative work. These lessons immersed students in Wigman's theory and practice of interrelating improvisation and composition. As she wrote in a handbook distributed to students, "From the happenstance of improvisation there flowers the final reality of composition."[37] The handbook describes how "the creative moment," which "remains a mystery even to ourselves," generates a "theme," a unified movement sequence that provides the basis for deliberate compositional development.[38] Once every month the entire school would gather in the evening to critique student works. Thimey recalls:

> There were certain times in the month when there would be a special evening for students to show their dances to Mary Wigman, to Elisabeth and to Hanya—to the faculty. We got assignments in our composition classes, of course, and if we wanted to, we could continue working on them and show the dances to the faculty. Or we could do something completely outside of our assignments, something extra—it was completely up to us. If you showed something that you had worked on in class, you had to do something more with it, develop it further. When you showed it, it had to be finished, as far as you were concerned.
>
> Those evenings were wonderful. You could work with costumes or without costumes. But, you had to say the name of the dance, what you had in mind, and whether you had designed or sewn the costume. Or, you had to say what you envisioned—a certain kind of design you could not afford, or music of a certain kind—obviously you could not get the symphony to play for you, and so on. Then, Mary would talk about your dance and criticize. And boy, then I realized that Mary was fantastic with language. I mean, she could

talk and talk and talk! And then, when she said, "Now, Hanya, don't you agree?"—Hanya would talk as least as long! (Laughter) Sometimes we were wondering whether we would *ever* be able to get home![39]

In reminiscence after reminiscence former students at the Wigman School emphasized their devotion to "Mary." (More than one called her a "goddess.") Many told stories of parents' opposing their desire to pursue a dance career and of how their encounter with "Mary" and the Wigman School enabled them to realize their "creativity," "artistry," "individuality," and "sense of self." None articulated a conscious conflict between Wigman's mentoring and their self-realization. Indeed, all attributed their self-realization to her mentoring.

The students who graduated to the dance company concurred. In rehearsal dancers cultivated their own movement imaginations at the same time that they became instruments for the realization of Wigman's choreographic ideas. Typically, Wigman would ask dancers to generate material through improvisation and then would edit the material and set the choreography. Tina Flade remembered how the choreographer made use of the dancers' contributions in a rehearsal atmosphere that was "incredibly disciplined and incredibly free at the same time." Her impression was that "Mary never came in with anything [definite] but only [developed] what happened in rehearsal."[40] Lilian Espenak was left with a somewhat different impression, believing that Wigman came to rehearsal with "definite ideas" and worked out "specific details" with the dancers. Nevertheless, she concurred with Flade's judgment that the improvisational rehearsal method enabled her own creative development.[41] Like the former students at the school, the former members of the dance company acknowledged no conflict between Wigman's authority and their individual self-realization. As Hanya Holm once unwittingly stated the paradox, "There was no dictatorship in this group which was a single body with one head, the head of the master."[42]

GROUP DANCES, 1921–1926

Wigman's group dances presented an extended commentary on the relation of the individual body and the collective body. The dynamic tension between the choreographer and her dancers grounded the action. As Hans Fischer remarked: "In all her group dances Wigman functions as leader, as center, or as opposition to the moving mass of dancers. She pulls the others after her without resistance, holds them in balance, allows them to circle her like planets around a sun."[43] As the dance group evolved in the early twenties, it became a metaphor for *Gemeinschaft,* a utopian reconciliation of the choreographer's authority and the dancers' autonomy.

In group dances from the Weimar period, the parody of eroticism in *The Queen,* composed on Monte Verita, went out of focus as subject matter. Rather, the format anticipated by *Dance of Death* became more characteristic of Wigman's group choreography— poised between representation and abstraction, peopled by *Gestalten* rather than characters, propelled by the transformation of image rather than by the trajectory of narrative. It was as if the choreographer associated the story-telling mode of nineteenth-century ballet with the subject matter of sexual relations and that to do away with the latter necessitated doing away with the former, and vice versa. The converse also held: to present a stage world inhabited only by women meant to reconfigure the relationship between the soloist and the chorus; the choreographer and her all-female ensemble took their identities from their ever-changing interactions. The movement away from narrative, the interchange between leader and group, and the all-female ensemble evolved in tandem.

The Seven Dances of Life (*Die sieben Tänze des Lebens*), premiered in December 1921, shows Wigman working through the subject matter characteristic of *The Queen* and moving toward the mode characteristic of her later compositions. Although the work does not yet dispense with narrative, it does erase the masculine presence in Wigman's group choreography. And in erasing that presence, it substitutes images of self-transformation and the all-female community as subjects for attention.

Wigman's solo appearances in 1920–1921 had been so well received that the Frankfurt Opera House invited her to premier a new work. For subject matter she turned to a "dance-poem" composed, but neither published nor staged, during her stay on Monte Verita.[44] Diederichs Verlag published *The Seven Dances of Life* at the time the work premiered.[45] To accompany the dance, the opera house commissioned a score from Heinz Pringsheim, which served, according to one reviewer, as effective *Gebrauchsmusik* (functional music), borrowing the chromaticism of Strauss's *Death and Transfiguration* and Wagner's *Tristan and Isolde*.[46] For the first time in her career Wigman had access to the resources of an opera house while staging a new group work.

A prologue, recited by a male actor before the curtain rose, supplied the narrative pretext for the action:

The King spoke:
"Know that you dance to save your life,
slave!
And if your dance
can unravel for me
life's meaning,
then you shall go free."
And the woman danced
the first Dance of Life,
the dance of longing, unfulfilled.
"Free her from her fetters,"
said the King.
And the woman
danced the Dance of Love.
"Do not yet kill her,"
shouted the King.
Whereupon the woman danced
the wild Dance of Lust,
tearing asunder all fetters
and transcending all confines.
The King hid his head:
"You will have to die
for that, woman!"
And the slaves
brought the black
veil of death.
But the dancer
did not heed the King
and danced past him
the Dance of Suffering.
And then she danced
the dark Dance
of the Demon,
stirring up all forces

hidden beneath the threshold of life.
And when the dance
had ended,
she bowed before the King:
"I am ready, my Lord."
And then she began to dance
the silent Dance of Death.
Again the slaves lifted
the veil of death
to cover her
with it forever.
But the King
kissed the dancer's forehead
and said:
"Your dance conquered Life
and it conquered Death.
Live now and be free!"[47]

Hedwig Müller advances a biographical reading of the work as a projection of Wigman's own confrontation with the "demon" of mental illness on Monte Verità.[48] However valid this interpretation of the private sources for the work, there remain important public sources as well—Laban's dances on Monte Verità and the Salome dances popularized by female soloists since the turn of the century.

Maud Allan made her name dancing Salome in England and the United States, and Gertrud Eysoldt and Tilla Durieux performed their versions of the legend in Germany.[49] In Deborah Jowitt's re-creation of Maud Allan's performance, the solo was structured as a flashback: "Descending the darkened palace stairs, Salome relives the triumph of her dance before Herod, starts in fear at the sight of a dark object—the head—and begins to dance lasciviously with it."[50] From the reviewers' accounts cited by Jowitt, it seems that Allan positioned the spectator as Herod, simultaneously attracted and repulsed by her performing.

In *The Seven Dances of Life*—its title recalling Salome's legendary dance of the seven veils—Wigman reworked the imagery of predecessors such as Allan. First, the German choreographer brought the Herod figure back onstage, the "King" referred to in the prologue, but in effigy—a "fantastic" puppet propped up on a throne placed upstage center.[51] This maneuver almost literally deflated the erotic potential of the male gaze, for the spectator—whether male or female—found it impossible to identify with the perspective of the lifeless effigy. Further, Wigman added an onstage audience of female dancers. Looking at her through the eyes of other women, the spectator saw a mistress of movement, not an object of desire. Finally, and perhaps most significantly, Wigman identified herself, the semblance of Salome, with John the Baptist. No longer the royal daughter, she becomes the slave, imprisoned like the prophet. And like the prophet, she undergoes a baptism, a transformation, experiencing symbolic death as prelude for the renewal of life. *The Seven Dances of Life* retraces the plot of Laban's *Sun Festival*: the passage from confinement to liberation, through darkness into light. Thus the work reconfigured Laban's choreography along with the female soloists' Salome dances.

Through the first half of the work, the narrative parallels the Salome tale, all the while defusing the eroticism of conventional stage representations by orienting Wigman's dance for the onstage audience of female dancers and an effigy-king. As the spoken prologue alerts the spectator, her dance at first pleases the effigy-king, but once her *Dance of Longing* and *Dance of Love* give way to her *Dance of Lust,* his pleasure turns to wrath. In reaction to her expression of sensuality "tearing asunder all fetters and transcending all confines," the effigy-king orders her death, as Herod orders the death of Salome at the end of the Strauss and Wilde opera.

From this point, the narrative diverges from the conventional Salome tale. According to the spoken prologue, the dancer resists the effigy-king's authority, ignoring his threat in her *Dance of Suffering.* Pursuing her own desires rather than the effigy-king's, she encounters the demon (*Dance of the Demon*) and confronts death (*Death Dance*). Finally, she joins with the other four female dancers, and together they perform an ending *Dance of Life.* The sequence of action suggests that the dancer's resistance to male authority enables her double confrontation with the realms of the demonic and death, and that her passage through darkness enables her creation of an all-female community. *The Seven Dances of Life* presages the emergence of Wigman's all-female dance group.

A reconstruction of the action demonstrates the significance of this sequencing.[52] After the male actor delivers the prologue and exits, the curtain parts and reveals two drummers kneeling at the downstage corners of an empty space. Then four female dancers, identified by the prologue as the king's slaves, enter and perform a greeting dance, pacing to a square rhythm supplied by the drummers. Their dance culminates in the opening of a back curtain to reveal Wigman, costumed in a silver gown, reclining on steps in front of the effigy-king, a life-sized puppet.

A flute solo accompanies the opening *Dance of Longing* (*Tanz der Sehnsucht*). The promptbook notes that "the dance is based on a wave-like body movement which beginning in the feet extends to the upraised arms. The spatial relations are only suggested. The expression lies in the concentration."[53] A photograph (fig. 8) shows the inward-focused quality of Wigman's wave-like body posture. According to the promptbook, once the dance ends, the four dancers help Wigman into a wide green skirt, her costume for the next dance.

She performs the *Dance of Love* (*Tanz der Liebe*) to full orchestral accompaniment that builds from a dominant three-quarters rhythm into a clear waltz theme. As she dances, the four others recline on the steps of the king's throne, watching her. As the promptbook notes, "the character of the dance is bright, radiant and warm, with brief grotesque-humorous moments and a passing sentimentality."[54] After Wigman exits, "broadly flowing harmonic music" sounds during the interlude of her absence.[55]

A gong announces her reentrance, costumed in red for the *Dance of Lust* (*Tanz der Lust*). To the accompaniment of drum and gong she circles the space, turning and spiraling toward the center. Once she reaches the center, the other dancers advance from the four corners of the space and gravitate toward her, as if her dance exerted a magnetic force. The four then whirl out as suddenly as they whirled in, and leave Wigman staggering, her energy spent. She quietly exits as the others reenter with the black veil of death and spread it out on the floor, then take up positions kneeling at each of its four corners. From this point Wigman no longer identifies with Salome, the female dancer who first arouses and then enrages the king, but with John the Baptist, the prophet and martyr. The multicolored veils that had served other Salomes as erotic drapery are transposed into a black sheet, a death shroud.

Wigman reenters costumed in violet to perform the *Dance of Suffering* (*Tanz des Leides*). She dances on top of the shroud in silence. The other dancers remain motionless, bowed down at the four corners of the black veil. A photograph (fig. 9) shows the relationship

Fig. 8.   Mary Wigman in *Dance of Longing*, from her 1921 group work *The Seven Dances of Life* (courtesy of the Mary Wigman Archive)

Fig. 9.   Mary Wigman and her dance group in *Dance of Suffering*, from her 1921 group work *The Seven Dances of Life* (courtesy of the Mary Wigman Archive)

of soloist and group. The group, subordinated to Wigman, frames her, focusing the spectator's attention on her dance, intensifying the effect of the silence. Without adopting conventional ballet poses, the four function much like a traditional corps de ballet. The promptbook notes that Wigman's dance "comprises deep, weighty gestures: the deep upswing with variations, the slow rotation with spiral accent of the arms, the profound effort slowly sinking low." [56] When she falls for the last time, the others rise to support her, as the flute melody heard during the *Dance of Longing* recurs. The first half ends with this tableau of the group supporting their leader.

After a pause comes the *Dance of the Demon (Tanz des Dämons)*. In near darkness Wigman cowers in a back corner, unmoving, as the demon's voice sounds, his monologue delivered by the same male actor who had recited the prologue, now concealed backstage. The staging deliberately confuses the echoing male voice and the cowering female figure, her brown costume barely discernible on the dimly lit stage. The voice of the demon intones:

I was,—
I am,—
I will be,—

You became aware of me
on one day of your life.
Shapeless, I wafted
through the spheres of
the world.
But you created me,
You gave me the form
in which I now
dwell in your life.
What could make you
fear me?
Is it not that agent
between nothingness and
being?
Why are you frightened
of the creation of your own
fantasy?
I come to you
in those lost hours
when life is silent.
I carry you through worlds
concealed from the eyes of
man.
I lift you to heights
which your human eye
can never measure.
I pour
of that life into your veins
of which man must die,
if the demon
does not protect him.
You will be no longer without me.
And would you ever want
to miss those dark hours
when your eyes have learned
to see more than can be seen?
when my powers penetrated you
and you became one
with the elements?—
Beloved!
The smile of horror
around your red lips
makes me thirsty.
I feed
on your warm blood—
Now I am quite close to you!

Do you feel
how the invisible dance
of my limbs holds you embraced?—
I was,—
I am,—
I will be,—
before you,
with you,
after you,
imperishable . . . [57]

Symbolizing the unconscious and the supernatural, the resounding male voice identifies itself as both muse and vampire. As the scene unfolds, the female dancer internalizes the male voice, and this internalization empowers her to act.

Once the demon's words fade away, Wigman recovers from her paralysis, and she slowly comes to life. She crawls along the floor, then finally jumps up and begins dancing to the "compelling rhythms" of Prinzheim's score.[58] The movements of her dance remain oriented toward the floor, and several times she collapses. A photograph (fig. 10) shows her standing, though bent forward with arms outstretched, her stare oriented toward an undefined focus outside the camera frame. According to the promptbook, she exits in the midst of the action, trailing the afterimage of her achievement of motility.

The stage darkens, and the two drummers leave their places. The four dancers close the curtains in front of the effigy-king, then bring in torches to illuminate the stage before withdrawing. Dressed in white—a communicant—Wigman reenters and performs the *Death Dance* (*Tanz des Todes*). She dances in silence, alone, the flickering torches concealing and revealing her form. As the promptbook notes, "The expression of the dance is of complete repose and solemnity, intensifying to rigidity, sinking to deep humility."[59] As the dance comes to an end, Wigman first kneels downstage, bowing her forehead to the floor, then withdraws upstage, opening the curtain concealing the effigy-king, and at last kneels on the lowest step. The effigy-king has become a religious icon.

The four dancers enter and cover Wigman, still kneeling on the lowest step, with the black veil, then lead her offstage. The stage remains empty, its emptiness preparing the spectator for the final transformation from the *Death Dance* to the *Dance of Life* (*Tanz des*

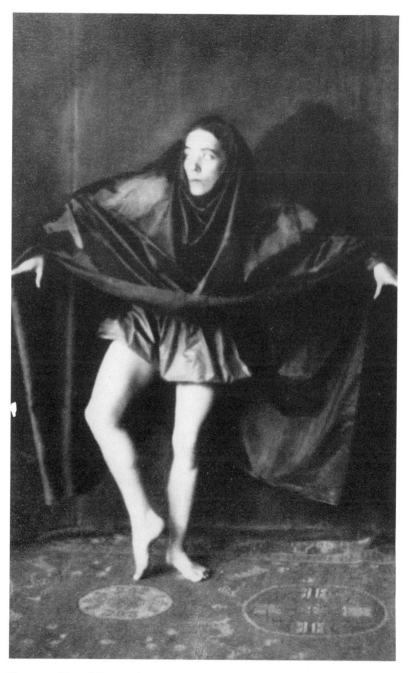

Fig. 10.   Mary Wigman in *Dance of the Demon*, from her 1921 group work
The Seven Dances of Life (courtesy of the Mary Wigman Archive)

Lebens). Then music sounds, increasingly louder and livelier, and the light becomes increasingly brighter. Once the drummers take their places again, Wigman, costumed in gold, and the four others reenter and for the first time dance together as equals. Meeting and parting, they swing through the space in a dance of celebration. The music shifts between duple and triple meters. The promptbook notes, "A flying and bounding quality characterizes the expression of the dance. The basic motif is the overcoming of gravity through jumps, swings, and suspensions. The entire dance is filled with a bright animation that can intensify into passion."[60]

Over the course of the dance the changing colors of Wigman's costumes signal her successive self-transformations: silver for the *Dance of Longing*, green for the *Dance of Love*, red for the *Dance of Lust*, violet for the *Dance of Suffering*, brown for the *Dance of the Demon*, white for the *Death Dance*, gold for the *Dance of Life*. Her self-transformations culminate in the changed relationship between the soloist and group. Until the final dance the group had remained separate from the soloist, much in the manner of a traditional corps de ballet. The four dancers help Wigman on with her skirt for the *Dance of Love*, enter into her energetic whirling in the *Dance of Lust*, support her limp form at the end of the *Dance of Suffering*, cover her with the black veil at the end of the *Death Dance*. But in the final *Dance of Life* soloist and group come together as equals, partners in the creation of the dance.

In retrospect, *The Seven Dances of Life* becomes a transitional work in Wigman's oeuvre, erasing the masculine presence and establishing the all-female community as the protagonist of her group choreography. From this point, no male—in effigy or in actuality—appeared in Wigman's works until 1930. And over the next two years the all-female ensemble expanded from four dancers to eighteen.[61] In January 1924 the expanded group premiered the final version of *Scenes from a Dance Drama* (*Szenen aus einem Tanzdrama*). Ironically titled, the new work presented neither "scenes" nor "drama," but rather eliminated narrative as a structuring principle. Or, perhaps more accurately, *Scenes from a Dance Drama* was the work that made drama out of Wigman's relations with her dancers and introduced the utopia of the all-female dance group.[62]

With *Scenes from a Dance Drama* Wigman initiated her collaboration with Will Goetze, a student of the expressionist composer Paul

Aron.[63] Her dissatisfaction with preexistent musical compositions and even with specially commissioned scores, like Pringsheim's for *The Seven Dances of Life*, led her to improvise with Goetze from the beginning of the choreographic process. As she later explained:

> I do not create a dance and then order music written for it. As soon as I conceive a theme, and before it is completely defined, I call in my musical assistants [Goetze until 1929, Hanns Hasting from 1929 until 1939]. Catching my idea, and observing me for atmosphere, they begin to improvise with me. Every step of the development is built up cooperatively. Experiments are made with various instruments, accents, climaxes, until we feel the work has indissoluble unity.[64]

Improvising with Wigman, Goetze would evolve a score for piano and percussion, which the composer then set for performance. Thus Wigman's improvisational work with Goetze paralleled her work with members of her dance ensemble. For both music and dance a strict line separated rehearsal from performance: improvisation structured the former but not the latter. As with the choreography, once the musical score was set, it was performed as exactly as possible.

With the creation of the expanded dance group and her collaboration with Goetze, Wigman no longer needed to rely on an opera house commission to prompt the creation of a group work, as she had for *The Seven Dances of Life*. She now commanded the resources to allow her work process with the dancers to dictate the evolution of her group choreography. That work process can be read as a utopian reconciliation of the choreographer's charismatic authority and her dancers' individual self-realization. In the *Gemeinschaft* staged by Wigman's group dances, her mentorship enabled her disciples' assertion of imagination and independence.

A comparison of photographs suggests the difference between the dance group conceived as a corps de ballet and as a *Gemeinschaft*. In *The Seven Dances of Life* (fig. 9) the group provided an almost geometric frame for Wigman's dancing. Whether seated with bowed heads or standing and gesturing toward the choreographer, the four dancers clearly subordinated themselves to Wigman. The spatial arrangement invites the spectator to focus on Wigman as soloist. In contrast, a photograph (fig. 11) of *Wandering* (*Wanderung*), the second of ten titled sections in *Scenes from a Dance*

Fig. 11.   Mary Wigman and her dance group in *Wandering*, from the 1924 work *Scenes from a Dance Drama* (courtesy of the Mary Wigman Archive)

Drama, shows Wigman in a spatial dialogue with her dancers. Although Wigman remains a visual focus within the camera frame, her placement directs the eye to the spatial tension between the two groups flanking her. Here the interplay between the soloist and the group provides the visual interest of the image.

A film clip of *Wandering* further evidences the *Gemeinschaft* of Wigman's dance group.[65] The two excerpts included on the clip demonstrate the stylistic reconciliation between the choreographer's authority and her dancers' autonomy. The first excerpt demonstrates how fluidly Wigman and the dancers exchange roles: at times Wigman functions as a soloist, at times as a group member, and the dancers too shift affiliations with ease. To begin, one group of two dancers and another of three pace in single file, their paths crossing one behind the other. Walking to a common measure, the two lines of dancers adopt contrasting attitudes: each of the threesome twists her torso to the side and holds her arms angled behind her, as if gliding into an open channel of space ahead, while each of the twosome adopts a flowing, wavelike motion of the upper body. The shared rhythm of their pacing unites the dancers, while their varied gestures lend them differentiation. Then Wigman appears in a long, light-colored gown. Although her costume sets her apart from the others in their dark-colored practice clothes, she is not isolated from the group. First she duets with another dancer as they turn around a common center point. Then her partner slips into line with the threesome, and Wigman dances alone, yet she remains connected to the group by echoing the rhythm of their walk.

The second excerpt demonstrates the difference between the group conceived as a mass and as a collection of individuals, presenting Wigman as both one among many and the first among equals. To begin, the group of dancers clusters together in a huddle. Breathing in unison, their bodies appear to expand and contract as one animate mass. Wigman stands apart from the group, the fluid foldings and unfoldings of her torso echoing its breathing form. Finally, she joins the huddle, becoming one with the mass. Her coming marks a closure, for once her body slumps forward over the others' limp forms, the mass becomes inert.

Breaking the stillness, Wigman initiates a procession. The dancers peel off from the huddle one by one and follow their mentor: the mass transforms into a collection of individuals, a column of dancers solemnly pacing in unison. A photograph (fig. 12) shows the dancers following Wigman, who already has left the camera frame. Each dancer assumes a different gesture. Some extend their arms somewhat away from the body, as if offering a gift. Others hold their arms closer, as if protecting a treasure. Although all are rapt in the order of the procession, each is involved in her own way. Devotion to charismatic authority does not suppress but rather supports her individuality. As Artur Michel remarked in his review of the work, "The self-development of the individual dancers presupposes the unbelievable effectiveness of the master teacher."[66]

The structure of *Scenes from a Dance Drama* makes the same point. The opening sections—*Summons* (*Aufruf*), *Wandering*, *Circle* (*Kreis*), and *Triangle* (*Dreieck*)—present a striving toward order that is never achieved due to opposition between Wigman and the group. The opposition climaxes in *Chaos* as the group overpowers the choreographer and she symbolically dies. In *Turning Point* (*Wende*) she revives and in *Vision* again confronts the group. This time the choreographer triumphs, reconciling herself with the group in *Gathering* (*Begegnung*). Reconciliation leads to the subor-

Fig. 12.   The Wigman dance group in *Wandering*, from the 1924 work *Scenes from a Dance Drama* (courtesy of the Mary Wigman Archive)

dination of the group to Wigman in *Salute* (*Gruss*), and this restoration of hierarchy leads in turn to the celebration of interdependence between choreographer and dance group in *Finale*.[67]

Eliminating narrative as conventionally conceived in Western theater dance, *Scenes from a Dance Drama* scripts a tale of the changing relations between soloist and ensemble. In this tale Wigman appears as the teacher-choreographer-artist whose student-dancers, her creative instruments, threaten to overwhelm her. She struggles to establish her authority, and once this is accomplished, freely interacts with her dancers as near equals. Alternately, Wigman represents a female Christ figure and undergoes the archetypal experience of the scapegoat, sacrificing herself in order to return to life and restore order to the community. The group turns against her at the beginning, only to idolize her as a goddess when she returns. Whether as teacher-choreographer-artist or as prophet and martyr, Wigman remains the *Führerin* (female leader) whose authority stabilizes the world of the dance and empowers its individual inhabitants.

Reviewers' descriptions and photographs demonstrate the significance of the work's structural progression. Hans Brandenburg describes the opening three sections:

> The first dance is a "summons": it is a call that resounds so strongly that an equally strong counter-call must answer, forming the group into a community. *Wandering* begins: three bell tones sound without interruption, as more and more dancers enter from every side. [The film excerpt begins at this point.] Everywhere there are paths: everywhere paths meet, cross, touch in passing. Suddenly, the bell tones become a torrent of buzzing and take hold of the striding dancers, whirling them into a vortex. But the lone path of the *Führerin* flows into its center, a solemn triad sounds, and the vortex becomes a long line. [The film excerpt ends at this point.] Three times the line is broken and temporarily makes a circle, where the first becomes last, the last first, and all become equal. At last the circle divides into a single line, and all kneel prayerfully. . . . Finally, in the next dance we experience the complete and lasting *Circle*: carried by the music, the circle is always undone and always united, undone into varying clusters and displays, united through a rocking impulse that once builds to a joyful climax.[68]

In Brandenburg's reading, the momentum of the opening sections builds toward the closure of the circle. But what remains at issue is the form of this closure. Is it the simple shape articulated thrice in *Wandering*, where, in Brandenburg's biblical echo, "the first becomes last, the last first, and all become equal?" Or is it the more complicated shape articulated in the aptly titled *Circle*, where the circular form embodies diversity within unity? These questions imply an analogous issue: how is community to be represented? As a configuration that confuses leader and follower, breaking down hierarchy in favor of equality? Or as a configuration that allows for difference and diversity? The subsequent course of events erases both forms of the circle, rejects both representations of community.

In the following *Triangle* and *Chaos* the community of the circle does not hold. Wigman becomes increasingly estranged from the others, until they finally turn against her. Brandenburg's description continues:

Fig. 13.   Mary Wigman and her dance group in *Chaos*, from the 1924 work *Scenes from a Dance Drama* (courtesy of the Mary Wigman Archive)

Then *Triangle* forms out of the circle: the *Führerin* joins with two others to become a threesome; these three stand apart from the rest. We see a disrupted and reversed movement figure, but only the two companions come within the net of the group; the *Führerin* remains outside and alone. Then rash chaos breaks out: the group is now only a mass, an element, the blind working of disunited forces accompanied by the hollow whirring and clapping of castanets. Following a solemn theme in the music, the *Führerin* enters this formless darkness like an animated and ordered sun, but she is swallowed by it.[69]

Hanya Holm's reminiscences echo Brandenburg's image of ingestion. She recalls the moment, "as if we were eating her."[70] A photograph (fig. 13), shot in the studio rather than outdoors, shows the group clustered around Wigman, threatening her with their clawed gestures. Wigman, kneeling on the floor, echoes their hand gestures, but in a way that pleads rather than threatens.

Chaos does not exhaust the possibilities for confrontation between the choreographer and dance group. In the subsequent *Turning Point* her limp form, left alone onstage after the group exits, revives, and she faces the threat of the group again in *Vision*. Brandenburg describes the action:

> Then comes the *Turning Point*, a resurrection from elemental death: first the resurrection of only the hands, which remain conscious of the earth, then of the entire *Gestalt*. The gong seems to sound of its own accord, to resound from the earth. The forces of the deep whirl in the figure and send her off on a new path, which she follows submissively. But the alien life also has revived and threatens her in *Vision*: a many-headed, many-limbed monster made of blood, whose hands are inescapable, like greedy claws even when carelessly hanging in a row.[71]

A photograph, not reproduced here, shows the "many-headed, many-limbed monster," the dancers huddled together so that they look like one organism with ten heads and ten pairs of arms and legs. In another photograph in the archive Wigman manages to fragment this collective body into individual bodies, but the effort leaves her spent. She and the dancers who had massed against her sprawl on the floor, united by their exhaustion.

Their confrontation past, the leader and group reconcile in *Gathering*, then celebrate their communion in *Salute* and *Finale*. Strikingly, as the community reforms, the configuration of the circle does not recur. Rather, the new community relies upon hierarchical organization. First, in *Gathering*, the dancers surround Wigman as if worshiping a goddess. Then, in *Salute*, ranked rows of dancers carry "a salute to the *Führerin*, a salute to us all," in Hans Brandenburg's words.[72] At last, in *Finale*, the recall of earlier movement themes culminates in "the unity of leader and group," in the words of Artur Michel.[73]

The ending three sections associate the principle of hierarchy with the interdependence of soloist and ensemble. As Hans Brandenburg describes *Gathering*: "One can never forget the sublimely weary, compelling gestures with which [Wigman] sinks back among her trusted children, blessing them while held and surrounded by them."[74] In a photograph not reproduced here, Wigman appears both to support physically the four dancers surrounding her and to be supported physically by them, evoking Brandenburg's description. Like a religious icon, the choreographer affords her disciples a central focus. In another photograph (fig. 14) Wigman,

Fig. 14.   Mary Wigman and two of her dancers in *Gathering,* from the 1924 work *Scenes from a Dance Drama* (courtesy of the Mary Wigman Archive)

costumed in a patterned metallic gown, visually opposes two of her dancers, costumed in dark robes. It is as if her physical presence were the exact equivalent of theirs together.

Another photograph (fig. 15) shows a moment from *Salute*: arranged in orderly rows, dancers step forward on one foot while raising the opposite arm overhead, a "salute" created by the gesture of the entire body. In contradistinction to the anarchy of the mass overpowering their leader in *Chaos,* order, hierarchy, and symmetry prevail.

Fig. 15.   The Wigman dance group in *Salute,* from the 1924 work *Scenes from a Dance Drama* (courtesy of the Mary Wigman Archive)

Finale summarizes the preceding action and celebrates the interdependence of choreographer and dance group. Artur Michel describes the action:

> Every dancer has her movement theme, her movement melody. . . . Groups led by individuals—individuals in opposition to groups—individuals let loose into a multitude—a closed unity—a bound mass from which each individual, pursuing her movement melody, breaks into dance, which in turn initiates a new grouping. . . . Finally, as a large group the collective tension returns as the group imitates the leader's strong swings, accompanied by a grand march theme, ending with the unity of leader and group.[75]

This ending section departed from the preceding sections in that it was performed to Liszt's *Rhapsodie* rather than to Goetze's score for piano and percussion. In fact, the section was not always performed with the others, perhaps because it seemed not only discontinuous but also superfluous.[76] After all, the remaining nine sections scripted a self-contained narrative about the breakdown and restoration of order. Whether performed in nine scenes or ten,

Scenes from a Dance Drama implicitly commented on the nature of community without explicitly telling a story. In the course of the action the equality and difference made possible by the circle give way to anarchy and chaos. Only once hierarchy and authority return does interdependence again become possible.

It is the progression from equality to interdependence between leader and follower that I read as both feminist and nationalist. For the "imagined community" represented onstage allowed younger women to realize their own potential without renouncing the mentorship of an older woman. At the same time, the "imagined community" allowed for the coexistence, and even reconciliation, of authoritarianism and individualism. Although quite inexplicable in terms of present-day politics, the *Gemeinschaft* dramatized by *Scenes from a Dance Drama* resonates with the paradoxes of Weimar feminism and democracy outlined by historian Claudia Koonz.

As Koonz explains, "women's suffrage, like democracy, came as a by-product of chaos and defeat rather than as the immediate result of a long and hard-fought battle."[77] The interim socialist cabinet that took control after the kaiser's abdication in 1918 instituted women's suffrage. But political rights did not directly translate into social revolution, for although "women heard themselves welcomed as citizens," in actuality they "experienced the erosion of their right to work, claim to equal pay, legal equality, and access to politics."[78] Koonz continues: "Women's suffrage, far from opening up new avenues of change, may have actually retarded further inroads on male hegemony. Reactionaries rallied as never before to prevent further progress, while the women's-rights advocates found their ranks seriously divided on questions related to protective legislation, divorce, welfare policy, rights of children out of wedlock, and education."[79]

Although exclusion from public life before 1918 had tended to unify women, now the differences between socialist and bourgeois women's organizations intensified. Weimar women responded with ambivalence to their supposed emancipation. Koonz concludes: "The fundamental dynamic of the Woman Question paralleled in important ways the problems of Weimar Germany generally. Politicians, artists, writers, and publicists balanced the promise of emancipation against the fear of chaos, weighing the prospect of an uncertain future against myths about the past."[80] Balancing "the promise of emancipation against the fear of chaos"—I could think of no more apt description of *Scenes from a Dance Drama.*

Scenes from a Dance Drama was arguably the most significant of Wigman's group dances choreographed during the twenties. According to Rudolf Lämmel, the work was given sixty-nine performances, far more than any other ensemble dance.[81] Moreover, Wigman's subsequent works for her group can be seen as variations on themes introduced by *Scenes from a Dance Drama.* Of the five group works Wigman choreographed after 1924 and before her company disbanded in 1928, I will reconstruct three—in this chapter, *Dance Fairy Tale* (1925) and *Dance of Death* (1926), and in the next chapter *Celebration* (1927–1928), the last work for her ensemble.[82] In the remainder of this section, my reconstructions will demonstrate how Wigman's group dances from 1925 to 1926 deployed the principle of the mask familiar from her solos and in so doing varied the theme of the choreographer's charismatic leadership.

Dance Fairy Tale (Das Tanzmärchen) struck a different tone from Wigman's other works in the twenties. Like *The Queen,* choreographed nearly a decade earlier on Monte Verita, *Dance Fairy Tale* functioned to parody the conventions of nineteenth-century story ballet. In the course of the action women are transformed into flowers rather than into dolls or swans, while good demons rather than good fairies triumph over their evil antagonists. But whereas *The Queen* made reference only to the story ballet, *Dance Fairy Tale* layered self-parody with the parody of the earlier tradition. Appearing as the Great Demon, Wigman mocked her own role as *Führerin* of the dance group.

Dance Fairy Tale departed from *The Queen* in another way as well. Whereas *The Queen* had supplied a scenario—so that the spectator could follow the story and its comic inversions of nineteenth-century conventions—*Dance Fairy Tale* supplied no scenario. Rather, the program listed only the generic title and a list of *Gestalten*—the Moon, Three Girls transformed into Flowers, the Five Guardians of the Flower Magic, the Youth, Ten Magicians (Five Drummers, Four Dancers, and the Chief Magician), and the Great Demon.[83] Thus the work demanded that spectators decode its parody, either by excavating the buried narrative or scripting their own associations with the action.

That a buried narrative did exist is evidenced by a scenario that Wigman wrote in 1920, titled "The Spellbound Flowers: A Dance Fairy Tale" ("Die verzauberten Blumen: Ein Tanzmärchen").[84] Presumably this scenario served as a starting point for the improvisational rehearsal process. As the work evolved in rehearsal, it was shaped by the individual dancers' improvisations. Wigman commented on the rehearsal process in comparison with that of *Scenes from a Dance Drama*:

> *Scenes from a Dance Drama* represented my personal conflict with the group as a totality, a mass. Its theme arose from my own world of expression. After working out the theme of *Dance Drama*, the young members of my group needed to take a rest from its seriousness and tragedy and to dance out their own worlds of expression. So I composed *Dance. Fairy Tale* purely out of their material. Their talents were lyrical, burlesque, restrained and austere, rhythmic and explosive—these talents wanted to speak their own languages and communicate. The originality and inflection of their varying talents gave rise to the forms of the fairy tale and its plot.[85]

Despite Wigman's insistence that the work arose from her dancers' individual qualities, reviewers' synopses of the action suggest that the production followed the general outlines of the 1920 scenario. Without access to the scenario, however, spectators often could not perceive the narrative logic and saw instead a succession of theatrical images. For example, the scenario clarifies the fairy-tale conceit whereby a demon has bewitched five girls so that they appear as flowers by day, assuming human form only when the moon shines at night. But the spectator in the theater had no reason to connect the entrance of a clown-like figure personifying the moon with the subsequent action of the flower guardians unsheathing their charges from their flower-like encasements. A photograph (fig. 16) shows what the spectators would have seen: *Gestalten* in body-distorting costumes—the moon encircled by a length of cloth gathered at the neck and attached to a wide hoop at the hip; the bewitched girls wrapped in yards of fabric that ruffle around their upper bodies, concealing their heads and arms; and the guardians in bodysuits and face masks, with bristly ruffles around their necks. The *Gestalten* invited spectators to project a story of their own devising.

It is important to note that the written scenario, the basis for the

Fig. 16.   The Wigman dance group in the 1925 work *Dance Fairy Tale* (courtesy of the Mary Wigman Archive)

improvisational rehearsal process, scripted only one of many possible narratives. However, since this narrative survives in more detail than those scripted by reviewers, it is the story told here. As noted before, reviewers' accounts suggest that although they read the general outlines of the story, they could not read the details. Yet in whatever story the spectator imaginatively scripted, only a few of the *Gestalten* took on recognizable identities as "he" or "she." On the contrary, most of the figures were of indeterminate gender.

According to the scenario, the girls, released from their bewitchment, come to consciousness and dance, watched over by their guardians. A young man passing by catches the eye of the most beautiful girl, and she soon steals away to join him. The guardians only notice her absence after her companions stop dancing and reassume their form as flowers. Once the guardians exit to search for the missing girl, the lovers emerge from the depths of the stage and dance a love duet. A photograph (fig. 17) shows the lovers stage left—two female dancers, one costumed in a skirt, the other in a tunic, both wearing bobbed hair. In contrast to the body-distorting and androgynous costume worn by the Moon seated stage right, the conventional silhouettes of the lovers' costumes signal their identities as "he" and "she."

The scenario continues: the guardians return and bind the girl

Fig. 17. The Wigman dance group in the 1925 work *Dance Fairy Tale* (courtesy of the Mary Wigman Archive)

in her flower-like encasement. Drums are heard in the distance, heralding a train of magic priests and drummers (the magicians listed in the program) who perform a dance of "ecstatic homage" for their leader, the great demon who remains offstage.[86] The young man rushes in, imploring the magician-priests to help him. At first they turn on him angrily, but his pleas have an effect, and the magician-priests bewitch him into repose before conferring on the best plan of action. They summon the great demon, a monstrous creature with twelve legs and a smiling face, who challenges the magician-priests: kill the guardians and the beautiful girl is freed, lose the fight and the young man loses his life.

A struggle between the magician-priests and guardians ensues. A photograph (fig. 18) shows the great demon, Wigman herself, presiding over the dueling forces. Finally, the magician-priests triumph and free the girls. While the others rejoice, the most beautiful girl crouches sadly, having seen her lover spellbound and believing him dead. But soon the magician-priests wake him from his spell, and the lovers rejoice at their reunion. As the scenario draws to a close, the head magician leads a celebratory procession offstage. At the end the figure who personifies the moon dances on the empty stage, unaware of the drama that just has transpired.

The magician-priests wear tall hats and bristly straw for hair.

Fig. 18.   Mary Wigman and her dance group in the 1925 work *Dance Fairy Tale* (courtesy of the Mary Wigman Archive)

The straw also decorates their costumes, forming bristly vests and short skirts. The great demon, Wigman herself, varies this costume with a long blond wig and more capacious skirts. Like the moon and guardians, the magician-priests do not have a recognizable gender. Their costumes transform them into figures of uncertain sexuality. Only the great demon and the young lovers and their companions appear legibly masculine or feminine, their sexual identities bestowed by the silhouettes of their costumes—the blond wig, the wide skirts, the tunic and trousers. In *Dance Fairy Tale* the performers' costumes bear their identities and their gender— whether masculine or feminine or androgynous or asexual. Identity and gender do not reside in the dancers' persons but in the costumes that mask their bodies.

Dance of Death (*Totentanz*), premiered one year later, made the divorce between the identity of the performer and the identity of the mask almost absolute. Unlike the figures in *Dance Fairy Tale*, the figures in *Dance of Death* did not exhibit much individuation or differentiation according to gender. Rather, their actual facial masks transformed them into *Gestalten* whose only identity came from their habitation of the realm of death. Within this desexualized realm, Wigman's charismatic leadership took a surprising turn, no longer an active force but a passive state of being.

Presumably, the scenario titled "A Dance of Death" that Wigman wrote on Monte Verità served as a basis for the dancers' improvisations.[87] As the dancers improvised with their masks, the original

Fig. 19. Mary Wigman and her dance group in the 1926 work *Dance of Death* (courtesy of the Mary Wigman Archive)

conception of the work subtly shifted. Wigman described the composition process:

> Originally I had envisioned this dance as a ghostlike *Reigen* [round dance], rushing back and forth across the dancing area, with all figures twitching and jerking in gesture and movement. But now that the masked shapes stood in front of me, they dictated their own will. They were not like individuals. However, seen one by one, they made the impression of variations on a theme, gaining independence in different phases, only to melt into a many-headed body in its tense grouping.[88]

In Wigman's account, the qualified "independence" of the figures stood in tension with their near interchangeability.

A photograph (fig. 19) vivifies the tension between individuality and anonymity highlighted in the choreographer's memoirs. As captured by the camera, the eight *Gestalten* wear masks carved by Viktor Magito and costumes, extending the mask principle, designed by Elis Griebel. Evoking "the impression of variations on a theme," six of the *Gestalten* wear nearly identical masks. Just as the masks conceal their faces, so dark hooded shawls and voluminous skirts conceal their bodies. The photograph shows two other *Gestalten* as well, differentiated from one another and from the others through their masks and costumes, yet with their offstage identities almost as equally well concealed. The threatened figure, costumed in a tube of boldly striped fabric, wears an elongated mask with downward-slanting lines for eyes and mouth; the threatening figure, costumed in a bloused bodysuit, wears a squared mask with straight lines for eyes and mouth. (The program notes only the title and does not even list the names of the eight dancers, although astute observers identified Wigman as the threatened figure and Ruth Berentson as the threatening figure.)[89]

As the action unfolds, the six nearly identical *Gestalten* find themselves pulled between the opposing two *Gestalten*. In Wigman's account:

> I resisted calling the dominating figure [Berentson] "Death." . . . This figure was much closer to a barbaric, beastlike creature which seemed to grope its way through a jungle of the unknown, in a greedy, gruesomely lustful manner, cracking an invisible whip over the dark obscurity of being. . . .
>
> This animallike masked figure . . . had its counterpart in a dancer [Wigman] standing there like an alien body, like someone who perhaps only came to pass through, as a plaything of irrational happenings. With this masked face acquiring human features, the entire figure experienced movement impulses from time to time which recalled a once-lived existence.
>
> Between these two soloists the group of masked creatures, like lemures with their soulless lives, moved as if driven by the master figures.[90]

The work begins with all the dancers lying inert on the floor, except for the death figure lurking in shadows upstage. Gradually, the *Gestalten* come to life. Wigman is the last figure to stir, and her memoirs relate how "lying on my back and, with my arms stretched out, reminiscent of the cross, it [appears] as if the ground beneath me would lift my rigid body, forcing me into a swaying movement that kept me from any motion of my own free will."[91] Once the *Gestalten* come to life, the death figure incites them into action, holding their arms and whipping them through space, grabbing and throwing Wigman. Near chaos ensues: "Then nobody could any longer have said who moved what and what whom."[92]

Through all this sounds a cacophony of percussion, created by

Goetze and a group of dancers crowded into a corner with an assortment of instruments—drums, gongs, a whistle, a flute. The sound alternates with durations of eerie silence, "through which the beast [moves] with catlike steps."[93] At a pitch of musical intensity, the six dancers "[stop] as if riveted to time and place, helpless, frozen."[94] Wigman alone remains in motion. Then she and the others fall back to the floor. "Everything [seems] to fade away while recalling the stage image of the opening moments of the dance."[95]

Wigman's role in *Dance of Death* differs from her role in earlier group dances, for she no longer functions as the absolute authority within the world of the dance. Rather, she submits to the finality represented by the realm of death, as personified in the *Gestalt* performed by Berentson. Her memoirs recall:

> My figure should have been reminiscent of something human, but was not supposed to react in a human way. This figure was called upon to let the devilish game happen without resisting it—to endure, as it were, but not to suffer from it. Exposed to the sadism of her beastly counterpart, she was driven around and overcome—and yet she was not allowed to play the part of a puppet, nor could she leave the route assigned to her.[96]

In *The Seven Dances of Life* Wigman had danced through death and affirmed life, identifying with the figure of John the Baptist. But her gesture of the cross served her differently in *Dance of Death*, allowing her to "endure," as she wrote, not to experience rebirth. In *Scenes from a Dance Drama* her resurrection had strengthened her efficacy as *Führerin*. But in *Dance of Death* her identification with the cross demonstrated her loss of absolute authority, as the gesture of the cross became a means of passive resistance to death. Or, perhaps more accurately, in *Dance of Death* the choreographer redefined leadership as endurance and submission to fate.

Despite this divergence, however, the 1926 work did not depart from the utopian reconciliation of authority and autonomy characteristic of her group works during the twenties. As her choreographic memoirs make clear and her dancers' reminiscences attest, Wigman's charismatic leadership—whether defined in negative or positive terms—did not preclude her dancers' self-realization. As a reviewer remarked: "Enticing first the mask and then the soul to dance, the figure of Death played as large a role as Wigman herself. The incredible togetherness of the group was evident here as well as in the chorus of masks. Through the perfect self-development of each dancer, the group becomes an instrument of singular artistic unity."[97]

It is easy to read the *Gemeinschaft* of Wigman's group dances from the mid-twenties in feminist terms. For, unlike the female characters in narrative ballets such as *Giselle,* Wigman's dancers did not define themselves in relation to men but rather in relation to one another. This female-identified community seemingly resolved the participants' conflicting needs for intimacy and for independence. Wigman's dances presented the solidarity of the Wilis transposed into another key, a solidarity that included the female spectator, who could imagine herself part of the same community, where her needs for affiliation and for self-realization did not conflict. That Wigman's ensemble functioned in this way for its participants is clear from oral history. It is harder to confirm the responses of women in the audience, since most of the surviving accounts—the reviews—were authored by men. However, it is clear that women in the audience enrolled at the Wigman School and affiliated studios in droves. Perhaps this was proof enough of their desire to experience something of the utopia they witnessed onstage.

It is more difficult to read the *Gemeinschaft* of Wigman's group dances in terms of nationalism than in terms of feminism. For neither the choreographer nor her dancers nor her critics read the *Gemeinschaft* as essentially German, as they would after 1933. In the mid-twenties her group dances did not essentialize national identity in the same way that they did later. However, in the context of the Weimar Republic, the *Gemeinschaft* of Wigman's group dances did take on a particular import. A nascent democracy, the republic attempted to chart a course between the militarism of the right and the millenialism of the left. Her group dances suggested that the visions of the right and left were not antithetical, that the *Führerprinzip* (leadership principle) was not incompatible with the liberation of the individual. That reviewers associated with journals of diverse political orientations—from the right-wing *Die Tat* to the left-wing *Sozialistische Monatshefte*—responded enthusiastically to Wigman's work suggests that spectators could interpret her dramatization of authoritarianism and individualism according to their own inclinations.

It is important to note that the presence of the *Führerprinzip* did not render her group dances from the mid-twenties "protofascist." It was not until the utopian reconciliation of authority and autonomy had given way to the dystopian counterpoint between the *Führerin* and the mass that "fascist" becomes an appropriate label for Wigman's dances. And that did not happen until the choreographer had disbanded her dance group and sought alternative conditions under which to create group choreography.

WITCH DANCE

A similar analysis holds for Wigman's solos from the mid-twenties. That is, to read them in feminist terms is easy, but to read them in nationalist terms is more difficult. Her deployment of the mask clearly undermined the spectatorial position of the male gaze and consolidated the possibility of female spectatorship in a way that challenged the Duncanesque dancer's reinscription of the erotic female body. Yet Wigman's challenge to Duncanesque dancing did not entirely do away with the assumptions of cultural feminism and nationalism, for spectators could view her solo performances as essentialized visions of Woman and the Germanic. All this becomes clear in a reconstruction of the 1926 *Witch Dance* (*Hexentanz II*).[98]

The revised *Witch Dance* made explicit what had been implicit in the identically titled solo presented twelve years earlier on her debut program. As in the earlier solo, the choreographer does not impersonate the character of a witch but rather embodies the quality of "witchness." However, her self-transformation is intensified and made more complete through her use of a facial mask, designed by Viktor Magito. As a reviewer described the effect: "She employs a small face mask, which doesn't hide all of her cheek, nor does it cover her hair. The eye openings of the mask allow her eyes to be seen. . . . [Her] partially covered body . . . lives no longer, but withdraws so far from life that each movement extinguishes all thought of human existence."[99]

A photograph (fig. 20) shows the oddly fitted mask and the bared body parts visible from beneath the folds of brocade. Wearing a mask, the female dancer objectifies herself rather than allowing herself to be objectified by the (male) spectator. Wearing a mask, she turns the gaze back on the spectator.

Fig. 20.   Mary Wigman in the second version of *Witch Dance,* a solo choreographed in 1926 (courtesy of the Mary Wigman Archive)

A film survives of the first half of the work.[100] Seated on the floor throughout, the *Gestalt* sways from side to side and claws at the air, as if straining against its boundness to the ground. Once set in motion, the mask and the exposed body parts appear animated by a life-force of their own. The dance reverses the usual relation of stillness and motion: rather than moments of stasis punctuating a continuum of motion, gestures punctuate the stillness. The alternation of sound and silence follows the same patterning. Underscoring the gestures, the percussive accents of drum, cymbals, and gong focus the spectator's attention on durations of silence. The interpenetration of sound and silence counterpoints the interplay of stillness and motion.

The gestures contain more energy than they release. As each gesture subsides into stillness, the potential energy contained by the *Gestalt* mounts. Pounding its feet against the floor, the figure propels itself into a circle, finally transforming gesture into locomotion but not yet transcending the limitations of its seated position. The film excerpt ends here, but from reviewers' accounts it is clear that the remainder of the dance releases the accumulation of potential energy. Rising to standing, the *Gestalt* leaps and circles wildly through the space. Rudolf Bach describes the action:

> With a powerful swing the [*Gestalt*] comes to its feet. Now everything happens in rapid, flowing, close succession. A complicated rhythmic movement sets in. . . . Like a giant, the red and gold, phantom-like figure rears up in the space. Now it leaps around in a circle, the right foot is thrown out, the hands of the speeding arms perform a kind of spurting throwing action. . . . The figure leaps out of the circle with fierce increased tempo. . . . Now comes a sudden, wild jump outwards. . . . The forearms cross over each other horizontally, as the fingers open and close. . . . it is as if something invisible were being severed with eerie industry, again and again.[101]

At the end the *Gestalt* collapses back to the floor. Yet at the final moment the masked face rears up to confront the spectator. The dance has not exhausted the potential energy of the *Gestalt*. Rudolf Bach describes the ending: "For a moment the [*Gestalt*] is like a gleaming, enthroned idol, but the body immediately falls over backward, a very powerful swing of both arms throws it forward again, it tumbles back on the ground, the hands support it, the head snaps up, the mask stares toward us in petrified madness. Darkness."[102]

During the final moments of *Witch Dance II* Wigman's mask reverses the direction of the gaze. The spectator becomes not only the viewer but also the viewed, not only the subject of vision but also the object of vision. It is as if the spectator and performer switch positions at the last moment. A reviewer described the effect: "A witch, vain and mad, wants to capture us. We see through her. She cannot have us. But almost. If we don't watch out, she could have us, suddenly. That is, insanity could have us. A shrill laugh. And the despairing, wretched, infamous emptiness."[103] The reversal of the gaze threatens the spectator, undermines the spectator's control over the interpretation of the dance. Is the solo a projection of the choreographer's personal "demon" or an archetypal image? If an archetype, is the witch essentially female or without recognizable gender, essentially German or universal? Does the *Gestalt* transcend history and culture or bespeak the Zeitgeist?

The solo supported antithetical interpretations. Its seemingly demonic energy erased the potential eroticism of the female body. At the same time, *Witch Dance II* threatened to redefine Woman as the Demonic, albeit in a way that celebrated rather than denigrated her otherness. Similarly, the solo both undermined attempts to ascribe national identity to the dancer and supported attempts to equate the Germanic and the Demonic. It was precisely such tensions, I would suggest, that gave *Witch Dance II* its power.

4

From Modernism to Fascism

In challenging the teleological narrative of absolute dance, I have endeavored *not* to substitute the teleological narrative of "all roads lead to fascism." Nowhere is this substitution more difficult to avoid than in the present chapter, for retrospect gives me as a historian a perspective unavailable to the contemporary spectator. This retrospective vantage point reveals how the shifts in Wigman's choreographic practice from 1928 to 1931 anticipated further shifts after 1933. Yet the changes evident around 1930 do not necessarily render Wigman's works from this period "protofascist," even though when viewed in retrospect, the changes initiate a transition from her modernist aesthetic of the mid-twenties to her fascist aesthetic of the mid-thirties. In only one case does the designation "protofascist" seem apt, the case of *Totenmal* (1930), which modeled strategies later adopted by Nazi spectacle. In other works from this period (*Celebration* [1928], *Shifting Landscape* [1929], *Sacrifice* [1931]), the label does not apply.[1]

What all Wigman's works from this period reveal is her response to changing working conditions. In 1928 financial difficulties forced her to disband her all-female dance group. Without this creative instrument she turned first to the solo format and created an extended solo cycle, *Shifting Landscape*. She then teamed up with poet Albert Talhoff and staged the multimedia spectacle *Totenmal*. During this period her career was marked by paradox, for she experienced increasing popular renown, yet increasing choreographic constraints. Without her dance group she no longer fully controlled the circumstances under which she worked.

My explanation for Wigman's passage from a modernist to a fascist aesthetic lies in the choreographic crisis she faced around 1930. This crisis cannot be separated from the crisis of *Ausdruckstanz* as a whole. For, like Wigman's career, the *Ausdruckstanz* movement occupied a paradoxical position around 1930: the movement seemed to have arrived, but where to go next seemed unclear. At a series of three dancers' congresses—held in 1927, 1928, and 1930—the movement appeared both to coalesce and to fragment. When the National Socialists came to power, they resolved the crises facing Wigman and *Ausdruckstanz,* and for this reason not only Wigman but also many other modern dancers struck up an accommodation with the new regime.

CRISIS

Through the mid-twenties a provocative tension between populism and elitism animated *Ausdruckstanz.* The *Technik* of improvisation blurred the boundary between professional and amateur dance, for stage dancers employed the same working method as devotees of *Tanz-Gymnastik.* A network of private studios supported *Ausdruckstanz.* Although a few offered professional-level training and sponsored concert dance groups, most focused on classes for amateurs. These amateur dancers provided a ready audience for the soloists and dance groups that toured from city to city. The artistry of *Ausdruckstanz* rested upon a mass movement.

Enrollment at the Wigman School increased exponentially in the mid-twenties, necessitating a renovation and an expansion in 1927. With funds raised from private supporters as well as from the city of Dresden, the state of Saxony, and the national government in Berlin, a new studio was built that increased the available rehearsal and teaching space by a factor of eight.[2] Wigman oversaw not only this project but also the founding of branch schools in Berlin, Hamburg, Erfurt, Frankfurt, Leipzig, Munich, Magdeburg, Freiburg, Riesa, and Chemnitz.[3] Directed by students who had completed the professional course at Dresden, the branch schools modeled their curriculum on Dresden, although they were financially independent. By the late twenties the Dresden school registered more than three hundred students, the Berlin school more than twice that number, and the branch schools altogether enrolled fifteen hundred students.[4] In addition, many students who had studied at Dresden opened private studios that further disseminated Wigman *Technik* among devotees of physical culture.

During the twenties Laban's work underwent a popularization similar to Wigman's. By 1927 he oversaw a network of more than twenty-five schools, from Hamburg to Munich.[5] Many of the schools supported "movement choirs" (*Bewegungschor*), a large-scale form of amateur dance involving anywhere from fifty to five hundred or more participants. As envisioned by Laban, the movement choir aimed to create a sense of community (*Gemeinschaft*) among members of an industrialized society (*Gesellschaft*).[6] Founded in association with churches, schools, and political unions, in addition to private dance studios, movement choirs blurred the distinction between professional and amateur dance.

Although Laban was commonly associated with a populist stance and Wigman with an elitist stance, both worked somewhere between the two positions. Wigman's school in Dresden offered lay courses in *Tanz-Gymnastik* as well as professional training. And the division of her oeuvre between solos and group dances mediated between the demands of individual talent and group participation. Laban innovated not only the form of the movement choir but also a system of movement notation. Although the notation system could serve as a means of transmission for the movement choir (small-group leaders could receive notated scores and rehearse their groups separately before the larger movement choir assembled), the elaboration of the system went far beyond the needs of amateur performance.[7] The complexity of the system foreclosed its widespread dissemination and required highly trained specialists for its deployment. Juxtaposing Wigman's *Tanz-Gymnastik* and Laban's notation system, it is hard to say whose practice was more "populist," whose more "elitist."

In the mid- to late twenties what had been a provocative tension between populism and elitism became a problem. At a series of dancers' congresses, followers of Wigman, the faction of "elitists," squared off against followers of Laban, the faction of "populists." Personal rivalries had played a role in the factionalization, although they did not explain it altogether. Piqued that she was not invited to perform at the First Dancers' Congress in 1927, Wigman boycotted the event, and many of her former students stayed away in support of her position. Hans Brandenburg commented: "Mary Wigman did not appear; she had set the condition that the [organizers] engage her to perform at the congress. Since this did not happen, she was justified in staying away."[8] In Wigman's absence, Laban dominated the first congress and became the de facto leader of the Tänzerbund (Dancers' Union) organized among participants at the congress.

The following year Wigman, her former students, and associates founded a rival organization, the Tanzgemeinschaft (Dance Circle), and the two organizations jointly sponsored the Second Dancers' Congress held in 1928. Given this background, it is not surprising that participants at the second congress continued their partisan debates, despite a carefully balanced program that gave equal time to the two camps.[9] The reporter for the *Sozialistische Monatshefte* commented on the event: "It was self-evident that two parties would form. One party was for drill and solid craftsmanship, whereby every dancer could develop according to his or her talent. The other party was for individuality and inspired *Technik*."[10]

This comment suggests that more than personal rivalries were at stake in the factionalization of *Ausdruckstanz*. At issue was not only whether modern dance should focus its efforts toward amateur participation or stage art, but also whether concert dance should follow the inspiration of individual improvisation or adopt the training methods of ballet. Indeed, the squaring off of "elitists" and "populists" revealed a new tension—between younger and older choreographers. A new generation of choreographers, students of Wigman and Laban, had appeared on the scene, and they saw the potential of the opera house as a patron for *Ausdruckstanz*. To realize this potential, modern dance had to divorce itself from its roots in physical culture and integrate the discipline and theatricality of ballet. Such was the view propounded at the Second Dancers' Congress by younger choreographers: Max Terpis, a former Wigman student and ballet master at the Berlin State Opera; Yvonne Georgi, another former Wigman student and ballet mistress at the municipal theater in Hannover; and Kurt Jooss, a former Laban student and director of the dance department at the recently established Folkwang School in Essen.[11]

The interest in the opera house among younger choreographers coincided with a glut of private studios that made it difficult for recently trained dancers to support themselves through amateur teaching as easily as had their predecessors. In the early twenties there seemed an insatiable demand among amateurs for instruction in the new art of movement. The market seemed infinitely expandable as private studio after private studio opened, many directed by former students of Wigman and Laban. But by the late twenties the market had reached a saturation point. The number of amateurs interested in dance instruction could not increase exponentially forever.

Even the Wigman School in Dresden felt the effects of the economic crisis. For the renovation and expansion in 1927 had over-extended the resources of the school and left Wigman financially vulnerable.[12] The following year financial difficulties became so acute that the choreographer was forced to disband her dance group—a decision she announced at the Second Dancers' Congress after a performance of what became her final work for the ensemble, *Celebration* (*Die Feier*).

Although financial difficulties played an important role in her decision—and provided its public rationale—other factors also contributed. Many members of the group had left to pursue careers on their own or to marry and start families. By the time *Celebration* was performed at the Second Dancers' Congress, only two of the dancers who had premiered *Scenes from a Dance Drama* remained with the troupe.[13] The turnover in personnel culminated with the departure of Will Goetze, who had decided to pursue his own career as a composer and to accept more secure employment elsewhere.[14] Choreographing *Celebration,* Wigman collaborated with Goetze for the last time.

Celebration was Wigman's most extended group composition to date, lasting an entire evening. The work moved away from the mask principle evident in *Dance Fairy Tale* and *Dance of Death.* Further, it departed from the buried narratives and representational imagery characteristic of the earlier masked dances and of *Scenes from a Dance Drama.* Unlike Wigman's earlier group dances, however, *Celebration* did not refer beyond itself but rather functioned self-reflexively. Its structure recalled motifs from earlier works as well as circling back and mirroring its own design. For the first time Wigman supplied her spectators with an extended program note, authored by Will Goetze. The program note associated the opening section, *The Temple* (*Der Tempel*), with "dancerly ecstasy"; the middle section, *In the Sign of Darkness* (*Im Zeichen des Dunklen*), with "dancerly tragedy"; and the closing section, *Festive Conclusion* (*Festlicher Ausklang*), with "solemn celebration."[15]

As reconstructed from reviews and an extended description by Rudolf Bach, *The Temple* introduces a new relation between Wigman and the dance group. The choreographer appears more independent of the group than in earlier works. Conversely, the group appears more independent of the choreographer. In the first two "monotonies," as Wigman termed the four subsections of *The Temple*, she appears as a soloist backed by the dance group. For the first section dancers enter carrying musical instruments, then seat themselves and play the instruments as the choreographer dances in front of them.[16] The dancers quite literally function as the accompanying orchestra for Wigman's appearance as soloist. This relation between choreographer and dance group becomes figurative in the second section, characterized by Rudolf Bach as a "danced concerto grosso."[17]

In the third "monotony" Wigman appears alone, spinning until she collapses. As Rudolf Bach describes the action:

> From the first moment a spell lies over the *Gestalt*. Her dreamlike movements . . . evidence only an apparent freedom of will. The dancing figure has as little power over her decisions as a stick of wood caught in a whirlpool. The center of the space becomes a magnet around which she begins to circle in spiral fashion. Soon she finds herself in the innermost ring. Slowly, she begins to turn around herself. Developing out of its own intensity, the tempo moves faster and faster, quickening by measured increments from stolid suffering through rebellion, despair, and fury to the last furioso of self-destruction. The wide spectrum with which Wigman inflects this process is incredible: changes from flat-footed turns to turns on the toes, from accented to unaccented turns, use of a continuous though strongly controlled transformation of arm and hand forms and of the torso, now erect, now swinging. Suddenly, in the middle of a raging whirl, an accumulated pause. Collapse.[18]

This solo seems almost detachable from the remainder of the action, and, indeed, it was, for the choreographer often presented this section on her solo programs as *Monotony Whirl (Drehmonotonie)*.

In the final "monotony" the group appears alone. Strikingly, in Wigman's absence members of the dance group take turns functioning as soloists.[19] Margarethe Wallmann comments:

> [In *Scenes from a Dance Drama* Wigman] was not bound as a part of the totality but rather opposed her individuality to the mass. Hence the heroic and cruel fight of two worlds. A transformation happened over the course of *Dance Fairy Tale* and . . . *Dance of Death. Celebration* no longer concerns the violent struggles of the dancers as in *Scenes from a Dance Drama.* . . . First, all the participants are arranged such that they can see neither one another nor the [onstage instrumental-

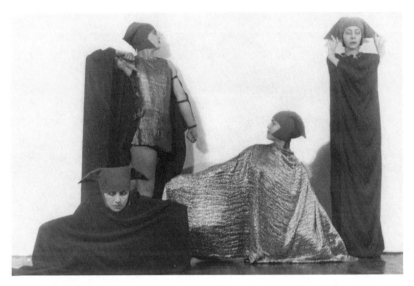

Fig. 21. The Wigman dance group in *In the Sign of Darkness*, from the 1928 work *Celebration* (courtesy of the Mary Wigman Archive)

ists.] Despite this, the dancers perform as a group, filled with the impetus of Mary Wigman and with an overpowering urgency. The group creates a unity as if led by an invisible hand. We know: although Mary Wigman is not present onstage, she is there in spirit.[20]

By the time they performed *Celebration*, the members of the dance group had fully internalized Wigman's authority. Their internalization of her authority empowered them to dance, however briefly, as soloists, individuals in their own right. The utopian reconciliation of authority and autonomy reached its apogee in *Celebration*.

The middle section, *In the Sign of Darkness*, recalls motifs from earlier group works. A photograph (fig. 21) shows the dancers wearing body-distorting costumes reminiscent of their costumes-as-masks from *Dance Fairy Tale*. Another photograph (fig. 22) shows Wigman in a silver dress with a long cape, which she manipulates as part of her dance.[21] The configurations of movement are reminiscent of *Dance of Death* and *Scenes from a Dance Drama*: Wigman, costumed in silver, rising from the floor and sinking back to the floor, commanding the group and imprisoned by the group.[22] But the structure of the section brackets these paraphrases of earlier works as exactly that—paraphrases that do not have referents outside Wigman's corpus. *In the Sign of Darkness* begins and

Fig. 22. Mary Wigman in *In the Sign of Darkness,* from the 1928 work *Celebration* (courtesy of the Mary Wigman Archive)

ends with the same image: the dancers spread through the space in "crouching groups, standing groups, pairs, singles."[23] Like the final "monotony" in *The Temple,* this closing differentiates the dancers, testifying to their individuality.

As its action unfolds, *Celebration* becomes increasingly self-reflexive. The final section, *Festive Conclusion,* recalls images from the first two sections, thus functioning as a summary of a summary.[24] As at the beginning of *The Temple,* the opening presents dancers carrying musical instruments. First five dancers carrying cymbals enter,[25] initiating a "joyously vibrant . . . march in canon," and then two flute players initiate a "pastoral."[26] Wigman next performs alone, replicating the sequence of *The Temple*. The subsequent action recalls *In the Sign of Darkness*, as the group assumes a block formation and temporarily imprisons Wigman. The conflict resolves as leader and group reunite, and Wigman leads the others in unison dancing. But the ending image, as at the close of *In the Sign of Darkness*, reasserts the individuality of the dancers: "All pause suddenly, distributed over the entire stage, each in a different position: sliding, upright, thrown back, bent over forward, kneeling, still in the shape of turning, stiff as if torn through by the force of a swing. Curtain."[27]

In *Celebration* the dancers' internalization of Wigman's authority had paradoxical effects. On the one hand, the dancers appeared as individualized presences, an impression underscored by the endings of all three sections. At the close of *The Temple* each performed briefly as a soloist; at the close of *In the Sign of Darkness* and *Festive Conclusion* each froze in a different position. On the other hand, the dancers appeared almost as automatons, focusing their gaze inward rather than toward one another, as Margarethe Wallmann noted. André Levinson confirmed her impression: "[*Celebration*] displayed the ceremonies of a cult devoted to an unknown god. It opened with a solemnly ordered procession, a figured march which evoked the splendors of a legendary Orient. The hierophants paraded, broke or closed their ranks in cadence: their eyes were set, their expression trance-like, like that of sleep-walkers."[28]

As Wigman became more independent of the group, her dancers became, paradoxically, more individualized and more anonymous. *Celebration* exposed the tension between Wigman's authority and her dancers' autonomy at the center of her group works. The production marked the end of an era in more ways than one, for it seemed to epitomize the utopian achievement of the dance group at the same time that it revealed the utopia's underlying contradiction. The dancers' need to break the bounds of the self came into open conflict with their need to subordinate themselves to a greater force. Although financial difficulties prompted the disbandment of the dance group, its dissolution testified to the breakdown of its raison d'être. Joseph Lewitan commented:

> After *Celebration* further development [of the dance group] no longer was conceivable, only a crass return and a cursory stab at new directions. The dance group, founded as a means toward the end of

absolute dance, in actuality served another purpose in the period after the war's end. Following the war and revolution, the group became a substitute for the masses' unsatisfied needs for military drill and religious ecstasy. However paradoxical it sounds, Mary Wigman's dance group was both. . . . This fascinated spectators for whom the idea of *order* was only the memory of an earlier time.[29]

In the utopia staged by the dance group, the order of the past coexisted with the possibilities of the present.

RESPONSE

Wigman's first response to the disbandment of her dance group was to focus on her solo choreography, and in 1929 she premiered the extended cycle *Shifting Landscape* (*Schwingende Landschaft*). The cycle juxtaposed the principle of the mask with a new image of the dancer: an identifiably feminine persona now shared the stage with the *Gestalt* that blurred gender. Wigman's contemporaries recognized her shift in representational strategy. Some deplored the change, such as the reviewer who remarked: "Times have changed. . . . The world no longer likes 'frenzy.' So one must be more 'womanly.' "[30] Others welcomed the change, such as Vera Skoronel, a former student of Wigman, who related the change to a heightened compositional clarity.[31] What contemporaries could not recognize was how the new image of the dancer—no longer a *Gestalt* but rather a feminine persona—anticipated Wigman's solo choreography during the Third Reich.

Like *Celebration*, *Shifting Landscape* displayed a formalization of means that responded to younger choreographers' interest in ballet. Although Wigman could not or would not integrate her improvisational *Technik* with ballet technique, she did respond to the Zeitgeist of *Neue Sachlichkeit* (new objectivity) and heightened attention to form. More tightly integrated than earlier solo cycles, *Shifting Landscape* comprised an exact sequence of variations on a theme. Wigman designed the cycle to be performed as a whole, not in separate parts. Her choreographic design was underscored by the musical accompaniment composed by Hanns Hasting, Goetze's successor. As with *Celebration*, the formalization of the choreography required a program note of explanation. Authored by Wolfgang Schumann, a critic and fan, the note summarized the shift in

Wigman's style: "No longer does an unknown artist manifest generalized and indefinite provocations and streams of consciousness. Rather a graspable, nameable fantasy-form experiences before the spectators' eyes singular and concrete events full of heartwarming impressions."[32]

The cycle comprises seven solos. The opening *Invocation* (*Anruf*) and *Seraphic Song* (*Seraphisches Lied*) project a quality of reverence. As the program states, in the first solo "a druidlike priestess calls on the blessing of the higher spirit." The second solo takes place "in the realm of the highest piety that knows nothing except humble rapture" as "the heavenly dance expresses all that is inner with a language gentle and urgent." *Face of Night* (*Gesicht der Nacht*) then introduces a dark note. According to the program:

> The night itself, embodied in form [*Gestalt*], enters the dark space. Expands itself over the land, furtively conquering. Not a sweet summer night of blessed moonlight. The night fumbles along pregnant with horror, threatening crime, spreading fear. Soon flung toward the ecstasy of power and the rage of victory, saturated by . . . power over the earthly realm. A phantasmagoria of universal experiences of fear.

The remaining four solos return to the lighter tone of the opening. *Pastorale* embodies "reflections, thoughts, dreams rambling over the world's breath." *Festive Rhythm* (*Festlicher Rhythmus*) displays "a sovereign . . . reveling in fighting postures and gestures," and *Dance of Summer* (*Sommerlicher Tanz*) presents "a summer goddess blessing the fruitful earth." *Storm Song* (*Sturmlied*) provides the finale described by the program: "In a dance of swings and jumps, cascades, whirls and catapults, the wind's bride herself rushes, flits, races over the panting land, thundering with the desire for movement, free, bold, born in a mood of jubilation, unfettered and lovestricken."

Photographs show that even though *Face of Night* and *Storm Song* deployed the costume-as-mask, the remaining solos lent Wigman a decidedly feminine, even at times autobiographical, persona. A photograph (fig. 23) of the opening solo, *Seraphic Song*, shows the dancer bringing her hands together in prayer while standing still. The spectator reads the gesture mimetically, as the image of a woman performing a familiar ritual of worship. A photograph (fig. 24) of the penultimate solo, *Dance of Summer*, reads more

Fig. 23.   Mary Wigman in *Seraphic Song*, from the 1929 solo cycle *Shifting Landscape* (courtesy of the Mary Wigman Archive)

Fig. 24.   Mary Wigman in *Dance of Summer*, from the 1929 solo cycle *Shifting Landscape* (courtesy of the Mary Wigman Archive)

Fig. 25.   Mary Wigman in *Storm Song*, from the 1929 solo cycle *Shifting Landscape* (courtesy of the Mary Wigman Archive)

ambiguously than does the opening image. Wigman poses on half-pointe, her arms angled and her torso bent in a gesture that at first recalls no familiar gesture but that on closer inspection looks like a pantomime with an invisible violin. Yet the spectator never doubts the dancer's female persona. Contrast the photograph (fig. 25) of the ending solo, *Storm Song*. Wigman's costume billows around her, nearly dematerializing the body, and her face stares out with a masklike expression. The female persona of the other solos has given way to an apparition.

Seraphic Song, Pastorale, and *Dance of Summer* also survive on film, vivifying the choreographer's more feminine persona in at least these solos.[33] Moreover, the film record of the three solos demonstrates a changed relation between the movement and music. Hasting's accompaniment—scored for piano, glockenspiel, harp, gong, flute, bells, pipes, and drums[34]—emphasizes repetitive melodies and simple harmonies, thus sounding more like traditional dance music than do Goetze's percussive compositions. In striking contrast to *Witch Dance II*, Wigman appears to dance to the music, and this change reinforces the corresponding shifts in movement quality and expression.

As recorded on film, Wigman solemnly paces through the space in *Seraphic Song*. She alternates the gestures of bringing her hands together over her chest or hip, as if praying, and opening her hands to the side, as if giving a blessing. (The still photograph reproduced as figure 23 shows the basic motif of palms pressed together.) In *Pastorale* she begins lying on the floor, luxuriating in the stillness. Over the course of the solo she languidly rises, as if waking from a nap, stirs herself into a burst of activity, then subsides into rest, as if returning to sleep. *Dance of Summer* captures the choreographer in a more show-offish mood. She playfully varies the initial impulse, a slight torso contraction almost like a sob, externalizing it in snaps of the wrist and stamps of the feet. It is as if she transforms what might have ended in sadness into happiness instead. (The still photograph reproduced as figure 24 shows one variation on the initial torso impulse.)

Wigman's memoirs relate that the cycle reflected her impressions of a summer holiday spent in France with Herbert Binswanger, a psychiatrist fourteen years younger than she and her lover for the past five years.[35] Although contemporary spectators had no awareness of this autobiographical source, they saw how the choreographer danced in dialogue with the "shifting landscapes" she represented. In all three solos recorded on film, her performance simultaneously represents external phenomena (the "shifting landscapes" of the title) and enacts her internal response (the emotions recollected in her memoir).

The film record of *Pastorale* vivifies this strategy of simultaneous representation. To the accompaniment of a flute melody, Wigman's hand lifts from her inert form and sways in the air. Her gesture both imitates the motion of warm summer breezes and replicates the sensation of being lulled awake by such breezes. Her doubled representation substitutes for the principle of the mask in staging a dialogue between the dancer and her "invisible partner."[36] Thus, although more decidedly feminine, her persona does not show off for the male voyeur but rather exposes the dancer's objectification of subjective experience. The solo exposes the process whereby the choreographer simultaneously recalls and abstracts her life experience.

In the context of the cycle as a whole, even the two solos that deploy the costume-as-mask, *Face of Night* and *Storm Song*, enact the strategy of simultaneous representation. In *Face of Night* Wigman both embodies the fearsome power of night and acts out the human fear of darkness. In *Storm Song* she represents both the force of the wind and the experience of being buffeted about by the wind. As shown in figure 25, her costume seemingly dematerializes her body. Her memoirs describe the ending of *Storm Song*:

> The feet race across the floor, chasing the body in wide curves through space, as though whipped by the winds, driven by the storm. Blindly, the body throws itself into mercilessly hammering rhythms. Seeking protection, it crouches, is being tossed about and bent—back and forth, back and forth—rearing up and falling like a tree hit by lightning. . . .
>
> The costume: a tremendously bright red chiffon mantle, obliterating the body outlines to a point of unrecognizability. The face, too, utterly depersonalized under the red veil mask.
>
> Above the swinging gestures of the arms, the light fabric swelled and was blown up and turned into cloudy images, stirring and drifting away only to tumble down like a torrent, rippling and slowly becoming smooth; then, during short moments of rest, the dancing body again received its human proportions and shivered under the onslaught of the storm.[37]

The choreographer's description shifts between the depersonalized body responding to the storm and representing the storm. The reader/spectator senses an antagonism between the power projected by the body and the submission of the body to that power. In solos choreographed after 1933, this plot took on a changed import in the context of the Third Reich.

An article published in 1929–1930, "The Dancer and the Theater," first anticipated Wigman's later accommodation with fascism. Envisioning a synthetic form of dance and theater that went far beyond what her dance group had accomplished in *Celebration*, Wigman opposed the integration of modern dance and ballet within the opera house advocated by younger colleagues such as Jooss. Rather, she proposed that the new synthesis of dance and theater required the dismantling of the conventions of opera house production. She further proposed that the decline (*Niedergang*) of the contemporary theater also signaled a process of transformation.

"The Dancer and the Theater" opens with a characterization of the contemporary situation:

[Theater today] is in the possession of society [*Gesellschaftsgut*] rather than in the possession of the *Volk* [*Volksgut*]. The theater has a public, but no community [*Gemeinde*]. Dedication to the work recedes in favor of dedication to the personality. The true protagonist—the ensemble, the chorus—is less important than the individual actors. The cult of the self [*der Kult des "Ichs"*] stands in the foreground and subjugates the idea.[38]

Wigman's rhetoric picks up on a tradition of reaction against the bourgeois theater that encompassed Emile Jaques-Dalcroze and Adolphe Appia's *Orpheus* and Rudolf Laban's *Sun Festival* as well as Max Reinhardt's productions of Greek plays at the Circus Schumann and of Hofmannsthal's *Everyman* at Salzburg. Aiming to eliminate the proscenium separating performer and spectator, this festival tradition chose outdoor settings or specially designed theaters that reunified the stage space and the auditorium space. Performances emphasized not the individual actor alone, but rather the group or the antithesis of the individual and group. According to the rhetoric that accompanied this festival tradition, the experience of the performance would build a sense of community (*Gemeinschaft*) among the spectators.

Where Wigman departs from Emile Jaques-Dalcroze, Rudolf Laban, and Max Reinhardt is in her focus on leadership (*Führerschaft*) as a constitutive element of community (*Gemeinschaft*). Her article continues: "The often-profaned idea of community [*Gemeinschaft*] is no utopian illusion. We do not deceive ourselves when we assume that impulses toward community characterize our time. Such impulses exist and are apparent everywhere. . . . Community requires leadership [*Führerschaft*] and recognition of leadership. The mass that refers to its own collectivity never forms a community."[39]

In terms of her group choreography from *Scenes from a Dance Drama* to *Celebration*, the concept of *Führerschaft* had implied Wigman's own role "as leader, as center, or as opposition to the moving mass of dancers," to quote Hans Fischer.[40] But in "The Dancer and the Theater" the term *Führerschaft* implies more, evoking a vision not yet realized. The remainder of the article extends the vision, proclaiming dancers ideally situated to realize the new theater in service of community. A typical comment: "Only when individual destiny reclaims and finds meaning in communal destiny will the theater fulfill its eternal and eternally new mission: to speak through symbols from person to person, and to reveal humankind's inner visage in its outward *Gestalt*."[41]

In June 1930 Wigman realized this vision of "communal theater" in collaboration with Albert Talhoff. Together they staged *Totenmal* (*Call of the Dead*), a multimedia spectacle memorializing soldiers killed in the First World War. Premiered at the Third Dancers' Congress held in Munich, the production combined a speaking choir and movement choir. Talhoff borrowed the form of the speaking choir from the working-class theater movement, while Wigman borrowed the form of the movement choir from the populist wing of the modern dance movement. Without her dance group the choreographer cast students drawn from her Dresden school, the Munich branch school, and the Dorothee Günther school in Munich.[42] She later commented on the transition from the dance group to the movement choir, from *Celebration* to *Totenmal*:

> It was no longer a matter of the play of forces with and against one another. . . . The potential matter of conflict was no longer to be solved within the group itself. What was of concern here was the unification of a group of human beings [that] strove from a unified viewpoint toward a common aim recognized by everyone; a viewpoint which no longer permitted any splitting into single actions. . . .
>
> In the same way as the choric creation demands its antagonist—whether or not it takes actual shape or takes effect as thematic idea above and behind the events—in many cases it also asks for a leader [*Anführer*] chosen by the chorus, for the one who conveys the message powerfully, who, supported and carried by the entire chorus, advances the thematic idea and brings it to its final execution.[43]

Totenmal occasioned more critical debate than any of Wigman's earlier group works. Although some critics considered the production an ambitious realization of the Wagnerian *Gesamtkunstwerk* (total work of art), others found it a disappointment, more hype than substance, and outdated as well. Many saw the work as a sign of the stagnation of the modern dance movement as a whole. For the tensions evident at the first and second dancers' congresses intensified at the third, and left many observers wondering if the organized movement indeed had a future.[44]

What contemporary observers could not see, of course, was the extent to which *Totenmal* modeled a prototype for Nazi theater—in its theme, the cult of the fallen soldier; in its format, the combination of a movement choir and a speaking choir; and, above all, in its strategy of not appearing "political." Only in retrospect can one see how Talhoff and Wigman, perhaps unintentionally, staged not a "theater above politics," as they believed, but a protofascist theater. Revising the tradition of festival, borrowing forms from the left and reorienting them toward the right, *Totenmal* set a precedent for Nazi dramaturgy.

In the preface to the published script Talhoff stated his intent to create an "alternative" to the "political theater" of Erwin Piscator, Bertolt Brecht, Kurt Weill, and others, "an alternative that points toward the universally human essence of existence, at once timely and timeless."[45] But Talhoff's script contradicted his preface, sounding "the cult of the fallen soldier" familiar from nationalist and militarist rhetoric of the time. Wigman's staging then obscured this association by lending the production an almost religious aura. The apparent contradiction between Talhoff's script and Wigman's staging was itself a protofascist gesture, projecting the illusion of community (*Gemeinschaft*) as a way of erasing the very real divisions of society (*Gesellschaft*).

The turn toward fascism evident in *Totenmal* accompanied a turn away from the feminism implicit in earlier dances. In this production Wigman again employed actual facial masks, carved by a Munich artist named Bruno Goldschmitt.[46] But the masks functioned to confer gender rather than to blur gender, as a masked choir of men—representing the spirits of men fallen in battle—confronted a masked choir of women—representing the men's wives, mothers, sisters, and lovers. The action turned on the women's attempt, led by Wigman, the only unmasked figure, to call the dead back to life.

Photographs show the distinct differences between the male and female choruses and between Wigman and the other women. One photograph (fig. 26) shows the female chorus as a jumble of bodies, each wearing a distinctive mask. In contrast, another photograph (fig. 27) shows the male chorus as a geometrical mass, all wearing nearly identical masks. Yet another photograph (fig. 28) highlights

Fig. 26.   The female chorus in *Totenmal*, a war memorial staged in 1930 by
Mary Wigman and Albert Talhoff (courtesy of the Mary Wigman Archive)

Wigman's unmasked visage as she opposes her masked antagonist,
the Demon.

For the first time since staging *The Queen* on Monte Verita, Wigman cast men as dancers in a group work, and the male presence
for the first time cast women in traditional roles. The women no
longer defined themselves as a self-sufficient female community,
but derived their identities from their relations with men. Their
masks no longer refused the male gaze, but rather assigned them
stereotypical female identities. That Wigman alone remained unmasked reversed the dynamic of earlier masked dances such as
Dance Fairy Tale and *Dance of Death*. In those dances the mask
had allowed both Wigman and her dancers to defy the antitheses
of male and female, human and demonic, living and dead. But
in *Totenmal* Wigman's unmasked presence mediated between the
women's chorus, the chorus of the living, and the men's chorus, the
chorus of the dead. Her unmasked persona embodied her near
superhuman stature.

As in the 1926 *Dance of Death*, Wigman's leadership became as-

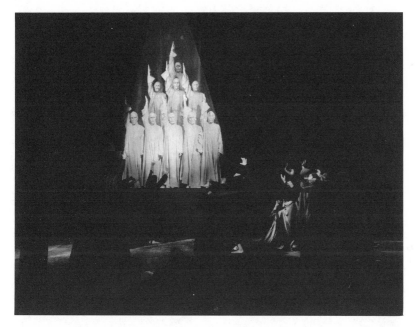

Fig. 27.   The male chorus in *Totenmal*, a war memorial staged in 1930 by Mary Wigman and Albert Talhoff (courtesy of the Mary Wigman Archive)

sociated with self-sacrifice. Through the first half of *Totenmal* she led through the example of action, confronting the spirits of the dead again and again, even though the other women fled. But at the crux of the work she subordinated herself to the Demon (Alexander Kamaroff), the personification of war, and thereafter the strength of her acquiescence became an example to the other women. For the first time since staging *The Seven Dances of Life*, Wigman externalized the demonic principle in the form of a male performer. Opposing herself to the male demon, she redefined leadership as female endurance. That she appeared unmasked reinforced the new gendering of her *Führerschaft*.

In the tradition of festival, the production of *Totenmal* took place in a specially designed hall, seating sixteen hundred spectators, built with a generous subsidy from the city of Munich. Also in the tradition of antibourgeois theater, the spectacle featured a mass of performers, about a hundred in all, divided between the speaking and movement choirs.[47] Talhoff's script was performed in a mode halfway between speech and song, a sort of chanting that employed

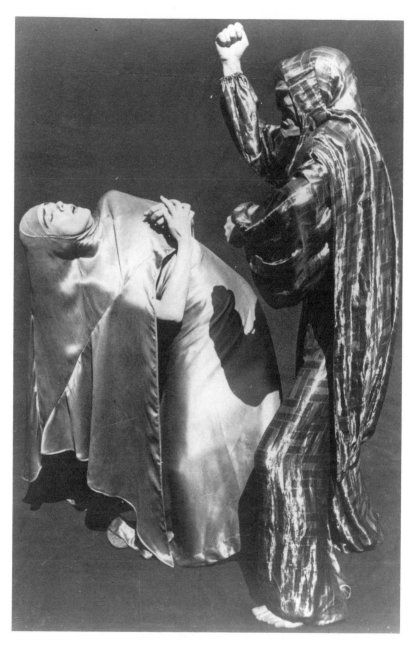

Fig. 28.   Mary Wigman and the Demon in *Totenmal*, staged in 1930 by Mary Wigman and Albert Talhoff (courtesy of the Mary Wigman Archive)

varied techniques for breath control. A few speakers were concealed in booths surrounding the auditorium. During interludes in the action these seemingly invisible voices read letters from soldiers killed in the war. (In interviews participants and spectators remember especially the quality of these voices, "haunting" and "chilling.")[48] The program alerted spectators that these letters were taken from actual collections published in Germany, France, and England. The remaining speakers were divided into two groups on platforms placed on both sides of the stage. Accompanying the speaking choir was a percussion orchestra (scored by Talhoff) as well as a color organ that coordinated sound and light effects. An American journalist reported:

> On either side of the stage, which was high and hung with black, were platforms for the chorus of forty . . . voices. . . . The chorus was supplemented by many cymbals and drums of widely different tone and volume, and even the sustaining pillars of the theater were arranged as mammoth cymbals by being covered with brass. In moments of great crisis the pillars were beaten by the dancers, making the whole place vibrate with rhythmic sound. At times the cymbals and chanting died away, and one heard the distinct and syncopated steps of the dancers who, draped either in black or in the deepest shades of purples, greens, and crimsons, afforded a striking background for the white, clear-cut masks which they wore. A light organ was used in the background upon whose pipes were thrown the changing colors, whose value and harmony expressed the same emotions as those portrayed by the chanting, the cymbals and the dancing. At moments of high tension the organ colors shot up to the end of the pipes, high narrow and red, and at times of despondency the colors fell down again, low wide and dreary.[49]

The spectacle divides into eight sections.[50] In the first, *Hall of Summons* (*Raum des Rufs*), the women enter up a ramp from the orchestra pit to the central platform, pausing one by one under a spotlight. Each dancer assumes a physical attitude corresponding to her mask. The masks are individualized yet stereotyped, suggesting the stages of a woman's life from youth to old age. The stage directions to the published script note:

> First *Gestalt*: Every movement is a scream. . . . Mask: mouth open, eyes without focus. . . . Second *Gestalt*: She walks as if behind a casket. . . . Mask: mouth paralyzed, eyes closed. . . . Third *Gestalt*: She walks transfigured. . . . Mask: Eyelids barely open; vacant

look. . . . Fourth *Gestalt*: Every movement possesses infinite tenderness. . . . Mask: eyes closed, mouth quietly smiling. . . . Fifth *Gestalt*: Every movement is executed with hostility. . . . Mask: eyes lowered, mouth like a cut. . . . Sixth *Gestalt*: Every movement is executed with shrill excess. . . . Mask: confused gaze, mouth a distorted laugh. . . . Seventh *Gestalt*: She doesn't realize that she's still living. . . . Mask: eyes like an abyss, chin hanging. . . . Eighth *Gestalt*: She moves in ecstasy. . . . Mask: eyes closed, lips gently arched. . . . Ninth *Gestalt*: She moves as if led. . . . Mask: lips softly advancing, gaze extinguished.[51]

Once all the women gather on the platform, Wigman directs them to huddle together. Fused into an anonymous mass, they set off the choreographer's larger-than-life quality. Suddenly, the spirits appear on an upstage platform, frightening the women. This is the moment shown in figure 27. According to the stage directions, all the women except Wigman flee.

In *Totenmal* the opposition between femininity and masculinity corresponds to the opposition between life and death, or in movement terms, between mobility and immobility, animation and stasis. The women's masks and movement styles are individualized (however stereotypically), but the men's costumes are identical, their masks nearly so, and they move in unison with a uniform quality. According to the stage directions: "[The men] wear cothurni. Their gestures are stenographically monotonous. Each spirit figure executes inexhaustible repetitions of the same assigned movement."[52] Wigman's dancing mediates between the oppositions of life and death, femininity and masculinity. Her performance embraces the extremes of mobility and immobility, encompassing a far broader range of movement qualities than either the male or female chorus.

Subsequent sections repeat and intensify the fundamental action of the first section: again and again the women encounter the spirits, and all except Wigman flee. During interludes in the action the voices of soldiers killed in the war resound through the space, each of their letters punctuated by the entire choir reciting, "From one who fell in Flanders. . . . From one who fell at Ypres. . . . From one who fell in Arras."[53]

The leader resumes her mission in *Hall of Oblivion* (*Raum der Vergessenheit*). At first Wigman dances alone, flanked by the group of women. Finally, they join her, magnifying her invocation of the dead. But as soon as the chorus of spirits reappears, the women flee once again. The choreographer remains, continuing her attempt to animate the chorus of spirits, but darkness soon blots out her figure and evokes the invisible voices of the fallen soldiers.

In *Hall of Conjuration* (*Raum der Bannung*) the choreographer renews her attempt to conjure the dead. The stage directions describe her dance as "the struggle between space and figure, between space-light and conjuring movement."[54] Finally, the chorus leader imitates her gesture, and it seems as if Wigman has succeeded in rousing the dead. Yet her success proves illusory: the chorus of spirits turns away from the pair, and the demon figure suddenly appears and jumps between the two. The section ends with a tableau of the Demon threatening Wigman (fig. 28). At this point her leadership shifts from actively confronting the spirits to enduring her defeat.

The choreographer makes a final effort to call the spirits back to life in *Hall of Echoes* (*Raum des Gegenrufs*). At first her steps are reverent, then agitated. Finally, the spirits are set in motion, and she withdraws into the shadows, her life-force drained by their coming to life. Figure 29 shows this moment. According to the stage directions, the chorus of the dead stamps in unison, and the rhythm of their stamping synchronizes with the voices of the speaking choir:

> Once again
> And again
> Must they sing,
> Sighing, chilly,
> Their sad song
> Softly, stilly
> In the night. . . .
>
> They must see
> If there are candles shining,
> If there are flowers lying,
> If their mothers
> If their sweethearts
> Keep ever watch. . . .
>
> They must know. . . .
> Oh, forbid it—
>
> If memorial flags are flying,
> Are their gravestones smoothly lying. . . . [55]

Fig. 29.   The male chorus momentarily comes to life in *Totenmal*, a war memorial staged in 1930 by Mary Wigman and Albert Talhoff (courtesy of the Mary Wigman Archive)

At a sudden cry darkness falls, cutting short the spirits' dance. Wigman revives and dances, first summoning reserves of energy, then weakening, finally whirling herself into exhaustion. She falls to the side as the spirits rush forward, waving their heavy gowns like flags. The rhythmic movements of the spirits synchronize with the voices of the speaking choir, which accuses the spectators of forgetting the dead:

> Come we by night,
> Ye flee us as ghosts.
> Come we by day,
> Ye flee us still!
> Alas, we must hence
> For none will release us.
> Nay, we must hence,
> For we find no justice,
> And so no peace,
> While our sisters laugh and love,
> Empty stand our shrines.
> Put out the lights!
> For the curse shall be spoken,

To be on you all
That forget our graves,
And leave us to perish.
On you be the curse,
The curse of thunder and lightning,
The curse of pestilence and death,
The curse of shame,
The curse of terror and of shame
Be on you all.[56]

Then the spirits retreat to their original formation. Wigman responds with a dance of sorrow, her movements nearly devoid of energy. She rises to standing, growing into the shape of a cross, then collapses, breaking the shape, and lies still as if dead. As in the earlier *Dance of Death,* her leadership becomes identified with sacrifice, and the cross associates her with the sacrificial leadership of Christ.

Extending this religious association, the final section, *Hall of Devotion (Raum der Andacht),* shifts the mode of presentation and focuses on images of sound and light. Voices alternately herald a new beginning through the power of God's love and damn the destructiveness of war and man's inability to break the vicious cycle of hate. Ultimately, faith triumphs over despair. An American journalist described the "emotional crescendo" of the end: "The light organ changed from dull to high, strong colors, the chanting grew in volume, the cymbals crashed, the organ blared red, and the mourners [the speaking choir] stood straight with their arms held high in token of victory and belief. An emotionally exhausted audience staggered to its feet."[57]

Why in the end cannot the living and the dead, the female chorus and the male chorus unite? Examined separately, the script and the staging suggest overlapping and contradictory answers. But when examined in tandem, the script and staging project a coherent ideological strategy, which retrospect reveals as protofascist.

The choreography posited an exchange of energies between the choreographer and the chorus of the fallen soldiers. Conjuring the dead to life, Wigman spent her own life-force. The duality of motion and stillness, animation and stasis, governed the world of the dance. Within this world arousing the inanimate required extinguishing the animate. Hence, there seemed a kinesthetic barrier between the living and dead, the male chorus and the female chorus.

The staging overlaid this kinesthetic barrier with religious import. As the dance images gave way to images of sound and light, the action suggested the fusion of living and dead not in actuality but in imagination. This imagined union analogized the ritual of Christian communion, the merging of the worshiper with Christ. That Wigman's final dance enacted the image of a cross underscored the religious import of the action. Friedrich Muckermann, a Jesuit priest, praised the production for "serving the Christian idea in the larger sense."[58]

The production's kinesthetic design and overt religiosity realized Talhoff's stated intent of creating "an alternative . . . to the political theater." But the script contradicted the staging and pointed not to a theater above politics but to a theater of ambivalent politics. Playing off what historian George Mosse has termed "the cult of the fallen soldier," the script confused militarism and pacifism.[59]

The speaking choir suggests that Wigman's attempt to bring the fallen soldiers back to life fails because the living community of spectators does not sufficiently remember the dead. In this way the text reinforced nationalist rhetoric that accused the home front of "backstabbing" the soldiers on the front and called for the nation to atone for and avenge the loss by taking up arms again. The wordplay of the title underscored this implication, for *Totenmal* plays on the connotations of both *Denkmal* (monument or memorial) and *Kainsmal* (Cain's mark, i.e., a symbol of guilt).

But the socialists also exploited the emotional impact of the memory of the war dead. Inverting nationalist rhetoric, socialists evoked the image of the fallen soldier as a warning against future militarist adventures. The script accorded with this pacifist program by including letters written by soldiers of all nations—not just German soldiers—killed in the First World War.

The script's confusion of militarism and pacifism was obscured by the production's personification of war in the figure of the Demon. Given human form, war seemed more a natural phenomenon than a sociopolitical event. Like the kinesthetic barrier between the living and the dead, war became a given, beyond human control and beyond human decision making. From this perspective, the distinction between militarism and pacifism appeared irrelevant.

The evidence suggests that most contemporary spectators considered *Totenmal* a pacifist statement. This is how it appeared to spectators and participants interviewed decades later, who remembered especially the haunting voices reading the soldiers' letters. Presumably, these "invisible voices" made the greatest impression on many other spectators as well, who easily might not have understood the chanted script or recognized its covert support for militarism. (However, the text was available for sale, in English and French translation in addition to the original German.) Certainly, the reviewer for the *Völkischer Beobachter,* organ of the Nazi party, interpreted the production as a statement of support for pacifism. The reviewer commented: "Thalhoff [*sic*] doesn't appear to be a Jew . . . but that his piece is dedicated to all soldiers fallen in the World War alone demonstrates his internationalist-pacifist orientation."[60] Only a few spectators were as perceptive as Ernst Iros, who wrote in *Die neue Zeit*: "The seemingly straightforward progression of the action is confusing, because it takes all sides, both affirming war and negating war. It is not above politics, as Talhoff believes, but rather feeble-minded and speculative."[61]

The ambivalent politics of *Totenmal* take on a particular significance in the context of contemporary political developments. Nineteen thirty was a year of crisis for the Weimar Republic. Under the pressure of mounting unemployment and worldwide economic collapse, the precarious coalition of Social Democrats and conservatives that had governed through the twenties fell apart. Political factionalism gave way to political extremism. In March the coalition cabinet resigned, and in September the Nazis scored their first big victory at the polls. Thus, during the summer that *Totenmal* played in Munich, an electoral battle raged between socialists and nationalists that, according to one historian, "plumbed new depths of demagogy and sheer violence."[62] Against this backdrop the production's dual advocacy of militarism and pacifism projected the middle-class desire not to have to choose between the extreme left and the extreme right. The spectators that longed for a "middle way" between nationalism and socialism also longed for a "theater above politics," and *Totenmal* seemed to provide both. The staging of the war memorial obscured its contradictory politics, effacing the necessity of choice. The protofascism of the spectacle lay in its strategy of concealing a highly politicized theater within an apolitical aura.

Kurt Jooss's *The Green Table* (*Der Grüne Tisch*), premiered in 1932, presents an illuminating comparison with *Totenmal*. Like Wigman's collaboration with Talhoff, Jooss's work staged a dance of death employing masks. But there the resemblance ends. In contrast to *Totenmal*, which protested the conventions of bourgeois theater, *The Green Table* embraced the possibilities for "dance theater" (*Tanztheater*) within the opera house. Set to a score by Fritz Cohen and designed by Hein Heckroth, the production cast dancers from the Essen Opera, where Jooss worked as ballet director.

Although originally a student of Laban, Jooss had little interest in the form of the movement choir. Rather he believed in the synthesis of modern dance and ballet. In 1927 he wrote: "The creative adventures of expressionism lie behind us, also the convulsive cries of early jazz, the primeval tones of expressionist poetry, and the free—in its way barbaric—*Ausdruckstanz*. We are living in an age which is rediscovering artistic form. . . . A creative compromise between free personal expression and formal compliance with objective, intellectual laws is developing."[63] At the Essen Opera, Jooss was responsible for choreographing operettas and opera interludes as well as creating independent works for the dance ensemble such as *The Green Table*. Addressing the Second Dancers' Congress, he noted:

> Economic possibilities for the practice of dance on any larger scale today almost only exist in the opera houses and to a lesser degree in the drama theatres. The dance world of today must therefore take two major aspects into account: satisfying the needs of the theatre on the one hand, but on the other hand, and at the same time, working unceasingly . . . on the overall idea of dance theatre.[64]

The Green Table departed from *Totenmal* not only in its adherence to the conventions of bourgeois theater but also in its unambiguous alignment with leftist politics. Although the protofascism of *Totenmal* becomes clear only in retrospect, the political affiliation of *The Green Table* was more apparent in 1932 than decades later, when the generalizing power of the work and its survival in the repertory have supported multiple interpretations. Created during the last year of the Weimar Republic, the production affirmed leftist politics through a simple structural device, the juxtaposition of framed and framing sections. While the framed sections associate the dance of death with war, the framing sections assign responsibility for war's dance of death to the Gentlemen in Black and to the Profiteer.[65]

The traditional dance of death exists outside chronological and geographical coordinates. As visualized by the fifteenth-century frescoes depicting the dance of death on the walls of a church in Lübeck, known as the Lübecker Totentanz and one of Jooss's sources for his work, the personification of death inhabits a generalized locale, symbolic of all times and places. Within this symbolic world-space he leads representatives of all classes of society—beggar, peasant, bishop, king—to their end. Revising this traditional conception, Jooss localized the dance of death within the arena of war. Within the framed sections Death summons his victims—young soldiers and their idealistic leader, an old woman, a young girl, and a female revolutionary. The action suggests that war destroys not only those who go off to fight but also those who stay home awaiting their loved ones. One photograph (fig. 30) shows Death leading away a young soldier, another (fig. 31) shows Death carrying off an old woman.

The Gentlemen in Black, masked and tuxedoed, appear in the opening and closing sections, framing the remainder of the action with their deliberations around a large green table. Although they gesture in disagreement, their debate reveals them going through the motions, as they repeat exactly the same steps at the end as at the beginning. The logic of sequence sets their ritualized discussion as the continuing cause of war. Undeterred by the destruction of the dance of death, they continue their machinations.

Who are the Gentlemen in Black? This is a key question for a political interpretation of the work. In the postwar period Jooss insisted upon the ambiguity of their identity. In an interview conducted in 1976, the choreographer noted that they represented "all the powers which can gain in a war, which in the end, through their machinations, cause a war." He added: "I didn't know and

Fig. 30.   Death leads away a young soldier in Kurt Jooss's 1932 antiwar ballet, *The Green Table* (courtesy of the Jooss Archive)

Fig. 31. Death carries off an old woman in Kurt Jooss's 1932 antiwar ballet, *The Green Table* (courtesy of the Jooss Archive)

I still don't know who 'The Gentlemen in Black' are, I don't
think they are diplomats. There may be one or two diplomats between them."[66]

That the choreography left the exact identity of the Gentlemen
in Black ambiguous and open to interpretation has led to multiple
interpretations of the work. When Jooss's company-in-exile toured
the work during the years of the Second World War, the masked
dancers were widely seen as Nazi leaders. When the Joffrey Ballet
revived the ballet in 1976, they were associated with the American
"military-industrial complex" responsible for the Vietnam War. In
other words, successive generations of spectators have identified
the Gentlemen in Black in terms of contemporary notions of a
power elite. Thus *The Green Table* has survived in repertory, its
message of continuing relevance.

The work did carry a particular import in the context of 1932,
however, and in this context contemporary spectators clearly saw
Jooss's alignment with leftist politics. As the choreographer later
noted, the work had two sources, his viewing of the Lübecker Totentanz and his reading of the leftist journal *Die Weltbühne*, which
featured the political satire of Kurt Tucholsky. Jooss remembered
one recurring refrain in Tucholsky's writing: "'Don't believe it,
don't believe it, these peace talks. It's all rubbish, it's all fake, they
are secretly preparing a new war.' He had true secrets which could
prove that he was right."[67] According to Tucholsky and other leftist
intellectuals associated with *Die Weltbühne*, a coalition of industrial-
ists and conservatives wielded the real power in the Weimar government, just as they had during the Wilhelmine Empire. Capitalism and militarism were allies.[68]

The choreography supports the thesis of an alliance between
capitalism and militarism by drawing a connection between the
Gentlemen in Black and the figure of the Profiteer. Through the
framed sections, the Profiteer lurks as an evil presence, presiding
over the brothel, stealing from the corpses of slain soldiers, profit-
ing from the social disruption and carnage of war. Significantly, the
Profiteer is the only figure within the framed sections to escape
Death, dropping to the floor and rolling offstage just before the
blackout that precedes the reappearance of the Gentlemen in
Black. As Marcia Siegel has pointed out, although the Profiteer's
movement qualities—the way he "shrinks, angles, hides"—contrast

the movement qualities of Death—"imposing, contained, direct, strong"—the Profiteer shares the quality of indirectness with the Gentlemen in Black.[69] Within the framed sections the Profiteer represents the workings of entrepreneurial capitalism, thus functioning as the Gentlemen's surrogate. His actions realize the large designs of capitalism on a day-to-day level.

Given the temper of leftist politics in the closing years of the Weimar Republic, such a reading of *The Green Table* was inescapable. The Nazis correctly interpreted Jooss's leftist leanings, and after they came to power, they harassed the choreographer. The municipal government of Essen dismissed Fritz Cohen and several other Jewish members of the company, and an article appeared in the local newspaper branding Jooss as "Moses' temple dancer." The attack read in part: "In the new Germany the artist has the damned duty to exercise spiritual and national discipline due to his public mission. If he cannot do this, he must leave the fairground of German art and display his creations where he finds spiritually and racially kindred souls!"[70] Jooss took the hint and, along with most members of his company, slipped across the border to Holland. The next day the local Gestapo arrived at his house with an arrest warrant. The company took up exile in England, and the choreographer did not return to Germany until 1949.[71]

In fall 1930 Wigman embarked on the first of three American tours. At this point her critical reputation in Germany was at a plateau. Although critics acknowledged her contribution to the development of modern dance, they divided over the value of her most recent work, in particular *Totenmal*. How different was her critical reception in America! To American critics Wigman seemed a revelation, and her performances prompted the passionate response accorded her works in Germany during the early twenties. Her appearances prepared the way for the development of American modern dance over the next decade.

Returning home from her third American tour in late March 1933, Wigman encountered a changed Germany. Two months earlier Paul von Hindenburg, commander of German forces during the First World War and the aging president of the Weimar Republic, had appointed Hitler as chancellor. And within a few days of

Wigman's return the Reichstag voted Hitler the power to govern without parliamentary consent, thus legalizing dictatorship. Almost immediately, Hitler appointed Joseph Goebbels as director of the Cultural Ministry. Among the many responsibilities of Goebbels's ministry was the *Gleichschaltung* (bringing into line) of German dance. Ironically enough, this reorganization resolved the crisis besetting the modern dance movement around 1930 and consolidated a new direction in Wigman's choreography. After 1933 her works completed a transition that retrospect reveals as the passage from modernism to fascism.

5

Body Politic

In January 1934 Wigman premiered the solo *Dance of Silent Joy* (*Tanz der stillen Freude*) under the rubric *Women's Dances* (*Frauentänze*). The solo featured the spinning that had become the choreographer's signature, but in a muted tone. As critic Artur Michel described the dance, it begins "with a soft and brightly sounding swaying" that "develops into a winged haste and concentrates in an immensely easy and elastic whirling dance."[1] Paired photographs (figs. 32 and 33) demonstrate what Michel characterizes as "an admirably spiritualized and quietly shining expression of inward happiness."[2] The animation of Wigman's facial expression and hand gestures suggests a mood of subdued gaiety in keeping with the title of the solo. It is as if the choreographer were holding a conversation with herself, absorbed in her own memories or imaginings.

What a contrast to the imagery of *Witch Dance II*! Wigman no longer deploys the principle of the mask. She neither wears an actual facial mask nor adopts a fixed facial expression nor employs the costume-as-mask. On the contrary, her costume—a dress that hugged the torso and flared from the hips—flatters her female form and underscores her identity as a woman. As Artur Michel remarks:

> It was no more a dancing of a human being in the charm of eerie forces, no dancing shadowed by the eminent danger of death, and no dancing in the glorifying sight of the grace of God. Now a woman was dancing who was nothing but a woman, a woman of this world, whose sorrow and whose happiness, whose life and whose fate we all share.[3]

As Michel implies, *Dance of Silent Joy* repositions the spectator. Seemingly absorbed in a conversation with herself, the choreographer introduces an autobiographical persona into her dancing. And her autobiographical persona merges with an archetypal

Figs. 32 and 33.   Mary Wigman in *Dance of Silent Joy*, a solo
choreographed in 1934 (courtesy of the Mary Wigman
Archive)

female persona suggested by the title *Women's Dances*. Like Isadora Duncan, she stages her own experience as Everywoman's
experience.

In dances created from 1934 to 1942, Wigman embraced the
representational strategies of autobiography and archetype that
she had eschewed through the teens and twenties. However, her
deployment of these representational strategies differed from
Duncan's. In contrast to Duncan, who had used autobiography and
archetype to stage female experiences that had not been represented before, Wigman used these devices to stage the traditional
images of women revalued by Nazi ideology—woman as wife and
mother, woman as mourner for the war dead, woman as heroic
martyr. These images exposed the notion of woman's separate
and special sphere implicit in Wigman's earlier dances. Revising
the choreographic imagery of her Weimar dances, Wigman suppressed their challenge and highlighted their assent to the (heterosexist) duality of gender.

In this chapter I examine Wigman's changing relation to the
Third Reich through her changing choreographic imagery. From
1933 to 1936 she supported the Nazi regime, declaring her allegiance both in print and on stage. After 1936 her allegiance wa-
ered. Although she never publicly questioned the Nazis, her
dances suggest her ambivalence. The division of her oeuvre during
the Third Reich evidences her changed attitude. From 1934 to
1936 she received Nazi subsidy to choreograph group dances, staging the body politic envisioned by fascist ideology. From 1937 until
her retirement from the stage in 1942, she choreographed only
solos. Her focus on solo choreography resulted from her loss of
Nazi subsidy, but it also enabled her to muse on the role of the
individual within the body politic of the Third Reich.

GROUP DANCES, 1934–1936

Ironically, when the Nazis came to power, they resolved the crisis
besetting modern dance in the last years of the Weimar Republic.
The depression had occasioned widespread unemployment among
dancers, as among the population at large. According to the 1933
census, just over fifty percent of the dancers were unemployed,
compared to just under thirty percent of the population overall.[4]

The difficult economic situation exacerbated tensions in the modern dance movement. At the 1930 Dancers' Congress, Fritz Böhme had warned about the impending oversupply of dancers, but he could not foresee the scope or the duration of the mass unemployment that beset Germany over the next three years. What he did see was that dancers needed new sources of funding to survive, and he led the chorus of demands that issued from the congress for opera houses, schools, youth organizations, municipal governments, and state bureaucracies to patronize modern dance.[5] These were exactly the sources of funding that materialized once the Nazis came to power.

Conflicting demands emerged from the 1930 Dancers' Congress. On the one hand, dancers called for greater professionalization, for the synthesis of ballet and modern dance techniques, and for the integration of dance and theater within the municipal opera-house system. On the other hand, dancers called for a revitalization of the amateur practice of modern dance and for the inclusion of modern dance in school curricula. Participants at the congress submitted a proposal to government agencies calling for the founding of a Conservatory for Dance (Hochschule für Tanzkunst), comparable to conservatories already established for music, theater, and visual art. The conservatory would train performers, choreographers, directors, and teachers for both professional and amateur dance.[6] This demand, along with the others articulated at the 1930 Dancers' Congress, was met by the Nazi *Gleichschaltung*.

Responding to the demand for a Conservatory for Dance, Goebbels's Cultural Ministry founded the German Master Institute for Dance (Deutsche Meister-Stätten für Tanz) in Berlin in 1936. However, the curriculum at the Master Institute significantly varied the emphasis of the curriculum proposed at the 1930 Dancers' Congress. The 1930 proposal had considered modern dance the primary subject and ballet and national dances secondary subjects, but the Master Institute emphasized the three forms equally. In addition, the Master Institute required classes in National Socialist ideology. The curriculum at the Master Institute accorded with the standardized curriculum and certification exams instituted by the Cultural Ministry in 1934 and 1935.[7] These initiatives responded with a vengeance to the demand for greater professionalization that had issued from the 1930 Dancers' Congress. In the Third

Reich the professionalization of dance meant the bureaucratization of dance, and the bureaucracy would only provide credentials to those dancers who could prove their "Aryan origins."

With credentials from the Cultural Ministry, modern dancers could take advantage of the new forms of patronage provided by the Nazi state. They could find employment teaching *Tanz-Gymnastik,* either in girls' schools or through youth and leisure organizations—Association of German Girls (Bund deutscher Mädel), Faith and Beauty (Glaube und Schönheit), Strength through Joy (Kraft durch Freude). Like the Hitler Youth, all three organizations made physical fitness an important part of their programs.[8] Alternately, modern dancers could take a steady position in an opera house or find work directing and performing *Thingspiel* (literally, "thing play"). Large-scale spectacles that drew on the festival tradition, *Thingspiel* required professional dancers to train and supervise the amateur dancers involved in their production.

In unexpected ways these new sources of patronage—schools, youth and leisure organizations, opera houses, *Thingspiel*—fulfilled the contradictory demands voiced at the 1930 Dancers' Congress. When dancers at the earlier congress had called for the revitalization of amateur dance, they imagined men and women, boys and girls, embracing the new dance voluntarily. They did not foresee that mostly girls and women would practice the form in the Third Reich and that their practice would be nonvoluntary. When dancers gathered at the 1930 congress had called for the reintegration of dance and theater, they imagined a rapprochement between modern dance and opera-house ballet or new possibilities for collaboration between choreographers and directors. *The Green Table* and *Totenmal* were their models, not the *Thingspiel* designed to celebrate the *Volksgemeinschaft* (folk, i.e., Aryan community).

That the Nazis resolved the crisis besetting modern dance in the last years of the Weimar Republic is one reason why *Ausdruckstanz* struck up an alliance with fascism. Another reason lay in shared intellectual roots. Like *Ausdruckstanz,* fascism drew on the neoromanticism, life reformism, and cultural pessimism of turn-of-the-century Germany. The same impulses that occasioned the founding of Hellerau and Monte Verita—the desire to escape urban industrialization and find a life more attuned to nature, the valuing of emotion and intuition over intellect and rationality, utopianism mixed with a sense of approaching apocalypse—also underlay Nazi ideology.[9] Many of the dancers heard in Nazi rhetoric an echo of their own beliefs. Had not they always believed that the body possessed a truth inaccessible to the mind? If so, then was it such a leap to embrace the cult of the irrational? Had not they always believed in dance as a way of creating community (Gemeinschaft)? If so, then was it such a leap to embrace the ideal of the Volksgemeinschaft?

In the early years of the Third Reich, Mary Wigman made this leap, as did many of her colleagues. Only a minority of the choreographers who had established reputations during the Weimar period emigrated. The majority of modern dancers remained in Germany and in varying ways came to terms with fascism.[10] For Wigman, and presumably for many of her colleagues, opportunism combined with ideological sympathy in their support for the Third Reich. The Nazis offered Wigman, and other modern dancers, status and subsidy as important German artists.

In 1934 Goebbels's Cultural Ministry organized a German Dance Festival in Berlin. The festival showcased the achievements of German choreographers—Mary Wigman, Yvonne Georgi, Gret Palucca, Harald Kreutzberg, Dorothee Günther, Valeria Kratina, Lizzie Maudrik, and Rudolf Laban.[11] All had appeared at the dancers' congresses during the Weimar period, and their reappearance evidenced not only the continuity but also the discontinuity between Weimar and Nazi dance. In contrast to the 1930 Dancers' Congress, which had included guest appearances from foreign artists, the 1934 festival included only German dancers who could prove their Aryan origin. Wigman had received a commission from the Cultural Ministry to choreograph a new work for the festival.[12] The commission allowed her to form a new dance group, but one that included only non-Jewish dancers. According to Pola Nirenska, the dance group that had accompanied Wigman to the United States in 1932–1933 had included several Jewish dancers, none of whom were rehired for the new group.[13]

Organized by Rudolf Laban, the 1934 festival comprised a week-long series of performances, supplemented by exhibitions on "Dance in Art" and "Dance in Photography" and by a published volume with essays from the participants.[14] There were no lectures or face-to-face debates between dancers with conflicting viewpoints

**Deutſche
Tanzfeſtſpiele
1934**

Berlin - 9.-16. Dezember

Fig. 34. An illustration on the front
cover of the program for the 1934
German Dance Festival, organized by
Goebbels's Cultural Ministry (courtesy
of the Mary Wigman Archive)

or competing interests, as at the Weimar dancers' congresses.
Rather, the Cultural Ministry framed the festival as an overview of
Deutscher Tanz (German Dance).

The program presented the spectator with the Cultural Ministry's reading of the significance of the festival. On the cover
(fig. 34), underneath a photograph of a female nude sculpted in
classical academic style, the text read:

German Dance [*Deutscher Tanz*] encompasses manifold forms. However, this diversity reveals a unified strength that springs from our
being. . . .

  We Germans often are considered coarse and graceless, and yet
the vigor of the German temperament and the depth of the German
soul often have conquered the world, not only through music and
poetry but also through the art of dance [*Tanzkunst*].[15]

According to the Cultural Ministry, the apparent diversity of German Dance reduced to an essential unity that reflected the German
spirit and German superiority. The forward-looking tone of the
text on the front cover contrasted the backward-looking tone of the
text on the back cover, illustrated with a print of Fanny Elssler
(fig. 35). As the anonymous "we" explained:

  We memorialize the great dancer Fanny Elssler and the fiftieth anniversary of her death. We memorialize as well the countless unknown and lesser-known dancers who have served and continue to
serve the art of German dance, with passion and ardor and with all
the intensity of their being. We were able to bring together two hundred of these enthusiasts, in order to bring the expressive language
of German movement closer to the people [*Volksgenossen*].[16]

The text slips from the remembrance of Fanny Elssler to the remembrance of all dancers who contributed to *Deutscher Tanz* to the
Volk, the racial community represented by the audience. In abbreviated fashion the linking of ballet, *Tanzkunst*, and *Volk* summarizes
the program of the Cultural Ministry: to integrate ballet and modern dance in a dance form expressive of the *Volk* and accessible to
the *Volk*.[17]

  The program's juxtaposed images of the classical female nude
and Fanny Elssler underscore the summary of the Cultural Ministry's stated dance aesthetic. First, the juxtaposed images identify
dance as a female art, despite the appearance of male choreographers and soloists at the festival. Second, the two images associate
Deutscher Tanz with alternate models of "classicism," Greek sculpture and Romantic ballet, erasing the historical connection between
the choreographers at the festival and Weimar artistic experimentation. Third, that no contemporary German dancer is singled out
for representation reinforces the paean to "unknown dancers."
The homage to unknown dancers evokes an association with the

Wir gedenken der großen Tänzerin **Fanny Elßler,** deren Todestag sich
soeben zum fünfzigsten Male gejährt hat. Wir gedenken auch der zahl-
lojen Unbekannten und wenig Genannten, die mit Leidenschaft und In-
brunst, mit aller Heiterkeit ihres Wesens der deutschen Tanzkunst dienten
und noch dienen.

Zweihundert dieser Begeisterten konnten wir verjammeln, um unjeren
Volksgenojjen die Sprache des deutschen Bewegungsausdrucks näher-
zubringen.

Zweihundert deutsche Tänzer und Tänzerinnen, die sich auf mannigfache
Art und Weise zum deutschen Tanz bekennen.

Die Nationalgalerie veranstaltet im Prinzejjinnenpalais eine Ausstellung
„Der Tanz in der Kunst"
Während der Tanzfestjpiele findet in den Wandelgängen des Theaters am
Horst Wejjel Platz eine Ausstellung „Der Tanz im Lichtbild" statt. Leitung:
Charlotte Rudolph

Fig. 35. An illustration on the back cover of the program for the 1934
German Dance Festival, organized by Goebbels's Cultural Ministry (courtesy of the Mary Wigman Archive)

cult of the fallen soldier prevalent in Nazi rhetoric, and the association implicitly defines the duty of the dancer: to serve her fatherland, not on the battlefield, but through her self-sacrificing devotion to *Deutscher Tanz*. These were terms that Mary Wigman could
accept.

The program note introducing Wigman's premiere, *Women's
Dances*, reflects the vision of Goebbels's ministry. (Who authored
the note is unclear, whether it was the choreographer, one of her
associates such as Hanns Hasting, or one of the organizers of the
festival.) The program read:

> [*Women's Dances*] encompass all five spheres of women's experience
> and symbolize female powers: girlish mirth, motherhood, passion,
> prophecy, and finally the abyss, which we recognize from Goethe's
> Walpurgisnacht. . . . Although not naturalistic, the individual sec-
> tions encompass no other content than that suggested by their titles.
> A dance such as *Lament for the Dead* creates an atmosphere similar
> to a commemorative ceremony (*Weihespiel*) at a memorial for the
> war dead.[18]

The assertion that the work represents essential dimensions of female experience accords with the Cultural Ministry's identification
of dance as a female art. Further, the reference to Goethe anchors
the work within a German classical tradition. Finally, the focus on
Lament for the Dead, the third of five sections of the work, accords
with the notion of art as a communal remembrance of the war
dead, like *Totenmal* and like the *Weihespiel* commissioned by the Nazis to mark the national days of mourning instituted on 16 March
and 9 November.[19]

Like *Dance of Silent Joy, Women's Dances* eschews the principle of
the mask and embraces the representational strategies of archetype
and autobiography. The dancers are not *Gestalten* but recognizably
female personae. As such, they enact the archetypes of female experience generalized by the program note and titles—bride (*Wedding Dance*), mother (*Maternal Dance*), widow or mourner (*Lament
for the Dead*), prophetess (*Dance of the Prophetess*), witch (*Witch
Dance*). The program note insists that the dances derive from archetypes alone, that "the individual sections encompass no other
content than that suggested by their titles." However, the spectator

Fig. 36.   Mary Wigman and Ruth Boin in *Wedding Dance,* from the 1934 group work *Women's Dances* (courtesy of the Mary Wigman Archive)

familiar with Wigman's oeuvre could also read the dances in auto-biographical terms, as a narrative of the choreographer's relation to her new dance group and to her past.

Women's Dances opens with *Wedding Dance* (*Hochzeitlicher Reigen*). To begin, Wigman, taking the role of a mother, performs a fare-well duet with her daughter and the bride-to-be, danced by Ruth Boin. A photograph (fig. 36) shows Wigman standing, Boin kneel-

Fig. 37.   The Wigman dance group in *Wedding Dance*, from the 1934 work *Women's Dances* (courtesy of the Mary Wigman Archive)

ing, and the two making hand and eye contact as if the mother (and choreographer) were passing the life-force onto her daughter (and student). Having taken leave of her mother, the bride then takes leave of her friends. As Artur Michel describes the action, "over and over again [the bride] ranks herself into the rows of her dancing friends, over and over again she is eliminated. But she always remains the center of the dance."[20] A photograph (fig. 37) shows Boin surrounded by fourteen other dancers, as if she now took the central role assumed by Wigman in earlier dances. Just as the daughter assumes the role of her mother through marriage, the student dancer assumes the role of her mentor.

In *Maternal Dance* (*Mütterlicher Tanz*) Wigman dances out the mother's response to the loss of her daughter. (Or does the nearly fifty-year-old choreographer respond to the necessity of passing on her art?) Michel describes the action: "A few motives are sufficient for revealing the sanctity and greatness of maternity: the kindness willing to embrace everything with love; the humility with which the blessedness of maternal mission is carried out; the power of complete devotion and sacrifice."[21] A photograph (fig. 38) shows a

Fig. 38.   Mary Wigman in *Maternal Dance,* a solo section from the 1934 group work *Women's Dances* (courtesy of the Mary Wigman Archive)

gesture that may well have closed the dance, Wigman kneeling and extending her arms forward, as if calling to a child no longer there.[22] Or is she sending the child off into the world? Or, with eyes closed, is she remembering the mixed emotions of wanting to both hold the child and let the child go? (Or is she experiencing the

Fig. 39.   Mary Wigman and her dance group in *Lament for the Dead,* from the 1934 work *Women's Dances* (courtesy of the Mary Wigman Archive)

mixed emotions of passing her art onto dancers so young that they could be her daughters?)

The lament of the mother for her daughter gives way to the group section titled *Lament for the Dead (Totenklage).* Michel describes the opening for Wigman and twelve dancers: "They start moving quietly in loose groups, [singly] or in couples or several together, each of them in her individual manner giving way to her mourning. So the expression of lamentation changes continually and grows into a perfect art of polyphonia."[23] A photograph (fig. 39) shows individuals and small groups clustering together, each dancer seemingly alone in her grief but also sharing her grief by joining in an imperfect circle. The spatial formation of the circle becomes more pronounced as the action progresses. Michel continues:

> This polyphonia collects into a strong homophonia: all combine movements and directions to a great circle; and the motion of the circle becomes a powerful lamentation of all. Once more the polyphonia wins the upper hand: again each of them is giving way to her sorrow. But the direction of the circle remains as it was before and, as a symbol of the sorrow they all have in common, it seizes the gestures of all the dancers: they all kneel down, and overwhelmed by

Fig. 40.   Mary Wigman and her dance group in *Dance of the Prophetess,* from the 1934 work *Women's Dances* (courtesy of the Mary Wigman Archive)

> the greatness of the sorrow they bend flatly onto the floor. One
> dancer passes into the middle of the circle, kneels down gently and
> bows her head.[24]

Is it Wigman who moves into the center of the circle? Michel does
not imply so, which suggests that one of the other dancers executes
this final gesture.[25] In the face of death, the choreographer becomes one mourner among others. (Or is it that, having passed her
leadership onto her younger dancers, she can retreat into the chorus, at least momentarily?)

Wigman reasserts her leadership in *Dance of the Prophetess* (*Tanz
der Seherin*). Mourning the dead, she may well have become her
students' equal, but looking toward the future, she displays powers
greater than theirs. Michel describes the dance as "a solo . . . accompanied by a group of six . . . dancers."[26] A photograph (fig. 40)
shows Wigman set off from the group of dancers, who imitate her
gesture of looking afar. The facial expressions of all six seem arti-
ficial, as if indicating an experience not internalized. Only Wigman
(even though her facial expression is somewhat blurred by the

camera) appears genuinely rapt by what she sees beyond the space of the stage. Michel notes: "The prophetess sees the future; she tries to resist the horror of what she has seen; but she is crushed down. At last she goes to face the inevitable fate in a solemn and sublime dance."[27]

In Michel's account, the choreographer becomes the primary actor in the dance. Wigman's retrospective choreographic notes depict the action somewhat differently. She terms the dance a "ritual" and describes the prophetess "trying to break out of it, but called back to the severe ritual by the priestesses."[28] In Wigman's account the group exerts power over its leader. The ambiguity rising from the two accounts suggests a complicated relation between the choreographer and the group. Having passed on her leadership to the group earlier, was the choreographer now reclaiming power? Having experienced power themselves, were the group members now loath to relinquish leadership?

Michel's and Wigman's accounts of the ending Witch Dance (Hexentanz) also differ in emphasis. In the choreographer's retrospective notes she shares leadership with another dancer (Drusilla Schroeder), and the two join with the larger group in "big spatial patterns, very wild, vital and strong in rhythm."[29] In Michel's account Wigman takes the leading role as the "mistress of witches," though the group always appears to threaten her command:

> At first a crowded, tangled heap, it starts vibrating slowly in ever increasing elastic and shaking movements, dissolves and darts out to the floor in somersaults and grotesque jumps. The mass comes in wild motion again, stiffens into a bizarre group, dissolves again, gallops into all directions, joins for a wantoning circle dance and rushes all disappearing from view. The mistress of witches entices them to come back, after a curious whirling dance. Once more the vibration and the shaking of the thronged witches. Once more a wild reeling circle dance. Then a raving whirling of all; and they rush to combine for the final group, a grotesque heap of heads and hands stretched out.[30]

A photograph (fig. 41) vivifies the ending image. The dancers crowd around the choreographer, playfully grimacing and clawing at the air, like schoolgirls in a charade of witches. Only Wigman's facial expression seems genuinely fearful and fearsome, reminiscent of her self-transformation in earlier solos. Enacted by her

Fig. 41. Mary Wigman and her dance group in *Witch Dance,* from the 1934 work *Women's Dances* (courtesy of the Mary Wigman Archive)

dancers, the demonic becomes another category of female experience, in accord with the program note. Enacted by Wigman, the demonic still retains the potential to defy categorization, to transform the human into a *Gestalt.*

In *Women's Dances* the dancers no longer could enter Wigman's world, as they could in her group dances from the Weimar period. The evidence of photographs and reviews suggests that the dancers appeared less individualized than in the Weimar dances. At the same time, Wigman's relationship to the group became more defined, more fixed. Over the course of the dance she passes the torch to a younger dancer, she laments alone, she joins the group lament, she reasserts her prophetic and demonic powers. It is as if the dynamic interplay between choreographer and group that provided the dramatic momentum of her Weimar dances had become formalized—and formulaic.

That Wigman was now a generation older than her dancers and that the ensemble assembled for *Women's Dances* did not have the collective experience of the earlier dance group undoubtedly contributed to the changed relation between leader and group. However, the changed relation also reflected the Nazi vision of the *Volksgemeinschaft*, which posited an anonymous collective in thrall to its *Führer*. In group dances choreographed during the early years of the Third Reich, the utopia of Wigman's Weimar dances broke down and was transformed. The dynamic relation of leader and group—defining themselves in relation to one another moment to moment—gave way to a static relation—enacting predetermined roles as charismatic leader and anonymous follower. Moreover, the dynamic roles of the Weimar dances had defined women in relation to one another, but the static roles of the Nazi dances posited women's separate and special sphere.

In 1935 Goebbels's ministry organized a second German Dance Festival in Berlin. Many of the choreographers and dancers presented the year before reappeared. Wigman premiered a new work commissioned by the ministry, as did Gret Palucca, Harald Kreutzberg, Dorothee Günther, and Lizzie Maudrik. In addition, Lotte Wernicke and Lola Rogge presented choreography for movement choir. As the program explained, in contrast to the previous festival, which had featured "well-known choreographers and performers . . . as well as a number of talented younger dancers," the current festival highlighted "the specific forms of German dance-making" in order to demonstrate "that German dance is the bearer of German culture and embodies the spirit of the new German life."[31] Even more than the 1934 festival, the 1935 festival intended to elevate German Dance over German dancers.

The Wigman group formed the previous year premiered *Hymnic Dances* (*Tanzgesänge*). The program note, authored by Wigman, associated the work with the Nazi rhetoric of "blood and soil" (*Blut und Boden*). As the program note explained:

> The dances convey man's deeply rooted love for all that binds him to the earth and to his homeland. Thus the various parts refer to exaltation (*Paean*), to painful burdens (*Road of the Suppliant*), to dark threats (*Song of Fate*), to elemental rhythm (*Fire Dance*), to the experience of nature (*Moon Song*), and to unending devotion (*Dance of Homage*).
>
> It seems to me superfluous to describe the dances in detail. They should speak for themselves. Any attempt to explain them through their content would not get very far, but in all circumstances would

be misunderstood. For what the dance can say through its artistic language cannot be said fully in words.

Better to allow the powerful feelings and experiences of the dance to cast their spell, the content-as-form awakening others to experience.[32]

In contrast to the program note for *Women's Dances*, which discouraged spectators from finding meanings beyond the verbal formulations of the section titles, this program note encouraged spectators to perceive nonverbal meanings. Did this encouragement introduce a spectatorial position beyond the control of Nazi rhetoric, as the choreographer's retrospective notes suggest? Or did the mystification of the artistic process simply reinforce the fascist cult of the irrational? Although the surviving evidence is contradictory, the weight of the evidence suggests that the work's seeming resistance to fascism served its thoroughgoing accommodation with fascism.

Penned in the mid-fifties, Wigman's retrospective choreographic notes singled out from *Hymnic Dances* a solo section, titled *Song of Fate* (*Schicksalslied*), as a premonition of the coming war. Wigman wrote, "Looking back, I must have had the war in my bones" and described *Song of Fate* as "dark, threatening, revolting" and culminating in "heroic [acceptance]."[33] A contemporary review described the action: "Costumed in a dark cloak and with her hand to her breast, the figure [*der Mensch*] senses the threatening doom and the inexorable power of fate. The figure wants to flee, retreat . . . rebels, laments, cries, threatens, curses, collapses. The figure recognizes human powerlessness against fate and goes to the end resigned, knowing, and upright."[34]

A pair of photographs vivifies the transformation from revolt to resignation. In the first photograph (fig. 42) the choreographer lunges backward and tensely flings her hands overhead, as if rearing away from a frightening apparition that her intense gaze attempts to stare down. In the second photograph (fig. 43) she leans backward, clasping one hand to her abdomen and raising her other overhead, and closes her eyes, as if submitting to the frightening apparition. Both images present the choreographer's persona responding to an externalized fate rather than simultaneously embodying an external power and her response, as in *Shifting Landscape*.

Wigman's retrospective choreographic notes present this shift in representational strategy as a premonition of war. But was this reading available to the spectator in 1935? In that context was it not more likely that the spectator identified the externalized fate as the Third Reich, a fate that the choreographer struggles against but accepts in the end?

In retrospect, it appears that Wigman's retrospective notes were part of her own attempt to suppress her accommodation with the Nazis. After the war she fabricated a story about how her dance had been banned as "degenerate art," a fabrication that went without challenge until after her death. In her memoirs she became the victim, not the victimizer. In a curious passage from her 1963 choreographic memoirs Wigman muses: "Later, I asked myself whether it might have been the external situation which forced [*Song of Fate*] to emerge, whether it was a matter of some compromise, even though a successful one. But I knew this could not have been the case. I knew that *Song of Fate* had *had* to be created."[35] Unwilling or unable to give up the mythology of her self-creation, Wigman remained oblivious to her admission of "successful compromise" with the Nazis.

A reconstruction of *Hymnic Dances* demonstrates the extent of the choreographer's "successful compromise." According to her retrospective notes, the opening *Paean* (*Lobgesang*) is "solemn in character and design."[36] Cast for a chorus of fourteen dancers with Wigman as the "leading figure,"[37] the dance reminds one reviewer of an "image of the heavenly host praising God."[38] A photograph (fig. 44) vivifies this impression: the choreographer kneels in the center of the space, flanked by symmetrical groups of dancers that bow toward her. The anonymity of the group is striking. As one reviewer comments: "Not that any one dancer stands out more strongly as an individual. Indeed, the individual voice barely has a special meaning in the great choric work. The dancers are ordered within the suprapersonal events of the dance."[39]

Next comes the solo *Song of Fate*, then the group dance *Road of the Suppliant* (*Bittgang*). Just as the solo moves from Wigman's revolt to her acceptance of an externalized fate, so too does her role within the group dance. A reviewer summarizes the action of *Road of the Suppliant*: "The artist moves from humble supplication to passionate rebellion to a bold summons that then shatters. The group

Figs. 42 and 43.   Mary Wigman in *Song of Fate*, a solo section from the 1935 group work *Hymnic Dances* (courtesy of the Mary Wigman Archive)

conveys fright, then consolation and comfort."[40] Wigman's retrospective choreographic notes cite *Road of the Suppliant*, in addition to *Song of Fate*, as a premonition of war. She describes her own role as the "leading figure" as less emphatic than in the other ensemble sections and pictures the other dancers "suffering, mourning, waiting in anxiety, threatened by visions of disaster and resigning, accepting, some of the women in sadness, some in resignation, some in revolt and some in deep belief of future life."[41]

In striking contrast to the image of the dancers' anonymity in *Paean,* a photograph (fig. 45) vivifies the individuation of the ensemble. Although all gesture with variations of hands clasped in prayer, each does so in a different way—pleading, begging, demanding, with Wigman swooning in their midst. Just as *Song of Fate* showed the choreographer coming to terms with an externalized fate, so *Road of the Suppliant* shows the ensemble coming to terms with the same fate, in each dancer's own way.

Fig. 44.   Mary Wigman and her dance group in *Paean,* from the 1935 work *Hymnic Dances* (courtesy of the Mary Wigman Archive)

The serious tone of *Paean, Song of Fate,* and *Road of the Suppliant* gives way in the second half of the work. It was as if having accepted their fate, the dancers can celebrate the new order. *Moon Song (Mondlied),* a solo for Wigman, recalls the spinning dances of the twenties, according to one reviewer.[42] According to the choreographer, the solo creates a "dreamlike, transparent . . . silvery atmosphere."[43] *Fire Dance (Feuertanz)* extends the "dreamlike" atmosphere to include the group. "Clad in red, with long transparent veils fastened to their right wrists," the dancers pictorialize fire.[44] The final *Dance of Homage (Huldigungstanz)* then returns to the "solemnity" of the opening *Paean* and transforms the "solemnity" into "jubilation."[45]

In Wigman's retrospective notes, *Hymnic Dances* substitutes a static relation between leader and group for the dynamic interplay characteristic of her Weimar dances. The two solos highlighting the choreographer's charismatic performing persona—*Song of Fate* and *Moon Song*—alternates with group dances—*Paean, Road of the Suppliant, Fire Dance, Dance of Homage*—in which the choreographer functions as a "leading figure." In contrast to the Weimar

Fig. 45.   Mary Wigman and her dance group in *Road of the Suppliant,* from the 1935 work *Hymnic Dances* (courtesy of the Mary Wigman Archive)

works, Wigman's charisma becomes more pronounced, rendering her followers less individualized and more anonymous. As a historian, I read this shift in the "imagined community" staged by Wigman's ensemble as evidence for her accommodation with fascist aesthetics. Thus my reading directly opposes the interpretation the choreographer advanced in her retrospective notes: that her work functioned as a premonition of future disaster.

The same year that saw the premiere of *Hymnic Dances* also saw the publication of *Deutsche Tanzkunst* (German dance art), Wigman's explicit statement of support for fascist aesthetics. A compilation of essays written over the preceding few years, the volume revised the choreographer's earlier published aesthetics to accord with Nazi ideology. At the same time, the collected essays countered the official view of *Deutscher Tanz* promulgated by the Cultural Ministry with Wigman's personal vision of *Deutsche Tanzkunst*. As long as Nazi aesthetics aggrandized her own achievements, Wigman embraced the rhetoric of Goebbels's ministry. Only when the official view undermined her position did she register her disagreement.

The volume opens with the title essay, "Deutsche Tanzkunst."

Wigman first poses the question, "What is German? What determines the essence of German art?"[46] She answers, "What one may term German in the best sense."[47] Then she elaborates:

> The Tragic, the Heroic—too often suppressed by the all-too-Playful—emerged and gave dance its new, its German face. Because this dance had the courage to confess to life, to life as the eternal mystique of weaving and working, because this dance searched for God and wrestled with the demon, because it gave form to the old Faustian desire for redemption as the ultimate unity of existence—because of all this, it is a German dance.[48]

Earlier Wigman had made statements such as, "Since Germany is the cradle of modern dance, so its living expression will reflect the essence of the German people."[49] But not until the National Socialists came to power was she compelled to define precisely what she meant by "the essence of the German people." Moreover, in contrast to her earlier writings, which had linked the Germanness of *Ausdruckstanz* to universal human experiences, her 1935 essay linked Germanness to the *Volk*. She wrote: "We German artists today are more aware of the fate of the *Volk* than ever before. And for all of us this time is a trial of strength, a measuring of oneself against standards that are greater than the individual is able to fathom. The call of the blood, which has involved us all, goes deep and engages the essential."[50]

Following the lead of Goebbels's ministry, Wigman revised her view of *Ausdruckstanz* to accord with the Nazi celebration of the *Volk*. In one respect, however, Wigman's vision of *Deutsche Tanzkunst* departed from the official view of *Deutscher Tanz*. As the programs for the Nazi dance festivals held in 1934 and 1935 made clear, the Cultural Ministry intended to elevate German Dance over German dancers. Wigman took exception to this maneuver. In her view "what one may term German in the best sense" neither inhered in all dances by Aryan choreographers nor could be mandated by bureaucratic proclamation. Rather, she believed that only the most talented choreographers, like herself, could realize Germanness "in the best sense." She wrote: "The new German dance is not the result of a predetermined program. It takes its mark from the few creative personalities who through unremitting struggle have given it the unity of form and content."[51]

The subsequent essay in *Deutsche Tanzkunst*, "Die natürliche

Bewegung als Grundlage des Tanzes" (Natural movement as the foundation for dance), undertakes an extended defense of the prerogatives of the talented. The defense turns on the meaning of the term "natural." Wigman carefully distinguishes the "natural" sources of dance—the experience of movement—from the "natural" talent that allows the artist to transform movement into dance. Again the terms were familiar from her earlier writings, which drew a similar distinction between *Gymnastik,* the experience of movement as a means for spiritual release and physical training, and *Tanz,* the translation of movement into symbolic representation. As she wrote in a 1928 essay, "Dance begins where *Gymnastik* ends."[52] But in the context of the Third Reich, this position took on a changed significance and aligned Wigman with the Cultural Ministry's policy of divorcing *Tanz-Gymnastik* from concert dance and promoting the former as a mode of female physical education and the latter as a mode of opera-house entertainment. As the following remarks demonstrate, Wigman accepted the Cultural Ministry's position regarding the integration of ballet and *Ausdruckstanz* on the stage:

> It must not be denied that a strident debate between "old" and "new," between "classical" and "modern," raged during the early phase of development of the new dance. . . . We may assume that this contested phase has come to a close, that a mutual respect and recognition not only has resulted in a truce but also guarantees and promotes the further development of artistic dance in Germany.[53]

In *Deutsche Tanzkunst* Wigman revised her defense of the talented by paraphrasing the rhetoric of the Cultural Ministry on the integration of ballet and modern dance, an integration that her own choreography never realized during the Third Reich.

The final essay in the volume revised the essay on "Der Tänzer und das Theater" (The dancer and the theater) first published in 1929–1930. When it first appeared, the essay's vision of a "cultic" theater had no actual referent. But five years later, it summarized the dramaturgy of the *Thingspiel,* a form promoted by the Cultural Ministry as an appropriate expression of the *Volksgemeinschaft.* Just as the proponents of *Thingspiel* looked back to the Greek theater for inspiration, so too did Wigman: "The Greeks had a theater that was inseparable from religion and the state, that embodied their being as *Volk,* nation, family, and individual. A theater that belonged to all, that served God and humanity, that became a festival [*Fest*] in the highest sense."[54] In *Deutsche Tanzkunst* Wigman revised her vision of *Ausdruckstanz* to conform to the forms of German Dance promulgated by Goebbels's Cultural Ministry: opera-house entertainment based on the integration of ballet and modern dance, and *Thingspiel.*

By 1935 the *Thingspiel* movement was well under way. The previous year the Cultural Ministry had issued a statement defining the elements of the form: "First, oratorio, that is, a combination of choirs and individual voices; second, pantomime—allegories, living pictures, flag ceremonies, ceremonial acts; third, procession—parades, ceremonial displays, gatherings; and fourth, dance—ballet, *Ausdruckstanz, Gymnastik,* sport festivals [*Sportfeste*]."[55] Nazi spectacle typically involved more than a thousand performers and around twenty thousand spectators, in other words, ten times as many participants as *Totenmal.* Yet like *Totenmal, Thingspiel* favored war remembrance themes and the combination of movement and speaking choirs, supplemented by processional elements characteristic of political rallies. Although Mary Wigman herself never choreographed a *Thingspiel,* her choreography for *Totenmal* was an unrecognized—or unacknowledged—model for the genre.[56]

However, Wigman did contribute to Nazi spectacle as part of a team that staged the opening-night festival for the 1936 Berlin Olympic Games. Collaborating with Gret Palucca, Harald Kreutzberg, and Dorothee Günther, she choreographed *Olympic Youth* (*Olympische Jugend*), a production staged on such a grand scale that it dwarfed even the typical *Thingspiel.* Just as the *Thingspiel* multiplied the proportions of *Totenmal* by a factor of ten, so *Olympic Youth* multiplied the proportions of *Thingspiel* by a factor of ten. Performed in the Olympic stadium, the spectacle involved more than ten thousand performers and one hundred thousand spectators.[57]

Like the games themselves, the production could be read on two levels: as a celebration of Olympic internationalism and as a celebration of German nationalism. Commentators then and now have debated whether the 1936 Olympics transcended or served Nazi ideology.[58] The American Olympic committee considered boycotting the games because of the Nazi ban on Jewish athletes, but

Avery Brundage convinced the committee that sports was above politics, and the American team participated. The black track star Jesse Owens won four gold medals, a fact prominently recorded in Leni Riefenstahl's documentary, *Olympia*. (Just as sports historians have debated the relation of the games to Nazi politics, so film historians have debated Riefenstahl's relation to fascism.)[59] The American dance community did boycott the international dance festival organized as part of the games, refusing to participate as a protest against the ban on Jewish dancers.[60] Dancers from Poland, Hungary, Bulgaria, Yugoslavia, Austria, Switzerland, Holland, Greece, and Italy did appear at the Olympic dance festival, along with the Wigman group dancing excerpts from *Women's Dances* and *Hymnic Dances*.[61]

Scripted by Carl Diem and directed by Hans Niedecken-Gebhard, *Olympic Youth* epitomized the fusion—and confusion—of nationalism and internationalism commentators have noted in the games and in Riefenstahl's documentary. Displaying the symbols associated with the games—the interlocking rings of the Olympic flag, the parade of flags from all nations, the Olympic bell, and the Olympic torch—the spectacle seemingly reflected the international spirit of Olympic competition. At the same time, the production fulfilled Goebbels's ideal of "invisible propaganda," staging the body politic of the Third Reich.[62] Like a magnified and distorted version of Renaissance and Baroque court entertainment, *Olympic Youth* explicitly celebrated a mythology on display while implicitly celebrating the presence of the monarch, the Führer who reviewed the work from the stands.

As reconstructed from the official scenario and photographs, the spectacle projects the illusion of unity and the actuality of division and exclusion. The festival seemingly includes all, performers and spectators alike, while actually dividing men from women, young from old, mass from leader, German from Jew. The illusion of unity depends not only on division according to age, sex, and status but also on the exclusion of non-Aryans and other "deviants." In other words, *Olympic Youth* functions as a metaphor for the *Volksgemeinschaft*.

A photograph of the opening section, *Children at Play* (*Kindliches Spiel*) (fig. 46), shows twenty-five hundred girls (aged 11 and 12) and nine hundred boys forming the design of the Olympic flag. While

Fig. 46. *Children at Play*, from *Olympic Youth*, the opening-night spectacle for the 1936 Berlin Olympic Games (from *The Eleventh Olympic Games Berlin, 1936: Official Report*)

the girls, costumed in white smocks and holding semicircular hoops, surround the field, the boys, costumed in warm-up suits in the Olympic colors, form the interlocking ring motif. Explicitly celebrating Olympic symbolism, the image implicitly differentiates the boys' and girls' gendered tasks. While the girls rely on hoops to properly space themselves, the boys line up in a more complicated pattern without the aid of props. In subsequent sections the boys abandon "round dances" altogether, as if growing up means leaving such games behind.

A photograph of the next section, *Maidenly Grace* (*Anmut der Mädchen*) (fig. 47), shows twenty-three hundred older girls (aged 14 to 18) sitting in large concentric circles, awaiting the appearance of

Fig. 47. *Maidenly Grace*, from *Olympic Youth*, the opening-night spectacle for the 1936 Berlin Olympic Games (from *The Eleventh Olympic Games Berlin, 1936: Official Report*)

Palucca, who "emerges . . . and dances a waltz."[63] Costumed in unbleached muslin dresses with red borders, the older girls watch Palucca, costumed in red, dance in the center of the circle. This costuming and spatial arrangement present Palucca as a role model for the girls. After she leaves, the girls perform with balls, hoops, and clubs.

Their peers, twenty-three hundred adolescent boys, take the field in the next section, *Youth at Play and in a Serious Mood* (*Jünglinge in Spiel und Ernst*). A photograph (fig. 48) shows the girls withdrawn to the sides of the field while the boys set up camp in the middle. Then a group of one thousand youths descends the marathon steps in a flag-swinging sequence, accompanied by a song that mingles slogans of German nationalism and Olympic internationalism:

Kampf der Kräfte, Kampf der Künste,
Kampf um Ehre, Vaterland,
Friede, Freude, Fest der Jugend,

Fig. 48. *Youth at Play and in a Serious Mood,* from *Olympic Youth,* the opening-night spectacle for the 1936 Berlin Olympic Games (from *The Eleventh Olympic Games Berlin, 1936: Official Report*)

Fest der Völker, Fest der Tugend,
Ewiges Olympia.[64]

(Fight of powers, fight of arts, / Fight for honor, fatherland, / Peace, joy, festival of youth, / Festival of peoples, festival of virtue, / Eternal Olympia.)

While the adolescent girls danced in circles and passively watched their role model, the adolescent boys actively engage in the sorts of paramilitary exercises practiced by the Hitler Youth.

The boys' exercises give way to mock war in the fourth section, *Heroic Struggle and Death Lament* (*Heldenkampf und Totenklage*). A speaker introduces the warrior's dance cast for sixty men, his words "calling to mind the spiritual significance of all games, the supreme sacrifice for one's native land":[65]

Allen Spiels
heil'ger Sinn;
Vaterlandes
Hochgewinn.
Vaterlandes höchst Gebot
in der Not:
Opfertod![66]

(All games / divine purpose; / fatherland / greatest win. / Fatherland's greatest command / in need: / Sacrificial death!)

After the men engage in mock war, eighty women led by Wigman lament the dead. Just as the adolescent girls looked to Palucca, so the lamenting women follow the choreographer's lead. In striking contrast, no male leaders are left on the field. Only the Führer remains, watching from a special box in the stands, where the spectators watch him spectating. Like a Renaissance monarch, Hitler stages himself at the center of his spectacle.

In the final scene, *Olympic Hymn* (*Olympischer Hymnus*), attention shifts from the Führer to the mass of participants, who return to the field for the last movement of Beethoven's Ninth Symphony and Schiller's "Lied an die Freude" ("Ode to Joy"). A photograph (fig. 49) shows the effect described in the scenario as "a vault like a dome of brilliant light above the arena" with "flames of fire [encircling] the edge of the Stadium."[67] This lighting effect quite literally brought all the spectators inside the spectacle. Sitting among the crowd, the spectator experienced the illusion of unity provided by the *Volksgemeinschaft*. As the official report explains, the festival was designed so that "everything was excluded which would, like a stage-play, appear to the onlooker as a spiritual happening that he would have to explain to himself."[68] Goebbels's "invisible propaganda" did the spectators' thinking for them.

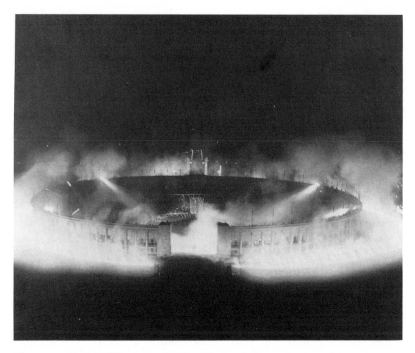

Fig. 49. *Olympic Hymn,* from *Olympic Youth,* the opening-night spectacle for the 1936 Berlin Olympic Games (from *The Eleventh Olympic Games Berlin, 1936: Official Report*)

Were all the spectators convinced by the "invisible propaganda"? It is interesting to compare reports by two American journalists. Although Frederick Birchall, writing for the *New York Times,* seemingly was convinced, Janet Flanner, writing for the *New Yorker,* clearly was not. Birchall read the explicit level of meaning, the celebration of Olympic symbolism. His report noted the display of Olympic symbolism that was concentrated at the opening and closing of the spectacle—the interlocking rings of the Olympic flag formed by the children near the beginning and the lighted torches and unfurling of flags from all nations at the end. In his account these images of Olympic internationalism frame the "moral" of the warrior's dance, the pacifist sentiment that both the aggressor and the defender lose: "The moral of this scene was supposedly that modern war destroys both the victor and the vanquished."[69] Was Birchall persuaded by the "invisible propaganda" that presented Germany's hosting of the Olympic Games as a signal of the nation's peaceful intentions within the international arena? Or did the use of the term "supposedly" reveal some skepticism? In contrast, Janet Flanner made no secret of her skepticism:

> That [opening] night, two hundred thousand . . . enthusiasts plodded back to the stadium to witness a *Festspiel*, heavily announced as symbolizing the ageless Olympic ideal, with pageant, dance, and melody, the whole being given, by a novel application of cinema principles, a brilliant new nocturnal beauty. Under faraway lamps, the arena's green grass and red-clay lanes looked like long shots in a colored movie. Under spotlights that could shine for a quarter of a mile, and floodlights which passed over vast dancing groups as pale sunshine impersonally passes between clouds over mountain meadows, the antics of ten thousand perfectly trained children, marching in exact tinted arabesques, the dancing of pink and saffron Greek ballet warriors, chieftained by Harald Kreutzberg, and their mournful female followers, in loops of varied gray, led by Mary Wigman, composed an ocular chef-d'oeuvre unique in European experience. As the finale, a giant chorus sang Schiller's words to Beethoven's Ninth Symphony; overhead seventeen searchlights, from far outside the arena, made a lofty birdcage of streaming light beams; from exterior flares, smoke and radiance broke to envelop the inevitable Hitler *Jugend* waving the inevitable flags of all the Olympic nations from the topmost layer of the stadium's many mounting rings.[70]

In keeping with the program of the Cultural Ministry, *Olympic Youth* placed no one artist at its center but rather a community unified through its allegiance to Hitler. When she contributed to the staging of the spectacle, Wigman saw no discrepancy between this concept of *Deutscher Tanz* and her own vision of *Deutsche Tanzkunst*. However, when next invited to contribute to Nazi spectacle, she became aware of the discrepancy, and apparently so did the Nazis.

As her biographer tells the story, in spring 1937 Albert Talhoff, then a party official in Bavaria, asked Wigman to choreograph the opening ceremony for the First German Art Exhibition in Munich. (This was not the exhibition of "degenerate art" but the exhibition of officially approved art.) The scenario Talhoff sent pictured the "decadent art" of the Weimar Republic giving way to the military parade of the Third Reich. The scenario made explicit what had remained implicit in *Olympic Youth*—the artist's displacement by the *Volksgemeinschaft*. Wigman no longer could remain unaware of the dissonance between the policy of the Cultural Ministry and her commitment to the prerogatives of the artist. But although she resented the implications, she dared not refuse the invitation. Yet on the day she mailed her acceptance, the party withdrew the offer.[71]

As preparations were under way for the First German Art Exhibition in Munich, Joseph Goebbels wrote in his diary: "Ufa is making a dance film. I have prohibited the philosophical dance of Wigman, Palucca and others from taking centerstage. Dance must be buoyant and must show beautiful women's bodies. That has nothing to do with philosophy."[72] After *Olympic Youth* Wigman never again received a commission from the Cultural Ministry, although she remained the figurehead of German Dance.

THE WIGMAN SCHOOL, 1934–1942

Wigman staged the body politic of the Third Reich not only through her group choreography from 1934 to 1936 but also at her school from its reorganization in 1934 until its closing in 1942. In a 1940 article she wrote: "The community ideal of dance education finds its fullest realization in the group studio at the school. . . . [The students] take part in the creative process from the first sketches of a work-in-progress to its final stage of realiza-ₗon. In so doing they learn what it means to be responsible for a project that demands the same contribution from all."[73] Did the students' experience of a "dancers' community" prepare them to contribute to the *Volksgemeinschaft*, as a 1934 brochure announcing the school's reorganization implied? Or did the experience of a "dancers' community" model an alternative to the *Volksgemeinschaft*, as the reminiscences of former students imply? The conflicting evidence of archival documents and oral history suggests both possibilities, as well as a third possibility: that the students' memories function as a denial of the fusion between the "dancers' community" and the *Volksgemeinschaft*.

The Cultural Ministry designated the Wigman School one of thirteen training centers fully in accord with Directive 48, the statute setting out the certification examination for "artistic dance."[74] The examination required students to prove their Aryan origin and familiarity with National Socialist ideology (Weltanschauung) as well as demonstrating their mastery of "German dance forms," "classical dance forms," and "folk dance forms." Beginning with the 1934–1935 academic year, the Wigman School had reorganized its curriculum to accord with Cultural Ministry policy. The brochure announcing the reorganization noted that the new curriculum would prepare the student to contribute to "the theater, the new festivals, and the physical education of the German *Volk*."[75] In other words, the new curriculum trained students to take advantage of new forms of dance patronage offered by the Nazi state.

As outlined in Directive 48, the required curriculum for *Deutscher Tanz* narrowed the limits of improvisation and pointed toward a codified vocabulary for *Ausdruckstanz*. The directive gave examples of improvisations to folk music ("German—Russian—Polish—etc."), to classical dance music ("Saraband—Gavotte—Waltz—March—etc."), and to "music of a dramatic or lyrical character" ("Serenade—elegiac march—practical stage tasks—etc.").[76] The catalog of movement techniques included:

> Walking patterns: on the balls of the feet and on the soles—in varied directions—with changing centers of balance—with temporal and rhythmic variations—etc.
>
> Running patterns: high and low—with changing torso positions—with sudden stops and drops—etc.
>
> Triplet patterns: relaxed and taut—free or tied to rhythmic and spatial components—etc.
>
> Skipping patterns: accented and unaccented—in 3/4 and 4/4 time—narrow and wide—high and low—etc.
>
> Spinning: half and full—in place and while traveling—rhythmically accompanied by arm, leg, or pelvis swings—gyrating turns—etc.
>
> Swings: pendulum swings, fore and aft swings, and circling swings with varying postures and spatial directions—etc.
>
> Jumps: bouncing jumps—high, wide, straddling, shifting, diving and staccato jumps—etc.[77]

The Cultural Ministry directive renamed *Ausdruckstanz* German Dance and installed German Dance within the required curriculum alongside the codified vocabularies of classical ballet and folk dance.

Oral history raises the issue of whether the Wigman School followed the letter or the spirit of the Cultural Ministry directive, both in terms of the National Socialist Weltanschauung (worldview) and in terms of the tripartite division of the curriculum. Although some students from the period deny that the school offered any training in Weltanschauung, others remember a teacher coming in from the outside to offer ideological training. At the 1986 gathering of former Wigman students at the Academy of Arts in West Berlin, both Drusilla Schroeder-Schwinghammer, an American dancer who graduated from the school in 1933 and performed with the Wigman dance group in 1934 and 1935, and Kurt Paudler, a student at the school from 1937 to 1939, denied that the school offered any classes in National Socialist ideology. But in separate interviews, Margrit Bassow, a student at the school from 1933 to 1936 who later emigrated, and Shirlee Dodge, an American student at the school from 1937 to 1939, remember teachers coming in from the outside to offer classes in Nazi ideology. Bassow remembered a young blond man, "quite good-looking," who taught the classes, and one day took her aside and "kindly suggested" that since she was Jewish, she had "little chance" of pursuing a dance career in Germany and recommended that she try her luck in Switzerland or Italy instead.[78] (Although Jewish students were technically barred from study, Wigman had secured special permission from the authorities to enroll Jewish students in her school.)[79] Shirlee Dodge remembered a female teacher who taught the classes in ideology and recounted in particular one class when Gundel Eplinius, a "fiercely anti-Nazi" student, came in late with heavy strides and defiantly turned her chair around and sat with her back to the teacher.[80]

Eplinius, a student at the school from 1937 to 1939, also participated on the 1986 panel at the Academy of Arts. Although she made no comment on the subject of ideology classes, she did emphasize that the school exams were separate from the certification exams required by the Cultural Ministry. She defended Wigman by asserting that the choreographer never believed in the ballet and folk dance taught at the school: "I believe that Mary Wigman included classical ballet within the curriculum out of practical reasons. I do not think she would have done so if it were not required, if we could have passed the exams without ballet training. . . . At the Wigman School folk dance was an absurdity. Mary viewed it with humor. But it was imposed. Swallowed exactly like classical

ballet was."[81] Eplinius pictured a Wigman School where the choreographer only superficially conformed to the Cultural Ministry
directive. From her viewpoint, the school was essentially "un-
changed" from the Weimar period. Kurt Paudler vigorously
agreed with her and noted the presence of foreign students, just as
during the Weimar period. As he stated: "At the school there were
Germans, Americans, British, Czechs, Greeks, Scandinavians. We
were international, and lived for dance alone."[82] How should one
interpret the defense of Wigman by her former students? As a denial of their own complicity? Or as a significant corrective to the
Cultural Ministry directive?

The evidence of oral history suggests that the archival documents tell only part of the story of the Wigman School during the
Third Reich. It seems that Wigman's teaching did not limit improvisation as narrowly as did the Cultural Ministry directive. Rather,
she interpreted the directive's multiple "etceteras" as freedom to
continue teaching as she had before. Moreover, oral history suggests that even though Nazi rhetoric pervaded the official publications of the school and the required classes in Weltanschauung, it
did not invade the dance studio. Rather, Wigman's teaching employed the rhetoric of self-realization she also had voiced during
the twenties.

The question remains of why Wigman sought special permission
for Jewish students. Her biographer suggests that it was partly because she needed the extra tuition.[83] Some former students give
her the benefit of the doubt and believe that she considered anti-
Semitism wrong. Margrit Bassow remembers the Wigman School
as a refuge from the pervasive anti-Semitism of the time,[84] and so
does Isa Partsch-Bergsohn. Partsch-Bergsohn studied with Wigman in Leipzig in 1943–1944, after the choreographer had sold
her Dresden school. Ostracized as a "half-breed" (*Mischling*), she
remembers her encounter with Wigman as a salvation.[85]

SOLOS, 1937–1942

Just as the Wigman School staged a more contested version of the
Nazi body politic than did the choreographer's group dances, so
too did her solos choreographed during the Third Reich. From

1937 until her retirement from the stage in 1942, Wigman premiered nearly twenty new solos. These solos consolidated the formal shifts characteristic of *Women's Dances* and *Hymnic Dances,* further eclipsing the principle of the mask, extending the strategies of autobiography and archetype, and introducing the frame of musical visualization. This consolidation completed her redefinition of dance as a space for female experience. As a male reviewer remarked in 1938:

> Mary Wigman's greatness lies in her dancing out woman's being, which she visualizes and crystallizes. Even the titles of her works evoke the world of woman. . . . an almost mystical world, in the end comprehensible only to women. One realizes this sitting in the audience, for it is the response of the women that makes sense of the happenings onstage. A man is only mildly interested. He ultimately does not comprehend this art.[86]

In her group dances choreographed from 1934 to 1936, Wigman's redefinition of dance as a space for female experience signaled her accommodation with the vision of *Deutscher Tanz* promulgated by the Cultural Ministry. But in the context of her solos created from 1937 to 1942, the redefinition asserted the dissonance between *Deutscher Tanz* and Wigman's vision of *Deutsche Tanzkunst.* In her late solos the space for female experience became a space where the individual body resisted the collective body. Within the seeming monolith of Nazi culture after 1937, Wigman's solos preserved a space, however limited, for individual vision.

Wigman's late solos reveal the fine line that separates female spectatorship from the reinvention of the male gaze in Duncanesque dancing. To address the female spectator by dramatizing a female-associated subjectivity invites the male viewer to bracket the dancing body as essentialized Woman. In her Weimar dances Wigman had avoided this slippage by deploying the principle of the mask, distancing her onstage *Gestalt* from her offstage persona, and subverting the viewer's conflation of the dancing body and the performer's gender. This subversion created a space within which the female spectator could imaginatively experience self-transformation without being limited to predetermined notions of women's separate and special sphere. But once Wigman's dances de-emphasized the principle of the mask, her performances limited female spectatorship in exactly that way. Now her dances set up categories and placed boundaries on female experience. Yet within the context of the Third Reich, Wigman's reversion to the notion of women's separate and special sphere gave her a place from which to comment on what she perceived as the masculinist and anti-individualist ethos of the fascist regime.

The choreographer's focus on solo choreography after 1936 had practical as well as ideological determinants. After collaborating on the production of *Olympic Youth,* she received no more commissions for group choreography from Goebbels's Cultural Ministry. Nor could she support a company with funds generated by school tuitions, as she had managed to do in the mid-twenties. Indeed, supporting the school became increasingly difficult through the thirties, for the number of foreign students declined considerably, as did the number of German students, now that Jews required special permission to enroll. (According to one estimate, twenty percent of the students during the twenties came from Jewish families.)[87] Moreover, Nazi youth organizations now absorbed the energies of amateur students who once had flocked to lay dance classes. What kept the school afloat after 1936 were receipts from solo tours.[88] Hence, when Wigman decided to retire from the stage in 1942, she also had to sell her school.

During this time Wigman came to see herself as a victim of Nazi cultural politics, and her retrospective view of the period only intensified this self-perception. According to her biographer, Goebbels personally vetoed her participation in a staging of Gluck's *Orpheus and Eurydice* planned for summer 1938.[89] And one week before she was scheduled to lecture and perform at a meeting of the Cultural Ministry in spring 1941, she received word that her appearance was canceled. In a letter to a friend she called the meeting a "farce," and her diary recorded the realization that she had been classed with the "decadent artists" (*Entarteten*).[90] These were the experiences that led her to identify herself in the postwar period as an artist branded by the Nazis. Such claims, however, clearly distorted her role within the Third Reich. Although her leadership of German dance was undermined, her status as the figurehead of the movement was never challenged. More important, neither her life nor her livelihood was ever endangered. In comparison with artists whose works were banned and whose existences were threatened by the Nazis, Wigman's position was relatively secure.

In reconstructing Wigman's solos from 1937 to 1942, I have found it difficult to separate her retrospective denial of collaboration from her limited resistance to fascism. A reconstruction of *Autumnal Dances* (*Herbstliche Tänze*), a solo cycle premiered in 1937, demonstrates this difficulty. Although Wigman's retrospective account clearly distorts her position within the Third Reich, archival evidence both counters the choreographer's distortion *and* demonstrates a dissonance with Cultural Ministry policy that can be read as limited resistance. The same holds for *Dance of Brunhild* and *Farewell and Thanksgiving*—solos choreographed for her farewell concert in 1942.

Wigman's postwar memoirs erase her collaboration with fascism by presenting herself as a victim of the Nazis. Describing *Autumnal Dances*, she writes: "These dances were created at a time of political unrest. The anathema 'degenerate art' had long since been pronounced about my work. Everything demanded utter caution. I have never known 'being careful' in my work and have always gone my own way as I had to. But to this very day I ask myself how *Autumnal Dances* could remain untouched by all outside tribulations and keep their innocent purity in experience as well as creation."[91]

Strikingly, not only the fact of Wigman's earlier collaborations with the Nazis but also the reconstruction of *Autumnal Dances* challenges the choreographer's assertion that the cycle remained "untouched by all outside tribulations." Indeed, the evidence suggests that the solo cycle conformed to a change in Cultural Ministry policy. For reasons that remain unclear, the Cultural Ministry withdrew support from the *Thingspiel* movement after 1936 and redirected support toward "classical" opera, theater, and dance. This meant that, in addition to promoting productions of Wagner and Goethe, the Cultural Ministry promoted dance that was more entertaining than artistically challenging. By 1937 the effect of compulsory ballet training began to be noticeable. For example, photographs collected in a coffee-table volume published that year, titled *Tänzer unserer Zeit*, show dancers posing in arabesques and attitudes, smiling at the viewer.[92]

Autumnal Dances responded to the Cultural Ministry's policy that de-emphasized dance as festival while revaluing dance as entertainment. Yet the cycle did not fully embody the shifting expectations, and as a result it can be read as both accommodation with and limited resistance to the prescribed aesthetics. The work accommodated the new policy of the Cultural Ministry by reversing a central tenet of Wigman's Weimar aesthetic: that dance remain independent of music. Dance that entertained meant dance accompanied by music, not dance to silence or percussive sounds. And so the program note for *Autumnal Dances*, authored by the composer Hanns Hasting, emphasized not the independence but the interdependence of dance and music. The program note framed the choreography as musical visualization:

> The music originates simultaneously with the dances. It would be wrong to measure this music against the standards set for absolute music. One can no more consider it alone than opera music without the accompanying text or than many songs whose melodic structure fuses with the lyrics. . . . It is also important that one not consider a dance without its accompanying musical form. It is not a matter of one standing back in favor of the other.
>
> In *Blessing* [*Segen*] we hear a fanfare theme interspersed with harplike arpeggios, which later are transformed into a quiet lyrical theme. Gong and kettledrum sparely support the tonality. The theme fades away into an ascending hymn.
>
> *Dance of Remembrance* [*Tanz der Erinnerung*]. A quiet song returns twice in modified form.
>
> *Hunting Song* [*Jagdlied*]. Trumpets and horns sound throughout the theme. Hunting fanfares and clattering of horses' hooves. The kettledrum supports this presentation.
>
> *Dance in the Stillness* [*Tanz in der Stille*]. Music of which one only becomes aware when it stops in the middle and when it later starts again, softly but with an accelerating tempo.
>
> *Bride of the Wind* [*Windsbraut*]. It is not the music's task to illustrate the wind. A glassy theme begins; cymbals give the sound support and color. A second theme, underscored by the gong, only sings gently with the movement in order later to accelerate with the dance into a raging whirlwind. This breaks off and a few large impulses lead to the conclusion.[93]

As reconstructed from photographs, reviews, and choreographic memoirs, *Autumnal Dances* juxtaposes the frame of musical visualization with references to Wigman's earlier works. A photograph of *Dance of Remembrance* (fig. 50) shows the dancer gesturing upward with head tilted back and eyes closed, as if absorbed in her

Fig. 50.   Mary Wigman in *Dance of Remembrance,* from the 1937 solo cycle *Autumnal Dances* (courtesy of the Mary Wigman Archive)

own memories. The image of inner reverie recalls her 1934 solo *Dance of Silent Joy.* Similarly, the retrospective descriptions of *Hunting Song* and *Bride of the Wind* recall the strategy of simultaneous representation characteristic of solos from the late twenties. In *Hunting Song* the choreographer becomes the caller and the called: "[The dancer] with fast feet running across the floor and suddenly coming to a halt; then tensely listening and looking, statue-like—Artemis, roaming through the forests, forcing her way in great delight, imperiously sounding the hunting call which is thrown back by its echo."[94]

In *Bride of the Wind* the choreographer embodies the power of the wind and the figure buffeted by the wind:

> It was wonderful once again to throw oneself into a large orbit, with the wide dance skirt swinging about, leaving the limitations behind so that it swelled and billowed like a sail in the wind. How wonderful to let oneself be driven, to offer oneself enraptured—moved by the wind, wedded to the wind—to lose oneself whirling down in all the uproar like a leaf falling from a tree, to reach the ground in a last flaring up with a last faint breath.[95]

A photograph of *Bride of the Wind* (fig. 51) shows Wigman stilled in a turn, her angled arm punctuating the momentum of the action. Unlike other dancers profiled in *Tänzer unserer Zeit*, she never looks at the camera. Her refusal to show off for the spectator undermined the entertainment value of her dancing and occasioned criticism that she remained too "tied to the demonic," however "decorative" she attempted to be. As one reviewer commented: "Not that [her lighter solos] lack charm and playfulness, but even in the intricate decoration of her movement Wigman remains tied to the demonic. . . . [Her] dances attract a distinct circle of people who don't consider dance as the creation of joy but as a temple rite or as the ecstasy of night and melancholy."[96] The reviewer's use of terms such as "temple rite" and "ecstasy" points toward Wigman's aesthetic from the twenties. In *Autumnal Dances* the frame of musical visualization compromised this aesthetic, but only to a degree. Beyond that point Wigman refused to abandon her earlier vision, and her defiance asserted the right of the individual artist not to conform to the collective.

In 1937–1938 Wigman toured a solo program titled "The Most Beautiful Dances" ("Die schönsten Tänze"), which included *Dance of Remembrance* and *Bride of the Wind* from *Autumnal Dances*, *Maternal Dance* from *Women's Dances*, *Song of Fate* from *Hymnic Dances*, plus four new solos and three solos from *Spanish Suite* (1922–1925). As a retrospective of Wigman's solo choreography, the program passed over her signature solo from the twenties, *Witch Dance II*, and chose to represent the Weimar period with the "lighter"

Fig. 51.   Mary Wigman in *Bride of the Wind,* from the 1937 solo cycle *Autumnal Dances* (courtesy of the Mary Wigman Archive)

solos of *Spanish Suite.* Thus the program presented her "lighter" solos as precedent for the shift in her solo choreography after 1933. What was unprecedented in "The Most Beautiful Dances" was the excision of the "darker" solos that had counterpointed her "lighter" solos on programs through the twenties.[97]

Solos choreographed for her farewell concert in 1942 conformed as closely as did previous works to Cultural Ministry policy, even while itensifying the defiance evident in *Autumnal Dances*. Like *Women's Dances, Dance of Brunhild* deloyed the representational strategy of female archetypes. Like *Autumnal Dances, Farewell and Thanksgiving* deployed the representational strategy of musical visualization. Yet both *Dance of Brunhild* and *Farewell and Thanksgiving* vivified internal oppositions and in so doing animated the resistance that counterpointed their accommodation with the prescribed aesthetic.

A scenario survives of *Dance of Brunhild* (*Tanz der Brunhild*) and recounts the tale of the proud and revengeful queen of Norse mythology. Cast as an interior monologue, the scenario narrates the queen's conflicting emotions and memories as she prepares for her wedding to the King of Burgundy. As Hedwig Müller has pointed out, this moment of transition in Brunhild's life story found resonance in Wigman's own life. Identifying with Brunhild, the choreographer also felt estranged from the changed world in which she found herself and betrayed by her intimates: Hanns Benkert, her lover of more than a decade and a high Nazi official, recently had married a younger woman for political reasons, and Hanns Hasting, her colleague of more than a decade, recently had pressured her to relinquish control of her school.[98] Dancing the archetype of Brunhild, Wigman danced her personal disillusionment.

The scenario begins with the tolling of the cathedral bells for the wedding ceremony. The queen first laughingly remembers the efforts of the ladies at the Burgundian court to teach her to dance:

> Her hand holds the hem of her wedding gown as she angrily shoves her foot into the pearl-covered slipper. Her lips hum the measure of the saraband that she later will dance at her kingly partner's side. She dances, yet her gestures are a bit angular, and she lacks the feminine grace that the women here so unconsciously possess. But her posture is queenly, and she resolutely marks the steps and figures of the dances. She knows that she will be admired, but will she be loved?[99]

A photograph (fig. 52) shows Wigman, costumed in a rich brocade gown and crownlike headpiece, holding the edge of her skirt as if attempting to court dance. There is both pride and self-mockery in her demeanor, as if she considers herself above the effort and

Fig. 52.   Mary Wigman in the 1942 solo *Dance of Brunhild* (courtesy of the Mary Wigman Archive)

finds it slightly ridiculous. Is the unfamiliar dance style an analogue for the diverting style prescribed by the Cultural Ministry?

The scenario continues the queen's interior monologue. She muses that the Burgundian countryside is beautiful and the sun warm but the people seem so strange with their free way of moving and their fine manners. It is "as if they didn't know the deathly seriousness of battle." [100] The queen closes her eyes, and the image of the most handsome of the Burgundians—the king, her betrothed—absorbs her thoughts. "He is . . . the only one who does not look at her with cold eyes. . . . But his presence will never feel close." [101] Her thoughts wander to her northern homeland, and in her mind she hears again the old woman who murmurs the prophecy of her birth: that she was born the daughter of gods with superhuman strength.

The queen remembers her first encounter with the King of Burgundy, how he struck her at first sight and sent a sensual trembling through her entire body. Then:

> She lifts an arm in greeting as if in a trance. A smile passes over her face. With swaying steps she nears the man whose image is so indelibly imprinted within her. He seems to call her from all sides at the same time. She must follow him, hold him. So she reels blindly though the space, here and there, until her outstretched hand hits against a wall, and the dream image is extinguished. [102]

All at once the queen experiences hate and the desire to revenge the humiliation of her pride. Yet she still desires to see her loved one, her hated one. Again a dream image obscures the present reality. She remembers going hunting in the icy landscape. This time she aims her spear at her lover's heart. A photograph (fig. 53) shows her gesture, a variation on the outstretched arm motif of her court dancing. As the scenario describes the action:

> Slowly she raises her arm. The action of balancing her body weight against the heavy projectile propels her forward, pushes her down, makes her rear. But her wildly swinging gestures cannot launch the spear. It falls from her. Her knees collapse.
>
> What has happened—is the divine strength that was bestowed upon her broken, destroyed? No, no, she crawls on her knees, throws herself over an imaginary stone mound on the floor. Her

Fig. 53. Mary Wigman in the 1942 solo *Dance of Brunhild* (courtesy of the Mary Wigman Archive)

body, shaking with effort, again and again tries to lift the heavy stone but in vain. Finally, overcome by the awareness of her weakness, she collapses and lies on the floor, deathly rigid.[103]

Brunhild's passion for the King of Burgundy—Wigman's passion for Benkert—has nearly destroyed her.

Then at the last moment she regains her strength. The scenario ends as it begins: cathedral bells sound. Thus the entire duration of the dance represents one complex moment of consciousness. The ending image is of doors opening, the sun streaming in as the queen stands tall. "Raising her right arm in greeting and assuming a queenly bearing, she goes to meet the fate . . . that had [been] prophesied."[104] A photograph, not reproduced here, shows what might have served as the closing gesture: Wigman stepping forward, raising her right arm overhead, looking into the distance with expectation yet resignation.[105]

In *Women's Dances* and *Hymnic Dances* the choreographer had visualized her response to an external force that shaped her actions, at first resisting and then accepting her "fate." This plot culminated in *Dance of Brunhild,* as her resistance was stretched to the limit. Was the spectator more impressed by the "deathly" rigidity of her collapse to the floor that climaxed the action or by the "queenly bearing" that she assumed at the final moment? Did the spectator read the solo as her disillusionment or as the "heroic" overcoming of her disillusionment? Did Wigman's resistance function as dissent or as accommodation? The evidence for *Dance of Brunhild* supports both interpretations.

The evidence for *Farewell and Thanksgiving* (*Abschied und Dank*), which survives on a film commissioned by the Cultural Ministry to mark the choreographer's retirement from the stage, also supports both interpretations.[106] The solo visualizes the lush sonorities and sustained rhythms of Aleida Montijn's score. (After 1939 Montijn replaced Hasting as Wigman's musical collaborator.) As recorded on film, Wigman returns again and again to the same pose, a lunge to the side with the arms wide from the shoulders and the head back. A still photograph (fig. 54) shows this pose, which often was followed by a wide leg swing. Wigman's choreographic memoirs describe the action as "a diagonally upward fluttering gesture which sought to fade out in space, but, at an arrested instant of its

Fig. 54. Mary Wigman in the 1942 solo *Farewell and Thanksgiving* (courtesy of the Mary Wigman Archive)

suspension, was caught by the swinging leg and brought to its end in an almost imperceptible, eluding hip movement of withdrawal."[107] Her memoirs interpret this action as an expression of the "renunciation without resignation" that marked the end of her performing career.

Viewing the film almost fifty years later, I experience double vision. Watching Wigman visualize the music, my memory contrasts this performance with the interpenetration of sound and silence in *Witch Dance II* and that solo's defiant assertion that music need not accompany movement. Watching Wigman's soulful gestures and facial expressions, my memory contrasts them with the demonic *Gestalt* of *Witch Dance II* and that solo's defiant assertion that the dancer need not perform Woman. Wigman seems to have reverted to a Duncanesque mode, bypassing her achievements of the Weimar years and compromising her performance in accordance with the aesthetic promulgated by Goebbels's ministry.

But then an official from the Cultural Ministry interviews the choreographer. As his clipped voice insists that she define her art, she answers elusively in the mystical rhetoric that her students remember, her eyes averting the camera and her offscreen interviewer. At that moment, her rhetoric seems not to support the cult of the irrational but to oppose the cult of efficiency. At that moment, her soulful dancing seems to secure a space for individual vision. And I wonder, was this how Wigman managed to preserve a sense of individual value and difference that empowered her students in the postwar period? Was this what Goebbels found objectionable?

In the end, I view not only the film record of *Farewell and Thanksgiving* but also the relation between Wigman and National Socialism with double vision. Taking advantage of the new patronage offered by the Nazi state, Wigman resolved a period of crisis in her choreographic career, and in so doing her staging of *Gemeinschaft* subtly transmuted into her staging of *Volksgemeinschaft*. The utopia of her all-female ensemble, based on the harmonious reconciliation of Wigman's authority with her dancers' individuality, reappeared as the dystopia of a dance group divided between its charismatic leader and an anonymous mass. Her vision subtly shifted once again after she had lost direct Nazi subsidy and returned to solo touring as her only choreographic venue. Her late solos ambivalently comment on the role of the individual, the artist, and the woman within the *Volksgemeinschaft*. Yet even after tracing Wigman's complex response to National Socialism, I still wonder: did her choreographic ambivalence serve as a limited resistance to fascist aesthetics or as a means of coming to terms with her accommodation? For me, that remains the vexing question of Wigman's career.

6

From *Ausdruckstanz* to *Tanztheater*

In this chapter I bring the story of Wigman's career to a close, tracing her activities from spring 1942, once she had retired from the stage and sold her Dresden school, to summer 1967, when she closed the school she had reopened after the war in West Berlin. I then begin to tell the story of Wigman's influence, focusing in this chapter on her German legacy and in the next and final chapter on her American reception.

Other narratives weave through my story of Wigman's last years and her influence from the fifties through the eighties. One is the continuing transformation of the cultural space inhabited by German Dance. The National Socialists had dismantled the network of private schools that supported *Ausdruckstanz* and installed modern dance within the opera house, where it remained in the postwar period. In effect, the National Socialists substituted government patronage for the patronage of amateur students, and both the Federal Republic (West Germany) and the Democratic Republic (East Germany) continued this practice.

In the fifties and early sixties, ballet eclipsed *Ausdruckstanz* as the preferred genre. Thus, as Wigman pursued her career in the postwar period, she encountered a dissonance between her work and the institutional practices of opera-house ballet. Although she received commissions from several opera houses, she found it difficult to work with ballet-trained dancers. And she never managed to attract many students to her school in West Berlin, for young dancers fixed their sights on ballet training, not on the study of what seemed an anachronism, *Ausdruckstanz*.

Within a few years of the closing of the Wigman School in 1967, interest in *Ausdruckstanz* began to revive, prompted by the emergence of an oppositional practice within the opera-house system called *Tanztheater*. Direct as well as indirect connections linked *Ausdruckstanz* and *Tanztheater*. Not only had Wigman and other survivors taught many of the choreographers who innovated *Tanztheater*, but also these innovators looked back to *Ausdruckstanz* as precedent for their assault from within on opera-house ballet. Thus, in retrospect, Mary Wigman and *Ausdruckstanz* appeared less marginal than they had during the fifties and early sixties.

A second narrative weaves through this story of the near disappearance and reappearance of *Ausdruckstanz*: how Wigman, her contemporaries, and her successors reread the German past. In her postwar dances and publications Wigman mythologized herself as a victim and as a dissenter, above all as a survivor of the Nazi period. She also assented to the view of ballet critics that the legacy of *Ausdruckstanz* was its contribution to the ballet revival. After her death in 1973 proponents of *Tanztheater* vigorously reversed these views, rewriting the history of German dance. Their rewriting not only acknowledged the alliance between *Ausdruckstanz* and fascism but also undermined the earlier celebration of the ballet boom. In the new history of German dance, the ballet boom suppressed the tradition of *Ausdruckstanz*, a tradition that reemerged as the practice of *Tanztheater*.

WIGMAN'S LIFE AND CAREER, 1942–1973

Although she had retired from the stage and sold her Dresden school in spring 1942, Wigman continued to work through the remainder of the war. She moved to Leipzig, where she had been invited by the mayor to head the dance department at the Conservatory for Music and Dramatic Art. It appears Goebbels vetoed her appointment as director, however, for in the end she was employed only as a guest instructor. Her employment lasted less than two years, for after Allied bombing destroyed the conservatory building in February 1944, the school closed.[1]

Determined to continue teaching her students, Wigman set up an impromptu school in her own apartment. She did not charge tuition but taught any students who appeared. Many were refugees who camped out on the floor for a short period and then moved on. Her housekeeper, Anni Hess, foraged for supplies and somehow managed to keep the students fed. A bombing raid in December 1944 left her apartment house one of the only buildings on its street standing, though somewhat damaged and without water, heat, or electricity for several weeks.[2] Nonetheless, Wigman persevered through the occupation of the city by American troops in April 1945, Germany's surrender in May, and the replacement of American by Soviet troops in June.

Students vividly remember this period. Gisela Colpe, a student at the conservatory in 1943–1944 and thereafter at Wigman's impromptu studio, recalls dancing during air raid alerts at night:

> There were orgies. When there was a full moon, we didn't black out the lights and we would improvise and create and play the piano and drums. Yes, that was fantastic. We wouldn't stay in our air-raid shelters. It was great. . . . And above all, you must not forget that one was glad for every day one still was alive. . . . That was perhaps one reason why the vitality of a person became almost superhuman, why one could develop powers without having anything to eat or anything else. It was quite crazy. One actually lived from such experiences.[3]

Jutta Ludewig, a student at the conservatory from 1942 to 1944 and thereafter at the impromptu school, recalls the period after the bombing stopped and refugees arrived:

> Many former Wigman students knew Mary's address, and when they didn't know where to go, they came to her—soldiers returning from the war or from a prison camp. Some stayed an hour, some stayed eight weeks. . . . Once I saw a young girl sitting across the way on a pile of rubble. She sat there the whole day. The next day she rang and said, so many loud young girls are coming here, what is happening? I answered, this is a dance school, the Wigman School. "What's that?" I answered, it's a school where one can learn to dance. "Does it cost anything?" No, I said, it doesn't cost anything. "Then I'll stay." And one day she was gone again. Such things happened again and again. And things kept changing. Extremely talented former students came as well, they taught us for a day or two, and then they were gone again.[4]

One would not think that much learning could take place under such conditions. But according to the half-dozen students from this period who gathered at the Academy of Arts in 1986, this was not the case. Isa Partsch-Bergsohn, yet another student from the 1943–1944 class at the conservatory who then studied at the impromptu Wigman school, summarized the general feeling among students from this time:

> During this period Mary taught with a special intensity and care, for teaching was her only artistic expression. She no longer had other opportunities to perform. She was so concentrated and centered. . . . I mean that with all the difficulties [of the last years of the war], this small group of students was very happy to have Mary as a teacher. We sensed this very strongly.[5]

In 1945–1946 the functioning of the school normalized. The Russian authorities in Leipzig granted official permission to reopen (as if the school ever had been closed!), and now students consistently attended class, paid tuition, and were divided into elementary, intermediate, and advanced levels.[6] The stabilization of the school gave Wigman the resource she needed to resume her choreographic career, namely, a group of trained students. In July 1946 she prepared new choreography for a student recital, and the following spring she staged Gluck's *Orpheus and Eurydice* at the Leipzig Municipal Opera for an ensemble that combined her students with opera-house dancers. This division between student recitals and opera-house commissions became characteristic of her choreographic production in the postwar period.

From the end of the war in May 1945 until the formalization of the political division between Soviet and Allied zones of occupation four years later, German theatrical life was in great flux. The bureaucracy of the Cultural Ministry no longer existed, and no successor or alternative had been formed at the national level. Thus it fell to municipal authorities to rebuild and restaff the many theaters and theater schools that had been destroyed during the war. During this period Mary Wigman entertained several offers of support. The director responsible for rebuilding Leipzig's Conservatory for Music and Dramatic Art offered to reemploy her as a fulltime teacher.[7] And the former producing director at the Leipzig Municipal Opera, who had taken up the same post in Wiesbaden, offered her a steady position there.[8]

In the end she took up an invitation from the mayor of Wilmersdorf, a suburb in the western sector of Berlin, to relocate her school in his jurisdiction. The positive draw was the promise of subsidy, for it was difficult to support a private dance school from student tuition alone. The negative push was the decision made by the new authorities of the German Democratic Republic to nationalize her school as of 1 May 1949. A month later Mary Wigman moved to West Berlin.[9]

During the four years in Leipzig following the war, Wigman had been contacted by artists and politicians committed to socialism, who invited her support for their cultural policy. She responded positively, and this interlude again raises the issue of the relationship between her art and the politics of the time. In December 1947 Wigman served as a delegate to the First German People's Congress for Unity and Peace in the Soviet Sector.[10] One month later she made a radio broadcast explicitly in support of German unity and implicitly in support of the position taken by the Socialist Unity party, the party that soon would govern the German Democratic Republic. She stated:

> For me, this is not a matter of politics—and certainly not party politics—I myself belong to no party. For me, this is a matter of the heart, of faith, of human and artistic conviction, of the deepest inner necessity of life. I love my homeland more than I can say in words. . . . And my homeland is not just the city, the region, the place where I live and work. All of Germany has become my homeland. . . . I love Germany and I suffer for Germany. . . . We want to determine our own fate! But we can realize our fate only as a common German fate, not as a fate divided among zones. I would like to be able and to be permitted to ask: Do not tear apart our land, which we love above all else![11]

How is one to interpret Wigman's actions in the Soviet zone? To American officials in 1948, her participation in the People's Congress branded her a "Communist," and they denied her application for a visa to visit the United States that year.[12] To her biographer Hedwig Müller, her radio talk evidences how once again she could not fathom the larger political consequences of her actions, how once again her determination "to serve her homeland, not a party" made her vulnerable to political manipulation.[13] In Müller's narrative, Wigman's devotion to her country runs parallel to her devotion to her art. And just as she was willing to accept subsidy from cultural bureaucrats irrespective of their political affiliation, so she was willing to proclaim the cause of a greater Germany, whatever party her voice supported, be it the National Socialist party or the Socialist Unity party.

From one perspective, Müller's assessment of Wigman's political involvements is apt. But from another perspective, the parallel Müller sets up between Wigman's entanglements with fascism and communism is misleading. For the choreographer did vote with her feet when the Communists came to power in a way that she did not when the Nazis came to power. Moreover, she never received patronage from a communist state, and her flirtation with the Socialist Unity party never marked her work as did her cohabitation with the National Socialist party. Perhaps, as Müller suggests, this was because she had learned her lesson about tangling with totalitarian regimes.[14]

Moving to West Berlin, Wigman intended to reestablish her school as it had existed in Dresden before 1933—as a private institution partially subsidized by municipal funds that functioned as a national center for training dancers. However, this never came to pass. Within a year Wigman lost her municipal subsidy, and her codirector, Marianne Vogelsang, a student of Gret Palucca, left to open a competing school in the eastern sector of Berlin.[15] Although a steady stream of American students helped finance the school, it led a precarious existence until its closing in 1967. Wigman's name no longer commanded the public recognition it had during the Weimar years, when she had relied on the renown of her performances to attract students. As Helmut Gottschild, a student from 1958 to 1962 and then a teacher at the Berlin school, recalled: "It happened so often that when I told people that I studied with Mary Wigman, they would ask, 'So she's still alive?' She was forgotten."[16]

In general, students from the Berlin period acknowledge conflict with their mentor more willingly than do their predecessors from Dresden and Leipzig. Not that students earlier had not experienced conflict and felt the need to strike out on their own. But although in retrospect students from Dresden and Leipzig occasionally admit their need for independence, they rarely admit overt tension with their mentor. Indeed, as discussed earlier, Wigman's prewar students see no contradiction between their continued allegiance to their mentor's authority and their own self-realization. For students after the war this was not necessarily the case. Often they tell a story of rebelling against Wigman while at the Berlin school and only afterward discovering how much she had taught them.

At the 1986 gathering of former Wigman students, Helmut Gottschild gave his account of rebellion and rediscovery. When he arrived at the Wigman School in 1958, he sensed an institution in decline. Now in her seventies, Wigman no longer possessed the strength and energy that had animated her teaching earlier. Generational conflict and the larger culture's indifference, if not hostility, to *Ausdruckstanz* also contributed to his impression of the school's stagnation. As he explained:

> We grew up in the years after the war or even during the war, and we had learned to mistrust big words. . . . We were the first generation to come to consciousness after the war. The first generation to ask our parents how it could have happened. And suddenly we were confronted with Mary Wigman's pathos. . . . Some of us could go along. But many of us—and I would have to say the more aware among us—could not go along. . . . This was the time of hunger or that was just past, we became established again, we rebuilt our apartments and were interested in refrigerators and we repressed much that was connected with the Third Reich. Meanwhile we heard that at least the pathos of Wigman's rhetoric was quite similar to . . . the pathos that had led us to the Third Reich. . . . On the one hand, the classical ballet had made a strong come-back, but we didn't want that, and we were too old [to acquire ballet technique]—most of us had started dancing later. On the other side, there was Mary Wigman with her words and her dance that appeared somewhat antiquated, at least superficially. Now when one later slowly mined the experience . . . much of great value came out, but in the first moment it appeared antiquated to us. We did not know where we belonged. So we went out and we said, we will now make a new dance.[17]

For Gottschild, Merce Cunningham's 1960 appearance in Berlin was a revelation, and two years later he joined with two other Wigman students—Brigitta Herrmann and Inge Katharine Sehnert—to found a dance group dedicated to a less expressive and cooler movement style, called Gruppe Motion.

Inge Katharine Sehnert, who studied at the Wigman School from 1955 to 1959 and from 1961 to 1963, also remembers the generational conflict, not only between mentor and students but also between students. As she recalls:

> When I came to the Wigman School in 1955, it was still in its late expressionist phase. The students . . . were of two types, those who were flipped out and those who were somewhat more normal. At first I had contact mostly with the flipped-out ones—black eyes, pale complexion, long hair in a pony tail, black leotard with high necks and long sleeves, long black skirt, tights. . . . Everything a bit gloomy, everything very expressive, with corresponding personal attitudes, from lightly neurotic to hysterical. . . . Suddenly, there was a revolution in outer appearance. We all cut our hair. We no longer wore

skirts, simply tights, and we wanted to see the body, see what actually happens under the skirt and how the legs can work, how they were visually formed and what they could do.[18]

This fascination with the functioning of the body motivated Gottschild and Sehnert to found Gruppe Motion in 1962.

The reminiscences of Susanne Linke, who studied at the school from 1964 to 1967, strike a somewhat different note. She too felt the need for a more rigorous training, and after the school closed, she transferred to the Folkwang School in Essen, where she could study ballet as well as modern dance. But, unlike Gottschild and Sehnert, she did not feel the need to distance herself from her mentor while at the Wigman School. She had been inspired to dance by the performances of Dore Hoyer, who had trained with Palucca and performed with Wigman, and the body awareness that she so admired in Hoyer she also saw embodied by Wigman. As she recalled:

> Mary . . . was the ideal of expressionism. When she would stand there . . . her expressivity was unbelievable, she was also so clear technically. Pure physicality, in every fiber of her body. That's what I found wonderful about Mary. I mean, she was an old woman, she could hardly stand, biologically she had died five times. . . . But even with her broken body, how perceptive she was with her water-blue eyes. . . . She once gave me a correction that I still remember twenty years later.[19]

Reconstructing Hoyer's *Affectos Humanos,* Linke has fashioned an *Ausdruckstanz* for contemporary audiences (see figs. 55 and 56).

The disaffection voiced by Gottschild and Sehnert, and to a lesser extent by Linke, point toward larger transformations that rendered the Wigman School marginal to the development of West German dance during the fifties and sixties. Once the municipal theater system was rebuilt, it favored the genre of ballet over *Ausdruckstanz.* Exponents of *Ausdruckstanz* found it difficult to command an audience for their performances. Even Dore Hoyer, widely considered the most talented soloist of her generation, had to rely increasingly on engagements in South America to support her art.[20] Although some dancers who had trained with Wigman successfully made the transition to opera-house ballet, many did not. And those who could not also found it difficult to support themselves by teaching amateurs interested in *Tanz-Gymnastik,* an important source of income for their predecessors between the wars. It appeared that *Ausdruckstanz* had lost its public and its patronage.[21]

These changes affected not only Wigman's students but also her own choreographic production during the postwar period. The precarious existence of the Berlin school ruled out the possibility of an affiliated company such as her Dresden troupe. However, student recitals remained an option, as did opera-house commissions, and her choreographic production between 1950 and 1961 was divided between these two formats. In the early fifties she concentrated her energies on student recitals, and then from 1954 to 1961 she received a series of opera-house commissions that consumed her choreographic efforts and precluded further student productions. However, only one of her opera-house commissions allowed her to stage a purely choreographic work, Stravinsky's *Le sacre du printemps.* The remaining commissions were to stage operas by Gluck, Handel, and Orff. In the era of the ballet boom it was not permissible to dance without music.

In January 1953 Wigman and her students premiered *Choric Studies II* (*Chorische Studien II*) at the Hebbel Theater in West Berlin. The choreographer had not intended to perform herself but had planned for Dore Hoyer to take the solo role. But when Hoyer canceled the engagement, Wigman herself took the role, more than a decade after her announced retirement from the stage.[22] Like *Celebration* (1928) and *Women's Dances* (1934), *Choric Studies II* dramatized the choreographer's relation to her dance group and narrated a retrospective account of her career. In contrast to her earlier works, however, *Choric Studies II* no longer presented Wigman as the mentor who enabled her followers' self-realization, or even as the charismatic leader who overshadowed her anonymous followers. Rather, the work framed the choreographer as an outsider, a survivor from another time. Just as her students now sensed a gulf between their teacher and themselves, so too did she.

Contemporary music composed by Ulrich Kessler and J. D. Link accompanies the action, which divides into four sections. In the first section, *Prophetess* (*Die Seherin*), Wigman appears as the title figure, and twenty students join together as a chorus. As she described her role: "Costumed in a blue-gray robe, I sat in the lap of a large, black, fateful figure . . . and slowly became conscious of a

Fig. 55. Dore Hoyer in her 1962 cycle *Affectos Humanos* (courtesy of the Deutsches Tanzarchiv)

Fig. 56.   Susanne Linke in her 1987 reconstruction of Dore Hoyer's *Affectos Humanos* (courtesy of Gert Weigelt)

Fig. 57. Mary Wigman and a member of her dance group in *Prophetess*, from the 1953 work *Choric Studies II* (courtesy of the Mary Wigman Archive)

premonition of disaster. The two halves of the chorus reacted in the background and gradually came together as one chorus in order to answer the repeated call with a definitive refusal."[23] A photograph (fig. 57) shows Wigman held by the "fateful figure" looming behind her, her body slumped almost lifeless, her weight yielding to the black-cloaked figure's support. No longer in possession of the physical strength that animated her earlier performances, the choreographer externalizes the principle of fate that her earlier performances had internalized and literally embodied. She appears as a prophetess overwhelmed by the disaster of her own visions, as the victim of the looming figure, not as the challenger of fate.

How did contemporary spectators interpret the action? Reviews confirm my own interpretation of Wigman's retrospective choreographic notes: that the fate against which Wigman stands powerless symbolizes her own and her nation's experience of the previous two decades. As one reviewer remarks, "Through an architectural use of the body, Wigman's symbolic style grasps the course of the difficult years."[24] And as Mary's sister Elisabeth wrote to their brother Heinrich: "[The work] is *the* theme of her last years: war, destruction, rebuilding."[25]

Wigman's retrospective choreographic notes describe the second section, *The Temple* (*Der Tempel*): "[an] architecture built by living people. Form of a pyramid in strong and severe rhythm and the crashing down of the sacred building."[26] Is the "sacred building" Wigman's utopian vision of the twenties that came "crashing down" in the thirties? Or is the "temple" a unified Germany that fragmented in the postwar period?

The third section, *Tears of the Nameless* (*Tränen der Namenlosen*), features the dancing of Manja Chmièl, who performed a solo lament for the lost, according to one reviewer.[27] (Inexplicably, Wigman's retrospective choreographic notes omit this section.)[28] The final section, *The Street* (*Die Strasse*), continues the motif of human architecture from *The Temple*. Wigman's choreographic notes describe the architectural formation of bodies: "The street, which was more [like] the crossing of three streets, was again built by people in an architectural form, vertical lines, like the facades of houses or walls, and there were six girls and six boys walking, dancing in this architecture, [while] the walls reacted to the mood and the movement of the living people."[29]

The Street further divides into five subsections. The titles of the first four—*Twilight* (*Zwielicht*), *Resounding Steps* (*Dröhnende Schritte*), *Danger* (*Gefahr*), and *Ghostly Darkness* (*Gespenstisches Dunkel*)—evoke images of a threatening urban environment. One reviewer describes the action: "A part of the group allegorized the houses along a street. The people within danced the tragedy of the last decades: playful frivolity, false heroism, death and ruin, devastation."[30] Does "the street" represent the postwar years as an anti-utopia, when the rebuilding of Germany substituted alienation for the unified "temple" of the prewar years? Or does the coming and going of the student dancers represent Wigman's own failed efforts to revive her utopian vision?

The final subsection of *The Street* is titled *Way* (*Weg*)—a title that alludes to an earlier group work—and reintroduces the choreographer as soloist.[31] Thus Wigman's appearances frame the cycle as a whole. Having seen disaster and found no response, she returns to "[help] first the dead-tired people out of their resignation and then [retire] into the background, and so [pass] the leadership to the young ones."[32] The ending reasserts the value of her vision: although she cannot prevent the "crashing down" of the "temple," she perhaps can show "the way" beyond "resignation." In my reading of her choreographic notes she distances her utopian vision from the antiutopia of the alienated present as well as from the dystopia of the Nazi past.

During the postwar years, Wigman never confronted the relation between her utopian vision and the dystopia of the Third Reich either in her work or in her life. Although she spoke rarely about the Nazi period,[33] when she did, her comments denied any possible relation between her own actions and the policy of the Cultural Ministry, a position contradicted by the historical record. In a speech made in 1949 she stated:

> The cultural dictatorship of the Third Reich kept German creativity bogged down as if by a rock around the German neck; it particularly crippled the German dance. I cannot resist recalling the slogan of that time, a slogan which determined the end of the development of dance in Middle Europe: "*Schmissiges Ballett und zackige Erotik*" ("Dashing ballet and bold eroticism"). It is hardly necessary to com-

ment on it. In these words are expressed the finality of misunderstanding of dance. In them are the utmost . . . contempt of the ethical and spiritual values we truly find in dance. By negation of its spiritual and moral content, dance was debased to the level on which it could function, if at all, purely as entertainment.[34]

During the Third Reich, Wigman did take exception to many aspects of the aesthetic promulgated by the Cultural Ministry. However, she also lent her tacit support to Nazi cultural policy by publishing *Deutsche Tanzkunst* in 1935; accepting commissions to choreograph *Women's Dances, Hymnic Dances,* and *Olympic Youth*; and altering her school curriculum in accord with official directives. After the war her public pronouncements focused only on her aesthetic disagreements with the Cultural Ministry, forgetting to mention her gestures of conformity.

In 1957 Wigman was commissioned by the Berlin Municipal Opera to choreograph Stravinsky's *Le sacre du printemps* (*The Rite of Spring*) as part of an annual festival of the performing arts. Funded by the western sector of the city, though open to residents in the eastern sector before the building of the Wall, the festival promoted West Berlin as a *Kulturstadt* (cultural center) devoted to artistic experimentation of the kind banned under National Socialism and banned in the Soviet bloc.[35] Surveying the 1957 festival—from musical premieres by Pierre Boulez and Hans Werner Henze to plays by Samuel Beckett and Eugène Ionesco to the revival of Kurt Weill's 1932 opera *Die Bürgschaft*—the critic from the *New York Times* concluded that "this year's festival has proven conclusively that the lively Berlin tradition of the Weimar Republic days and earlier was not killed by the Nazis; it was only interrupted."[36] This was exactly the message that the organizers of the festival intended to convey.

The premise of the festival—that the postwar avant-garde had picked up where Weimar modernism had left off—also informed Wigman's staging of *Le sacre du printemps*. Reviewers assumed a continuity between *Ausdruckstanz* during the twenties and the 1957 production, unaware of how much Wigman's working conditions had changed and consequently unaware of how much her representational strategies had changed. Her choreographic notes parallel the reviewers' implicit bracketing of the Nazi years. Like her notes for *Choric Studies II*, her scenario for *Le sacre du printemps* reveals the choreographer's self-mythologization as the survivor, the victim of fate.

In contrast to the 1953 work, Wigman herself did not appear onstage, and so the roles of survivor and victim were split between other female dancers. Dore Hoyer took the role of the fated victim, the chosen maiden (*die Erwählte*) who sacrifices herself for the community, and Lilo Herbeth took the role of the survivor, a Mother Figure (*Mütterliche Gestalt*) who mentors the maiden.[37] In the original scenario an older woman and older man frame the first half of the work, but it is the male elders who witness the virgin's self-sacrifice. In Wigman's scenario the Mother Figure is joined by two priestesses, and the three older women remain with the virgin throughout her sacrificial ritual.[38] In her scenario the older women prepare the virgin for her sacrifice and imbue her with a sense of the holiness, indeed the heroism, of her mission:

> Filled with belief in the magical powers of pure virginal self-sacrifice, the Chosen One loses herself in the ecstasy of the sacrificial dance, as she sheds her blood and thereby effects the renewed blessing of the earth for her tribe. She knows her destiny. For on long winter evenings she was initiated into the ritual secrets by the female elders [*Mütter*], who gave her instruction in suffering and endurance, in self-absorption and self-illumination. They will stand by her through the last and most difficult moments of self-transcendence and self-divestment.[39]

One photograph (fig. 58) shows the Mother Figure and the two priestesses standing behind the maiden as she bends over, her body bound by a rope. (To initiate the ritual action, the community had wrapped her thus.) The Mother Figure turns toward the maiden, as if supporting her in this crucial moment, while the two priestesses turn away, as if petitioning supernatural powers for support. Another photograph (fig. 59) shows the Mother Figure and two priestesses joining the circle of other celebrants around the virgin, raised aloft by bare-chested men. I read the female elders as Wigman-the-survivor and Dore Hoyer as her younger self, who had sacrificed herself for the greater good of her art and her nation and who had become the victim of fate. In my reading, the choreographer's rescripting of Stravinsky's scenario supports her self-mythologization in the postwar period.

Strikingly, reviewers did not comment on the addition of the female elders to the scenario. Rather, they commented on the in-

Fig. 58.   Dore Hoyer and members of the Berlin Municipal Opera in Mary Wigman's 1957 staging of *Le sacre du printemps* (courtesy of the Dance Collection, New
York Public Library for the Performing Arts, Astor, Lenox and Tilden Foundations)

tensity of Hoyer's performance, on the "spatial language" (*Raum-
sprache*) of Wigman's choric formations, on the visualization of the
complex rhythms of Stravinsky's score, and on Wilhelm Reinking's
design that rejected references to pagan Russia in favor of an abstract stage world. The dancers wore simply cut garments associated with no cultural or historical period and performed on a
raked oval platform against a curtained backdrop.

Wigman's choreography exploited the raked platform, setting
endless variations on circular patterns. Photographs and her notational drawings show the dancers huddled in a central mass and
then separating into single and double circles; the group clustering
around the Mother Figure in a whirling mass and the mass then
breaking apart into spinning flanks of young women and young
men; dancers moving along arched pathways in counterpoint to
stationary formations of dancers; the group clustering around the
male sage and holding him aloft.[40] As Horst Koegler remarked:
"There are formations . . . that would make an architect proud.

Fig. 59. Dore Hoyer and members of the Berlin Municipal Opera in Mary Wigman's 1957 staging of *Le sacre du printemps* (courtesy of the Dance Collection, New York Public Library for the Performing Arts, Astor, Lenox and Tilden Foundations)

The structure provides a formal analysis of Stravinsky's score with a clarity not seen before."[41]

In general, the reviewers praised Wigman for successfully staging a work that had stymied so many ballet choreographers. Again Horst Koegler: "Mary Wigman's attempt at a scenic realization belongs among the two or three even discussable stagings that this score has ever had."[42] Passionate advocates of ballet, Koegler and his colleagues were less concerned with the scripting of gender than with international standards and universality. Thus they overlooked the unprecedented appearance of the female elders in Wigman's scenario and focused instead on her choreographic ability to meet the demands of the ballet stage. As another reviewer remarked:

> The means of classical ballet . . . do not correspond to the wild spirit of . . . this score. Can the naturalness, the spontaneity, the expressive

power of *Ausdruckstanz* do it justice? . . . The paradoxical question remains: is it even possible to dance . . . the most important ballet score of our epoch? What is possible Mary Wigman has done: she has solved a problem that until now found no resolution, and won an unexpected victory for *Ausdruckstanz*.[43]

In reconstructing Wigman's *Le sacre du printemps*, the dissonance between her scenario and the reviews is telling. From her perspective, the invitation to stage *Le sacre du printemps* offered her an opportunity to restate the themes that had preoccupied her between the wars: the nature of cultic festival, the association between leadership and sacrifice, the heroism of Woman, the relation between the individual body and the collective body. Since few of her critics in the fifties had seen her group dances in the twenties and early thirties, they viewed her staging of *Le sacre du printemps* not in the context of her career but rather in the context of the ballet boom. Yet however much her reviewers' perspective diverged from Wigman's own, they conspired in her self-mythologization during the postwar period, imagining the continuity of her work between the Weimar period and the mid-fifties.

As noted before, Hedwig Müller also stresses the continuities rather than the discontinuities marking Wigman's choreographic career, and her analysis of *Le sacre du printemps* is no exception. She sees the production as a realization of the "central theme of Wigman's entire oeuvre: to sacrifice oneself in service to a suprapersonal ideal."[44] This view overlooks how Wigman's changed working environment had subtly transformed her "central theme." In works from the twenties and thirties she had conflated her sacrifice with charismatic leadership. But in the fifties she conflated her sacrifice with her victimization. Not only had her "central theme" shifted but so too had her form of absolute dance. Rather than collaborate with a composer as she had through the twenties and thirties, she worked from a preexistent musical score and with its preexistent associations. Rather than improvise with dancers she had trained herself, she adapted a familiar scenario and worked with ballet-trained dancers, adapting her techniques to their abilities. My reconstructions of *Le sacre du printemps* and of her earlier works make the same point: that ideology, form, and context exist in a complicated interplay and must be examined in tandem.

Perhaps the most obvious discontinuity between the interwar and postwar periods was Wigman's involvement with opera productions. In 1921 she had staged an opera by Hans Pfitzner, *The Rose in the Garden of Love* (*Die Rose vom Liebesgarten*), but once she had trained and developed her dance group, she lost interest in opera-house commissions. But during the war and after, Wigman no longer could command or finance a professional dance ensemble, and so she came to rely on opera-house commissions as a choreographic outlet. From 1943 to 1961 opera productions constitute most of the entries on her choreochronicle: Carl Orff's *Carmina Burana* (Leipzig, 1943) and *Catulli Carmina/Carmina Burana* (Mannheim, 1955); Handel's *Saul* (Mannheim, 1954); and Gluck's *Alcestis* (Mannheim, 1958) and *Orpheus and Eurydice* (Leipzig, 1947, and Berlin, 1961).[45]

Just months after the building of the Berlin Wall in 1961, Wigman ended her choreographic career staging the same work in which she had made her first stage appearance almost forty years earlier as a student at Hellerau—Gluck's *Orpheus and Eurydice*. Although she did not choreograph after 1961, Wigman continued to teach until 1967. Finally, at age eighty, she closed her school, and six years later she died, on 18 September 1973.

In the November 1973 issue of *Theater Heute* Horst Koegler reflected on Wigman's career. Significantly, his article acknowledged the alliance between *Ausdruckstanz* and fascism. Just one year before, he had broken the taboo within the dance world against public discussion of dance in the Third Reich, and his appreciation of Wigman's career restated the thesis that underlay his just-published research: that *Ausdruckstanz* had reached a point of exhaustion before 1933 and thus had no alternative except to "conform compliantly to the Nazi ideology of blood and soil with its dream of a new festival culture."[46] In other words, National Socialism killed what was already half-dead, and thus no revival was possible after 1945.

When Koegler turned to the question of Wigman's legacy, he downplayed the influence of *Ausdruckstanz* on American modern dance and highlighted its influence on modern ballet. Like most American critics writing at the time, he believed that *Ausdruckstanz* exerted only a "minimal" influence on its American counterpart, "an independent American form, which arose from American thinking on American ground."[47] Koegler believed that *Ausdruckstanz* had exerted a more substantial influence on contemporary German ballet. As authority for this view, he cited Mary Wigman, who had spoken on the subject the year before on a radio interview with Koegler. His appreciation concluded with an extended quotation from that interview, when Wigman had stated:

> I find that, in its final effect, the German *Ausdruckstanz* has fulfilled its task by pushing something that was a bit tired, dusty, and petrified, namely the German ballet. There the modern dancer has done a marvelous job in cleaning the ballet from its dust, giving it new ideas. For, in principle, the classical ballet is the traditional dance, the traditional European dance. It was here before, strongly anchored, it became a bit tired and needed some fresh blood. This it did receive and quite a bit of it through the German *Ausdruckstanz*. I assure you, we can no longer speak of a classical ballet. The classical has gone. Everything has become modern ballet.[48]

The same autumn that Horst Koegler penned his obituary for Mary Wigman, Pina Bausch assumed the position of resident choreographer at the Wuppertal municipal theater. As *Tanztheater* came into its own over the next two decades, its critical advocates would rewrite the history of German dance in quite different terms.

DANCE IN DIVIDED GERMANY, 1973–1989

In 1975 Pina Bausch premiered her version of Stravinsky's *Le sacre du printemps* at Wuppertal, and a comparison with Wigman's version from 1957 illuminates the relations between *Ausdruckstanz* and *Tanztheater*. Staging *Le sacre du printemps*, Wigman had come to terms with the ballet boom that otherwise rendered her choreography marginal. Staging *Le sacre du printemps*, Bausch signaled her determination to move beyond the ballet boom.

Like Wigman's, Bausch's production was based on the original scenario. Whether Bausch intended the parallel or not remains unclear. However, that a parallel exists becomes evident when one considers the stage history of *Le sacre du printemps*, for the three productions that immediately preceded Bausch's on the West German stage—by Erich Walter in 1970, John Neumeier in 1972, and Glen Tetley in 1974—all had radically departed from the original scenario. In Walter's production, the men appeared to gang-rape the Chosen One at the end. In Neumeier's, a male solo of breakdown preceded the ending female solo of breakdown. And in Tetley's, a young man took the role of the Chosen One and evoked an association with Christ.[49]

Departing from her male predecessors, Bausch reinterpreted the original scenario, and in so doing, her approach recalled Wigman's precedent. The program for Bausch's production noted:

> Here one sees the original libretto as if viewed from afar: the adoration of the earth, the veneration of the forces of nature, the glorification of life at the beginning of spring; the group which needs, searches, and finds its sacrificial victim; the anxiety over who will be the sacrificial victim; the fear of the sacrificial victim in the face of death; the power that radiates from the executor of the group will (the oldest or the wise one or the chief); the relentlessness of the group that is damned to sacrifice in order to live; and then the breaking out of the forces of nature within us and around us (the spring); and not least the purpose that the living give to the sacrificial victim and that the sacrificial victim gives to those who survive.[50]

Just as Bausch's recall of Wigman's precedent may have been witting or unwitting, so too was her departure from her female predecessor. Whether intentionally or not, the 1975 production rejected the transcendent tone that reviewers had noted in 1957. In the earlier version Dore Hoyer had not seemed to sacrifice herself in vain. Rather, her ritual death seemed to serve the greater good of the onstage community, and with this awareness the community supported and witnessed her dance of death. In contrast, in Bausch's production it is not clear until near the end which dancer will take the role of the sacrificial victim. And when Marlis Alt finally assumes this role, she seems to enact a purposeless death. Despite the rhetoric of purpose in Bausch's program note, the production undermines the legitimacy of such social rituals. In my viewing of the work in performance and on video, the "as if" of the program note sets the frame for interpretation: "The original libretto as if viewed from afar"—and when so viewed, the social ritual that frames the woman as victim becomes shockingly clear.[51]

Rejecting the elevated tone of Wigman's staging, Bausch's production also rejects the essentialism that informed her predecessor's vision. Wigman's *Le sacre du printemps* never questioned that the female elders and Dore Hoyer represented Woman and that Woman represented endurance and self-sacrifice. In contrast, Bausch's *Le sacre du printemps* questions why a woman invariably

Fig. 60.   Wuppertal Tanztheater in Pina Bausch's 1975 staging of *Le sacre du printemps* (courtesy of Gert Weigelt)

serves as a victim of social violence. The formal device of repetition makes this point. Near the beginning one of the women lies face down in the dirt that covers the stage floor, on top of a piece of red cloth that the subsequent action will reveal as the dress in which the sacrificial victim performs the dance of death. Later the male leader of the group performs the same action (fig. 60), but his gender inflects the gesture with an aura of authority rather than an aura of vulnerability. For soon after, he dresses one of the women in the dress, and she, like an automaton, proceeds to dance herself to exhaustion and a metaphorical death (fig. 61).[52]

Bausch's *Le sacre du printemps* marked a point of transition in her career and anticipated motifs in her later works: the disintegration of social life into primitive violence; the interchangeability of victims; and the power play implicit in the action of one performer undressing and dressing another. Later works interrelate these motifs in powerful stage images. For example, near the beginning of *Bluebeard* (*Blaubart*, 1977) a woman lies on her back, clutching a man whose head rests on her stomach, and drags the two of them

Fig. 61.   Marlis Alt and members of the Wuppertal Tanztheater in Pina Bausch's 1975 staging of *Le sacre du printemps* (courtesy of Gert Weigelt)

across the floor strewn with dead leaves. Near the end the man reverses the action and drags the woman across the floor, her body rigidly bloated by layers of dresses. In *1980* one woman has a row of men drop their drawers, exposing their buttocks to the audience, while she walks in front of them inspecting their genitals. Later the women line up, and a man walks down the line inspecting the jiggle in their breasts. In *On the Mountain a Cry Was Heard (Auf dem Gebirge hat man ein Geschrei gehört*, 1984), a woman repeatedly lies down on the floor in front of a man, pulling her skirt up over her head so that he can draw a red *X* on her bare back. But even when he stops marking her back, she continues to prostrate herself before him.[53]

As these stage images make clear, Bausch's *Tanztheater* stresses the social construction of gender. Female performers alternately cross-dress and play Woman, and in so doing they undo the essentialism that underlies *Ausdruckstanz*. Men too alternately cross-dress and play Man, yet their performance of gender functions differently than that of the female performers. For their parodies of Woman and Macho always threaten women onstage. Even when playing Woman, the men still possess a physical strength that they may choose to unleash on women. Bausch draws the attention of the spectator to this physical asymmetry, a sign of the imbalance of power between men and women in society at large.

Although gender is Bausch's overt subject, I often wonder if history is not her covert subject. She often sets her works in an indeterminate period that evokes the thirties as well as the fifties. Snatches of popular song from mid-century, spiked heels and satin evening gowns for the women, tuxedos and business suits for the men—do the dancers represent the generation of Bausch's parents, the generation that lived through the Nazi period? If so, then this generation provides a clear referent for the role-playing in Bausch's work, the apparent interchangeability of victim and victimizer that actually masks an asymmetry of power. For was it not the previous generation, the generation of Mary Wigman, that had confused the roles of victim and victimizer, believing themselves victims of the Nazis and denying their complicity in the victimization of Jews and other outsiders?

I also see a historical reference in the way that Bausch's dancers consume the material resources of the opera-house stage. By the end of most productions the stage is littered with debris—costumes discarded by the performers, objects that they have used and then thrown aside—all mixed with the floor coverings that are a Bausch signature—leaves, dirt, water, grass. Her works epitomize the gross consumption of postindustrial society. Is this a way of rejecting or reinforcing the materialism of the postwar decades?

In the Federal Republic the critical reception of Bausch's works has divided along generational lines. Although Horst Koegler and many of his generation admire Bausch's talent, their respect does not approach the passionate response accorded her works by their younger German colleagues—Jochen Schmidt, Norbert Servos, Hedwig Müller, Claudia Jeschke, Susanne Schlicher. Not that the younger critics avoid negative criticism of Bausch altogether, but their criticism never challenges the social and aesthetic ideals of *Tanztheater*. In effect, their writing functions as critical advocacy for the practice of *Tanztheater*. It is my contention that the critical debate among dance critics implies a debate over the interpretation of the German past. In the remainder of this chapter, I first follow the contest through the historiography of *Tanztheater* and then enter the debate, aware of my position as an outsider.[54]

Constructing a German tradition for *Tanztheater*, its critical advocates emphasize both its direct connections to and family resemblances with *Ausdruckstanz*. The teaching of survivors figures prominently in the historiography: Susanne Linke and Gerhard Bohner studied with Mary Wigman in West Berlin, Pina Bausch and Reinhild Hoffmann studied with Kurt Jooss at the Folkwang School, which Jooss had rebuilt after his return from exile in 1949. Jooss's student Hans Züllig taught both Hoffmann and Susanne Linke at the Folkwang School. The historiography of *Tanztheater* also emphasizes its formal similarities to *Ausdruckstanz*: the predominance of female choreographers, attention to the scripting of gender, the revival of solo dancing, the return to improvisation, the reappearance of the "mask," social consciousness. After all, it was Kurt Jooss who first coined the term *Tanztheater* to differentiate his oppositional works such as *The Green Table* from *Theatertanz,* or the more usual variety of opera-house ballet.[55]

The continuity between *Ausdruckstanz* and *Tanztheater* that Norbert Servos theorizes as a return to "the language of the body" other writers (Jochen Schmidt, Claudia Jeschke, Susanne Schlicher) contextualize within the ethos of the late sixties. Disgruntled with the hierarchy of ballet companies, committed to collective decision making, demanding social and political relevance—proponents of *Tanztheater* pursued collaborative means for choreography and management, rediscovered improvisation as a working method, and exploited techniques for agitprop. Responding to the rediscovery of Brecht and Artaud, the influence of Grotowski and the Living Theatre, the parallel development of *Regietheater* (directors' theater) by Peter Stein and others—proponents of *Tanztheater* combined text and image and blurred the boundaries between what had been considered "dance" and "theater." Reacting against the neoclassicism of official culture in the fifties and its embrace of the internationalized vocabulary of ballet, proponents of *Tanztheater* sought German precedents for their rebellion. In so doing, they challenged the previous generation's denial of the German past and attempted to understand that past differently.

Unlike Mary Wigman, who never seemed consciously to confront the connection between *Ausdruckstanz* and Nazi culture, the critical advocates of *Tanztheater* acknowledge this connection. In so doing, they build on the research first undertaken by Horst Koegler, although they radically revise Koegler's view of relations between *Ausdruckstanz* and fascism. In contrast to Koegler, who viewed the *Ausdruckstanz* impulse as exhausted before 1933, critical advocates of *Tanztheater* see *Ausdruckstanz* as still viable at the end of the Weimar Republic. According to Koegler, the National Socialists imposed their vision of German Dance on the dancers who had lost their own sense of mission. According to the critical advocates of *Tanztheater*, the National Socialists exploited the protofascist tendencies within *Ausdruckstanz* and thus deformed the movement. From their viewpoint, *Tanztheater* recovered those dimensions of *Ausdruckstanz* that remained resistant to National Socialist appropriation.

Further, the critical advocates of *Tanztheater* view the Third Reich as not the only interruption between Weimar and an authentic postwar culture. Rather they posit a double interruption, the Third Reich *and* the Adenauer era, the period from 1949 to 1963, when Konrad Adenauer served as chancellor of West Germany. In retrospect, they associate those years with the consumerism that supported the West German "economic miracle," the "Americanization" of daily life, and the spirit of "Restoration" and "classicism" in the arts. They view with suspicion the ballet boom of the Adenauer years, which Horst Koegler hailed as the legitimate successor to *Ausdruckstanz*. According to their view, it was only by rejecting both Nazi culture *and* the culture of the Adenauer years that German artists could reconnect to Weimar modernism. With subtle variations this narrative informs the overviews of *Tanztheater* penned by Jochen Schmidt and Claudia Jeschke.

In his 1983 overview of *Tanztheater*, Jochen Schmidt equivocates when acknowledging the entanglement between *Ausdruckstanz* and Nazi culture. He prefers to explain the rejection of *Ausdruckstanz* in terms of the Zeitgeist, not in terms of politics. He writes:

> The fact that after 1945 German dancers and choreographers refused to return to . . . *Ausdruckstanz*, . . . the only important (and, cum grano salis, politically "clean") tradition in the German dance, is one of the curious phenomena in the history of ballet. . . . Quite obviously *Ausdruckstanz* was, after 1945, not what the West Germans wanted. Perhaps to a generation rebuilding a new world from the ruins it seemed too heavy, too oppressive, too close to the ground, even too realistic in its form of expression and possibilities. They wanted something lighter, the art of the *danse d'école*, aspiring to heaven, defying gravity.[56]

In contrast to Horst Koegler, who celebrates the German domestication of the *danse d'école*, Schmidt deflates the "German ballet miracle." In particular, he undercuts the achievement of the Stuttgart Ballet under John Cranko, whose leadership of the company from 1961 to 1973 established its international reputation. Schmidt writes:

> It is doubtful whether the Germans would have achieved under their own steam what the Americans at the beginning of the seventies called the "German ballet miracle." But the question is an idle one, we already know the answer. With imported choreographers and choreographies, especially from the Anglo-Saxon countries, with John Cranko's move to Stuttgart in 1961 and his exemplary work there after that date, the German ballet pulled itself up to ever greater heights, from which it finally drifted gently into the restoration: the dancers' ever improving technique led to little more than constant new attempts at *Swan Lake* and *Cinderella, Giselle* and *Nutcracker*, at most to attempts at the heritage of the Diaghilev epoch and at the reproduction and imitation of Balanchine's work.[57]

"Imitation" of foreign models, importation of "Anglo-Saxon" personnel, ever-improving technical standards, "restoration"—Schmidt challenges the economic and cultural pieties of the Adenauer era. Although he would never dare formulate the question explicitly, he implicitly asks whether the Nazi years or the Adenauer years posed the more serious threat to German culture.

In her 1989 overview of *Tanztheater*, Claudia Jeschke pens a more straightforward account than Schmidt's, though she clearly shares his bias against ballet and for *Ausdruckstanz* and *Tanztheater*. Nonetheless, she unequivocally acknowledges the link between *Ausdruckstanz* and Nazi culture and explains the rejection of *Ausdruckstanz* after 1945 as a result of its association with fascism. She writes:

> Lived and experienced in the group, [expressionist dance was] supposed to develop more natural and healthier people, restore their unity with the cosmos, help to overcome negative effects of the industrial revolution and contribute to international understanding. This outlook allowed the expressionist dance community to integrate itself slowly into the national community after 1933. It is precisely for this reason that after World War II the fear of being tainted by contact with all that had been infected (or could have been

infected) by National Socialism may have resulted in expressionist dance no longer being able to build on its prewar momentum.[58]

As Jeschke continues her chronicle, "an oversaturation with expressionism" led to a "flight into the formal and objective" that was realized through the establishment of ballet within the municipal opera houses.[59] She writes:

> After 1945 . . . dance/ballet is found almost exclusively at the established, government-financed opera houses, but without receiving an appropriate share of their high subsidies. The artistic vision negates the innovations of the prewar period: it caters to the taste of its audience, to the educated classes with their regressive taste for all that is nineteenth century. Various small ballet centers develop without much vision, cut off from one another, and without any exchange of ideas [from] abroad.[60]

Jeschke concedes that the Stuttgart Ballet transcended the provincialism of other German companies. But she considers Cranko's innovations, however "trend-setting" and "unconventional," as inherently limited, for his choreography never rejected the format of narrative ballet.[61]

Unlike Schmidt and Jeschke, I write not as a critical advocate of *Tanztheater* but rather as an American historian of German dance. And it is from this vantage point that I wish to enter the debate among German critics. Just as I have challenged Hedwig Müller's scripting of Wigman's career as an essential continuity, so I would like to challenge her and her colleagues' view of an essential continuity between *Ausdruckstanz* and *Tanztheater*. Not that I dispute the commonalities linking the two practices. But I weigh the divergences between the two practices differently than do my German colleagues. To catalog these divergences: *Tanztheater*'s break with the "organic form" of *Ausdruckstanz* and its reliance on repetition, fragmentation, and collage; *Tanztheater*'s abandonment of the "poor theater" of *Ausdruckstanz* and its embrace of the visual spectacle made possible by the opera house; and the decline of the patronage of the amateur student in the postwar period and *Tanztheater*'s reliance on government patronage. In the remainder of this chapter I focus on the change in patronage, for it brings into view two continuities that the critical advocates of *Tanztheater* overlook in their construction of a tradition: first, the continuity between German Dance in the Third Reich, the ballet boom during the Adenauer era, and *Tanztheater*; and second, the continuity between *Tanztheater* in what had been the Federal Republic and the Democratic Republic.

With few exceptions, the leading choreographers of West German *Tanztheater* work within the government-subsidized operahouse system, and that system provides relatively secure employment as well as rehearsal and performing space, scenery and costume shops, and administrative staff—in other words, all the apparatus of the proscenium theater without the constraints of the commercial stage. Pina Bausch in Wuppertal (since 1973); Johann (Hans) Kresnik in Bremen (1968–1978), in Heidelberg (1980–1989), and again in Bremen (since 1989); Reinhild Hoffmann in Bremen (1978–1986) and in Bochum (since 1986)—all work in theaters subsidized by the state.

Yet it must be noted that the emergence of *Tanztheater* has prompted the development of a "free dance scene" in West Germany, that is, dance outside the established municipal theaters. Susanne Linke, Gerhard Bohner, Rosamund Gilmore (founder of the Laokoon Dance Group), and the members of Tanzfabrik Berlin all have presented works independently. But even the free dance scene remains dependent on government subsidy, if only indirectly. For many of the free dancers received their training as members of municipal theater ensembles. And subsidized institutions such as the Academy of Arts in West Berlin and the Goethe House network abroad have provided production and touring opportunities that otherwise might not exist. Moreover, municipalities have begun to give direct grants to free dance groups. For example, in 1987 Tanzfabrik Berlin received more than eighty percent of its operating expenses from the Berlin Senate.[62] Although free dancers lead a more precarious financial existence than do choreographers attached to municipal theaters, both groups work within a system shaped by government patronage. The patronage of amateur students that supported *Ausdruckstanz* has not revived.

Government patronage means that *Tanztheater* carries the legacy not only of *Ausdruckstanz* but also of *Deutscher Tanz*. For however much inspiration exponents of *Tanztheater* draw from the formal and ideological concerns of *Ausdruckstanz*, they rely on the material resources first offered modern dance by National Socialism. For it was Nazi cultural policy that effectively dismantled the network of private schools that had supported *Ausdruckstanz* and that centered modern dance within the opera-house system, where it necessarily cohabited with ballet.

Ironically, the postwar ballet boom that critical advocates of *Tanztheater* attribute to Anglo-American influence actually had foundations in the Nazi period. For however much the Adenauer era revolutionized balletic style in accord with Anglo-American models, the postwar boom made use of the ballet training mandated for all professional dancers by Goebbels's Cultural Ministry. Does this make sense of Jochen Schmidt's curious comment that *Ausdruckstanz* represented the only politically "clean" tradition in German dance? Did he mean to imply that ballet had been more tainted than *Ausdruckstanz* by exposure to Nazism?

The government patronage of modern dance introduced by National Socialism continued in the German Democratic Republic from 1949 to 1990. The development of East German dance provides an interesting comparison with that of West German dance. Just as West Germany looked to Anglo-American models through the fifties and early sixties, so East Germany looked to Soviet models. Schools and opera houses engaged Russian teachers and ballet masters, and aspiring East German dancers often finished their professional training in the Soviet Union. As in West Germany, the teaching of *Ausdruckstanz* survivors inspired a younger generation of choreographers in East Germany. Tom Schilling studied with Mary Wigman and Dore Hoyer. Harald Wandtke studied with Gret Palucca and with Jean Weidt, known in the early thirties for his Communist agitprop dances. (An exile during the Nazi period, Weidt returned to East Germany in 1948 and took up a position at the Komische Oper in East Berlin.) Dietmar Seyffert and Arila Siegert also studied with Palucca. Indeed, the Palucca School in Dresden served as a center for the training of East German choreographers.[63]

Strikingly, the East German choreographers who studied with Palucca and Weidt cast their dances under the rubric *Tanztheater*. Although the precedent set by Kurt Jooss may have been the deep source for the term, the immediate source was Walter Felsenstein's concept of *Musiktheater* (music theater). Felsenstein, the founder of the Komische Oper who engaged Schilling as a choreographer in

1964, used the term *Musiktheater* to characterize his socialist approach to opera production, an approach that Schilling adapted for dance. As Dietmar Fritzsche, an East German critic, explains this approach:

> Inspired by Felsenstein's concept of music theater, Schilling evolved a concept of dance theater from "the stylistic means and expressive forms of modern dance, ballet, folklore, pantomime, and pure movement." Working with Felsenstein, Schilling discovered that "behind every artistic expression there must be a thought as well as a commitment" in order to arouse a specific emotion, a specific intended impression within the spectator. Thus he derived his responsibility "to make clear the truth, above all the social truth of the piece" in his productions.[64]

Although Fritzsche presents Schilling's choreography as a fusion of Soviet and German influences, it is difficult for outside observers to differentiate Schilling's approach from Soviet models. This has been my impression, as well as Jochen Schmidt's, who once dismissed my questions about East German *Tanztheater* with the comment, "narrative ballet in the mode of socialist realism."[65] Of the few performances of East German dance that I have seen, Arila Siegert's solo performances stand out. Her reconstructions of dances by Marianne Vogelsang, the codirector of Wigman's Berlin school for a brief time, reveal an expressive intensity that counters the literalness of much ballet in the Soviet pattern.

Despite its identical rubric, East German *Tanztheater* diverged from its West German counterpart. From the early fifties, the Democratic Republic institutionalized the influence of *Ausdruckstanz* survivors, installing Gret Palucca in the Dresden school that bore her name and Jean Weidt at the Komische Oper. Integrating the teaching of Palucca and Weidt with training in Soviet ballet, East German choreographers evolved a form of *Tanztheater* that functioned not as an oppositional practice but rather as a performance genre that supported the political status quo. The onstage integration of German and Soviet influences served the offstage integration of East Germany within the Soviet sphere.

Now that East and West Germany have reunited, what will be the fate of the two *Tanztheaters*? Will there be a radical change in personnel—in effect, a de-Sovietization—at opera houses in the eastern half of Berlin, Dresden, and Leipzig? Or will the Federal

Republic reemploy the choreographers formerly under the employ of the Democratic Republic? Will choreographers who achieved reputations in what was East Germany now reject Tom Schilling's prescription for *Tanztheater*? If so, will they emulate the model of their "Western" colleagues or modify their previous practice in response to the new context? And how will choreographers who have worked all along in the Federal Republic react to the dismantling of the Berlin Wall? As I write, less than a year after reunification, these questions do not yet have answers.

Equally unclear is the impact of reunification on the historiography of *Tanztheater*. Before 1990 critical advocates of Pina Bausch and Tom Schilling rarely compared the development of *Tanztheater* in East and West Germany. To an outsider, the parallels were striking, as were the differences, but insiders seemed to avoid the issue of comparison altogether. When I raised the question of comparison at the panel sponsored by Goethe House New York in October 1989, the West German panelists responded with bafflement and derision. Now that the Berlin Wall has fallen, will German critics and historians examine the convergences and divergences of *Tanztheater* in what were East and West Germany?

Further, will the *Ausdruckstanz* revival, apparent in both the Federal Republic and the Democratic Republic during the eighties, gain momentum or lose steam? Will critics reify or critique the continuity between *Ausdruckstanz* and *Tanztheater*? If critics in what were East and West Germany choose to focus on the common heritage of *Ausdruckstanz*, will their construction of a unified German tradition bracket the troubling issues surrounding the postwar division? As with the (re)organization of German dance, these questions are not yet answered.

On 3 October 1990, the official date of reunification, Susanne Linke presented a lecture-demonstration at the Chicago Arts Club. The timing was sheer coincidence, for since November 1989 political change had happened so rapidly that what was originally planned as an event to publicize Linke's artistry turned into her impromptu celebration of German reunification.

As the lecture-demonstration began, Linke expressed the euphoria she felt over reunification. She then reflected on the German national character, characterizing German identity as a constant conflict between nihilism and arrogance, between an embrace of struggle and a longing for happiness. She noted that these tensions always had found expression in German dance. She stated, "We don't know who we are in Central Europe, and so our dance expresses what we are not and want to be."

Linke then turned to a discussion of her dances, marking the choreography through gestures. Describing *Bathtubbing* (*Im Bade wannen*), a solo in which she dances around and in a cast-iron bathtub, she talked about the prop as a metaphor for a partner, a uterus, a grave. Describing *Flood* (*Flut*), a solo in which she unravels and wraps herself in a long length of cloth, she talked about the image of drowning—drowning in monotony, drowning in despair, drowning in materialism.

Watching the lecture-demonstration, I experienced a sense of déjà vu. For the event made palpable not the discontinuity but rather the continuity between *Ausdruckstanz* and *Tanztheater*. A charismatic performer standing on a podium, voicing belief in an essential German experience transformed through her dances, talking like no American modern dancer has talked since mid-century: was this 1990, or was this 1930, when Mary Wigman made her first American tour to wild acclaim?

7

Mary Wigman and
American Dance

When I first began to study dance history, it was a commonplace
that modern dance was as American as jazz or apple pie. But then
came the emergence of modern dance troupes across Europe, Asia,
and Latin America as well as the revival of interest in European
modern dance during the first decades of the century. By the late
eighties it no longer was possible to posit the Americanness of the
art form, as Marcia Siegel had asserted—plausibly—just a decade
earlier. In *The Shapes of Change: Images of American Dance* (1979)
Siegel wrote:

> It's not possible to identify the real beginnings of a phenomenon as
> diversified and as organic to our American cultural development as
> modern dance. Some people automatically consider Isadora Duncan
> as the founder, others give credit to Ruth St. Denis, but we could as
> well trace some of the roots of American dance to the levees of the
> Mississippi or the free-thinking religions of the nineteenth century.[1]

From the perspective of the early nineties, it is clear that modern
dance did not arise "organically" from American culture but rather
that American modern dancers worked hard during the thirties to
create a national identity for their practice.

To follow Wigman's reception in the United States is to realize
how constructed is the Americanness of American modern dance.
As I will argue, the nationalization of modern dance in the United
States informed both the critical response to Wigman's three trans-
atlantic tours (1930–1933) and the practice of her disciples. The
image of the German choreographer became a projection through
which John Martin, Lincoln Kirstein, and their colleagues debated
which genre—ballet or modern dance—was the appropriate form
for American dance. Advocates of ballet saw Wigman as a negative

argument for their cause; advocates of modern dance saw her as an inspiration and a competitive spur.

Yet opinion within the modern dance community was not unanimous. Believing that modern dance represented an international movement, some proponents called for the adoption of *Ausdruckstanz*. Other proponents countered that modern dance represented the Zeitgeist of a particular culture and called for distinctly American forms. This debate within modern dance informed the borrowing of Wigman's methods. To what extent could her methods be transplanted? To what extent did they require modification for American dancers? Those questions confronted every German dancer who had emigrated and every American dancer who had studied at Dresden.

During the early thirties the direction that modern dance should take in the United States remained a matter of debate. By the late thirties, however, a consensus had emerged that modern dance should take a distinctly American form as defined by the choreographers associated with the Bennington Festival—Martha Graham, Doris Humphrey, Charles Weidman, and Hanya Holm. In the postwar period the history of American modern dance was written as the story of the "four pioneers," as the title of a documentary film termed the Bennington choreographers.[2] The postwar historiography mythologized the Americanness of modern dance, glossing over the precedent of *Ausdruckstanz*. Moreover, the standard literature mentioned neither the controversy that flared over Wigman's Nazi affiliation nor the existence of an organized group of leftist dancers, centered around the magazine *New Theatre*, that provoked the controversy in the mid-thirties.

My narrative recovers these dimensions of the history of American modern dance as it examines the consensus that emerged during the thirties. At the center of my narrative stands Hanya Holm, who emigrated from Germany in 1931 to become director of the New York branch of the Mary Wigman School, which she renamed the Hanya Holm Studio in 1936. Holm's career epitomizes the consensus forged at Bennington, and partly for this reason she became the best known of Wigman's disciples in the United States. That I center my story around her career is not to reinforce the marginality of other German immigrants but to bring into focus the way that the domestication of Wigman contributed to the nationalization of modern dance and the mythologization of its Americanness.[3]

THE RECEPTION OF WIGMAN'S
AMERICAN TOURS

When Mary Wigman departed for her first American tour in December 1930, her critical reputation in Germany had reached a plateau and her career a point of crisis. Since disbanding her company more than two years earlier, she had premiered a new solo cycle, *Shifting Landscape*, and the choric work *Totenmal*. Both works received an ambivalent critical reception. Reviewing a solo concert in April 1929, Joseph Lewitan remarked: "Having not seen Mary Wigman for about a year, my first general impression is of stagnation."[4]

During the summer that Wigman disbanded her dance group, in 1928, she entered into negotiations with impresario Sol Hurok over the possibility of an American tour.[5] By the time the planning became a reality, the tour provided the choreographer a respite from the controversy that had marred the Third Dancers' Congress and the premiere of *Totenmal*. Although exceedingly taxing physically, the tour brought Wigman the sort of critical acclaim she had not experienced in Germany since the early and mid-twenties. As Joseph Lewitan commented on the disparity in her critical reception: "This is not the first time that something becomes fashionable in America when it is already 'passé' in Europe, and that there people are 'crazy' about things that already have been played out here."[6] From Lewitan's perspective, American culture lagged behind Europe and turned what had been a serious style into a frivolous fashion. From my perspective, American critics constructed a Wigman that diverged from the image of the German choreographer created by her compatriots, and the American image of Wigman reflected the repertory chosen for her Hurok tours as well as her critics' polemical disagreements over American dance.

The dissonance between the reception of Wigman in Germany and the United States can be explained partly as a consequence of her repertory for the three Hurok tours. Showcasing solos rather than group works, Wigman's tours left the impression that her achievement rested in the solo genre. This assessment contradicted the image of Wigman held by her German critics, for although they celebrated her genius as a soloist, they considered her group works of equal if not greater significance than her solos. From the Germans' point of view, it was her achievement in group choreography that distinguished her from her predecessors, such as Isadora Duncan, who never managed the transition from brilliant solo dancing to effective handling of an ensemble.

Since American critics had little opportunity to see Wigman's group works, they based their assessment of her achievement on the solos performed on her American tours—among others, *Witch Dance II, Monotony Whirl, Shifting Landscape,* and *Sacrifice.* The one group work that American critics did see, *Pilgrimage (Der Weg),* most judged a failure.[7] As John Martin, one of her most ardent supporters, summarized the general impression: "It would be useless to deny that Mary Wigman's first appearances in this country with a group were a bitter disappointment to those who have been stirred by the power and the depth of her solo performances."[8] Commissioned by Hurok for Wigman's third tour in 1932–1933, *Pilgrimage* also had failed with German critics when it premiered in Berlin just before the choreographer and her student ensemble departed for the States. As Fritz Böhme remarked: "One can only regret that Wigman is taking this work to America. There it will be taken as representative, and that it certainly is not."[9]

As Böhme predicted, since American reviewers could not place *Pilgrimage* in relation to Wigman's earlier group works, most dismissed her as a group choreographer on the basis of this one critical failure. Not surprisingly, they viewed Wigman as a charismatic soloist who could not translate her genius into group choreography. In other words, American critics constructed her in much the same terms as they—and their German counterparts—constructed Isadora Duncan.

Yet the selection of Wigman's repertory for her Hurok tours does not fully account for the tenacity with which American critics fixed her image as the successor to Duncan. For they did have access to her own writings and to the writings of her German critics in English translation, excerpted in the souvenir program for the first American tour. As the choreographer herself asserted in an essay translated for the American public: "Solo dancing achievement is not the essential for the future. . . . The younger generation should cultivate and range itself with group dancing. There are the great possibilities of the future."[10] In choosing to overlook such statements, Wigman's American critics demonstrated their determination to view her achievement in terms of the solo genre. In so doing, they pursued their own polemical disagreements over whether America should adopt the genre of modern dance or ballet. For ballet apologists, Wigman's presumed ineptness as a group choreographer simply supported their view of the inherent limitations of modern dance. For advocates of modern dance, Wigman's perceived failure as a group choreographer worked in a more complicated fashion to support their formulation of a distinctly American practice of modern dance.

To understand how the image of Wigman the charismatic soloist came to serve the polemical ends of American critics requires retracing the controversy that erupted in the dance world over the German choreographer. Although ballet supporters were united in their rejection of Wigman, proponents of modern dance were divided in their judgments. Some, such as John Martin, passionately defended Wigman, but others, such as Doris Humphrey, challenged her influence. In May 1931 *Dance Magazine* published a symposium titled "What Dancers Think about the German Dance," surveying the range of opinions pro- and anti-Wigman.

To proponents of ballet Wigman's dancing undermined the values they associated with the high art of their own practice. According to Michel Fokine, the German dancer possessed neither technique nor professionalism nor musicality. His contribution to the symposium in *Dance Magazine* stated:

> [Wigman's] "innovation" is built upon a total absence of knowledge of laws of the dance, its technique, and its grammar.
>
> It is the development of dilettantism unparalleled in the history of the dance. . . .
>
> The dances of Wigman are announced as "new art" while they really contain nothing new. She is being glorified as the "mistress" of all schools, while she herself has no technique, no skill, no knowledge.
>
> In order to glorify her a novel method is used: Wigman is not beautiful in movements, therefore beauty is condemned as something old fashioned.
>
> She is not feminine, therefore femininity, it is said, no longer

should belong to women. She has poor musical sense, therefore there is no music.[11]

In a review for *Hound and Horn,* Lincoln Kirstein seconded Fokine's opinion. Kirstein wrote:

> Wigman herself is dangerous because by the strength of her personal appeal she can seduce such passivity into mistaken dancing. She believes and teaches that any one can dance. It requires no particular dedication; it is an idiom which she can provide. In a similar manner any one can indulge in the therapeutic writing of "poetry," any one can paint "pictures." . . . Mary Wigman is a destructive dancer. . . . She has completely disintegrated the continuous flow of pose and gesture into a series of static or abruptly shifting positions. She is at a complete loss . . . when she attempts to negotiate a turn. She chooses to "interpret" only the most cosmic of "ideas," which is convenient, since it irons out any exact meaning into a flat generalization of the ambiguous, subjective, and equivocal. Bliss, ecstasy, release, revolt, terror, enchantment lead finally, pursued to their inevitable climax, to what but exhaustion? And so Mary Wigman finishes almost every dance by falling in a collapsed heap on the floor.[12]

Four years later Kirstein summarized his critique of Wigman in *Dance: A Short History of Classic Theatrical Dancing* (1935), presenting her practice as the negation of the balletic values his polemical history espoused: the legibility of form, the discipline of referentiality, the subordination of self to tradition. Implicit in his commentary, as well as in Fokine's remarks, is the image of Wigman the charismatic soloist, who elevates personal idiosyncrasy into art and who does not possess the requisite skills for group choreography.

Supporters of modern dance viewed Wigman with far less unanimity than did proponents of ballet. In the *New York Times* John Martin represented one pole of opinion, championing Wigman's art and holding her up as a model for American modern dance. Summarizing her first tour, he wrote: "It was not until Wigman arrived upon the [American] scene that the newest element of modernism was presented by an acknowledged master, one who had become the symbol of a movement. The response was instantaneous and electrical."[13] American modern dancers took Martin's comments as an indirect attack on their own methods. They resented his suggestion that were they as masterful as Wigman they too would win the large audiences that the German dancer commanded. In the symposium in *Dance Magazine* Doris Humphrey penned a retort that countered Martin's perspective. She wrote:

> We must remember that German dancing is not for us. We must not copy in this country if we are to develop. Imitation is at once our greatest talent and our greatest vice.
>
> We adopted ballet, we adopted Spanish dancing, we adopted Oriental dancing—are we never to have a dance that is our own? We will never produce a great German dancer in this country, no matter how hard some of our most talented concert artistes may try. . . . And the pity of it is that we cannot as a nation see and admire a genius like Mary Wigman without throwing everything else overboard and copying her style without going through the underlying developments which make her dances genuine, and for the lack of which ours must necessarily be insincere.[14]

As readers familiar with the history of American dance already know, John Martin came to share Doris Humphrey's view by the mid-thirties, and the contest represented by their views in the early thirties resolved in consensus. Over the course of the decade, Martin's writings both reflected and shaped the consensus that emerged around the nationalization of modern dance. That consensus held that American modern dance reflected the conditions and possibilities of a national experience shared by dancer and spectator. In other words, the aesthetic associated with Bennington essentialized national identity and mythologized the Americanness of modern dance.

As Martin articulated the Bennington aesthetic, his views of Mary Wigman underwent a decided change. Although in one sense he remained her advocate, he pushed her name from the center to the margins of the history of American dance. Over the course of the thirties his writings revealed and resolved a tension between his awareness of *Ausdruckstanz* as a precedent for American modern dance and his determination to celebrate the Americanness of the form. From *The Modern Dance* (1933) to *America Dancing* (1936) to *Introduction to the Dance* (1939)—his books resolved this tension in two ways: first, by constructing an American tradition for modern dance that included Wigman as a predecessor along with Isadora Duncan and positioned both as charismatic soloists; second, by emphasizing how decisively German-trained dancers, notably Hanya Holm, had adapted their methods in response to their new environment. From Martin's perspective, America remade *Ausdrucks-tanz* in its own image.

In *The Modern Dance*, a published series of lectures delivered at the New School during 1931–1932, Martin reaffirmed his championship of Wigman, although in more restrained terms than earlier. The published lectures proposed to give a theoretical underpinning to the emergent movement of modern dance, and at this time Martin had not yet placed the movement in a specifically national frame. As he notes in the introduction, "These theoretical deductions are based not on any preconceived point to be proved, but upon the practice of the leading dancers of the day, both American and European."[15] Among the "leading dancers" whom the critic mentions by name are Martha Graham, Doris Humphrey, Helen Tamiris, Rudolf Laban, and Mary Wigman. He cites these choreographers' practice as illustrative of the characteristics he considers fundamental to modern dance. His discussion links Rudolf Laban with dynamism, the "only purely muscular rhythm," and Mary Wigman with metakinesis (kinesthesia).[16] Martin writes:

> At its highest point of development we find the so-called expressionistic dancing with Mary Wigman as an outstanding practitioner. This class of dance is in effect the modern dance in its purest manifestation. The basis of each composition in this medium lies in a vision of something in human experience which touches the sublime. Its externalization in some form which can be apprehended by others comes not by intellectual planning but by "feeling through" with a sensitive body.[17]

In Martin's theory of modern dance the process of metakinesis allows the spectator to reexperience the sensation that the dancer objectifies in movement terms.

Three years later Martin published *America Dancing,* and in a striking departure from *The Modern Dance,* framed modern dance as a specifically American practice. Fulfilling the promise of the book's title, the introduction established a tradition for American modern dance by looking back to Isadora Duncan. Martin wrote:

> In her autobiography . . . Isadora Duncan recorded her "vision of America dancing," and the dance she saw was one of such heroic sweep and nobility as to match the prophecy of Whitman which she paraphrased. . . .
> But his prophecy, for all its priority, is still for the future, while

hers is in the process of being fulfilled. America is dancing, and just such a "new great vision of life" infuses its dance. It is fairly safe to assume that Isadora would not recognize it as the dance of which she spoke, for its forms have departed radically from her forms; but it is nonetheless deeply and fundamentally the fruit of her prophecy, her ideal, her work.[18]

Surveying the development of American dance, Martin sees the years 1926 to 1928, the "two years of which Isadora's death marks almost the middle point," as the formative period, when Martha Graham, Helen Tamiris, Doris Humphrey, and Charles Weidman all made their choreographic debuts.[19] In Martin's narrative what coalesced the efforts of individual dancers into a national movement was the appearance of collective structures for creating dance, notably the founding of the Bennington Festival in 1934. However, the critic does not limit his discussion to Bennington but also points out the collective activity connected with the Neighborhood Playhouse, the Federal Theatre Project, and the New Dance League.

Where did the new historiography of *America Dancing* place Mary Wigman? Martin considered her influence "indirect" in that it was mediated through Hanya Holm, whose "[keen sensitivity] to the American scene" rendered Wigman's methods "amenable to the American temperament."[20] The critic concluded: "In [Holm's] hands the admirable Wigman technique is in no danger of becoming just another imported orthodoxy but is already undergoing processes of adaptation, both conscious and unconscious, to free its potentialities in a new environment. . . . If there are any other foreign influences at work [in American modern dance], they have been thus far singularly ineffective."[21]

The year before *America Dancing* appeared, Lincoln Kirstein had published his polemical *Dance: A Short History of Classic Theatrical Dancing,* outlining the Great Tradition of ballet and dismissing the countertradition of modern dance. Martin's subsequent volume, *Introduction to the Dance,* attempted to reverse Kirstein's polemic by opposing the Great Men of ballet, or "spectacular dance," with the Great Women of modern dance, or "expressional dance." Published in 1939, *Introduction to the Dance* placed less emphasis on collective structures than had the earlier *America Dancing* and isolated the individual artists associated with Bennington as precisely that—individual artists. Thus the march of Great Women began with Isadora Duncan, continued with Mary Wigman and Ruth St. Denis, and culminated with Martha Graham, Doris Humphrey, and Hanya Holm. Martin now clearly positioned Wigman's formal innovations—her spatial awareness and achievement of absolute dance—as an advance beyond Duncan's representational strategies. He wrote:

> [Before Wigman, creative dance] had been at best simply an emanation from a person, as when Isadora by her irresistible power to awaken sympathetic experience was able to project an emotional concept directly into the minds of her audience. . . .
>
> With Wigman's sense of space as a tangible symbol of universal forces, the dancer is supplied with something outside himself, which he may shape to his purposes, and toward which he may direct his emotional reactions so that even his most subjective experiences become visibly externalized. . . .
>
> With Wigman the dance stands for the first time fully revealed in its own stature.[22]

As in *America Dancing*, Martin emphasized how sensitively Holm had adapted Wigman's methods for American dancers. But in a new departure he differentiated between the Germanness that had infused Wigman's dancing and the universal applicability of her methods. Acknowledging Wigman's essential Germanness allowed him to posit the essential Americanness of the modern dance created by Graham, Humphrey, and Holm. Moreover, essentializing the national identities of both movements enabled Martin to assert no mutual influence. He wrote:

> Wigman is too nearly contemporaneous with the American leaders to have influenced them in any tangible way, even if they had not been traveling divergent roads. . . .
>
> In this essential divergence it is possible to see the effects of different national environments, the contrasts between an old civilization and a new, between what is peculiarly German and what is peculiarly American. Wigman's dance is a dance of acquiescence; the American dance is one of affirmation.[23]

In the progressive tradition sketched by Martin, just as Wigman overtook Duncan, so younger American dancers would overtake Wigman. Martin locates the achievement of Graham, Humphrey, and Holm in their group compositions. Thus he implies that however much Wigman's dancing transcended Duncan's example, the

German dancer remained more effective as a soloist than as a group choreographer. In so doing, he strikes up an unlikely alliance with Lincoln Kirstein, and as standard sources for the postwar history of American dance, *Introduction to the Dance* colluded with *Dance: A Short History of Classic Theatrical Dancing* to present the image of Wigman the charismatic soloist to the American reader.

Despite the consonance of their images of Wigman, Martin and Kirstein remained on opposing sides in the contest over American dance during the thirties. Martin never wavered in his belief that modern dance constituted the appropriate genre for America, and Kirstein never questioned that American dance should domesticate ballet. In the postwar period the conflict between their viewpoints resolved in a compromise, and a double consensus came to govern the practice and historiography of dance in the United States: that American ballet descended from the Russian tradition as reinterpreted by George Balanchine and that American modern dance descended from the "four pioneers" associated with the Bennington Festival.

LEFTISTS, HUMANISTS, AND HANYA HOLM

For modern dance to arrive at the consensus represented by Bennington required more than John Martin coming to share Doris Humphrey's mission. Indeed, the consensus demanded that the "leftist" wing of the modern dance movement give way to the "humanist" wing. The terms are my own, intended to illuminate a dispute that largely was written out of the postwar historiography of American dance. In this dispute, leftist dancers asserted the necessity to connect dance directly with political activism, while humanist dancers viewed the connection between dance and politics in more indirect terms. In one sense, these two positions marked the endpoints of a continuum along which modern dancers worked during the thirties, as they in varying ways reconciled the demands of political engagement and artistic commitment. But as the history of American dance came to be written, the leftist end of the continuum became obscured. The dancers who elevated art over politics—Martha Graham, Doris Humphrey, Charles Weidman, Hanya Holm—became enshrined as the "four pioneers"; the dancers who saw a direct relation between art and politics—Edith Segal, Edna Ocko, Nadia Chilkovsky, Miriam Blecher—disappeared from the annals. And the dancers who staked out positions midway along the continuum—Helen Tamiris, Anna Sokolow, Jane Dudley, Sophie Maslow—were remembered more for their humanist credentials than for their leftist commitments.

This is not to deny that there was considerable overlap between the humanist and leftist camps: members of the Graham and Humphrey-Weidman companies presented works on concerts sponsored by the Workers Dance League, and Graham and Humphrey lent their support to initiatives undertaken by the New Dance League, as the Workers Dance League was renamed in 1934. Yet it is clear that during the early and mid thirties modern dancers worked between two opposing positions, one of which had all but disappeared by the late thirties. And it is also clear that the postwar historiography of modern dance either mocked or ignored the position staked out by the leftist dancers. When the leftist position was remembered, it was remembered as a youthful enthusiasm that faded as dancers matured and accepted the rightness of the humanist ethic. The literature simply assumed the superiority of the Bennington aesthetic. Typical was this comment in Margaret ⸲Lloyd's *The Borzoi Book of Modern Dance* (1949):

> There are no reds in modern dance today. Once there were left-wingers who, with bare feet thrust up from the ankles and fists doubled out from the wrists, outdid dancing with polemics. "Dance is a Weapon" was their battle-cry. We heard a lot about Dances of Protest in those days. The militants were anti-Nazi when more conventional people were unaware of what the Nazis were up to. They denounced the bombing of women and children in Spain; they recognized the nucleus of another world war. They thought the miners, the Negroes, and several million other people who did not cut coupons once or twice a month, were getting a tough break. Their ardor was restrained by progress (their own, not the world's) as they learned to distinguish between political diatribes and dance—long before it became dangerous to follow any but the two-party line.
>
> Now, of course, the left wings are all tucked out of sight. Only right wings (with a liberal spread) are to be seen.[24]

In this passage, Lloyd recalls how once the leftist dancers made "progress," that is, learned to separate aesthetics from politics, they abandoned "protest," even before McCarthyism made their earlier allegiances a liability.

To date, Stacey Prickett's research has most fully recovered the work of the leftist dancers. As she has documented, eleven workers' dance groups in the New York area banded together to found the Workers Dance League in 1932. These groups organized lay dance classes for workers and for their children, presented performances at union meetings and Communist political rallies, and collaborated with the workers' theater movement in a national organization that published the magazine *New Theatre*. The same year that the Workers Dance League was formed, a group of six students from the Holm studio organized the New Dance Group to promote socially conscious dance, and within a year they had rallied three hundred other dancers to their cause. By 1934 the Workers Dance League listed eight hundred members, and its membership broadened further when it changed its name to the New Dance League and reoriented its efforts around the battle cry of the Popular Front—"Unite against War and Fascism" (see figs. 62 and 63). In 1936 it was reported that the New Dance League had two thousand members.[25] In *America Dancing* John Martin captured the spirit of the times when he proclaimed that "[dance] has refused to be a class art any longer and has made up its mind to be a mass art."[26]

The leftist wing of American modern dance viewed the precedent of German dance in quite different terms than did the humanist wing. For the humanist wing was dedicated to Americanizing the form, but the leftist wing was more internationalist in orientation. The Workers Dance League looked to German and Russian models for workers' theater and emulated the festivals staged in both countries with its own choreographic competition, called Spartakiade, organized in 1933.[27] And German methods were among the methods of choice for leftist dancers. Founded by students from the New York Wigman School, the New Dance Group promoted the movement choir at a time when Holm herself was turning away from the form. As Margaret Lloyd remembered, "For [ten cents a class] the crusaders [at the New Dance Group] offered one hour of Wigman technique, one of creative work, and one of discussion."[28]

The leftist dancers saw the relations between professional and amateur dance in quite different terms than did the humanist dancers. The humanist dancers aimed to professionalize the practice of modern dance among the middle class, but the leftist dancers aimed to broaden the participation of amateurs by introducing

Fig. 62.   Poster for a fund-raiser sponsored by *New Theatre* (from *New Theatre*, March 1935)

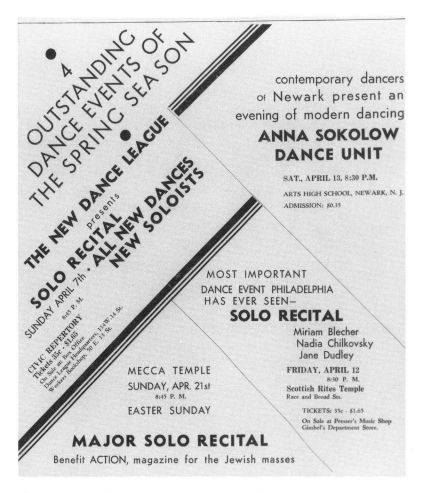

Fig. 63.   Poster for a concert series sponsored by the New Dance League (from *New Theatre*, April 1935)

modern dance to the working class. In effect, the Workers Dance League restructured the patronage of amateur students by turning away from the network of private studios and affiliating instead with unions and socialist organizations. Working with the Needle Trades Industrial Workers Union and with Jewish and German leisure organizations such as Nature Friends, the leftist dancers cast themselves as "professional" revolutionaries who aimed to instill political consciousness in the "amateur" masses.

The humanist dancers also restructured the patronage of ama-

teur students, but in a strikingly different direction. Affiliating with
university physical education departments, the humanist dancers
consolidated a new source of amateur patronage—the college student. The Bennington Festival stood at the center of this development, for it trained a generation of college dance instructors.
Moreover, Bennington initiated the direct link between physical
education (and later dance) departments and the private studio
system in New York. As this connection consolidated during the
forties and fifties, aspiring professionals first studied through a college program and then completed their training at a New York
studio. This career path often included a summer or two spent
at the successor to the Bennington Festival, the American Dance
Festival, housed at Connecticut College from 1948 to 1978 and
since then at Duke University. Training at a New York studio
in turn became a prerequisite for teaching in a university dance
department.

To dancers and dance scholars, this patronage system is so familiar as to be self-evident. But what is perhaps less obvious is how
the consolidation of university patronage and the New York studio
system accompanied the decline of the leftist wing of the modern
dance movement and the ascent of the humanist wing. In the early
to mid-thirties leftist dancers looked to the workers' theater movement and to the Popular Front for support. After 1935 they also
found patronage from the federal government through the Federal Theatre Project, as did dancers from the humanist camp. But
government patronage proved short-lived, for Congress cut funding for the Federal Theatre Project in 1939. By then the workers'
theater movement and the Popular Front had collapsed, and so
leftist dancers had to turn to the same sources that supported
the humanist dancers: New York studios, university dance departments, and Broadway musicals. Some leftist dancers, including
many of the leaders, stopped working. Others embraced the consensus forged by the humanist dancers at Bennington.[29]

To recover the tension between leftist and humanist dancers is
to understand the Americanization of Hanya Holm in different
terms from those of John Martin. Or, more precisely, to set Hanya
Holm's early career against the backdrop of tension between leftists
and humanists is to understand how profoundly the agenda of nationalization informed the practice of modern dance in the United

States. As formulated over the course of the thirties, the agenda of nationalization converged with the humanist wing of the modern dance movement. In many ways, the convergence was overdetermined, for it united the patronage of the university and the New York studio system with the necessity for artistic legitimation. In the context of the thirties, modern dance had to compete against the domestication of ballet, and as an alternate genre of "high art" humanist practice proved more viable than leftist practice. Elevating art over politics, the humanists developed techniques that approximated the formal values of ballet, that is, techniques that could form the basis for both training and composition and that could be codified and transmitted fluently from teacher to student. At Bennington, Martha Graham, and Doris Humphrey and Charles Weidman, focused on developing exactly such codified movement techniques, establishing American modern dance as an alternative to American ballet. Bennington marked the convergence between humanism, artistic legitimation, and nationalization.

The early years of Holm's career in the United States illuminate the fault line separating humanist from leftist dancers. Within a few years of founding the New York branch of the Mary Wigman School in 1931, Holm had evolved Wigman's *Technik* in the direction of American "technique." In so doing, she was motivated not only by her "sensitivity to the American environment," as she herself stated and Martin reiterated, but also by her decision to affiliate with the humanist wing rather than with the leftist wing of the dance movement. The invitation to teach at Bennington from 1934 to 1939 formalized her affiliation. Her alliance with the humanist dancers had important consequences, for it allowed her to survive the controversy over Wigman's fascism launched by the leftist dancers in the mid-thirties. Asserting her belief in the independence of art and politics, Holm distanced herself from her mentor's entanglement with the Nazis.

When the New York branch of the Mary Wigman School opened in 1931, the curriculum approximated that offered at Dresden. Although some classes were designed for amateurs and others for professionals, the choric class, emphasizing "mass or communal expression," admitted both lay and professional students. As at Dresden, the professional curriculum comprised "class lessons," devoted to improvisational explorations of movement concepts;

technique classes, focused on perfecting the body as an instrument; and "group classes," concerned with the varied ways of moving as a group.[30]

By 1936–1937, the year the school was renamed the Hanya Holm Studio, the curriculum had undergone significant modification. The disappearance of the choric class meant that amateur and professional students now were segregated. At the same time, the professional curriculum dropped the group class and was rearranged and divided into technique and composition classes.[31] Now professional students focused more on individual mastery than on group involvement, more on the acquisition of technical and compositional skills than on the experience of community. Although Holm never abandoned the method of improvisation, she reoriented improvisation so that it no longer constituted a *Technik* in the German sense but rather approximated a "technique" in the American sense.

What occasioned this change? Although the shift accorded with the Bennington consensus, other factors contributed as well. First was the internal dynamic of Holm's own practice. It seems that the independence of her working situation in New York intensified her pedagogical style evident earlier. According to students in Dresden, Holm had provided clearer theoretical explanations for Wigman's methods than any other teacher there, including the choreographer herself. Holm's ability to clarify and even codify the principles of Wigman's methods sharpened during the early years in New York. As she trained an advanced group of students, she crystallized the principles of her method through a series of lecture-demonstrations, which she and her students toured across the country. A typical "demonstration program" presented not "finished dances" but "studies to illustrate the various problems," such as:

> Harmonious relation between dancer and space—Space shattered by explosive quality arising from inner excitement of the dancer whose body is the focal point—Conflict between the attractions of two opposing focal points—Space as scenery suggested through descriptive movement—Effervescent movement motivated by excitement coloring space—Attraction toward depth—Suspension—Resurgent plunging into depth.[32]

In clarifying the formal principles of Wigman's methods, Holm was assisted by Louise Kloepper, an American dancer who had studied at the Wigman School in Dresden. Kloepper joined Holm during her second season and remained for ten years. (Fé Alf, another recent graduate of the Dresden school, had accompanied Holm to America to assist at the school but left after the first year to help found the New Dance Group.) A native of Seattle, Kloepper had studied ballet as a child and then had completed her dance training in Germany. As Kloepper remembers the early years of the Wigman School in New York, many students enrolled at first but then left because of the "lack of technique." So she and Holm together evolved a "more technical basis" for Wigman's methods, employing balletic turn-out and repetitive exercises to build skill. They developed a rigorous warm-up to use at the beginning of technique classes before moving on to improvisations around a theme such as falls, turns, or jumps. Composition classes also were based on improvisation, although Holm emphasized the compositional principles developed through her lecture-demonstrations.[33]

A student's published account of her study at the Wigman School evidences the resistance to "free improvisation" and the demand for "technique" that Holm and Kloepper encountered during their early years in New York. Describing herself as "a young, discriminating, social-minded modern dancer," Blanche Evan recorded her experiences at the Wigman School during summer 1934 for the readers of *New Theatre*. Although at first she found improvisation a more useful method than the rote exercises demanded at the Graham School, her enthusiasm was ambivalent. She wrote:

> We have two classes daily, one in improvisation and one in so-called technique. So-called because even the technical classes are built on improvisation. . . . For instance, today our lesson was built on body falls. Louise gave us varied falls to do and then we proceeded to invent our own. We experimented with different dynamic uses of the body contacting the ground: sinking "passively" into it, and then falling "actively"; not to submit but to receive an "electric shock" from the floor that sent us bouncing from place to place; running into the ground only to tear away from it, or the opposite, running into space on a crescendo and pitching from this height down to the floor in a kind of final extinction. . . . We had been worked up into a kinesthetic hypnosis in which we lost all fear. I wonder now how I did it. I wonder moreover how constructive this kind of training is if, in such immediate retrospect, I cannot hang on to any one specific thing,—except that the use of movement in contact with the floor-spatial-level has dynamic possibilities of which I had never dreamt. I

have seen several Graham demonstrations at the New School and each year the girls repeated the same six falls—patterns which are known by now as "Graham falls." . . . At least through the Wigman method of improvisation, I am avoiding the pitfall of regarding the dance as an academic vocabulary of technical patterns.[34]

As Evan continued her course at the Wigman School, her initial enthusiasm for improvisation faded, and her subsequent journal entries probe her disaffection. Her dissatisfaction arose partly from the lack of "technique," in the sense of acquired skills. As she explained:

> Today's lesson was on elevation. A number of the girls came down with a thud but no technical criticism was given: only the qualitative one, that their movement had too much *down* in it. . . . Their thud was due plainly to lack of resiliency in ankle and knee. All the talk about "height and depth" could not possibly help them. . . . Hanya's explanation was very refreshing for those professionals in the class who had mastered the technique before coming to the Wigman School. But for the majority it was futile and dangerous. . . . If only the school would *teach* fundamental technique, as a base, its stress on quality would really be fruitful.[35]

Not only the absence of technical explanations disturbed Evan, but also the "mysticism" she associated with the method of improvisation. As she described her disillusionment:

> A lesson on "Vibration." . . . It was the nearest thing to a primitive worship-cult celebration that I had ever experienced. . . . I went wild, broke into a run,—a run that was stronger than the strongest run I had ever executed in my whole dancing career—then into spinning turns, the body doing all kinds of uncontrolled movements. Yet this happened not as if I set out to *do* a wild dance but as a result of an hypnotic rhythmic state. . . .
> This hypnotic way of achieving power in movement is like a poisonous gift. What you want, happens, once you are really *in* the "state." Everything in my intellectual make-up resents it. Everything in the dance takes on an unreal mysticism.[36]

Evan concluded that the Wigman School had "not achieved a balance between discipline and freedom."[37] Although she disapproved of the "technique, technique, technique" characteristic of ballet training and study at the Graham School, she equally disapproved of the "mystic kind of free expression [that leads] to the annihilation of technique" at the Wigman School.[38] Evan was searching for a methodological starting point that the teachers associated with Bennington could not provide.

That Evan published her report in *New Theatre* suggests her affiliation with the leftist wing of the modern dance movement. Indeed, her comments reveal a subtext linked to the controversy over Wigman's fascism launched by *New Theatre* the previous year. Although Evan reflects on her study at the Wigman School during summer 1934, her article appeared almost two years later. In the interim *New Theatre* had published revelations concerning Wigman's collaboration with the Nazis, and Evan's retrospective account implicitly asks how the "mysticism" of Wigman's methods might have contributed to her affiliation with fascism.

Just as Wigman's American tours ignited conflict between advocates of ballet and modern dance and among modern dancers, so the controversy over Wigman's involvement with National Socialism inflamed tensions between leftist and humanist dancers. The controversy flared in the pages of *New Theatre*, the official organ for the leftist dancers, and *Dance Observer*, the unofficial organ for the humanist dancers founded by Louis Horst. Coincidentally, both journals published their inaugural issue in January 1934. However, while *New Theatre* ceased publication after April 1937, *Dance Observer* continued to appear until 1964. In the end this difference in longevity determined the outcome of the trial over Wigman's fascism. For once the prosecution mounted by *New Theatre* lost its voice, the defense mounted by *Dance Observer* won the case.

The controversy began in August 1935 when *New Theatre* published an article titled "Mary Wigman—Fascist." Authored by Nicholas Wirth, the article paraphrased recent articles by Wigman that had appeared in German, notably the essay "German Dance Art" ("Deutsche Tanzkunst"), later published as the title essay of her 1935 volume. Wirth commented:

> In their efforts to preserve the last remnants of culture in Germany, thousands are facing persecution and death—while Mary Wigman, who belongs in the vanguard of that struggle, deserts. She openly supports the rule of the exploiters, closing her eyes, ignoring the misery; many of her best pupils are working in the other camp, fighting for a new society; and recently, these pupils addressed a letter to Mary Wigman. While they extol the old Mary Wigman, she

who did so much for the art of the dance throughout the world, they must mourn that Mary Wigman who gives way to Goebbels. When her art had no national bounds, they followed; now, they must leave that memory, while she is Fascist.[39]

Although Wirth did not list which dancers had signed the letter to Mary Wigman, the letter received the official endorsement of the New Dance League.

The editors of *Dance Observer* did not respond directly to Wirth's accusations. Rather in the October 1935 issue they printed Virginia Stewart's "German Letter," a factual account of recent developments in the Third Reich: the 1934 Dance Festival sponsored by Goebbels's Cultural Ministry, the reorganization of the professional curriculum at the Wigman School, and plans for an international dance festival to be held in conjunction with the 1936 Olympic Games.[40] The following month they printed an article by Hanya Holm on Mary Wigman that celebrated the German choreographer's artistry. Like Stewart, Holm described Wigman's recent activities in a straightforward manner: "[*Women's Dances*] was the high point of the Dance Festival held in Berlin. . . . At this writing, Mary Wigman is working on a new program [*Hymnic Dances*] which she expects to be ready for presentation in November."[41]

New Theatre reacted with outrage at the refusal of *Dance Observer* to engage the question of Wigman's alliance with National Socialism. Edna Ocko, dance editor of *New Theatre*, sent a letter of protest to her colleagues at *Dance Observer,* pointing out that Virginia Stewart's "German Letter" had only strengthened the case of the leftist dancers against Wigman. She stated: "Although the *Dance Observer* admittedly is concerned with the American dance, surely the status of a dancer, whose influence in America is still nationwide, cannot be glossed over by silence and tolerant non-commitment."[42] To their credit, the editors of *Dance Observer* did print Ocko's letter, although they reserved any editorial comment and did not "take a stand" as she had demanded.

In the November 1935 issue of *New Theatre,* Ocko continued the case for the prosecution with an article titled "The Swastika Is Dancing." Reiterating Wirth's charges on the basis of the factual evidence supplied by Stewart, Ocko advocated a boycott of the international dance festival planned for 1936. She called on dancers "as social-minded artists, whether conservative, liberal or radical" to "join with the rest of the clear-thinking world and not permit

HITLER'S ONE-MAN SHOW: THE NAZI DANCE FESTIVAL

Fig. 64.   Cartoon intended to rally support for the dancers' boycott of the 1936 Olympics (from *New Theatre*, May 1936)

themselves to succumb to the tantalizing and desperate endeavors of the German government, aided and abetted by people like Wigman, to make Germany seem to the outsider, a patron of the arts, and an encourager of free artistic creation."[43]

American dancers did rally to Ocko's cause, and humanists and leftists joined together to support the boycott, organized by the New Dance League, of the 1936 International Dance Festival (see fig. 64). Among the supporters of the boycott were Martha Graham, Doris Humphrey, Charles Weidman, Helen Tamiris, Anna Sokolow, Sol Hurok, and Lincoln Kirstein.[44] Notably absent from the roster was Hanya Holm.

Surprisingly, the editors of *Dance Observer* stood somewhat aloof from the boycott, despite the advocacy of their constituents. An editorial in the April 1936 issue quoted Graham's statement declining an invitation to participate in the festival, although without any editorial statement of support.[45] The October issue printed a review of the festival by Artur Michel, a longtime dance critic and a German Jew who had faced persecution by the Nazis. An editorial alerted readers to his situation, asserting that "such a critic should not be lost to the dance world."[46] It seems that the politics of *Dance Observer* sanctioned intervention on behalf of individuals while remaining aloof from collective initiatives.

This inclination to protect individuals ultimately led the editors of *Dance Observer* to defend Wigman and Laban against the accusations of the left. In the March 1937 issue an editorial on the status of Wigman and Laban finally appeared and characterized their situation as unclear. The editorial presented the German dancers more as victims than as perpetrators of fascism: "It is known that Mary Wigman has been forced to disband her professional group, indicating that she has received no support from the Reich; that Laban is in bad favor and has temporarily been asked to stop working; and that others have been intimidated into acquiescence to the system because their families were threatened."[47] That the editors' long silence had resulted in part from their distrust of leftist politics became clear as the editorial continued. Noting that "America has its own enemies within," the editorial stated that "such hysteria can be curbed only by united resistance against it, and dancers and other artists must know and play their part with others in that resistance."[48]

The dance press never resolved the issue of Wigman's collaboration with the Nazis. Two months after *Dance Observer* finally took a stand, *New Theatre* ceased publication. Once the prosecution went silent, the issue was dropped, and *Dance Observer* never again brought up the question of Wigman's relations with the Nazis. The humanist defense of Wigman rested its case with the 1937 editorial. For decades afterward, the notion that Wigman had been a victim of the Nazis survived in the literature. Typical was Walter Sorell's statement in *The Mary Wigman Book* (1975):

> The question has often been asked why Mary Wigman did not leave Nazi Germany, when she knew she would have been received with open arms in Switzerland, England, or America. Her motivations for staying may shed some light on certain features of her character. She was a German who had grown up and risen to fame in her country. She felt she had no right to leave her native soil and her contemporaries at their time of greatest and gravest trial. She did not think of saving herself, not even when she was denounced as a leftist and Jew-lover and put on the blacklist of the Nazis. She thought she could be of greater help while staying where she belonged and continuing her work, saying in dance form what could not be said in words. But the pressures of the National Socialist Party grew stronger, and the Party took control of her school. . . . At the relatively early age of fifty-five she gave up, or rather had to give up, her career as a dancer. . . . From then on she lived in the shadow of her time and self-willed fate.[49]

Like so many other of Wigman's friends and disciples, Sorell defended her to her death and beyond.

Not surprisingly, the controversy over Wigman's fascism also implicated Holm. During the period when *New Theatre* printed accusations of Wigman's Nazi connections, the leftist dancers initiated a boycott of the New York branch of the Mary Wigman School. As Holm later recounted the mid-thirties:

> I was not representing any faction, certainly not. I was interested in the dance. Period. . . .
>
> [When Hitler came to power,] people who were on top of the Communist party came and said I should make a statement that Wigman had nothing to do with the Hitler government though she was living over there. Well, she was left alone, and I said I'd make no statement because that might cost her head. . . . All right if you boycott. And they boycotted. They threw stones in the window. At the same time I wrote Wigman and I said, listen, the situation is not easy. It would be easier for me if I would use my own name and not affiliate with the Wigman school, and she said fine.[50]

In November 1936 the school officially became the Hanya Holm Studio (see fig. 65). Announcing the name change, Holm reaffirmed, "My respect and admiration for the artist Mary Wigman is today the same as ever." However, since "time and distance [had] automatically brought about a complete dissociation" of the New York branch from the Dresden school, she believed it important to underscore the status of the school as an "independent institution."[51] Her statement continued: "A racial question or a political question has never existed and shall never exist in my school. In my opinion there is no room for politics in art. I most emphatically refuse to identify myself with any political creed which strangles the free development of art, regardless of whether these political straitjackets are imported from Europe or manufactured here."[52] In this statement Holm distanced herself both from the fascism attributed to Wigman and from the socialism advocated by the leftist dancers in the United States. Embracing the humanist credo, she asserted her belief in the separation of art and politics.

The same fall that the Mary Wigman School of New York became the Hanya Holm Studio, the Hanya Holm Concert Group made its formal debut. The following summer the concert group premiered *Trend* at Bennington, a work that "established [Holm]

hanya
holm

school of dancing

and

concert group

formerly

NEW YORK WIGMAN SCHOOL

*will be conducted
under her own name*

hanya holm studio

215 West 11 Street
New York, N. Y.
WA. 9-6530

Fig. 65.   Announcement of name change for the Hanya Holm Studio (from *Dance Observer*, November 1936)

beyond question as one of the important figures in the American dance world," to quote John Martin.[53] The critic saw the work as a synthesis of "the dynamic quality" of American dance with "the more subjective qualities" of the German dance, especially "its sense of space, its fluency, its unbroken relationship of movement to emotion."[54] Martin concluded:

> Her acceptance of the rhythms of American life as her own, and America's acceptance of her without question as its own, bring not only a new artist into the field but the seeds of a new maturity. Those principles of Wigman's dance which are without race or country but belong to the universal aspects of the art, have been planted in perhaps the only manner in which their growth is assured. . . . In the fullness of time their universality may very well come to blossom in a new soil with all the hardiness of an indigenous growth.[55]

Identifying "universality" with the "indigenous" development of American modern dance, Martin set the terms for the appreciation of Hanya Holm in the postwar period.

Having embraced the humanist credo during the thirties, Holm departed from the career paths of her Bennington colleagues in the late forties. After *Trend* she choreographed a number of other dances for her concert group, but by 1945 financial difficulties forced her to disband her company. In 1948 she commenced a new career choreographing Broadway musicals. Among her many successes were *Kiss Me Kate* and *My Fair Lady*. In 1967, the same year that the Wigman School in Berlin closed, she retired from an active professional career. Holm lived for another twenty-five years, until her death on 3 November 1992.[56]

THE POSTWAR HISTORIOGRAPHY OF
MODERN DANCE

In the postwar period few commentators questioned the innate Americanness of American modern dance. Don McDonagh's *The Rise and Fall and Rise of Modern Dance* (1970) popularized the historiography given a theoretical basis by Jill Johnston's 1967 essay, "The New American Modern Dance." In McDonagh's narrative, just as the "historic generation" of Martha Graham, Doris Humphrey, and Charles Weidman had rebelled against the "first generation" of Isadora Duncan, Loie Fuller, and Ruth St. Denis, so contemporary modern dancers such as Merce Cunningham and the choreographers associated with Judson Church rebelled against the choreographers affiliated with Bennington. Strikingly, McDonagh mentioned Mary Wigman and Hanya Holm only in passing. Focusing solely on American-born choreographers, McDonagh streamlined the genealogy familiar from Martin's *Introduction to the Dance.* The abbreviated genealogy supported McDonagh's contention that modern dance "had been created out of the American experience in the same improvisational manner in which jazz had been created."[57] Given the de-emphasis on improvisation as a working method by Graham and Humphrey, his assertion makes an unwitting irony.

Holm had a larger role in McDonagh's subsequent survey, *The Complete Book of Modern Dance* (1976). Outlining the family tree of American modern dance, the critic no longer could ignore the German-born choreographer. The 1976 encyclopedia broadened the tradition implicit in the 1970 volume in other directions as well. Not only Hanya Holm but also Angna Enters, Lester Horton, Edwin Strawbridge, and Helen Tamiris joined the generation of "the founders." The encyclopedia then placed contemporary dancers in genealogical relation to their predecessors. Thus Hanya Holm became the founder of an "extended choreographic family" through her training of Mary Anthony, Valerie Bettis, Don Redlich, Glen Tetley, and Alwin Nikolais. Nikolais in turn extended Holm's legacy through his training of Murray Louis, Phyllis Lamhut, Beverly Schmidt, and others. Wigman received more mention than she had in the previous volume, because she could be placed as the precursor to Holm's lineage.

During the seventies, students of modern dance had access not only to McDonagh's volumes but also to Martin's *Introduction to the Dance* and Kirstein's *Dance: A Short History of Classic Theatrical Dancing,* which remained standard references. In addition, Walter Sorell had translated two volumes of Wigman's writings, *The Language of Dance* (1966) and *The Mary Wigman Book* (1975). Thus the footnote status granted Wigman within McDonagh's chronicles coexisted with the image of the charismatic soloist in Martin and Kirstein and the rhapsodic voice in Sorell's translations. Together with the early sound film of Wigman's solos recovered during the mid-seventies, these sources created the impression of an eccentric precursor to American modern dance. This was the Wigman I first encountered in my dance history class—the mystical rhetoric of *The Language of Dance* juxtaposed against the grainy images of the dancer performing *Witch Dance II* and *Shifting Landscape*.

Beginning in the late seventies, American critics began to take more notice of *Ausdruckstanz* as a precedent for American modern dance. In *Where She Danced* (1979) Elizabeth Kendall devoted several pages to German modern dance, noting its connection to the physical culture movement and speculating on its possible influence in the United States. Kendall wrote:

> Denishawn had thrown its graduates into the hands of German dance credos by undermining the school's training with the idea that dance is finally something you make up yourself, according to what you have sniffed out about the progression of Art. Germany provided firm and compelling philosophic underpinnings that Denishawn . . . hadn't been able to provide even with all its talk of religion, eugenics, sex philosophy, Greek elitism, and Delsarte.[58]

Kendall's recovery of German modern dance formed part of a broad-ranging cultural history of early modern dance. Indeed, her book reflected a revival of interest in early modern dance that began during the seventies. Through staged reconstructions and symposia, the revival brought Mary Wigman back into view as well as her American contemporaries Isadora Duncan and Ruth St. Denis.

It seems more than coincidental that the revival of early modern dance accompanied a stasis in the development of American modern dance. After the Judson Church choreographers broke away from their mentor Merce Cunningham in the early sixties, the Greenbergian (and Oedipal) logic of American modern dance seemed to come to a standstill. At that point, interest turned to the origins of the practice. It also seems more than coincidental that the revival arose with the feminist movement of the seventies. That early modern dance comprised a cultural movement and artistic practice led by women now became a subject worthy of attention.

The revival and consequent revisualization of *Ausdruckstanz* as precedent for American modern dance inform Deborah Jowitt's *Time and the Dancing Image* (1988). Following up Kendall's lead in *Where She Danced,* Jowitt surveys the interest in German dance evident in New York during the late twenties and early thirties—appearances by Harald Kreutzberg, Tilly Losch, Yvonne Georgi, Eugene von Grona, Jan Veen, Margarethe Wallmann, and, of course, Mary Wigman's tours and the opening of the New York branch of the Wigman School by Hanya Holm. Jowitt notes that "quite a few early reviews presuppose some influence from Germany on the major American modernists, if only as a catalyst."[59] However, she backs away from making this argument herself, stating that "it remains a moot point how directly and to what extent [the German dancers] may have [influenced the Americans]."[60]

In an odd way, Jowitt's *Time and the Dancing Image* circles back to Martin's writings during the thirties. For both critics acknowledge *Ausdruckstanz* as a potential influence on American modern dance but then equivocate over whether this potential was realized. Hesitating over the question of German influence, Martin and Jowitt demonstrate their desire to view modern dance as an inherently American art form.

EPILOGUE

Beginning my research, I thought it possible to set aside the critical habit of seeing German dance through the lens of American dance, a critical habit that seemed to distort much of the English-language literature on *Ausdruckstanz* and *Tanztheater*. But now I realize the extent to which this study has rewritten *Ausdruckstanz* as a mirror for American modern dance. In this mirror, the ideological complication of feminism and nationalism in American modern dance looms large.

As the first chapter suggested, this complication marked the dancing and writing of Isadora Duncan. Dancing Woman, Duncan also danced the American Self. She pictorialized the Greek Dance as well, a pictorialization that universalized the American Self. Duncan's dancing and writing imagined America in terms of Hellenism, terms that excluded the "African savage." At the same time, her America required the liberation of Woman. As Duncan wrote:

> It is not only a question of true art, it is a question of race, of the development of the female sex to beauty and health, of the return to the original strength and to natural movements of woman's body. It is a question of the development of perfect mothers and the birth of healthy and beautiful children. The dancing school of the future is to develop and to show the ideal form of woman.[61]

Reading such a passage, it is hard not to reject Duncan's feminism, given its subtext of eugenics. But her dancing did provide the possibility of female spectatorship for white, middle-class women in an era when such possibilities were few, and for this reason her example cannot be discounted. What is difficult to accept is how intertwined were her feminism and nationalism. Both were tainted, her feminism with eugenics, her nationalism with the possibility of female spectatorship. In the end, the two dimensions of her work cannot be segregated and evaluated independently.

A similarly complicated judgment holds for the career of Mary Wigman. That her Weimar dances created a utopian space for her female dancers—and female spectators—cannot be discounted. Nor can the transmutation of this utopian space into a dystopian space—and its further transformation into a space for ambivalence under the Third Reich—be overlooked. Her dances exemplify the paradox of resistance and reinscription, whereby avowedly oppositional works reinforce some dimension of the status quo, and even intently affirmative works retain some dimension of subversion. From my perspective, wholly dismissing Wigman's career would be as absurd as uncritically celebrating her example. An either/or judgment simply is not possible.

Notes

Since the selected bibliography includes only published sources, archival documents referred to in the notes are identified according to the following abbreviations: MWA (Mary Wigman Archive, Academy of Arts, Berlin); DTA (Deutsches Tanzarchiv Köln); AdK-DDR (Akademie der Künste der DDR, Leipzig); NYPL-DC (New York Public Library for the Performing Arts, Dance Collection). Unless otherwise noted, all translations are by the author.

INTRODUCTION

1. Although I have read many of the articles frequently cited in discussions of the male gaze and female spectatorship (by Laura Mulvey, E. Ann Kaplan, Mary Ann Doane, and others), I have found Sue-Ellen Case's and Ann Daly's paraphrases of feminist theory more useful to my own work. See Sue-Ellen Case, *Feminism and Theatre* (New York: Methuen, 1988), 112–32, and Ann Daly, "The Balanchine Woman: Of Hummingbirds and Channel Swimmers," *Drama Review* 31:1 (Spring 1987), 8–21.

2. Benedict Anderson, *Imagined Communities: Reflections on the Origin and Spread of Nationalism* (London: Verso, 1983).

3. Joseph Goebbels, *Die Tagebücher von Joseph Goebbels: Sämtliche Fragmente* vol. 3, pt. 1 (Munich: K. G. Saur, 1987), 187. The full quotation is given in chapter five, note 72.

4. The expressionism–*Neue Sachlichkeit* scheme organizes Peter Gay's *Weimar Culture* (New York: Harper and Row, 1968) as well as John Willett's *Art and Politics in the Weimar Period* (New York: Pantheon, 1978). Neither survey mentions Mary Wigman. The dancer does figure in surveys of German theater organized according to the expressionism–Epic Theater scheme, but barely and somewhat misleadingly. Willett's *The Theatre of the Weimar Republic* (New York: Holmes and Meier, 1988), 184–85, associates her with Leni Riefenstahl, who had studied with her. In Michael Patterson's *The Revolution in German Theatre, 1900–1933* (London: Routledge and Kegan Paul, 1981), 138, she appears incorrectly associated with Piscator's production of *Hooray, We're Alive*. (Wigman-trained dancers, not Wigman herself, choreographed and performed the Charleston.)

5. Fredric Jameson's anthology *Aesthetics and Politics* (1977; reprint, London: Verso, 1980) translates the key essays in the "expressionist debate." Suspicious of the "mysticism" and "irrationalism" of *Ausdruckstanz,*

Jost Hermand and Frank Trommler dismiss Wigman and in so doing pursue a Lukács-like line of reasoning in their survey of *Die Kultur der Weimarer Republik* (Munich: Nymphenburger, 1978), 216–18. Hedwig Müller's account of Wigman's activities under the Third Reich tends to follow Bloch's reasoning. My own argument falls between these two positions.

In an essay written after completing this book, I reflect more self-consciously than I do here on my theory of the relations between ideology and form. See my essay "Modern Dance in the Third Reich: Six Positions and a Coda" in *Choreographing History*, ed. Susan Foster (Bloomington: Indiana University Press, 1993).

6. Stephanie Barron et al., *"Degenerate Art": The Fate of the Avant-Garde in Nazi Germany* (Los Angeles: Los Angeles County Museum of Art, 1991), 9, 250, 319.

7. Willett, *The Theatre of the Weimar Republic*, 179–212; John Rouse, *Brecht and the West German Theatre* (Ann Arbor: UMI Research Press, 1989), 9–24; Akademie der Künste, *Theater im Exil, 1933–1945* (Berlin: Akademie der Künste, 1973).

8. Horst Koegler, "Eine vitale Vielseitigkeit," in *Tanz in Deutschland: Ballett seit 1945*, edited by Hartmut Regitz (Berlin: Quadriga, 1984), 8–9.

9. Peter Bürger, *Theory of the Avant-Garde*, trans. Michael Shaw (Minneapolis: University of Minnesota Press, 1984). My reading of Bürger is indebted to Andreas Huyssen's *After the Great Divide: Modernism, Mass Culture, Postmodernism* (Bloomington: Indiana University Press, 1986).

10. Although this is not the place to pursue an overview of the disciplinary formation of dance studies, it is the place to acknowledge that I am not alone in my endeavors. My own efforts to imagine an (inter)discipline of dance studies have been encouraged and emboldened by Susan Foster's *Reading Dancing* (Berkeley and Los Angeles: University of California Press, 1986), Lynn Garafola's *Diaghilev's Ballets Russes* (New York: Oxford University Press, 1989), Cynthia Novack's *Sharing the Dance* (Madison: University of Wisconsin Press, 1990), and Mark Franko's *Dance as Text: Ideologies of the Baroque Body* (New York: Cambridge University Press, 1993).

11. Raymond Williams, *The Sociology of Culture* (New York: Schocken Books, 1982). See notes 1 and 2 for other references.

12. This remains so even when a film record shot under ideal conditions exists. For example, the choreographic works preserved and disseminated by public television's Dance in America series provide only the semblance of a New Critical text. Yes, they can be repeatedly viewed by multiple viewers, just as novels can be read and reread by many readers. But the film documents only a single performance reblocked to heighten the illusion of three-dimensional space made possible by sophisticated camera techniques, and the camera directs the viewer's gaze. In the theater the viewer chooses where to look, senses the performer's presence, participates in the event of performance. So even when an accurate film record exists, the dance scholar must read through the celluloid to the performance event, which remains the most elusive of texts.

13. Hodson's reconstruction of *Le sacre du printemps* has been documented by Dance in America. Also see Millicent Hodson, "*Sacre*: Searching for Nijinsky's Chosen One," *Ballet Review* 15:3 (Fall 1987), 53–66, and "Ritual Design in the New Dance: Nijinsky's Choreographic Method," *Dance Research* 3:2 (Autumn 1985), 35–45, and 4:1 (Spring 1986), 63–77.

14. "Tänze, die immer gelten: Gespräch mit Susanne Linke über ihr Dore Hoyer-Programm," *Tanzdrama* 1 (1987), 10; Anna Kisselgoff, "Modern Dances of Bones Rather Than Flesh," *New York Times* (5 November 1989), H:14; Mark Franko, "Repeatability, Reconstruction, and Beyond," *Theatre Journal* 41:1 (March 1989), 56–74.

15. Although dance and theater scholars often have deployed performance reconstruction as a working method, they have not reached agreement over the stylistic conventions for writing up the results of their research. In *Democracy's Body: Judson Dance Theater 1962–1964* (Ann Arbor: UMI Research Press, 1983) Sally Banes casts her performance reconstructions in the past tense, as if to underscore the choreography's ephemerality and its boundedness to the historical moment of its creation. In *The Shapes of Change: Images of American Dance* (Boston: Houghton Mifflin, 1979) Marcia Siegel pens her dance reconstructions in the present tense, as if to underscore the self-sufficiency and relevance of the choreographic design, irrespective of any single performance. My reconstructions make both sorts of claims and hence sandwich the fictional present tense within the past tense: the fictional present draws attention to the textuality of my reconstructions, while the past tense draws attention to the historicity of my interpretations.

1. IDEOLOGY AND ABSOLUTE DANCE

1. Rudolf von Delius, "Eine neue Tänzerin," *Die Propyläen* 5:28 (1914), 21.

2. In a series of essays published in the forties and fifties, Clement Greenberg articulated and popularized a theory of modern art that finds many analogues in theories of modernism in the other arts, most especially in Western theater dance. In an essay titled "'American-Type' Painting," Greenberg wrote, "It seems to be a law of modernism—thus one that applies to almost all art that remains truly alive in our time—that the conventions not essential to the viability of a medium be discarded as soon as they are recognized." In his view, the New York School furthered the modernist project of the School of Paris by creating a "new kind of flatness," thus acknowledging the essential nature of the picture plane. Greenberg was well aware that in making these claims he would be "accused of chauvinist exaggeration," but he insisted, "I make no more allowance for American art than I do for any other kind." In other words, that dance critics have conjoined overt critical advocacy with a belief in the formal logic of modernism finds ample precedent and parallel in Greenberg's writing.

"'American-Type' Painting" is reprinted in Clement Greenberg, *Art and*

Culture (Boston: Beacon Press, 1961). The quotations above are from pages 208, 226, 228, and 229, respectively.

3. Jean Georges Noverre, *Letters on Dancing and Ballets*, trans. Cyril W. Beaumont (New York: Dance Horizons, 1966), 16. As used here, "pictorial ballet" refers not only to Noverre's *ballet d'action* but also to the Romantic ballet and post-Romantic ballet, that is, to the varied genres of Western theater dance from 1700 to 1900 that pictorialized motifs familiar from literature and visual art. My understanding of pictorialism is indebted to Martin Meisel's *Realizations* (Princeton: Princeton University Press, 1983).

4. André Levinson, "The Spirit of the Classic Dance," *Theatre Arts Monthly* (1925), reprinted in Selma Jeanne Cohen, ed., *Dance as a Theatre Art* (New York: Harper and Row, 1974), 113, 114.

5. My critique of the master-narrative of absolute dance develops (and supersedes) a line of thinking I first presented in "Modernist Dogma and 'Post-Modern' Rhetoric: A Response to Sally Banes' *Terpsichore in Sneakers*," *Drama Review* 32:4 (Winter 1988), 32–39.

6. Fritz Böhme, *Tanzkunst* (Dessau: C. Dünnhaupt, 1926), 157. In an era of prolific dance critics Böhme was one of the most prolific, author of seven books and innumerable articles and reviews. For a biographical overview of his career, see Frank-Manuel Peter, "Wegbereiter des modernen Tanzes: Der Tanzpublicist Fritz Böhme," *Tanzdrama* 9 (1989), 23.

7. Böhme, *Tanzkunst*, 162, 23–53 passim.

8. Böhme, *Tanzkunst*, 128–62.

9. Böhme, *Tanzkunst*, 126–27.

10. John Martin was dance critic for the *New York Times* from 1927 to 1962. Before taking up that post, he had studied theater in Germany. That he was familiar with Böhme's theories seems evident from his writing, although he never acknowledged the influence of the German critic.

11. John Martin, *Introduction to the Dance* (1939; reprint, New York: Dance Horizons, 1965), 231, 235.

12. Martin, *Introduction to the Dance*, 224–47.

13. Martin, *Introduction to the Dance*, 197, 200.

14. Lincoln Kirstein, *Dance: A Short History of Classic Theatrical Dancing* (1935; reprint, New York: Dance Horizons, 1969), 305–6.

15. Kirstein, *Dance*, 306.

16. Kirstein, *Dance*, 284.

17. Kirstein, *Dance*, 289, 317.

18. Johnston's essay "The New American Modern Dance" was originally published in Richard Kostelanetz, ed., *The New American Arts* (New York: Collier, 1967), 162–93, and has been reprinted several times. This citation is from the reprint in *Salmagundi* 33/34 (Spring/Summer 1976), 149.

19. Johnston, "The New American Modern Dance," 165.

20. Johnston, "The New American Modern Dance," 152.

21. Johnston, "The New American Modern Dance," 152.

22. Johnston, "The New American Modern Dance," 153.

23. Johnston, "The New American Modern Dance," 150–51.

24. David Michael Levin, "Balanchine's Formalism," *Dance Perspectives* 55 (Autumn 1973), 32.

25. Levin, "Balanchine's Formalism," 30–37.

26. In a more recent essay Levin has refined his definition of dance modernism and used it as a basis for defining postmodernism in dance, without abandoning his indebtedness to Greenberg's insights. On a chart accompanying the essay, Mary Wigman appears under the rubric "avant-garde modern dance," and Balanchine and Cunningham mark the "modernist" phase, and Twyla Tharp the "postmodernist" phase, of "postmodern dance." See David Michael Levin, "Postmodernism in Dance: Dance, Discourse, Democracy," in Hugh Silverman, ed., *Postmodernism—Philosophy and the Arts* (New York and London: Routledge, 1990), 207–33.

27. Selma Jeanne Cohen, "Avant-Garde Choreography," *Criticism* 3 (1961), 16. Although Wigman warrants no mention in Cohen's account, this oversight cannot be read in the same way as her near disappearance in Johnston and her absence in Levin, for Cohen surveys contemporary developments rather than constructing a genealogy for dance modernism.

28. Norbert Servos, *Pina Bausch Wuppertal Dance Theater, or, The Art of Training a Goldfish* (Cologne: Ballett-Bühnen-Verlag, 1984), 19.

29. Servos, *Pina Bausch Wuppertal Dance Theater*, 19.

30. Servos, *Pina Bausch Wuppertal Dance Theater*, 23.

31. Servos, *Pina Bausch Wuppertal Dance Theater*, 26.

32. Hedwig Müller, *Mary Wigman: Leben und Werk der grossen Tänzerin* (Berlin: Quadriga, 1986), 305.

33. Joseph R. Roach, "Theatre History and the Ideology of the Aesthetic," *Theatre Journal* 41:2 (May 1989), 157.

34. Anderson, *Imagined Communities*, 15.

35. In *The Modern Dance* (1933; reprint, New York: Dance Horizons, 1965), 15, Martin asserts that "no conscious artistic use was made of metakinesis until the modern dance arose." The early modern dancer's reliance on kinesthesia raises interesting questions about the relation of an essential body to a constructed body. Do the movement vocabularies of early modern dance, based on physiological events such as the alternation of inhalation and exhalation, reveal an essential body? Or do these movement vocabularies construct and deploy a natural body for the purposes of artistic legitimation? Or does early modern dance give choreographic form to the tension between the essential body and the constructed body, revealing the two bodies to be endpoints of a continuum rather than antithetical alternatives? Although I do not pursue these questions, I raise them in order to suggest the relevance of early modern dance to contemporary debates on the status of the body.

36. For a thorough inquiry into this construction, see Tracy C. Davis, *Actresses as Working Women: Their Social Identity in Victorian Culture* (London and New York: Routledge, 1991).

37. Deborah Jowitt, *Time and the Dancing Image* (New York: William

Morrow, 1988), 67–102; Elizabeth Kendall, *Where She Danced* (New York: Alfred Knopf, 1979), 17–68; Nancy Ruyter, *Reformers and Visionaries* (New York: Dance Horizons, 1979), 17–73; Gertrud Pfister and Hans Langenfeld, "Die Leibesübungen für das weibliche Geschlecht—Ein Mittel zur Emanzipation der Frau?" in *Geschichte der Leibesübungen*, ed. Horst Ueberhorst (Berlin: Bartels und Wernitz, 1980), vol. 3, 485–521; Helmut Günther, "Gymnastik- und Tanzbestrebungen vom Ende des 19. Jahrhundert bis zum Ersten Weltkrieg," in *Geschichte der Leibesübungen*, ed. Ueberhorst, vol. 3, 569–93.

38. Cyril Beaumont's *The Ballet Called Giselle* (1945; reprint, Princeton: Princeton Book Co., 1988), 126–34, provides a production history and an account of changes made by Marius Petipa. Beaumont (39–52) also translates the libretto printed at the time the work premiered, which credits the ballet to Gautier, Henri de Saint-Georges, and ballet master Jean Coralli. (According to contemporary accounts, Jules Perrot, husband of Carlotta Grisi, the ballerina who played the leading role, also contributed to the choreography.) The libretto departs in some details from the scenario Gautier published a week after the premiere, translated in Ivor Guest's collection, *Gautier on Dance* (London: Dance Books, 1986), 94–102. Since my interpretation centers on the 1841 production, my analysis of the choreographic structure privileges the libretto and scenario over productions "after Petipa."

39. Guest, *Gautier on Dance*, 101.

40. Guest, *Gautier on Dance*, 101.

41. Guest, *Gautier on Dance*, 97.

42. Both the libretto and scenario note the pantomime with the daisy. In the Kirov version "after Petipa" documented on video, the pantomime gives way to a duet in which the two lovers dance in unison, with Albrecht mirroring a signature phrase first performed by Giselle. The unison suggests a partnership of equals; their two bodies remain two bodies. At the end of the first act, after the revelation of Albrecht's betrayal, Giselle reiterates the signature phrase, but only marks the steps, as if remembering what she cannot quite believe.

43. In the Kirov version "after Petipa," the unison dancing of the first act gives way in the second act to lifts and partnering that display the two bodies as one body.

44. Lynn Garafola, "The Travesty Dancer in Nineteenth-Century Ballet," *Dance Research Journal* 17:2/18:1 (Fall 1985/Spring 1986), 35–40.

45. Although neither John Chapman nor Evan Alderson use the term "the male gaze," their readings of *Giselle* in many ways parallel mine. See John Chapman, "An Unromantic View of Nineteenth-Century Romanticism," *York Dance Review* 7 (Spring 1978), 28–45, and Evan Alderson, "Ballet as Ideology: *Giselle*, Act II," *Dance Chronicle* 10:3 (1987), 290–304.

46. Guest, *Gautier on Dance*, 22.

47. See the references given in note 37

48. Although I have seen reconstructions by many third-generation

Duncan dancers, I have found Annabelle Gamson's to be the most persuasive. Her performances are recorded on a video titled *On Dancing Isadora's Dances*. Isadora Duncan's *The Art of the Dance*, edited by Sheldon Cheney and originally published in 1928 (available as a reprint from Theatre Arts Books), still provides the most useful single-volume anthology of visual images and writings by the dancer and her contemporaries.

49. Jowitt, *Time and the Dancing Image*, 77–84.

50. Jowitt, *Time and the Dancing Image*, 77.

51. The dating of the dance, like the dating of most dances by Isadora, is approximate. Isadora created two versions of the dance, a solo and a group dance for herself and her students. My comments relate to the solo version. For descriptions of the group version, see Kendall, *Where She Danced*, 169–70, and Fredrika Blair, *Isadora* (New York: McGraw-Hill, 1986), 246–47.

52. The same analysis could apply to *Mother*, set to Scriabin, as reconstructed by Annabelle Gamson. This is not to say that all Duncan's dances relied on the image of the mother, but rather that archetypes—whether borrowed from literary and pictorial sources, as in *Orpheus* and *Iphigenie in Aulis*, or fashioned in response to World War I and the Russian Revolution, as in *Marseillaise* and *Marche Slav*—often served as framing devices for her dancing. That I take *Ave Maria* as representative of her oeuvre is not to overlook the stylistic change often noted from her earlier to later dances. In fact, Duncan choreographed *Ave Maria* at the moment of stylistic transition. Her earlier dances emphasized light weight and free flow (in the terms of Labanalysis); her later dances emphasized strong weight and bound flow. Nonetheless, the choreographic frames I discuss persisted from her earlier to her later period, and it is this repertoire of representational strategies—archetype, autobiography, musical visualization, kinesthesia—that grounds my reading of Duncanesque dancing.

53. Duncan, *The Art of the Dance*, 21–22.

54. Duncan, *The Art of the Dance*, 21.

55. Duncan, *The Art of the Dance*, 17.

56. Mabel Dodge Luhan, *Movers and Shakers* (1936; reprint, Albuquerque: University of New Mexico Press, 1985), 319–20.

57. Duncan, *The Art of the Dance*, 7.

58. Hans Fischer, *Körperschönheit und Körperkultur* (Berlin: Deutsche Buch-Gemeinschaft, 1928), 228.

59. My argument counterpoints Ann Daly's reading of Duncan, outlined in her article "Dance History and Feminist Theory: Reconsidering Isadora Duncan and the Male Gaze," in *Gender in Performance*, ed. Laurence Senelick, 239–59 (Hanover: University Press of New England, 1992). Daly posits the kinesthesia of Duncan's dancing as a realization of Kristeva's conception of chora and as a perceptual mode that undermines the male gaze. In contrast, I see the kinesthesia of her dancing as an avenue not only for female spectatorship but also for the reinvention of Woman.

60. Duncan, *The Art of the Dance*, 61.

61. In *Fit for America* (New York: Pantheon, 1986) Harvey Green documents the link between national chauvinism and the turn-of-the-century interest in health, fitness, and sport. Oddly enough, he does not include early modern dance in his survey.

62. Duncan, *The Art of the Dance*, 48–49.

63. Duncan, *The Art of the Dance*, 48.

64. Duncan, *The Art of the Dance*, 39.

65. Note my shift in terminology from Duncan to Duncanesque dancer. Although a photograph of Duncan serves as a basis for comparison, my argument opposes the representational strategies fashioned by Wigman with those strategies—autobiography, archetype, musical visualization—associated with Duncan *and* her many followers. As I note in chapter two, Wigman saw Duncan perform only once, in 1916, a performance that she found "horrible." When Wigman made her choreographic debut in 1914, however, Duncanesque dancing was widespread in Germany, and she presumably reacted in the first instance against Duncan's many imitators, not against the innovator herself.

66. Here and throughout the remainder of the book I do not employ mechanical reproductions as primary texts in the way that art historians do. Rather I employ prints and photographs as one of the traces left by the performance event, and I segue from reading the image to reading the event, which in almost all cases I have reconstructed from a variety of media. The synthesis of visual and verbal evidence—live performances, films, photographs, reviews, choreographic notes, memoirs—creates the reconstruction, the semblance of a performance event. In the end it is the reconstruction—not the mechanically reproduced image—that I read.

67. Delius, "Eine neue Tänzerin," 21.

68. The most complete choreochronicle of Wigman's dances is appended to Hedwig Müller's biography.

69. Although the phrase *Gestalt im Raum* is my own invention, critical writing by and about Wigman often employed the two terms. In the twenties it became a critical commonplace that Laban and Wigman had developed the spatial dimension of movement (*Raum*) to a degree unknown before. It also became common for critics to describe Wigman in performance as a *Gestalt*, as a design in space and time rather than as a character or persona. Indeed, Wigman used both terms to title her dances, notably the solos premiered as part of the *Visions* cycle from 1925 to 1928.

70. Elizabeth Selden, *Elements of the Free Dance* (New York: A. S. Barnes, 1930), 36.

71. Delius, "Eine neue Tänzerin," 21.

2. GESTALT IM RAUM

1. Hedwig Müller, "Mary Wigman: Lebenslauf," *Tanzdrama* 8 (1989), 23; Müller, *Mary Wigman*, 11–14.

2. Heinrich later became an engineer, and Elisabeth ultimately joined

her older sister in Dresden and helped direct the Wigman School. Personal communication with Marlies Wiegmann Heinemann, 17 September 1991; Müller, *Mary Wigman*, 16; Gerhard Schumann, "Gespräche und Fragen: Mary Wigman," *Arbeitshefte* no. 36 (Berlin: Akademie der Künste der DDR, 1982), 37; James Albisetti, *Schooling German Girls and Women* (Princeton: Princeton University Press, 1988), 288.

3. Schumann, "Gespräche und Fragen: Mary Wigman," 36–38; Müller, *Mary Wigman*, 14–17.

4. Müller, *Mary Wigman*, 17–18.

5. Schumann, "Gespräche und Fragen: Mary Wigman," 38.

6. Schumann, "Gespräche und Fragen: Mary Wigman," 39.

7. Müller, "Lebenslauf," 23; Leonhard Fiedler and Martin Lang, eds., *Grete Wiesenthal* (Salzburg and Vienna: Residenz, 1985), 181.

8. Schumann, "Gespräche und Fragen: Mary Wigman," 38–39.

9. Schumann, "Gespräche und Fragen: Mary Wigman," 38.

10. Müller, "Lebenslauf," 23; Müller, *Mary Wigman*, 19–20; Walter Sorell, ed. and trans., *The Mary Wigman Book* (Middletown, Conn.: Wesleyan University Press, 1975), 187.

11. Quoted in Werner Otto, "Die Hellerauer Schulfeste von 1912 und 1913," in *Musikbühne 76*, ed. Horst Seeger (Berlin: Henschelverlag, 1976), 150.

12. Quoted in Selma Landen Odom, "Wigman at Hellerau," *Ballet Review* 14:2 (Summer 1986), 45.

13. Bildungsanstalt Jaques-Dalcroze, *Der Rhythmus: Ein Jahrbuch* (Jena: Eugen Diederichs, 1911), 72–73. I would like to thank Selma Odom for sharing this, as well as other sources, with me.

14. Odom, "Wigman at Hellerau," 46–47. I quote at length rather than paraphrase because the original is so precise as to the practice of Dalcroze's method at Hellerau.

15. Sorell, *The Mary Wigman Book*, 28, 188.

16. Schumann, "Gespräche und Fragen: Mary Wigman," 39–40; Müller, *Mary Wigman*, 36.

17. Sorell, *The Mary Wigman Book*, 26–27.

18. Sorell, *The Mary Wigman Book*, 33. For a comprehensive overview of Laban's early years, see Valerie Preston-Dunlop and Charlotte Purkiss, "Rudolf Laban—The Making of Modern Dance," *Dance Theatre Journal* 7:3 (Winter 1989), 11–16, 25, and 7:4 (Spring 1990), 10–13.

19. Course prospectus, *Tanz-Ton-Wort*, Laban School, c. 1914, MWA.

20. Sorell, *The Mary Wigman Book*, 34–36.

21. Sorell, *The Mary Wigman Book*, 38–40.

22. Martin Green, *Mountain of Truth* (Hanover: University Press of New England, 1986), 117–83.

23. Quoted in Green, *Mountain of Truth*, 129.

24. Müller, *Mary Wigman*, 45.

25. Green, *Mountain of Truth*, 83–115.

26. Sorell, *The Mary Wigman Book*, 47.

27. Sorell, *The Mary Wigman Book*, 41.

28. Sorell, *The Mary Wigman Book*, 50.

29. Sorell, *The Mary Wigman Book*, 50–51.

30. Müller, *Mary Wigman*, 64.

31. Program, Pfauen Theater, Zurich, 18 June 1917, MWA.

32. Rudolf Lämmel, *Der moderne Tanz* (Berlin: Oestergaard, 1928), 110.

33. H. B., "Tanzdichtungen von Mary Wiegmann," *Berner Tagblatt* (1 March 1916), MWA.

34. Müller, "Lebenslauf," 23.

35. Quoted in Müller, *Mary Wigman*, 60.

36. Lämmel, *Der moderne Tanz*, 110.

37. Program, Laban School, Zurich, 7 December [1917], MWA; "Bibi" [Berthe Trümpy], "Erster Abend ritueller Tanzkunst," typescript, 10 November 1917, MWA. I follow Hedwig Müller's choreochronicle in dating the premiere according to Trümpy's typescript rather than according to the extant program, which presumably documents a second performance.

38. The argument could be made that the shifting gender of the personal pronoun simply reflects the linguistic differences between German and English. However, my argument links the linguistically shifting gender to the shifting gender of Wigman's performing persona as visualized by Trümpy.

39. Since Müller's biography quotes nearly the entirety of Trümpy's typescript, references are given to the published version. Müller, *Mary Wigman*, 62.

40. Müller, *Mary Wigman*, 62.

41. Müller, *Mary Wigman*, 62.

42. Müller, *Mary Wigman*, 62.

43. Müller, *Mary Wigman*, 63.

44. Müller, *Mary Wigman*, 63.

45. Lämmel, *Der moderne Tanz*, 111.

46. Otto Flake, quoted in "Mary Wigman: Kritiken der schweizer Presse," Konzertdirektion Kantorowitz, 1919, 2, MWA.

47. Reviewer for *Zürcher Post*, quoted in "Mary Wigman: Kritiken der schweizer Presse," 6.

48. Frank Wohlfahrt, quoted in "Mary Wigman: Kritiken der schweizer Presse," 1.

49. Müller, "Lebenslauf," 23, and *Mary Wigman*, 66; Programs, MWA.

50. Böhme, *Tanzkunst*, 145–46.

51. Hugo Ball, *Flight out of Time: A Dada Diary* (New York: Viking Press, 1974), 102, 110.

52. Annabelle Melzer, *Latest Rage the Big Drum: Dada and Surrealist Performance* (Ann Arbor: UMI Research Press, 1983), 89.

53. Melzer, *Latest Rage the Big Drum*, 103–4. Similar arguments inform Naima Prevots's "Zurich Dada and Dance: Formative Ferment," *Dance Research Journal* 17:1 (Spring/Summer 1985), 3–8, and Harold Segel's discussion of Cabaret Voltaire in *Turn-of-the-Century Cabaret* (New York: Columbia University Press, 1987), 355–61.

54. Ball, *Flight out of Time*, 102.

55. As additional evidence for my reading of Wigman's divergence from the Dadaists, I cite the fact that she never performed at the Cabaret Voltaire. Were she so inclined, she presumably had as much opportunity to do so as the other members of Laban's circle who did perform there.

56. Susan Valeria Harris Smith, *Masks in Modern Drama* (Berkeley and Los Angeles: University of California Press, 1984), 12. Smith's analysis also encompasses "the heroic mask of the drama of myth, ritual, and spectacle" (49); masks that "make visible and real . . . dream images, hallucinations, and mental conflicts" (89); and the social mask that "emphasizes the false dimension of social interaction" (127).

57. I have been unable to identify the provenance of the dance depicted in the photograph beyond the ascription of "mathematician." Nor can Valerie Preston-Dunlop, coauthor with John Hodgson of *Rudolf Laban: An Introduction to His Work and Influence* (Plymouth, England: Northcote, 1990), which appends a detailed choreochronicle of Laban's work. Perhaps the masked figure took part in one of his group works. Preston-Dunlop does note, however, that the mask is "quite untypical." More typical were "hats/headgear which go across the face" (personal communication, 9 October 1991). In comparing images of Wigman and Laban, my intent is not to summarize Laban's oeuvre but rather to underscore the originality of Wigman's deployment of the mask principle.

58. Ball, *Flight out of Time*, 102.

59. The choreochronicle appended to Hodgson and Preston-Dunlop's *Rudolf Laban* details the productions staged by Laban from 1913 to 1917 in which Wigman appeared.

60. Richard Beacham, *Adolphe Appia: Theatre Artist* (Cambridge: Cambridge University Press, 1987), 77–78.

61. Sorell, *The Mary Wigman Book*, 188; Müller, *Mary Wigman*, 31; Beacham, *Adolphe Appia*, 78.

62. Quoted in Beacham, *Adolphe Appia*, 67.

63. In January 1991 a team of collaborators that included Selma Odom and Richard Beacham staged a reconstruction of the Hellerau *Orpheus* at the University of Warwick. Since I did not see this staged production, my interpretation is based solely on the descriptive reconstruction provided by Beacham in *Adolphe Appia*. For Odom's account of the reconstruction process, see the appendix to her dissertation on "Dalcroze Eurhythmics in England: History of an Innovation in Music and Movement Education" (University of Surrey, 1991), 215–30.

64. Emile Jaques-Dalcroze, *Rhythm, Music, and Education* (1921; reprint, London: Dalcroze Society, 1980), 167–68.

65. Horst Koegler, "Aus Rhythmus geboren—Zum Tanzen bestellt: Hellerau-Laxenburg und die Anfänge des modernen Tanzes," in *Ballett: Chronik und Bilanz des Ballettjahres* (Velber bei Hannover: Friedrich, 1977), 44.

66. Green, *Mountain of Truth*, 104–5; Müller, *Mary Wigman*, 61.

67. Hodgson and Preston-Dunlop, *Rudolf Laban*, 91.

68. Rudolf Laban, *A Life for Dance*, trans. Lisa Ullmann (New York: Theatre Arts Books, 1975), 159.

69. Laban, *A Life for Dance*, 159.

70. Laban, *A Life for Dance*, 160. Details in my reconstruction not found in Laban are from Edmund Stadler, "Theater und Tanz in Ascona," in *Monte Verita, Berg der Wahrheit*, ed. Harald Szeeman (Milan: Electa Editrice, 1978), 129–30.

71. Program, Der Freie Tanz, Museum Hall, Munich, 28 April 1914, MWA; Hans Brandenburg, *Der moderne Tanz* (1913; rev. ed. Munich: Georg Müller, 1917), 77.

72. Lämmel, *Der moderne Tanz*, 110; H. B., "Tanzdichtungen von Mary Wiegmann."

73. Program, "Die Königin: Tanz Pantomime," [Laban School, Zurich,] c. 1916, MWA. The program lists neither location nor date. That the program credits the design studio of the Laban School for the costumes and decor suggests that informal venue. That the program cites Mary Wiegmann as the choreographer places the work before 1918. My guess is that the work premiered in the second half of 1916. In February and March of that year the choreographer had presented her concert titled "The Self in Rhythm and Space." By winter 1917 she probably was preparing her Pfauen Theater program and soon thereafter began preparations for *Ecstatic Dances*. This suggests a date for *The Queen* in fall 1916, perhaps as Wigman's way of taking a break from the labor of solo choreography. But the dance could have been presented as early as winter 1914–1915, judging from the list of participants. Since no reviews are extant, the following interpretation is based solely on the scenario printed in the program.

74. Mary Wiegmann, "Ein Totentanz," manuscript, 5 pp., MWA. Since the handwritten scenario is signed "Wiegmann," it must date from the period before 1918. Although Lämmel notes that the Pfauen Theater program included a "group dance" set to Saint-Saëns titled *Dance of Death*, the Pfauen Theater program does not list any dancers other than "Wiegmann." Thus it is not clear how directly the scenario related to the 1917 concert. Also according to Lämmel, Wigman staged a second version of *Dance of Death* in 1921 for a group comprising Berthe Trümpy, Lena Hanke, and Gret Palucca. Since the relationship of the scenario to this production is equally unclear, I base my interpretation on the scenario alone, that is, on the choreographer's conception though not necessarily her realization. Lämmel, *Der moderne Tanz*, 110, 112.

3. MASK AND *GEMEINSCHAFT*

1. Fischer, *Körperschönheit und Körperkultur*, 233.

2. Bundesfilmarchiv, *Wege zu Kraft und Schönheit*, 2041. The film also includes clips of Laban, Niddy Impekoven, Dalcroze eurhythmics, Mensendieck exercises—and Tamara Karsavina! As a primary document for the movement culture of Weimar Germany, the film deserves closer scrutiny.

3. Wigman's best-known male students were Harald Kreutzberg and

Max Terpis. Both studied at the school in the early twenties and then left to pursue independent careers, Kreutzberg as a soloist and Terpis as ballet master at the Berlin State Opera.

4. Sorell, *The Mary Wigman Book*, 129.

5. Müller, *Mary Wigman*, 72.

6. Müller, *Mary Wigman*, 73–75.

7. Müller, *Mary Wigman*, 76–83; Schumann, "Gespräche und Fragen: Mary Wigman," 45–46; Berthe Trümpy, "Die Anfänge der Wigman Schule," *Tanzgemeinschaft* 2 : 2 (1930), 8–12.

8. During the mid-twenties Trümpy presented concerts of her own works. In 1926 she opened a studio in Berlin with Vera Skoronel, who had studied with Laban and Wigman on Monte Verita.

9. Müller, *Mary Wigman*, 81–83, 103.

10. Müller, *Mary Wigman*, 134; publicity brochure, "Mary Wigman: die Tänzerin, die Schule, die Tanzgruppe," 1927, NYPL-DC; announcement, "Berufsausbildung in Tanz," Wigman School, 1927, DTA. The first diploma exams were given in 1925.

11. According to Lilian Espenak, her parents allowed her to attend the Wigman School after consulting with a local dance teacher in her hometown of Bergen, Norway, who said that she most certainly would give a job to a Wigman graduate. Interview, 26 January 1988.

12. Müller, *Mary Wigman*, 88. Müller, 88–145 passim, chronicles the difficulties Wigman faced maintaining the balancing act described below.

13. Interview on 11 October 1987 with Tina Flade, a member of the dance group in 1923–1924 and a teacher at the Wigman School from 1928 to 1931.

14. The reminiscences of Wigman students from the 1920s who participated in the 1986 centennial conference at the Academy of Arts in West Berlin—Corrie Hartong, Else Lang, and Julia Tardy-Marcus—confirm the impressions of students from this period whom I have interviewed—Fé Alf, Lilian Espenak, Tina Flade, Truda Kaschmann, Louise Kloepper, Pola Nirenska, and Erika Thimey.

15. Interview with Flade, 11 October 1987.

16. Interview with Espenak, 26 January 1988.

17. Another student during this period, Pola Nirenska, remembers that the school was "rather expensive" and that her father, a Warsaw businessman, bought a building in Berlin and had the profits sent to Dresden to pay her tuition. She also does not remember any scholarship aid available. Interview with Pola Nirenska, 14 March 1985.

18. "Berufsausbildung in Tanz," DTA.

19. "Berufsausbildung in Tanz," DTA.

20. Interview with Nirenska, 14 March 1985.

21. Dianne Hunt, "The Wigman Years—Part One of the Thimey Transcripts," *Washington Dance View* 2 : 3 (February/March 1981), 25. In this interview Thimey describes the difference between technique classes and class lessons.

22. Interview with Louise Kloepper, 1 November 1987.

23. The most comprehensive overview of Laban's system is Vera Mal-etic's *Body-Space-Expression: The Development of Rudolf Laban's Movement and Dance Concepts* (Berlin: Mouton de Gruyter, 1987).

24. Quoted in Ewald Mathias Schumacher, "Körperkultur und Tanz-schulen," *Deutsches Musikjahrbuch* 1 (1923), 248. Wigman also wrote about her relation to Laban in "Rudolf von Labans Lehre vom Tanz," *Die neue Schaubühne* 3:5/6 (September 1921), 99–106.

25. Kaschmann made this remark while teaching a demonstration class on early Laban at the Society of Dance History Scholars, 18 February 1984.

26. Hunt, "The Wigman Years—Part One of the Thimey Transcripts," 24.

27. Quoted in Lämmel, *Der moderne Tanz*, 75.

28. The following analysis is based on Wigman's pedagogical note, titled "Die Schrittskalen," preserved at the Mary Wigman Archive, as well as on Rudolf Bach's firsthand observations of her teaching in *Das Mary Wigman Werk* (Dresden: Carl Reissner, 1933) and on oral history. For a more detailed analysis of this material, see Vera Maletic, "Wigman and Laban: The Interplay of Theory and Practice," *Ballet Review* 14:3 (Fall 1986), 86–94.

29. Bach, *Das Mary Wigman Werk*, 36.

30. Hunt, "The Wigman Years—Part One of the Thimey Transcripts," 23–24.

31. Schumann, "Gespräche und Fragen: Mary Wigman," 48.

32. Interview with Fé Alf, 18 October 1987.

33. Sorell, *The Mary Wigman Book*, 52.

34. Bach, *Das Mary Wigman Werk*, 38–39.

35. Hunt, "The Wigman Years—Part One of the Thimey Transcripts," 23.

36. Bach, *Das Mary Wigman Werk*, 39–44.

37. Sorell, *The Mary Wigman Book*, 86.

38. Sorell, *The Mary Wigman Book*, 88.

39. Hunt, "The Wigman Years—Part One of the Thimey Transcripts," 25–26.

40. Interview with Flade, 11 October 1987.

41. Interview with Espenak, 26 January 1988.

42. Quoted in Walter Sorell, *Hanya Holm* (Middletown, Conn.: Wes-leyan University Press, 1969), 22.

43. Fischer, *Körperschönheit und Körperkultur*, 241–42.

44. Müller, *Mary Wigman*, 91.

45. Mary Wigman, *Die sieben Tänze des Lebens—Tanzdichtung* (Jena: Diederichs, 1921). Walter Sorell translates the libretto in *The Mary Wigman Book*, 71–80.

46. Quoted in Müller, *Mary Wigman*, 91.

47. Sorell, *The Mary Wigman Book*, 73–74.

48. Müller, *Mary Wigman*, 92.

49. In *Time and the Dancing Image*, 105–23, Deborah Jowitt gives an

overview of the Salome craze. For documentation on German Salomes, see Frank-Manuel Peter, *Valeska Gert: Tänzerin, Schauspielerin, Kabarettistin* (Berlin: Frölich und Kaufmann, 1985), 22–26.

50. Jowitt, *Time and the Dancing Image,* 111. Further documentation can be found scattered through Felix Cherniavsky's *The Salome Dancer: The Life and Times of Maud Allan* (Toronto: McClelland and Stewart, 1991).

51. Mary Wigman, promptbook for *Die sieben Tänze des Lebens,* manuscript, 37, MWA.

52. My reconstruction is based on the promptbook at the Mary Wigman Archive. Müller's biography quotes a long passage from the promptbook. Where possible, references cite her biography rather than the manuscript.

53. Müller, *Mary Wigman,* 95.

54. Müller, *Mary Wigman,* 96.

55. Promptbook, *Die sieben Tänze des Lebens,* 42, MWA.

56. Müller, *Mary Wigman,* 97.

57. Sorell, *The Mary Wigman Book,* 78–79.

58. Müller, *Mary Wigman,* 91.

59. Müller, *Mary Wigman,* 99.

60. Müller, *Mary Wigman,* 101.

61. The discrepancy between the fourteen members of the dance group recorded in the ledgers of the Wigman School (see note 12) and the eighteen members of the actual company presumably results from the fact that members of the company who also taught at the school, such as Hanya Holm, were paid salaries as staff rather than provided expenses as dancers. Personal communication with Hedwig Müller, 12 December 1991.

62. *Circle, Triangle,* and *Chaos* were premiered on 22 April 1923 with fourteen dancers. Four more dancers had joined the group by the time that *Finale* and the first versions of *Summons* and *Wandering* premiered on 30 June 1923. Although the number of dancers remained the same when the final version of the work premiered on 4 January 1924, the cast had changed. Gret Palucca and Yvonne Georgi had left the company, and new dancers had joined. Thus Wigman had to deal with a changing cast as she choreographed the work, a challenge that surely informed the subtext of conflict between the choreographer and the ensemble. Details of casting from programs, MWA.

63. Müller, *Mary Wigman,* 83, 314.

64. Mary Wigman, "Composition in Pure Movement," *Modern Music* 8:2 (January/February 1931), 21.

65. This clip is part of *Ways to Strength and Beauty.* It also is included in Allegra Fuller Snyder and Annette Macdonald's documentary, *Mary Wigman, 1886–1973: "When the Fire Dances between the Two Poles,"* available on videocassette (Pennington: Princeton Book Co., Dance Horizons Video, 1991).

66. Artur Michel, "Das getanzte Drama Mary Wigman und ihre Schule," *Vossische Zeitung* (29 May 1923), MWA.

67. *Finale* was alternately titled *Rhapsodie.* No German titles are given when the English and German spellings are identical, as is the case for *Chaos, Vision,* and *Finale.*

68. Hans Brandenburg, *Das neue Theater* (Leipzig: Haessel, 1926), 433.

69. Brandenburg, *Das neue Theater,* 433–34.

70. Interview with Hanya Holm, 3 February 1984.

71. Brandenburg, *Das neue Theater,* 434.

72. Brandenburg, *Das neue Theater,* 434.

73. Michel, "Das getanzte Drama Mary Wigman," MWA.

74. Brandenburg, *Das neue Theater,* 434.

75. Michel, "Das getanzte Drama Mary Wigman," MWA.

76. As evidenced by programs and reviews at the Mary Wigman Archive, the Berlin premiere in January 1924 omitted *Finale.* But Frankfurt performances the following month restored the ending, which already had been shown on earlier programs.

77. Claudia Koonz, *Mothers in the Fatherland: Women, the Family, and Nazi Politics* (New York: St. Martin's Press, 1987), 22.

78. Koonz, *Mothers in the Fatherland,* 49.

79. Koonz, *Mothers in the Fatherland,* 49.

80. Koonz, *Mothers in the Fatherland,* 36.

81. Lämmel, *Der moderne Tanz,* 115.

82. The two group works not reconstructed here, *Hymns in Space* (*Raumgesänge*) and *Russian Suite* (*Russische Suite*), premiered on the same program as *Dance of Death.* The two dances are reconstructed in my dissertation, "Body Politic: The Dances of Mary Wigman" (Columbia University, 1987), 225–28, where I argue that their representational strategies anticipated those in *Celebration.*

83. Programs, MWA.

84. Mary Wigman, "Die verzauberten Blumen: Ein Tanzmärchen," manuscript, 1920, 15 pp., MWA.

85. Mary Wigman, "Aus einer tänzerischen Werkstatt," typescript, 1926, 2, MWA.

86. Wigman, "Die verzauberten Blumen," 8, MWA.

87. A complete translation of the scenario is given at the end of chapter two.

88. Sorell, *The Mary Wigman Book,* 99–100.

89. Among the reviewers who singled out Berentson was Hans Fischer in *Körperschönheit und Körperkultur,* 252.

90. Sorell, *The Mary Wigman Book,* 97–98.

91. Sorell, *The Mary Wigman Book,* 100–101.

92. Sorell, *The Mary Wigman Book,* 100.

93. Sorell, *The Mary Wigman Book,* 103.

94. Sorell, *The Mary Wigman Book,* 103.

95. Sorell, *The Mary Wigman Book,* 104. This account of the ending is confirmed by an anonymous review in the *Dresdner Volkszeitung* (27 March 1926), MWA.

96. Sorell, *The Mary Wigman Book*, 101.

97. Anonymous review, *Der Tag* (March 1928), MWA.

98. *Witch Dance II* was part of a longer solo cycle titled *Visions*, composed over a three-year period from 1925 to 1928. Only once did Wigman perform all eight solos on a single program. Otherwise she excerpted two or three in combination with other solo cycles. The entire cycle is reconstructed in my dissertation, "Body Politic," 87–105, which argues that the principle of the mask reached its high point in the cycle.

99. Gustav Grund, "Maskentanz," unidentified clipping, DTA.

100. The film was shot around 1930, perhaps as publicity for Wigman's first American tour. The clip is included in Snyder and Macdonald's documentary, *Mary Wigman, 1886–1973: "When the Fire Dances between the Two Poles."* For commentary on the film, see John Mueller, "Films: A Glimpse of Mary Wigman," *Dance Magazine* 50:3 (March 1976), 96.

101. Bach, *Das Mary Wigman Werk*, 29–30. English translation provided by the Dance Film Archive, University of Rochester.

102. Bach, *Das Mary Wigman Werk*, 31. English translation provided by the Dance Film Archive, University of Rochester.

103. Anonymous review, *Hannoverscher Kurrier*, 20 January 1929, MWA.

4. FROM MODERNISM TO FASCISM

1. *Celebration, Shifting Landscape,* and *Totenmal* are reconstructed in this chapter. For a reconstruction of the solo cycle *Sacrifice* (*Das Opfer*), see my dissertation, "Body Politic," 123–33. There I argue that the shift in Wigman's representational strategies evident in *Shifting Landscape* also was found in *Sacrifice.*

2. Müller, *Mary Wigman*, 134–35.

3. Müller, *Mary Wigman*, 134; Elly Müller-Rau, "Mary Wigman," *Kunst und Kritik* no. 16 (1929), 193–95.

4. G. Joachimstal, "Die neue Wigman-Schule in Dresden," *Der Tanz* 1:4 (1928), 26; Marguerite Bartholomew, "Margarethe Wallmann Speaks at the Club," *Foreword* 18:2 (November 1930), 14.

5. "Verband der Labanschulen," 1927 brochure, AdK-DDR. Reprinted in Hodgson and Preston-Dunlop, *Rudolf Laban*, 126–27.

6. Rudolf Laban, "Vom Sinne der Bewegungschöre," *Schrifttanz* 3:2 (June 1930), 25–26; Martin Gleisner, "Laban als Schöpfer von Laientanz und Bewegungschor," *Schrifttanz* 2:4 (1929), 69–70; Hodgson and Preston-Dunlop, *Rudolf Laban*, 43–47, 128–29.

7. Rudolf Laban, *Schrifttanz* (Vienna: Universal Edition, 1928); Hodgson and Preston-Dunlop, *Rudolf Laban*, 15–25, 130–31. For a detailed overview of Laban's system, see Maletic, *Body-Space-Expression*.

8. Hans Brandenburg, "Zur Einführung!" *Die Tat* 19:8 (November 1927), 570. This special issue of *Die Tat* printed the proceedings of the First Dancers' Congress.

9. For an overview of the congress, see Hans Kuznitzky, "Der zweite Tänzerkongress in Essen," *Melos* 7:8/9 (1928), 439–45.

10. Heinrich Spaemann, "Tänzerkongress," *Sozialistische Monatshefte* 34:9 (September 1928), 826.

11. Horst Koegler, "In the Shadow of the Swastika: Dance in Germany, 1927–1936," *Dance Perspectives* no. 57 (Spring 1974), 11.

12. Müller, *Mary Wigman*, 144.

13. Müller, *Mary Wigman*, 144.

14. Müller, *Mary Wigman*, 144.

15. Although the programs do not identify the author of the note, a typescript preserved at the Mary Wigman Archive does. Will Goetze, "Über das neue Gruppenprogramm Mary Wigmans," typescript, 1 p., MWA.

16. Bach, *Das Mary Wigman Werk*, 49–50.

17. Bach, *Das Mary Wigman Werk*, 50.

18. Bach, *Das Mary Wigman Werk*, 50–51.

19. Bach, *Das Mary Wigman Werk*, 51.

20. Margarethe Wallmann, "Mary Wigman und ihre Gruppe," *Tanzgemeinschaft* 2:2 (1930), 8.

21. Bach, *Das Mary Wigman Werk*, 52.

22. Bach, *Das Mary Wigman Werk*, 51–53. In *The Language of Dance*, trans. Walter Sorell (Middletown, Conn.: Wesleyan University Press, 1966), 90–92, Wigman offers a more abbreviated description of *Celebration* than does Bach.

23. Bach, *Das Mary Wigman Werk*, 53.

24. In February 1927 Wigman premiered a first version of *Celebration*. The version presented at the Second Dancers' Congress, premiered in March 1928, included a substantially revised ending, which is the version described here. For a comparison of the two endings, see my dissertation, "Body Politic," 228–36.

25. Wigman, *The Language of Dance*, 91.

26. Bach, *Das Mary Wigman Werk*, 53.

27. Bach, *Das Mary Wigman Werk*, 54.

28. André Levinson, "The Modern Dance in Germany," *Theatre Arts* 13:2 (February 1929), 151.

29. Joseph Lewitan, "Mary Wigman," *Der Tanz* 2:7 (1929), 20–21.

30. Anonymous review, *Berlin am Morgen* (4 February 1930), MWA.

31. Vera Skoronel, "Mary Wigmans Kompositionsstil," *Schrifttanz* 3:3 (November 1930), 50.

32. Unlike the program for *Celebration*, which did not credit Goetze, the program for *Shifting Landscape* gave a by-line to Schumann. This and the following excerpts come from the program for the performance at the Staatliches Schauspielhaus sponsored by the Dresdener Volksbühne on 1 December 1929 (MWA).

33. These solos survived on the same early sound film as *Witch Dance II* and are included in Snyder and Macdonald's documentary, *Mary Wigman, 1886–1973: "When the Fire Dances between the Two Poles."*

34. Mary Watkins, "To the Beat of Drums and Gongs," souvenir program for second American tour, 1931–1932, NYPL-DC.

35. In *The Language of Dance*, 47, Wigman refers to a "lighthearted and carefree" vacation. Müller's biography, 159, identifies her traveling companion as Binswanger.

36. The term is Wigman's. As she wrote in *The Language of Dance*, 17, "[All solos enact] something like a dialogue for the spectator, a dialogue in which the dancer holds a conversation with himself and with an invisible partner."

37. Wigman, *The Language of Dance*, 60.

38. Mary Wigman, "Der Tänzer und das Theater," *Blätter des Hessischen Landestheater* 7 (1929/1930), 50.

39. Wigman, "Der Tänzer und das Theater," 52.

40. Fischer, *Körperschönheit und Körperkultur*, 241.

41. Wigman, "Der Tänzer und das Theater," 52–53.

42. Program, Festspielbühne, Munich, Summer 1930, MWA.

43. Wigman, *The Language of Dance*, 92–93.

44. For commentary on *Totenmal* and the Third Dancers' Congress, see Hans Eckstein, "Tänzerkongress und Totenmahl [*sic*] in München," *Das Werk* 17 (September 1930), 283–85; Ernst Kallai, "Tänzerkongress," *Sozialistische Monatshefte* 36:9 (September 1930), 941–42; Alfred Schlee, "Tänzerkongress in München," *Schrifttanz* 3:3 (November 1930), 54–55; Werner Schuftan, "Der 3. Deutsche Tänzerkongress," *Singchor und Tanz* 47:13/14 (15 July 1930), 210–14; and Bruno Goetz, "Zum dritten deutschen Tänzerkongress in München," *Das National Theater* 2 (1929/1930), 470–74. More recently, Hedwig Müller has compiled "Dokumentation: 3. Deutscher Tänzerkongress, München 1930," *Tanzdrama* 13 (1990), 17–29.

45. Albert Talhoff, *Totenmal: Dramatisch-chorische Vision für Wort, Tanz, Licht* (Stuttgart: Deutsche Verlags-Anstalt, 1930), 12.

46. "Masken für das *Totenmal*," Chorische Bühne, Munich, 1930, DTA.

47. Program, Summer 1930, MWA; Fritz Böhme, *Über Totenmal* (Munich: Chorische Bühne, 1930).

48. These terms were used by Louise Kloepper, then a student at the Wigman School, who saw the production. Hanya Holm, Fé Alf, and Pola Nirenska—all participants in the production—confirm Kloepper's reminiscences.

49. Louise Munroe quoted in Julie Ripley, "Music and the Dance," unidentified clipping, NYPL-DC.

50. My reconstruction derives from Talhoff's published script, Wigman's promptbook (available at the Mary Wigman Archive), and a brief silent film. The original film is available at the Bundesfilmarchiv in Koblenz; a substantial excerpt is included in Snyder and Macdonald's documentary *Mary Wigman, 1886–1973: "Where the Fire Dances between the Two Poles."* At the time of the premiere the script was translated into English by M. A. Moralt and published under the title *The Call of the Dead* (Stuttgart: Deutsche Verlags-Anstalt, 1930). Where I quote the text, I rely upon

the preexistent translation. However, the English-language version does not contain the extensive stage directions included in the German publication, which contributed substantially to my reconstruction.

51. Talhoff, *Totenmal*, 22–24.

52. Talhoff, *Totenmal*, 62.

53. Talhoff, *The Call of the Dead*, 24.

54. Talhoff, *Totenmal*, 45.

55. Talhoff, *The Call of the Dead*, 45. These ellipses are found in the text.

56. Talhoff, *The Call of the Dead*, 47–48.

57. Ripley, "Music and the Dance," NYPL-DC.

58. Friedrich Muckermann, "Ein Weihespiel der Nation," *Der Gral* 24:8 (May 1930), 675.

59. George Mosse, "National Cemeteries and National Revival: The Cult of the Fallen Soldier in Germany," *Journal of Contemporary History* 14:1 (1979), 1–20. Mosse later expanded upon this argument in his book-length study *Fallen Soldiers: Reshaping the Memory of the World Wars* (New York: Oxford University Press, 1990).

60. "Wer ist Albert Thalhoff [*sic*]?" *Völkischer Beobachter* 163 (17 July 1929). Published the summer before *Totenmal* had its premiere, this article criticizes the commission of Talhoff to script the work. The article makes no mention of Mary Wigman.

61. Ernst Iros, "Uraufführung von Albert Talhoffs *Totenmal*," *Die neue Zeit* 12 (1930), 12.

62. Gay, *Weimar Culture*, 160.

63. Quoted in Anna and Hermann Markard, eds., *Jooss* (Cologne: Ballett-Bühnen-Verlag, 1985), 15.

64. Quoted in Markard, *Jooss*, 17.

65. The analysis presented here is based on viewing the work in performance and on the 1982 "Dance in America" video of the Joffrey production.

66. Quoted in Markard, *Jooss*, 49.

67. Quoted in Markard, *Jooss*, 49.

68. In *Weimar Germany's Left-Wing Intellectuals: A Political History of the Weltbühne and Its Circle* (Berkeley and Los Angeles: University of California Press, 1968), 36–48, Istvan Deak overviews Tucholsky's politics.

69. Marcia Siegel, "*The Green Table*—Sources of a Classic," *Dance Research Journal* 21:1 (Spring 1989), 20.

70. Quoted in Markard, *Jooss*, 51.

71. Markard, *Jooss*, 53–65.

5. BODY POLITIC

1. Artur Michel, "The Development of the New German Dance," in Virginia Stewart and Merle Armitage, eds., *The Modern Dance* (New York: E. Weyhe, 1935), 12.

2. Michel, "The Development of the New German Dance," 12.

3. Michel, "The Development of the New German Dance," 11.

4. "Tänzer und Tanzlehrer in der deutschen Reichsstatistik," *Der Tanz* 10:6 (June 1937), 23.

5. "Die Tagungen des Tänzerkongresses," *Der Tanz* 3:8 (August 1930), 8–9; Müller, "Dokumentation: 3. Deutscher Tänzerkongress," 18–19.

6. "Hochschule für Tanzkunst," *Singchor und Tanz* 47:12 (15 June 1930), 198–99.

7. "Hochschule für Tanzkunst"; Franz Büchler, ed., *Deutsches Tanz Jahrbuch 1941* (Berlin: Volkskunst Verlag, 1941), 95–98, 109–20. This volume reprints all the directives issued by the Cultural Ministry from 1933 to 1941 and appends a directory of dancers certified by the ministry.

8. Stephen Kern, *Anatomy and Destiny: A Cultural History of the Human Body* (Indianapolis: Bobbs-Merrill, 1975), 221–37; Hans Peter Bleuel, *Sex and Society in Nazi Germany* (Philadelphia and New York: J. B. Lippincott, 1973), 120–44.

9. George Mosse, *The Crisis of German Ideology* (1964; reprint, New York: Schocken, 1981); Martin Green, *Mountain of Truth*, 238–53.

10. Although no scholar has yet undertaken a census of all the dancers involved, it is possible to compile informal statistics on the leading dancers. At the 1930 Dancers' Congress forty German choreographers presented their works on ten programs, along with thirty-five younger dancers who shared a single program and presented a solo apiece. (A twelfth program was dedicated to guest artists from abroad.) Of the forty established choreographers who presented their works, I have been able to trace the subsequent careers of thirty-one. While two died before the National Socialists came to power (Heinrich Kröller and Vera Skoronel), another two had established careers abroad for other reasons before 1933 (Corrie Hartong and Käthe Wulff). Of the remaining choreographers whose careers I have been able to trace, twice as many remained in Germany and collaborated with the National Socialists as did not. All together, eighteen of the leading choreographers in 1930 came to terms with the National Socialists: Rosalia Chladek, Dorothee Günther, Günter Hess, Jens Keith, Jutta Klamt, Albrecht Knust, Rudolf Kölling, Valeria Kratina, Manda von Kreibig, Else Lang, Maja Lex, Lizzie Maudrik, Rudolf Laban (until his emigration in 1938), Frances Metz, Gret Palucca, Gertrud Wienecke, Mary Wigman, and Heide Woog. (This list does not include Yvonne Georgi and Harald Kreutzberg, whose solo careers were at a peak in 1930. Both later appeared under National Socialist auspices.) Of the leading choreographers in 1930, the remaining nine either emigrated after 1933 or stopped working in dance for reasons related to the rise of National Socialism: Olga Brandt-Knack, Jenny Gertz, Kurt Jooss, Gertrud Kraus, Sigurd Leeder, Ruth Loeser, Martin Gleisner, Oskar Schlemmer, and Margarethe Wallmann. (This list does not include Jean Weidt and Valeska Gert, both of whom emigrated. In 1930 Gert was an established actress and dancer, Weidt an agitprop performer and organizer.)

It is important to note that the division between dancers who collaborated and dancers who emigrated did not necessarily result from differing ethnic origins. Of the nine leading dancers who left Germany or stopped working after the National Socialists came to power, I have been able to ascertain that only two (Gertrud Kraus and Margarethe Wallmann) acted primarily on the basis of their Jewish identity. The others were censored for their leftist or Communist politics. Whether or not they were "Jewish," I do not know. In any case, to search out which dancers had Jewish grandparents strikes me as too close to National Socialist precedent for comfort.

11. Program, "Deutsche Tanzfestspiel 1934," Theater-am-Horst-Wessel-Platz, 9–16 December 1934, MWA; Koegler, "In the Shadow of the Swastika," 38.

12. Müller, *Mary Wigman*, 226.

13. Interview with Nirenska, 14 March 1985.

14. Rudolf Laban, ed., *Deutsche Tanzfestspiele 1934* (Dresden: Carl Reissner, 1934).

15. Program, 9–16 December 1934, MWA.

16. Program, 9–16 December 1934, MWA.

17. A perusal of archival documents suggests that a tension between Goebbels's Cultural Ministry and Alfred Rosenberg's Fighting League for German Culture created contradictions within Nazi dance policy. In 1933 the Fighting League issued a statement, authored by Rudolf Bode and others, titled "The Spiritual Foundations for Dance in a National Socialist State," which declared that "it is necessary to fight against every relapse to the old ballet technique, just as it is necessary to fight against every recourse to the weak self-indulgence that so often passed for art-dance over the last decade" (Kampfbund für deutsche Kultur, "Die geistigen Grundlagen für Tanz im Nationalsozialistischen Staat," *Der Tanz* 6:11 [November 1933], 3). Advocating *Tanz-Gymnastik* as the appropriate form for the *Volk*, the Fighting League opposed the Cultural Ministry's policy of support for a fusion of ballet and *Ausdruckstanz*. A Cultural Ministry directive issued in 1935 countered by declaring that "teachers whose main subject is *Gymnastik*, body awareness, sports, *Turnen*, and the like do not belong in the Cultural Ministry" (Büchler, ed., *Deutsches Tanz Jahrbuch 1941*, 120). From this point Goebbels's Cultural Ministry took responsibility for stage dance, and Rosenberg's Fighting League took responsibility for dance as physical education.

Since Wigman's group dances were subsidized by the Cultural Ministry, the following discussion focuses on the policy issuing from Goebbels's ministry. Further research is required to uncover the full story of the contradictions between the two bureaucracies responsible for dance in the Third Reich. A first attempt is made in my article "German *Rites*: A History of *Le sacre du printemps* on the German Stage," *Dance Chronicle* 14:2/3 (1991), 136–37.

18. Program, 9–16 December 1934, MWA. In January 1934 Wigman had premiered two solos under the title *Women's Dances: Dance of Silent Joy*,

discussed at the beginning of this chapter, and *Farewell* (*Abschied*). The program does not list *Dance of Silent Joy* as part of the group work titled *Women's Dances,* contrary to the claim made by Hedwig Müller in *Mary Wigman,* 227.

19. Bleuel, *Sex and Society in Nazi Germany,* 89–91.

20. Michel, "The Development of the New German Dance," 12.

21. Michel, "The Development of the New German Dance," 12–13.

22. In a sequence of photographs illustrating the dance that are appended to the end of Wigman's *Deutsche Tanzkunst* (Dresden: Carl Reissner, 1935), this photograph is placed last.

23. Michel, "The Development of the New German Dance," 13.

24. Michel, "The Development of the New German Dance," 13.

25. The photographic sequence of *Lament for the Dead* appended to Wigman's *Deutsche Tanzkunst* neither confirms nor denies this supposition.

26. Michel, "The Development of the New German Dance," 13.

27. Michel, "The Development of the New German Dance," 13.

28. Mary Wigman, "Dances," typescript, c. 1956–1957, 2–3, MWA. That the typescript is in English and describes dances choreographed from 1934 to 1955 suggests that it was written in preparation for Wigman's American visit in spring 1958.

29. Wigman, "Dances," 3, MWA.

30. Michel, "The Development of the New German Dance," 13–14.

31. Program, Deutsche Tanzfestspiel 1935, Theater am Horst-Wessel-Platz and Staatsoper unter den Linden, Berlin, 3–10 November 1935, MWA.

32. Program, Schauspielhaus, Hannover, 16 February 1936, MWA.

33. Wigman, "Dances," 3–4, MWA.

34. "L. D.," unidentified clipping, MWA.

35. Wigman, *The Language of Dance,* 74.

36. Wigman, "Dances," 3, MWA.

37. Wigman, "Dances," 3, MWA.

38. "L. D.," unidentified clipping, MWA.

39. "L. D.," unidentified clipping, MWA.

40. Otto Socher, "Deutsche Tanzfestspiele in Berlin: Der Wigman Abend," *Dresdner Nachrichten,* n.d., MWA.

41. Wigman, "Dances," 4, MWA.

42. Anonymous review, "Deutsche Tanzfestspiel 1935," *Der Tanz* 8:12 (December 1935), 7.

43. Wigman, "Dances," 4, MWA.

44. Wigman, "Dances," 4, MWA.

45. Wigman, "Dances," 4, MWA.

46. Wigman, *Deutsche Tanzkunst,* 12.

47. Wigman, *Deutsche Tanzkunst,* 15.

48. Wigman, *Deutsche Tanzkunst,* 15–16. This translation is by Hedwig Müller and appears in her article "Wigman and National Socialism," *Ballet Review* 15:1 (Spring 1987), 66.

49. Mary Wigman, "Das 'Land ohne Tanz,'" *Tanzgemeinschaft* 1:2 (April 1929), 12.

50. Wigman, *Deutsche Tanzkunst,* 11–12.

51. Wigman, *Deutsche Tanzkunst,* 15.

52. Mary Wigman, "Tanz und Gymnastik," *Der Tanz* 1:6 (April 1928), 6.

53. Wigman, *Deutsche Tanzkunst,* 35.

54. Wigman, *Deutsche Tanzkunst,* 69.

55. Quoted in Henning Eichberg et al., *Massenspiele: NS-Thingspiel, Arbeiterweihespiel und olympisches Zeremoniell* (Stuttgart–Bad Cannstatt: Fromann-Holzboog, 1977), 34.

56. For background on the *Thingspiel,* see Eichberg et al., *Massenspiele.* English-language sources include Eichberg's "The Nazi *Thingspiel*: Theater for the Masses in Fascism and Proletarian Culture," *New German Critique* no. 11 (1977), 133–50; Glen Gadberry, "The Thingspiel and Das Frankenberger Würfelspiel," *Drama Review* 24:1 (March 1980), 103–14; George Mosse, *The Nationalization of the Masses* (New York: Howard Fertig, 1975); and Bruce Zortman's *Hitler's Theater* (El Paso: Firestein Books, 1984). After 1937 the *Thingspiel* lost official support at the national level, although locally originated productions were not banned. The reasons why are not entirely clear. One possible explanation is that the *Thingspiel* simply did not work as a theatrical and dramatic form. Another hypothesis is that turf wars between the Cultural Ministry, responsible for approving the texts, and the Fighting League for German Culture, responsible for building the outdoor sites, led to the demise of the form. Yet another hypothesis is tied to the radicalization of the regime in 1937 that historians have noted. From this point, anti-Semitic measures intensified, and the Nazi party increased its control over the economy to divert funds to remilitarization. As more than one commentator has pointed out, once the Nazis abandoned the revolutionary activity that marked the first years of their regime, they also abandoned *Thingspiel.*

57. *The Eleventh Olympic Games Berlin, 1936: Official Report* (Berlin: William Limpert, 1937), 586–87.

58. Richard Mandell, *Nazi Olympics* (New York: Macmillan, 1971); Duff Hart-Davis, *Hitler's Games* (New York: Harper and Row, 1986); John Hoberman, *The Olympic Crisis* (New Rochelle, N.Y.: Caratzas, 1986), 88–106.

59. Opposing sides in the debate are represented by Susan Sontag's "Fascinating Fascism," *New York Review of Books* (6 February 1975), 23–30, and Andrew Sarris's "Fascinating Fascism Meets Leering Leftism," in his *Politics and Cinema* (New York: Columbia University Press, 1978), 107–15. The debate also informs the special "Leni Riefenstahl" issue of *Film Culture* (no. 56/57 [Spring 1973]). The history of *Olympia* is chronicled in Cooper C. Graham's *Leni Riefenstahl and Olympia* (Metuchen, N.J.: Scarecrow Press, 1986).

60. "Editorial: Olympic Protest," *Dance Observer* 3:4 (April 1936), 38;

Emanuel Eisenberg, "Danse Macabre," *New Theatre* 3:5 (May 1936), 22–23, 37.

61. Program, Internationale Tanzwettspiele 1936, Theater am Horst-Wessel Platz, Staatsoper Unter den Linden, Deutsches Opernhaus, Berlin, 15–31 July 1936, MWA; Artur Michel, "International Dance Tournament—Berlin, 1936," *Dance Observer* 3:8 (October 1936), 89, 93.

62. Goebbels once wrote, "Even entertainment can be politically of special value, because the moment a person is conscious of propaganda, propaganda becomes ineffective. However, as soon as propaganda as a tendency, as a characteristic, as an attitude, remains in the background and becomes apparent through human beings, then propaganda becomes effective in every respect." Quoted in David Welch, *Propaganda and the German Cinema: 1933–1945* (Oxford: Oxford University Press, 1983), 45.

63. *The Eleventh Olympic Games Berlin, 1936*, 577.

64. Program, Olympische Jugend Festspiel, Berlin Olympic Stadium, 1 August 1936, 9, MWA.

65. Program, 1 August 1936, 24, MWA.

66. Program, 1 August 1936, 11, MWA.

67. *The Eleventh Olympic Games Berlin, 1936*, 578–79.

68. *The Eleventh Olympic Games Berlin, 1936*, 577.

69. Frederick Birchall, "100,000 Hail Hitler," *New York Times* (2 August 1936), sec. 1, 33.

70. Janet Flanner (Genêt), "Berlin Letter," *New Yorker* (15 August 1936), 35.

71. Müller, *Mary Wigman*, 244–46. For an account of the spectacle that did result, see Berthold Hinz, trans. Robert and Rita Kimber, *Art in the Third Reich* (New York: Random House, 1979), 1–6.

It is important to note that I have not been able independently to confirm Müller's story, which she infers from Wigman's personal papers. According to Talhoff scholar Frank Simon, Talhoff did not serve as a cultural bureaucrat during the Third Reich. However, Simon writes that "there can be no doubt that Talhoff in the thirties—like a lot of 'intellectuals' in Germany—had some sympathies for the new regime." Simon does not know why the project *Spectacle at King's Square* (*Das Spiel vom Königlichen Platz*) was dropped. He does note that after 1937 Talhoff went into an "inner emigration" and that he even made contact with student resisters associated with the Scholls in Munich. Simon does not believe that Talhoff was ever a member of the Nazi party (personal communication, 18 August 1988). However, at the Berlin Document Center, Talhoff's response to a questionnaire from the Cultural Ministry, dated 1939, cites his association with the SS since 1934 (Talhoff file, Berlin Document Center). Clearly, Talhoff's story, like Wigman's, is a complicated one and demands further research.

72. Joseph Goebbels, *Die Tagebücher von Joseph Goebbels: Sämtliche Fragmente* vol. 3, pt. 1 (Munich: K. G. Saur, 1987), 187. This entry is dated 27

June 1937. I would like to thank Jim Van Dyke for calling this entry to my attention.

73. Mary Wigman, "Die Wigman-Schule," *Der Tanz* 13 : 8 (August 1940), 106.

74. Büchler, ed., *Deutsche Tanz Jahrbuch 1941*, 167.

75. Prospectus, "Die Berufs-Ausbildung," Mary Wigman–Zentralschule, Dresden, 1934, 6, MWA.

76. Büchler, ed., *Deutsche Tanz Jahrbuch 1941*, 117.

77. Büchler, ed., *Deutsche Tanz Jahrbuch 1941*, 116.

78. Interview with Margrit Bassow, 21 January 1988.

79. So Hedwig Müller related at the 1986 gathering of former Wigman students at the Academy of Arts (transcript, Mary Wigman Conference, Academy of Arts, Berlin, second folder, 24, MWA). At the conference Else Lang, a student at the Wigman School from 1927 to 1929 who later opened her own school in Cologne, remarked that she too had received special permission to enroll Jewish students.

80. Interview with Shirlee Dodge, 22 January 1988.

81. Transcript, Mary Wigman Conference, second folder, 22–23, 25, MWA.

82. Transcript, Mary Wigman Conference, second folder, 23, MWA.

83. Hedwig Müller, recorded at Mary Wigman Conference, transcript, second folder, 24, MWA.

84. Interview with Bassow, 21 January 1988.

85. Interview with Isa Partsch-Bergsohn, 23 September 1986.

86. Jürgen Petersen, "Die Tänze der Mary Wigman," *Deutsche Zukunft* (December 1938), MWA.

87. Interview with Nirenska, 14 March 1985.

88. Müller, recorded at Mary Wigman Conference, transcript, second folder, 25, MWA; Müller, *Mary Wigman*, 250.

89. Müller, *Mary Wigman*, 251.

90. Müller, *Mary Wigman*, 254–56.

91. Wigman, *The Language of Dance*, 80.

92. Siegfried Enkelmann et al., *Tänzer unserer Zeit* (Munich: R. Piper, 1937).

93. Program, Bachsaal, Berlin, 12 March 1937, MWA.

94. Wigman, *The Language of Dance*, 80.

95. Wigman, *The Language of Dance*, 79–80.

96. Henry Bleckmann, "Ihre schönsten Tänze: Mary Wigman—Gastspiel im Essen," *Rote Erde/Westfälische Landeszeitung* (15 January 1938), MWA.

97. For a fuller description of Wigman's solo programs from 1937 to 1939, see my dissertation, "Body Politic," 313–19.

98. Müller, *Mary Wigman*, 256–59.

99. Mary Wigman, "Tanz der Brunhild," typescript, c. 1942, 1, MWA.

100. Wigman, "Tanz der Brunhild," 1, MWA.

101. Wigman, "Tanz der Brunhild," 2, MWA.

102. Wigman, "Tanz der Brunhild," 3–4, MWA.

103. Wigman, "Tanz der Brunhild," 4–5, MWA.

104. Wigman, "Tanz der Brunhild," 5, MWA.

105. Müller's *Mary Wigman* reproduces this image, along with other photographs of *Dance of Brunhild*, on page 253.

106. The film is excerpted in Snyder and Macdonald's documentary *Mary Wigman, 1886–1973: "When the Fire Dances between the Two Poles."* The complete film, available at the Bundesfilmarchiv in Koblenz, includes two takes of the dance plus an interview with the choreographer.

107. Wigman, *The Language of Dance*, 87.

6. FROM *AUSDRUCKSTANZ* TO *TANZTHEATER*

1. Müller, "Lebenslauf," 25.

2. Müller, *Mary Wigman*, 261; transcript, Mary Wigman Conference, second folder, 53, MWA.

3. Transcript, Mary Wigman Conference, second folder, 52, MWA.

4. Transcript, Mary Wigman Conference, second folder, 65–66, MWA.

5. Transcript, Mary Wigman Conference, second folder, 55, MWA.

6. Müller, *Mary Wigman*, 268; transcript, Mary Wigman Conference, second folder, 70–71, 80, MWA.

7. Müller, *Mary Wigman*, 272–73.

8. Müller, *Mary Wigman*, 276–77.

9. Müller, *Mary Wigman*, 268, 276–77, 279.

10. Müller, *Mary Wigman*, 275.

11. Quoted in Müller, *Mary Wigman*, 276.

12. Müller, *Mary Wigman*, 275.

13. Müller, *Mary Wigman*, 275.

14. Marion Kant, a dance historian formerly employed by the Academy of Arts of the German Democratic Republic, provides a differently nuanced account of Wigman's activities in the Soviet zone. She views Wigman's decision to relocate to West Berlin as the result of "a [deep-seated] anti-Communism and anti-Bolshevism imprinted on her from the time of the Weimar Republic and intensified under National Socialism" ("Propositions on the History of Dance in East Germany," position paper circulated as part of the Choreographing History Conference, University of California, Riverside, February 1992, 7).

15. Müller, *Mary Wigman*, 277–80.

16. Transcript, Mary Wigman Conference, fifth folder, 6, MWA.

17. Transcript, Mary Wigman Conference, fifth folder, 3–5, 7–8, MWA.

18. Transcript, Mary Wigman Conference, fifth folder, 13–14, MWA.

19. Transcript, Mary Wigman Conference, fifth folder, 26–27, MWA.

20. Hedwig Müller, "Zu jung für ein Begräbnis: Dore Hoyers Tanzkunst," *Tanzdrama* 1 (1987), 7.

21. These comments generalize the reminiscences of participants at a

conference on *Ausdruckstanz* in the postwar period, "Wigman, Balanchine, und Rock 'n' Roll," organized by the Mary Wigman Society in Cologne, 13–15 November 1987. For my report on the conference, see "Wigman, Balanchine, and Rock 'n' Roll Conference," *Dance Research Journal* 19:2 (Winter 1987–1988), 54–55.

22. Müller, *Mary Wigman*, 286.

23. Quoted in Müller, *Mary Wigman*, 289.

24. Vorlinde, "Studien von Mary Wigman," *Telegraf* (13 January 1953), DTA.

25. Letter from Elisabeth Wigman to Heinrich Wiegmann, 11 January 1953. I would like to thank Marlies Wiegmann Heinemann for sharing with me this source and others from her personal archive.

26. Wigman, "Dances," 8, MWA.

27. Vorlinde, "Studien von Mary Wigman," DTA.

28. On this point the program confirms the reviews (program, Hebbel Theater, Berlin, 11 January 1953, MWA).

29. Wigman, "Dances," 8, MWA.

30. Georg Zivier, "Neue Aktualität: Mary Wigman," *Die neue Zeitung* (7 February 1953), DTA.

31. The earlier work was titled *Der Weg*, choreographed especially for Wigman's 1932–1933 American group tour and discussed in chapter seven.

32. Wigman, "Dances," 8, MWA.

33. Interview with Walter Sorell, 20 January 1984.

34. Sorell, *The Mary Wigman Book*, 164.

35. Henning Müller, *Theater der Restauration: Westberliner Bühnen, Kultur und Politik im Kalten Krieg* (Berlin: Edition neue Wege, 1981), 190–97. In his study Müller focuses on the significance of the Berlin Festival in the context of the Cold War.

36. Paul Moor, "Experimental Spirit in Berlin," *New York Times* (3 November 1957), sec. 10, 9.

37. Program, Städtische Oper, Berlin, 24 September 1957, MWA.

38. The gender of the different roles in the original scenario only became clear with Millicent Hodson's 1987 reconstruction for the Joffrey Ballet. In the descriptive accounts from which choreographers before Hodson worked—including Stravinsky's program note and reviews of the original production—the male sage and the male elders are the prominent characters. Hence Wigman may not have realized an older woman opened— and then disappeared from—the original production, which makes her addition of the Mother Figure all the more noteworthy.

39. Mary Wigman, "*Sacre*: Ueber den Inhalt," typescript, 2, MWA. Although the program differentiates between the Mother Figure and the two priestesses, the scenario refers to all three as "mothers."

40. Dietrich Steinbeck, ed., *Mary Wigmans Choreographisches Skizzenbuch* (Berlin: Edition Hentrich, 1987), 79–145.

41. Horst Koegler, "Ein Monstrum von Ballett, doch ein Gewinn," *Die Welt* (25 September 1957), NYPL-DC.

42. Koegler, "Ein Monstrum von Ballett, doch ein Gewinn," NYPL-DC.

43. Anonymous review, "Fug und Unfug des Tanzes," *Der Tagesspiegel* no. 3664 (26 September 1957), 4.

44. Müller, *Mary Wigman*, 298.

45. Steinbeck's *Mary Wigmans Choreographisches Skizzenbuch* includes notational drawings for the Mannheim productions and for the Berlin *Orpheus and Eurydice.*

46. Horst Koegler, "Mary Wigman ist im September in Berlin gestorben," *Theater Heute* 14:11 (November 1973), 4. The obituary referred to Koegler's "Tanz in die dreissiger Jahre," in *Ballett: Chronik und Bilanz des Ballettjahres* (Velber bei Hannover: Friedrich, 1972), 39–51, excerpted in his *Dance Perspectives* monograph, "In the Shadow of the Swastika." A second installment on dance in the Third Reich appeared as "Tanz in den Abgrund," in *Ballett: Chronik und Bilanz des Ballettjahres* (Velber bei Hannover: Friedrich, 1973), 57–61.

47. Koegler, "Mary Wigman ist im September in Berlin gestorben," 4.

48. Koegler, "Mary Wigman ist im September in Berlin gestorben," 4. This translation comes from Walter Sorell, *The Mary Wigman Book*, 198.

49. For details on these productions, see my article "German *Rites*: A History of *Le sacre du printemps* on the German Stage."

50. Wuppertaler Bühnen, Opernhaus, Spielzeit 75/76, Theaterzettel 7, DTA.

51. A video of Bausch's *Le sacre du printemps* is available for viewing at the Dance Collection, New York Public Library for the Performing Arts.

52. Norbert Servos provides a descriptive account of the ballet in his *Pina Bausch Wuppertal Dance Theater*, 29–40.

53. For further descriptions of Bausch's works, see Servos's *Pina Bausch Wuppertal Dance Theater* as well as my article "An American Perspective on Tanztheater," *Drama Review* 30:2 (Summer 1986), 57–79.

54. In the following discussion I generalize the views of Schmidt, Servos, Müller, Jeschke, and Schlicher. Although their writings reveal some differences of opinion, the five critics essentially agree on the family resemblances between *Ausdruckstanz* and *Tanztheater.* One of the few German critics to challenge the assumption of resemblance is Helmut Scheier. For the skeptical views of an insider, see Scheier's "What Has Dance Theatre to Do with Ausdruckstanz?" *Ballett International* 10:1 (January 1987), 12–17.

55. For the Second Dancers' Congress held in Essen in 1928, Jooss titled his lecture "Tanztheater und Theatertanz." Hedwig Müller quotes from the lecture in her contribution to Markard's *Jooss*, 12–17.

56. Jochen Schmidt, "From Swan Lake to the Weed Garden: The Development of Ballet and Dance Theatre in the Federal Republic of Germany since 1967," in Manfred Linke, ed., *Theater/Theatre, 1967–1982* (Berlin: International Theatre Institute, 1983), 77.

57. Schmidt, "From Swan Lake to the Weed Garden," 77–78.

58. Claudia Jeschke, "Identity and Order: Trends in Dance Theatre in Germany," in *Blickpunkte II* (Montreal: Goethe Institute, 1989), 20.

59. Jeschke, "Identity and Order," 24.

60. Jeschke, "Identity and Order," 24.

61. Jeschke, "Identity and Order," 25.

62. Gerda Ehrlenbruch, *Die freien Gruppen in der Tanzszene der Bundesrepublik* (Frankfurt: Peter Lang, 1991), 188.

63. Dietmar Fritzsche, "Die sowjetische Ballettkunst wirkte befruchtend: Anmerkungen zum Ballett in der DDR," in H. Regitz, ed., *Tanz in Deutschland: Ballett seit 1945*, 142–53.

64. Fritzsche, "Die sowjetische Ballettkunst wirkte befruchtend," 147–49. For an overview of Schilling's career, see Bernd Köllinger, *Tanztheater: Tom Schilling und die zeitgenössische Choreographie* (Berlin: Henschelverlag, 1983).

65. Our exchange took place on a panel titled "Dance-Theatre-Tanztheater," jointly sponsored by Goethe House New York and the New York Public Library for the Performing Arts on 16 October 1989. In print Schmidt has stated: "in East Berlin and the German Democratic Republic, dance theatre refers to something different [than in the Federal Republic,] namely a specific kind of action ballet" (Jochen Schmidt, "At the Summit—Or Already on the Decline? German Dance Theatre at the End of the 1980s," in *Blickpunkte II* [Montreal, Goethe Institute: 1989], 11).

7. MARY WIGMAN AND
AMERICAN DANCE

1. Siegel, *The Shapes of Change*, 23.

2. *Dance: Four Pioneers* (1966) is distributed by University of California Extension.

3. Dancers who transplanted Wigman's methods include, among others, Fé Alf, Tina Flade, Louise Kloepper, Truda Kaschmann, Lilian Espenak, Eugene von Grona, Erika Thimey, Jan Veen, Pola Nirenska, Suria Magito Saint Denis, Steffi Nossen, Margaret Gage, Margaret Dietz, Lotte Goslar, Margarethe Wallmann, Til Thiele, Isa Partsch-Bergsohn, and Helmut Gottschild.

4. Joseph Lewitan, "Mary Wigman," *Der Tanz* 2 : 7 (May 1929), 20.

5. Müller, "Lebenslauf," 24.

6. Quoted in Müller, *Mary Wigman*, 205.

7. The title translates literally as "the way." H. T. Parker, one of the few American reviewers to like the work, provided the free translation *Pilgrimage* (Olive Holmes, ed., *Motion Arrested: Dance Reviews of H. T. Parker* [Middletown, Conn.: Wesleyan University Press, 1982], 196–99).

8. John Martin, "Frau Mary Wigman and Her Company," *New York Times* (15 January 1933), sec. 9, 2.

9. Quoted in Müller, *Mary Wigman*, 213. For a reconstruction of *Der Weg*, see my dissertation, "Body Politic," 272–76.

10. Souvenir program, Mary Wigman's 1930–1931 American tour under the sponsorship of Sol Hurok, 8, NYPL-DC.

11. Quoted in "What Dancers Think about the German Dance," *Dance Magazine* (May 1931), 14.

12. Lincoln Kirstein, "Dance Chronicle," *Hound and Horn* 4:4 (1931), 576, 575. The quotation is given as later excerpted in *Literary Digest*.

13. John Martin, "Mary Wigman's Successful Tour Provides a Great Stimulus," *New York Times* (8 March 1931), sec. 8, 4. A consummate publicist, Sol Hurok reprinted Martin's paean in the souvenir program for her second American tour in 1931–1932.

14. "What Dancers Think about the German Dance," 15.

15. Martin, *The Modern Dance*, 2.

16. Martin, *The Modern Dance*, 32.

17. Martin, *The Modern Dance*, 59.

18. John Martin, *America Dancing* (New York: Dodge Publishing, 1936), 3–4.

19. Martin, *America Dancing*, 4.

20. Martin, *America Dancing*, 171.

21. Martin, *America Dancing*, 171.

22. Martin, *Introduction to the Dance*, 231–32, 235.

23. Martin, *Introduction to the Dance*, 237, 238.

24. Margaret Lloyd, *The Borzoi Book of Modern Dance* (1949; reprint, New York: Dance Horizons, 1974), 173–74.

25. Stacey Prickett, "From Workers' Dance to New Dance," *Dance Research* 7:1 (Spring 1989), 47–64, and "Dance and the Workers' Struggle," *Dance Research* 8:1 (Spring 1990), 47–61. Since writing this chapter, I have read Ellen Graff's dissertation, "Stepping Left: Dance and Politics in New York City, 1928–1942" (New York University, 1992), which provides even fuller documentation than Prickett's published articles on what Graff terms "revolutionary dance" and the movement's interrelation with "bourgeois dance."

26. Martin, *America Dancing*, 15.

27. Prickett, "Dance and the Workers' Struggle," 60.

28. Lloyd, *The Borzoi Book of Modern Dance*, 174.

29. Lynn Garafola provides a differently nuanced account of the decline of leftist modern dance in "Dance in the City: Toward an American Dance," in Leonard Wallock, ed., *New York: Culture Capital of the World, 1940–1965* (New York: Rizzoli, 1988), 157–87.

30. Prospectus, New York Wigman School of the Dance, c. 1933–1934, NYPL-DC.

31. Prospectus, Hanya Holm Studio, 1936–1937, NYPL-DC.

32. Program, Hanya Holm and her Dance Group, Wadsworth Atheneum, c. 1936. Walter Sorell's biography, *Hanya Holm*, reproduces this program on page 49.

33. Interview with Kloepper, 1 November 1987.

34. Blanche Evan, "From a Dancer's Notebook," *New Theatre* 3:3 (March 1936), 17.

35. Blanche Evan, "From a Dancer's Notebook," 28.

36. Blanche Evan, "From a Dancer's Notebook," 28.

37. Blanche Evan, "From a Dancer's Notebook," 28.

38. Blanche Evan, "From a Dancer's Notebook," 28.

39. Nicholas Wirth, "Mary Wigman––Fascist," *New Theatre* 2:8 (August 1935), 5.

40. Virginia Stewart, "German Letter," *Dance Observer* 2:7 (October 1935), 80–81.

41. Hanya Holm, "Mary Wigman," *Dance Observer* 2:8 (November 1935), 92.

42. Edna Ocko, "Anti-Fascism," *Dance Observer* 2:8 (November 1935), 93.

43. Edna Ocko, "The Swastika Is Dancing," *New Theatre* 2:11 (November 1935), 17.

44. Eisenberg, "Danse Macabre," 37. Eisenberg lists additional supporters.

45. "Editorial: Olympic Protest," 38.

46. Artur Michel, "International Dance Tournament—Berlin, 1936," *Dance Observer* 3:8 (October 1936), 89, 93. The editorial, titled "Artur Michel," is found in the same issue on page 86.

47. "Editorial: A Dancer and an Educator on Fascism," *Dance Observer* 4:3 (March 1937), 26.

48. "A Dancer and an Educator on Fascism," 26.

49. Sorell, *The Mary Wigman Book*, 162.

50. Interview with Hanya Holm conducted by Marcia Siegel, "Mary Wigman, 1886–1973: A Tribute," *Dance Magazine* 47:11 (November 1973), 80.

51. Quoted in Sorell, *Hanya Holm*, 45.

52. Quoted in Sorell, *Hanya Holm*, 45.

53. Martin, *Introduction to the Dance*, 267.

54. Martin, *Introduction to the Dance*, 267.

55. Martin, *Introduction to the Dance*, 268–69.

56. In addition to Sorell's biography, see the monograph on Holm edited by Marilyn Cristofori, "Hanya Holm: A Pioneer in Modern Dance," *Choreography and Dance* 2:2 (July 1992).

57. Don McDonagh, *The Rise and Fall and Rise of Modern Dance* (New York: Outerbridge and Dienstfrey, 1970), 1.

58. Kendall, *Where She Danced*, 204.

59. Jowitt, *Time and the Dancing Image*, 168.

60. Jowitt, *Time and the Dancing Image*, 167.

61. Duncan, *The Art of the Dance*, 61.

Selected Bibliography

DANCE

Akademie der Künste der DDR. *Mary Wigman—Sprache des Tanzes.* Berlin: Henschelverlag, n.d.

Alderson, Evan. "Ballet as Ideology: *Giselle,* Act II." *Dance Chronicle* 10:3 (1987): 290–304.

"Aleida Montijn." *Tanzdrama* 9 (1989): 34.

Aschengreen, Erik. "The Beautiful Danger: Facets of the Romantic Ballet." *Dance Perspectives* no. 58 (Summer 1974).

Atkinson, Madge. "Round the German Schools." *Dancing Times* no. 237 (1930): 242–47.

Bach, Rudolf. *Das Mary Wigman Werk.* Dresden: Carl Reissner, 1933.

Banes, Sally. *Democracy's Body: Judson Dance Theater, 1962–1964.* Ann Arbor: UMI Research Press, 1983.

Bartholomew, Marguerite. "Margarethe Wallmann Speaks at the Club." *Foreword* 18:2 (November 1930): 14.

Bättig, Joseph. *Einführung in das Werk und die Persönlichkeit Albert Talhoffs.* Littau-Luzern: Bühlmann-Fenner, 1963.

Baxmann, Inge. "Stirring Up Attitudes: Dance as a Language and Utopia in the Roaring Twenties." *Ballett International* 12:2 (February 1989): 13–19.

Beaumont, Cyril. *The Ballet Called Giselle.* 1945. Reprint. Princeton: Princeton Book Company, 1988.

Behne, Adolf. "Die neue Tanz-Legende." *Die Weltbühne* 20:10 (1924): 307–8.

Bell-Kanner, Karen. *The Life and Times of Ellen von Frankenberg.* Chur, Switzerland: Harwood, 1991.

Benov, Ruth Gordon, ed. *Collected Works by and about Blanche Evan.* San Francisco: Blanche Evan Dance Foundation, 1991.

Berber, Anita, and Sebastian Droste. *Die Tänze des Lasters, des Grauens, und der Ekstase.* Vienna: Gloriett Verlag, 1923.

Berg, Shelley. *Le sacre du printemps: Seven Productions from Nijinsky to Martha Graham.* Ann Arbor: UMI Research Press, 1988.

Bergengruen, Siegfried. "Der Tanz erobert die Bühne." *Der Tanz* 3:7 (1930): 2–4.

Bie, Richard. "Eros, Tanz, und Emanzipation der Frau." *Der Scheinwerfer* 1:11/12 (1927/28): 7–10.

Birringer, Johannes. "Pina Bausch—Dancing across Borders." *Drama Review* 30:2 (Summer 1986): 85–97.

Blair, Fredrika. *Isadora.* New York: McGraw-Hill, 1986.

Blass, Ernst. *Das Wesen der neuen Tanzkunst.* Weimar: Erich Lichtenstein, 1922.

Bloch, Paul J. "Der Münchener Tänzerkongress." *Melos* 9:10 (1930): 437–39.

Blom, Lynne Ann, and L. Tarin Chaplin. *The Moment of Movement: Dance Improvisation.* Pittsburgh: University of Pittsburgh Press, 1988.

Blümner, Rudolf. "Tanz und Tanz, oder Kunsttanz und Tanzkunst." *Der Sturm* 17:4 (1926): 50–56.

Bode, Rudolf. *Bewegung und Gestaltung: Von der Kulturaufgabe der körperlichen Erziehung.* Berlin: Widukind, 1936.

Boehn, Max von. *Der Tanz.* Berlin: Wegweiser, 1925.

Böhme, Fritz. "Labans tänzerischer Ausdruck." *Schrifttanz* 2:4 (1929): 66–68.

————— "Materialien zu einer soziologischen Untersuchung des künstlerischen Tanzes." *Ethos: Vierteljahresschrift für Soziologie, Geschichts- und Kulturphilosophie* 1:2 (1925): 274–93.

————— "Der musiklose Tanz." *Zeitschrift für Ästhetik und Allgemeine Kunstwissenschaft* 19 (1925): 365–68.

————— "Podiumtanz und Theatertanz." *Singchor und Tanz* 47:12 (1920) 185–87.

————— "Der Radius des Tanzkunstwerks." *Der Scheinwerfer* 1:11/12 (1927/1928): p14–17.

————— "Die Raumlehre der tänzerischen Bewegung." *Gymnastik* 1:9/10 (1926): 133–42.

————— "Tanz als Weg zu neuer Volksgemeinschaft." *Deutsche Frauenkultur und Frauenkleidung* 34:5 (1930): 130–31.

————— *Der Tanz der Zukunft.* Munich: Delphin, 1926.

————— "Tanzgeschichte?" *Der Tanz* 13:5 (1940): 36–37.

————— *Tanzkunst.* Dessau: C. Dünnhaupt, 1926.

————— *Über Totenmal.* Munich: Chorische Bühne, 1930.

————— "Vorstellung und Erlebnis im Tanz." *Schrifttanz* 3:2 (1930): 37–39.

————— "Wachsen und Gestalten." *Kontakte: Körper, Arbeit, Leistung* 1:3 (1933): 33–40.

Brandenburg, Hans. "Chorische Bühne und *Totenmal.*" *Singchor und Tanz* 47:6 (1930): 81–82.

————— "Erinnerungen an Labans Anfänge. *Schrifttanz* 2:4 (1929): 70–71.

————— *Der moderne Tanz.* Munich: Georg Müller, 1913; rev. ed., 1917; 2d rev. ed., 1921.

————— *München leuchtete: Jugenderinnerungen.* Munich: Neuner, 1953.

————— *Das neue Theater.* Leipzig: Haessel, 1926.

————— "Die sieben Tänze des Lebens." *Die Tat* 14:7 (1922/1923): 538–39.

————— "Der Weg zum Nationaltheater: Ein Zwiegespräch." *Die neue Literatur* 37 (1936): 399–403.

———— "Zur Einführung!" *Die Tat* 19:8 (November 1927): 569–72.

Brandstetter, Gabriele, and Brygida Ochaim. *Loie Fuller: Tanz-Licht-Spiel-Art Nouveau*. Freiburg: Rombach, 1989.

Bremer Tanztheater—Reinhild Hoffman. With photos by Klaus Lefebvre. Bremen: Theater der Freien Hansestadt Bremen, 1986.

Büchler, Franz, ed. *Deutsches Tanz Jahrbuch 1941*. Berlin: Volkskunst Verlag, 1941.

Burger, Hanns. "Das Ballett im nationalen Deutschland." *Der Tanz* 6:8 (1933): 8–9.

Chapman, John. "An Unromantic View of Nineteenth-Century Romanticism." *York Dance Review* 7 (Spring 1978): 28–45.

Cherniavsky, Felix. *The Salome Dancer: The Life and Times of Maud Allan*. Toronto: McClelland and Stewart, 1991.

Cohen, Selma Jeanne. "Avant-Garde Choreography." *Criticism* 3 (1961): 16–35.

———— *Next Week, Swan Lake: Reflections on Dance and Dances*. Middletown, Conn.: Wesleyan University Press, 1982.

Copeland, Roger. "Founding Mothers: Duncan, Graham, Rainer, and Sexual Politics." *Dance Theatre Journal* 8:3 (Fall 1990): 6–9, 27–29.

———— "In Defense of Formalism: The Politics of Disinterestedness." *Dance Theatre Journal* 7:1 (Spring 1990): 4–7, 37–39.

Coton, A. V. *The New Ballet: Kurt Jooss and His Work*. London: D. Dobson, 1946.

Cristofori, Marilyn, ed. "Hanya Holm: A Pioneer in American Dance." *Choreography and Dance* 2:2 (July 1991).

Cunz, Rolf. "Das Problem Mary Wigman." *Deutsches Musikjahrbuch* 2/3 (1925): 237–38.

Daly, Ann. "The Balanchine Woman: Of Hummingbirds and Channel Swimmers." *Drama Review* 31:1 (Spring 1987): 8–21.

———— "Classical Ballet: A Discourse of Difference." *Women and Performance* 3:2 (1987/1988): 57–66.

———— "Dance History and Feminist Theory: Reconsidering Isadora Duncan and the Male Gaze." In *Gender in Performance*, edited by Laurence Senelick, 239–59. Hanover, N.H.: University Press of New England, 1992.

———— "Movement Analysis: Piecing Together the Puzzle." *Drama Review* 32:4 (Winter 1988): 40–52.

———— "Unlimited Partnership: Dance and Feminist Analysis." *Dance Research Journal* 23:1 (Spring 1991): 2–5.

Dance: Four Pioneers. Film directed by Charles Dubin for National Educational Television. 1966. Distributed by the University of California Extension.

d'Andrea, Gisela. "The New German Dance in the Weimar Republic." In *Germany in the Twenties: The Artist as Social Critic*, edited by Frank D. Hirschbach et al., 86–97. Minneapolis: University of Minnesota, 1980.

De Keersmaeker, Anna Teresa. "Valeska Gert." *Drama Review* 25:3 (1981): 55–66.

Delius, Rudolf von. "Eine neue Tänzerin." *Die Propyläen* 5:28 (1914): 21–22.

—— *Mary Wigman.* Dresden: Carl Reissner, 1925.

DeMille, Agnes. *Martha: The Life and Work of Martha Graham.* New York: Random House, 1991.

Diem, Liselott. *Die Gymnastikbewegung.* Sankt Augustin: Academia Verlag, 1991.

Dixon, C. Madeleine. "Mary Wigman." *Theatre Arts* 15:1 (1931): 37–42.

Duncan, Irma. *Duncan Dancer: An Autobiography.* Middletown, Conn.: Wesleyan University Press, 1966.

Duncan, Isadora. *The Art of the Dance.* 1928. Reprint. Edited by Sheldon Cheney. New York: Theatre Arts Books, 1969.

—— *My Life.* New York: Boni and Liveright, 1927.

—— *Der Tanz der Zukunft.* Leipzig: Eugen Diederichs, 1903.

Ebler, Grete. "Die sieben Tänze des Lebens." *Neue Blätter für Kunst und Literatur* 4:5 (1922): 72–74.

Eckstein, Hans. "Tänzerkongress und Totenmahl in München." *Das Werk* 17 (September 1930): 283–85.

"Editorial: A Dancer and an Educator on Fascism." *Dance Observer* 4:3 (March 1937): 260.

"Editorial: Olympic Protest." *Dance Observer* 3:4 (April 1936): 38.

Ege, Friedrich. "Die Mary Wigman Tanzschule." *Deutsches Musikjahrbuch* 2/3 (1925): 234–46.

Ehrlenbruch, Gerda. *Die freien Gruppen in der Tanzszene der Bundesrepublik.* Frankfurt: Peter Lang, 1991.

Eisenberg, Emanuel. "Danse Macabre." *New Theatre* 3:5 (May 1936): 22–23, 37.

Emmel, Felix. "Neue Sachlichkeit im Tanz." *Tanzgemeinschaft* 2:3 (1930): 4.

—— "Tänzerische Verwirklichung." *Tanzgemeinschaft* 2:2 (1930): 2–4.

Enkelmann, Siegfried, et al. *Tänzer unserer Zeit.* Munich: R. Piper, 1937.

Evan, Blanche. "From a Dancer's Notebook." *New Theatre* 3:3 (March 1936): 16–17, 28–29.

—— "Road to the Dance." *Theatre Arts* 19:1 (1935): 27–34.

Fiedler, Leonhard, and Martin Lang, eds. *Grete Wiesenthal.* Salzburg and Vienna: Residenz, 1985.

Fischer, Hans. *Hamburger Kulturbilderbogen.* Berlin and Munich: Gebr. Paetl, 1923.

—— *Körperschönheit und Körperkultur.* Berlin: Deutsche Buch-Gemeinschaft, 1928.

—— "Der neue Tanz in seiner symptomatischen Bedeutung." *Die Form: Zeitschrift für gestaltende Arbeit* 1:13 (1926): 281–92.

—— *Das Tanzbuch.* Munich: Langen, 1924.

Fischer, Lothar. "Getanzte Körperbefreiung." In *"Wir sind nackt und nennen uns Du": Eine Geschichte der Freikörperkultur,* edited by Michael Andritzky and Thomas Rautenberg, 106–23. Giessen: Anabas, 1989.

————— *Tanz zwischen Rausch und Tod: Anita Berber 1918–1928 in Berlin.* Berlin: Haude und Spener, 1984.

Foster, John. *The Influences of Rudolph Laban.* London: Lepus Books, 1977.

Foster, Susan. *Reading Dancing: Bodies and Subjects in Contemporary American Dance.* Berkeley and Los Angeles: University of California Press, 1986.

Franko, Mark. *Dance as Text: Ideologies of the Baroque Body.* New York: Cambridge University Press, 1993.

————— "Repeatability, Reconstruction, and Beyond." *Theatre Journal* 41 : 1 (March 1989): 56–74.

Frentz, Hans. *Niddy Impekoven und ihre Tänze.* Freiburg i.Br.: Urban, 1929.

Freund, Liesel, ed. *Monographien der Ausbildungsschulen für Tanz und tänzerische Körperbildung.* Berlin: L. Alterthum, 1929.

Gamson, Annabelle. *On Dancing Isadora's Dances.* Portchester, N.Y.: Dance Solos, 1988. Videocassette.

Garafola, Lynn. "Dance in the City: Toward an American Dance." In *New York: Culture Capital of the World, 1940–1965,* edited by Leonard Wallock, 157–87. New York: Rizzoli, 1988.

————— *Diaghilev's Ballets Russes.* New York: Oxford University Press, 1989.

————— "The Travesty Dancer in Nineteenth-Century Ballet." *Dance Research Journal* 17 : 2/18 : 1 (Fall 1985/Spring 1986): 35–40.

Gerhard Bohner—Tänzer und Choreograph. Berlin: Edition Hentrich, 1991.

Gert, Valeska. *Ich bin eine Hexe: Kaleidoskop meines Lebens.* Munich: Franz Schneekluth, 1968.

————— "Mary Wigman und Valeska Gert." *Der Querschnitt* 6 : 5 (1926): 361–62.

————— "Tanzen." *Schrifttanz* 4 : 1 (1930): 5–7.

Giertz, Gernot. *Kultus ohne Götter: Emile Jaques-Dalcroze und Adolphe Appia.* Munich: Kitzinger, 1975.

Gleisner, Martin. "Laban als Schöpfer von Laientanz und Bewegungschor." *Schrifttanz* 2 : 4 (1929): 69–70.

————— *Tanz für alle: Von der Gymnastik zum Gemeinschaftstanz.* Leipzig: Hesse und Becker, 1928.

Goetz, Bruno. "Zum dritten deutschen Tänzerkongress in München." *Das National Theater* 2 (1929/1930): 470–74.

Goetze, Will. "Tänzerische Musiklehre." *Tanzgemeinschaft* 1 (April 1929): 6–9.

Gottschild, Helmut. "Late Awakening: The Re-Emergence of German Dance." *Ballett International* 8 : 2 (March 1985): 12–15.

Graff, Ellen. "Stepping Left: Dance and Politics in New York City, 1928–1942." Ph.D. diss., New York University, 1992.

Grauerholz, Hermann. "Der Nationalsozialismus als gestaltgebende Kraft für den Bewegungschor." *Der Tanz* 6 : 9 (1933): 3–4.

Grayburn, Patricia. *Bodenwieser.* Guilford, Australia: National Resource Centre for Dance, 1990.

Grell, Tamara. "Maskentänze: Der Schnitzer Viktor Magito." *Der Tanz* 10 : 2 (1937): 9–11.

Grund, Gustav. "Maskentanz." *Hellweg* 6:40 (1926): 692–93.

——— "Opernbühne und neuer Tanz." *Singchor und Tanz* 45:3 (1928): 27–28.

Grünthal, Ernst. "Der Tanz als Kunstwerk." *Die neue Schaubühne* 2:4 (April 1920): 85–89.

Guest, Ivor. *Gautier on Dance.* Selected, translated, and annotated by Ivor Guest. London: Dance Books, 1986.

——— *The Romantic Ballet in Paris.* Middletown, Conn.: Wesleyan University Press, 1966.

Günther, Alfred. "Der Tanz der Mary Wigman." *Die neue Schaubühne* 3:5/ 6 (1921): 106–8.

Günther, Dorothee. "Tanzwissenschaft." *Tanzgemeinschaft* 1 (April 1929): 10–11.

Günther, Dorothee, and Gustav Fischer-Klamt, eds. "Tänzerische Körperbildung." *Der Tanz* 14:3 (1941): 50–62.

Günther, Helmut. "Dorothee Günther." *Das Tanzarchiv* 23:11 (November 1975): 386–87.

——— "Die Entstehungsgeschichte des Triadischen Balletts." *Das Tanzarchiv* 26:4 (April 1978): 133–36.

——— "Gymnastik- und Tanzbestrebungen vom Ende des 19. Jahrhunderts bis zum Ersten Weltkrieg." In *Geschichte der Leibesübungen,* edited by Horst Ueberhorst, vol. 3, 569–93. Berlin: Bartels und Wernitz, 1980.

——— "Der Mensch—Ein raumbehextes Wesen: Über das Tanzwerk Oskar Schlemmers." *Das Tanzarchiv* 13:9 (1966): 257–63.

Hasting, Hanns. "Die Entwicklung der musikalischen Form in den Tänzen Mary Wigmans." *Deutsche Tanz-Zeitschrift* 1:2 (1936): 4–6.

——— "Klang und Raum." *Schrifttanz* 4:2 (1931): 31–32.

——— "Musik und der künstlerische Tanz unserer Zeit." *Der Tanz* 10:6 (1937): 5–7.

——— "Musik und Tanz." *Der Kreis: Zeitschrift für künstlerische Kultur* 9:12 (1932): 688–92.

——— "Der Tänzer und die Musik." *Tanzgemeinschaft* 1 (April 1929): 1–6.

"Helen Tamiris." *Studies in Dance History* 1:1 (Fall/Winter 1989–1990).

Heymann, Jeanne Lunin. "Dance in the Depression: The WPA Project." *Dance Scope* 9:2 (Spring/Summer 1975): 28–40.

Hildebrandt, Fred. *Die Tänzerin Valeska Gert.* Stuttgart: W. Hädecke, 1928.

——— *Tänzerinnen der Gegenwart.* Zurich: Orel Füssli, 1931.

Hirschbach, Denny, and Rick Takvorian, eds. *Hilde Holger: Die Kraft des Tanzes.* Bremen: Zeichen und Spuren Verlag, 1990.

"Hochschule für Tanzkunst." *Singchor und Tanz* 47:12 (15 June 1930): 198–99.

Hodgson, John, and Valerie Preston-Dunlop. *Rudolf Laban: An Introduction to His Work and Influence.* Plymouth, England: Northcote, 1990.

Hodson, Millicent. "Ritual Design in the New Dance: Nijinsky's Choreographic Method." In two parts. *Dance Research* 3:2 (Autumn 1985): 35–45 and 4:1 (Spring 1986): 63–77.

——— "*Sacre*: Searching for Nijinsky's Chosen One." *Ballet Review* 15:3 (Fall 1987): 53–66.

Hoerisch, Werner. "Zwei unterschiedliche Tanzschöpfungen an der Berliner Städtischen Oper." *Theater der Zeit* 12:11 (1957): 50–52.

Hoghe, Raimund. *Pina Bausch—Theatergeschichten*. Frankfurt am Main: Suhrkamp Taschenbuch, 1986.

Holm, Hanya. "Mary Wigman." *Dance Observer* 2:8 (November 1935): 85, 91–92.

——— "The Mary Wigman I Know." In *The Dance Has Many Faces*, edited by Walter Sorell, 182–91. New York: Columbia University Press, 1966.

Holmes, Olive, ed. *Motion Arrested: Dance Reviews of H. T. Parker*. Middletown, Conn.: Wesleyan University Press, 1982.

Howe, Dianne Shelden. "Manifestations of the German Expressionist Aesthetic as Presented in Drama and Art in the Dance and Writings of Mary Wigman." Ph.D. diss., University of Wisconsin, Madison, 1985.

——— "The Notion of Mysticism in the Philosophy and Choreography of Mary Wigman, 1914–1931." *Dance Research Journal* 19:1 (Summer 1987): 19–24.

Huber, Lotti. *Diese Zitrone hat noch viel Saft! Ein Leben*. Berlin: Edition Dia, 1990.

Hunt, Dianne. "The Wigman Years—Part One of the Thimey Transcripts." *Washington Dance View* 2:3 (February/March 1981): 1, 23–28.

Huxley, Michael. "Early European Modern Dance." In *Dance History: A Methodology for Study*, edited by Janet Adshead and June Layson, 147–61. London: Dance Books, 1983.

Ibel, Rudolf. "Die deutsche Tänzerin." *Der Kreis: Zeitschrift für künstlerische Kultur* 9:12 (December 1932): 692–96.

Iros, Ernst. "Uraufführung von Albert Talhoffs *Totenmal*." *Die neue Zeit* 12 (1930): 12.

Jaques-Dalcroze, Emile. *Rhythm, Music, and Education*. 1921. Reprint. London: Dalcroze Society, 1980.

Jeschke, Claudia. "Identity and Order: Trends in Dance Theatre in Germany." In *Blickpunkte II*, 18–27. Montreal: Goethe Institute, 1989.

Joachimstal, G. "Die neue Wigman-Schule in Dresden." *Der Tanz* 1:4 (1928): 26–27.

Jockel, Nils, and Patricia Stöckemann. *"Flugkraft in goldene Ferne . . .": Bühnentanz in Hamburg seit 1900*. Hamburg: Museum für Kunst und Gewerbe, 1989.

Johnston, Jill. "The New American Modern Dance." *Salmagundi* 33/34 (Spring/Summer 1976): 149–74.

Jowitt, Deborah. *Time and the Dancing Image*. New York: William Morrow, 1988.

Jürgens, Alfred. *Spiegelungen: Miniature, Theater, und Tanzskizzenblätter*. Bensheim: G. Berger, 1927.

Kallai, Ernst. "Tänzerkongess." *Sozialistische Monatshefte* 36:9 (September 1930): 941–42.

———— "Wigman." *Sozialistische Monatshefte* 36:7 (1930): 713.

———— "Zwischen Kulttanz und Varieté." *Schrifttanz* 4:1 (1931): 1–4.

Kampfbund für deutsche Kultur. "Die geistigen Grundlagen für Tanz im Nationalsozialistischen Staat." *Der Tanz* 6:11 (November 1933): 2–3.

Kandinsky, Wassily. "Tanzkurven: Zu den Tänzen der Palucca." *Das Kunstblatt* 10:3 (1926): 117–20.

Kant, Marion. "Ballett als eine Auskunft zur Frauenfrage." *Weimarer Beiträge* 33:12 (1987): 2026–43.

———— "Giselle—Die schöne Tod." *Musik und Gesellschaft* 38 (March 1988): 129–35.

———— "Propositions on the History of Dance in East Germany." Position paper circulated as part of Choreographing History Conference, University of California, Riverside, February 1992.

Kendall, Elizabeth. *Where She Danced.* New York: Alfred Knopf, 1979.

Kirstein, Lincoln. *Ballet: Bias and Belief.* New York: Dance Horizons, 1983.

———— *Dance: A Short History of Classic Theatrical Dancing.* 1935. Reprint. New York: Dance Horizons, 1969.

———— "Dance Chronicle." *Hound and Horn* 4:4 (1931): 573–80.

Klamt, Jutta. *Vom Erleben zum Gestalten: Die Entfaltung schöpferischer Kräfte im deutschen Menschen.* Berlin: Dorn, 1936.

Knab, Armin. "Mary Wigman: Visionen." *Schrifttanz* 2:3 (1929): 55–56.

Knust, Albrecht. "Vom Laientanzspiel." *Deutsche Tanz-Zeitschrift* 1:4 (July 1936): 75–76.

Koegler, Horst. "Aus Rhythmus geboren—Zum Tanzen bestellt: Hellerau-Laxenburg und die Anfänge des modernen Tanzes." In *Ballett: Chronik und Bilanz des Ballettjahres,* 40–51. Velber bei Hannover: Friedrich, 1977.

———— "In the Shadow of the Swastika: Dance in Germany, 1927–1936." *Dance Perspectives* no. 57 (Spring 1974).

———— "Laban." In *Intellektuelle im Bann des Nationalsozialismus,* edited by Karl Corino, 165–79. Hamburg: Hoffmann und Campe, 1980.

———— "Mary Wigman ist im September in Berlin gestorben." *Theater Heute* 14:11 (November 1973): 1–4.

———— "Tanz in den Abgrund." In *Ballett: Chronik und Bilanz des Ballettjahres,* 57–61. Velber bei Hannover: Friedrich, 1973.

———— "Tanz in die dreissiger Jahre." In *Ballett: Chronik und Bilanz des Ballettjahres,* 39–51. Velber bei Hannover: Friedrich, 1972.

Köllinger, Bernd. *Tanztheater: Tom Schilling und die zeitgenössische Choreographie.* Berlin: Henschelverlag, 1983.

Kraus, Hildegard. *Johann Kresnik.* Frankfurt am Main: Fischer Taschenbuch, 1990.

Kuxdorf, Manfred. "The New German Dance Movement." In *Passion and Rebellion, the Expressionist Heritage,* edited by Stephen Eric Bronner and Douglas Kellner, 350–60. South Hadley, Mass.: J. F. Bergin, 1983.

Kuznitzky, Hans. "Betrachtungen zum Tänzerkongress in Magdeburg." *Melos* 6: 8/9 (1927): 392–96.

———— "Der zweite Tänzerkongress in Essen." *Melos* 7 : 8/9 (1928): 439–45.

Laban, Rudolf. "Geist und Form des Tanzes." *Der Tanz* 1 : 2 (1927): 2–5.

———— *A Life for Dance.* Translated and annotated by Lisa Ullmann. New York: Theatre Arts Books, 1975.

———— "Meister und Werk in der Tanzkunst." *Deutsche Tanz-Zeitschrift* 1 : 2 (May 1936): 1–4.

———— *Schrifttanz.* Vienna: Universal Edition, 1928.

———— "Der Tanz als Eigenkunst." *Zeitschrift für Ästhetik und Allgemeine Kunstwissenschaft* 19 (1925): 356–64.

———— "Titan: Ein Bewegungschor und eine Forderung." *Der Kreis: Zeitschrift für künstlerische Kultur* 5 : 1 (1928): 30–32.

———— "Über Choreographie und Tanztheater." *Deutsches Musikjahrbuch* 1 (1923): 238–39.

———— "Vom Sinne der Bewegungschöre." *Schrifttanz* 3 : 2 (June 1930): 25–26.

———— *Die Welt des Tänzers.* Stuttgart: Walter Seifert, 1920.

————, ed. *Deutsche Tanzfestspiele 1934.* Dresden: Carl Reissner, 1934.

Lachmann, Ismar. "Artur Michel: Champion of Modern Dance." *Dance Observer* 14 : 1 (January 1947): 4–5.

Lämmel, Rudolf. *Der moderne Tanz.* Berlin: Oestergaard, 1928.

Levin, David Michael. "Balanchine's Formalism." *Dance Perspectives* 55 (Autumn 1973): 29–48.

———— "Postmodernism in Dance: Dance, Discourse, Democracy." In *Postmodernism—Philosophy and the Arts,* edited by Hugh Silverman, 207–33. New York and London: Routledge, 1990.

Levinson, André. *Ballet Old and New.* Translated by Susan Cook Summer. New York: Dance Horizons, 1982.

———— "The Modern Dance in Germany." *Theatre Arts* 13 : 2 (February 1929): 143–53.

———— "The Spirit of the Classic Dance." In *Dance as a Theatre Art,* edited by Selma Jeanne Cohen. New York: Harper and Row, 1974.

Lewitan, Joseph. "Germany at the Crossroads: Classical Ballet or Wigman." *Dancing Times* no. 296 (May 1935): 128–30.

———— "Mary Wigman." *Der Tanz* 1 : 2 (1927/28): 26.

———— "Mary Wigman." *Der Tanz* 2 : 7 (1929): 20–22.

———— "Mary Wigman." *Der Tanz* 3 : 1 (1930): 5–6.

———— "Mary Wigman." *Der Tanz* 4 : 6 (1931): 15–16.

———— "Mary Wigmans Heimkehr." *Der Tanz* 5 : 7 (1932): 14.

———— "Mary Wigman." *Der Tanz* 5 : 12 (1932): 9–10.

———— "Mary Wigman." *Der Tanz* 6 : 1 (1933): 4–5.

———— "Totenmal von Albert Talhoff." *Der Tanz* 3 : 8 (1930): 15–16.

Linder, Kurt. *Die Verwandlungen der Mary Wigman.* Freiburg i.Br.: Urban, 1929.

Lisman, H. "Mary Wigman, Dancer." *Musical Courier* 82 : 26 (1921): 6.

Litterscheid, Richard. "Mary Wigman und das Theater." *Der Tanz* 2 : 3 (1929): 2.

Lloyd, Margaret. *The Borzoi Book of Modern Dance.* 1949. Reprint. New York: Dance Horizons, 1974.

Loesch, Ilse. *Mit Leib und Seele: Erlebte Vergangenheit des Ausdruckstanzes.* Berlin: Henschelverlag, 1990.

Loring, Elinor. "German Dance Schools." *Dancing Times* no. 267 (1932): 237–39.

Maack, Rudolf. "Schöpfung und Wandlung." *Der Kreis: Zeitschrift für künstlerische Kultur* 9:12 (December 1932): 677–88.

———— *Tanz in Hamburg: Von Mary Wigman bis John Neumeier.* Hamburg: Christians, 1975.

Magriel, Paul, ed. *Nijinsky, Pavlova, Duncan: Three Lives in Dance.* New York: Da Capo Press, 1977.

Maletic, Vera. *Body-Space-Expression: The Development of Rudolf Laban's Movement and Dance Concepts.* Berlin: Mouton de Gruyter, 1987.

———— "Wigman and Laban: The Interplay of Theory and Practice." *Ballet Review* 14:3 (1986): 86–94.

Manning, Susan. "An American Perspective on Tanztheater." *Drama Review* 30:2 (Summer 1986): 57–79.

———— "Body Politic: The Dances of Mary Wigman." Ph.D. diss., Columbia University, 1987.

———— "From Modernism to Fascism: The Evolution of Wigman's Choreography." *Ballet Review* 14:4 (1986): 87–98.

———— "German Dance: Mary Wigmans Erbe in Amerika." *Tanzdrama* 3 (1988): 6–8.

———— "German *Rites*: A History of *Le sacre du printemps* on the German Stage." *Dance Chronicle* 14:2/3 (1991): 129–58.

———— "Ideology and Performance between Weimar and the Third Reich: The Case of *Totenmal.*" *Theatre Journal* 41:2 (May 1989): 211–23.

———— "Lotte Goslar: Interview." *Tanzdrama* 5 (1988): 18–21.

———— "Modern Dance in the Third Reich: Six Positions and a Coda." In *Choreographing History,* edited by Susan Foster. Bloomington: Indiana University Press, 1993.

———— "Modernist Dogma and 'Post-Modern' Rhetoric: A Response to Sally Banes' *Terpsichore in Sneakers.*" *Drama Review* 32:4 (Winter 1988): 32–39.

———— "The Mythologization of the Female: Mary Wigman and Martha Graham." *Ballett International* 14:9 (September 1991): 10–12, 14.

———— "*Pina Bausch Wuppertal Dance Theater* and *Jooss: A Documentation.*" *Dance Research Journal* 17:2 and 18:1 (Fall 1985/Spring 1986): 93–94.

———— "Pina Bausch's *The Seven Deadly Sins* in Brooklyn." *Kurt Weill Newsletter* 4:1 (Spring 1986): 19–20.

———— "Reinterpreting Laban." *Dance Chronicle* 11:2 (1988): 315–20.

———— "Tänzerinnen weiblicher Geschichte: Mary Wigman und Martha Graham." *Tanzdrama* 15 (1991): 7–13.

———— "*Valeska Gert, Anita Berber,* and *Auf der grossen Strasse: Jean Weidts Erinnerungen.*" *Dance Research Journal* 18:2 (Fall 1986): 70–73.

——— "Wigman, Balanchine, and Rock 'n' Roll Conference." *Dance Research Journal* 19:2 (Winter 1987/1988): 54–55.

Manning, Susan, and Melissa Benson. "Interrupted Continuities: Modern Dance in Germany." *Drama Review* 30:2 (1986): 30–45.

Markard, Anna, and Hermann Markard. *Jooss*. Cologne: Ballett-Bühnen-Verlag, 1985.

Martin, John. *America Dancing*. New York: Dodge Publishing, 1936.

——— *Introduction to the Dance*. 1939. Reprint. New York: Dance Horizons, 1965.

——— *The Modern Dance*. 1933. Reprint. New York: Dance Horizons, 1965.

Mary Wigman Gesellschaft. *Tanzdrama*. Quarterly journal, 1987 to present.

McDonagh, Don. *The Complete Guide to Modern Dance*. Garden City: Doubleday, 1976.

——— *The Rise and Fall and Rise of Modern Dance*. New York: Outerbridge and Dienstfrey, 1970.

Michel, Artur. "The Development of the New German Dance." In *The Modern Dance*, edited by Virginia Stewart and Merle Armitage, 3–17. New York: E. Weyhe, 1935.

——— "International Dance Tournament—Berlin, 1936." *Dance Observer* 3:8 (October 1936): 89, 93.

——— "Mary Wigman—On Her Sixtieth Birthday." *Dance Observer* 13:9 (November 1946): 108–9.

Michel, Marcelle. "Marie Wigman." *L'avant-scène: Ballet/Danse* (August/October 1980): 64–67.

Milward, Joe U. "Mary Wigman—Adventurer in Rhythm." *The Arts* 4:1 (1923): 45–47.

Moenius, Georg. "Totenmal." *Allgemeine Rundschau* 27:31 (2 August 1930): 529–33.

Moss, Suzan. "Spinning through the Weltanschauung: The Effects of the Nazi Regime on the German Modern Dance." Ph.D. diss., New York University, 1988.

Muckermann, Friedrich. "Ein Weihespiel der Nation." *Der Gral* 24:8 (May 1930): 675–76.

Mueller, John. "Films: A Glimpse of Mary Wigman." *Dance Magazine* 50:3 (March 1976): 96.

Müller, Hedwig. "At the Start of a New Era: Tenth Anniversary of the Death of Mary Wigman." *Ballett International* 6:12 (1983): 6–13.

——— "Dokumentation: 3. Deutscher Tänzerkongress, München 1930." *Tanzdrama* 13 (1990): 17–29.

——— "Emile Jaques-Dalcroze: The Beginnings of Rhythmic Gymnastics in Hellerau." *Ballett International* 8:6/7 (1985): 24–27.

——— "Mary Wigman and the Third Reich." *Ballett International* 9:11 (1986): 18–23.

——— *Mary Wigman: Leben und Werk der grossen Tänzerin*. Berlin: Quadriga, 1986.

———— "Mary Wigman: Lebenslauf." *Tanzdrama* 8 (1989): 23–25.

———— "Palucca: Zum Geburtstag einer Meisterin." *Tanzdrama* 18 (1992): 20–25.

———— "Wigman and National Socialism." *Ballet Review* 15:1 (Spring 1987): 65–73.

———— "Zu Jung für ein Begräbnis: Dore Hoyers Tanzkunst." *Tanzdrama* 1 (1987): 6–9.

Müller, Hedwig, Frank-Manuel Peter, and Garnet Schuldt. *Dore Hoyer—Tänzerin.* Berlin: Edition Hentrich, 1992.

Müller, Hedwig, and Norbert Servos. "Expressionism? *Ausdruckstanz* and the New Dance Theatre in Germany." *Dance Theatre Journal* 2:1 (January 1984): 10–15.

———— "From Isadora Duncan to Leni Riefenstahl." *Ballett International* 5:4 (April 1982): 14–23.

Müller, Hedwig, and Patricia Stöckemann. "*Der grüne Tisch:* Eine choreographie von Kurt Jooss." *Tanzdrama* 15 (1991): 22–28.

Müller-Rau, Elly. "Mary Wigman." *Kunst und Kritik* no. 16 (1929): 193–95.

———— "Stil und Technik: Ein Problem der Wigman-Tanzkultur." *Der Tanz* 3:1 (1930): 6–8.

Niedecken-Gebhard, Hans. "Bedeutung des Tanzes für das Kulturtheater." *Die deutsche Bühne* 19:6 (1927): 109–10.

Niehaus, Max. *Isadora Duncan: Leben, Werk, Wirkung.* Wilhelmshaven: Heinrichshofen, 1981.

Nikolaus, Paul. "Agonie des Bühnentanzes?" *Die neue Schaubühne* 3:5/6 (1921): 112–14.

———— "Tanz und Tanz-Kritik." *Die neue Schaubühne* 2:11 (1920): 310–12.

Novack, Cynthia. "Looking at Movement as Culture: Contact Improvisation to Disco." *Drama Review* 32:4 (Winter 1988): 102–19.

———— *Sharing the Dance: Contact Improvisation and American Culture.* Madison: University of Wisconsin Press, 1990.

Noverre, Jean Georges. *Letters on Dancing and Ballets.* Translated by Cyril W. Beaumont. New York: Dance Horizons, 1966.

Ocko, Edna. "Anti-Fascism." *Dance Observer* 2:8 (November 1935): 93–94.

———— "The Swastika Is Dancing." *New Theatre* 2:11 (November 1935): 17.

Odom, Maggie. "Mary Wigman: The Early Years, 1913–1925." *Drama Review* 88 (1980): 81–92.

Odom, Selma Landen. "Dalcroze Eurhythmics in England: History of an Innovation in Music and Movement Education." Ph.D. diss., University of Surrey, 1991.

———— "Wigman at Hellerau." *Ballet Review* 14:2 (Summer 1986): 41–53.

Oskar Schlemmer—The Triadic Ballet (Dokumentation 5). Berlin: Akademie der Künste, 1985.

Otto, Werner. "Die Hellerauer Schulfeste von 1912 und 1913." In *Musikbühne 76,* edited by Horst Seeger, 143–69. Berlin: Henschelverlag, 1976.

Ould, Hermon. "The Art of Mary Wigman: Some Notes on a New Dance

Form." *Dancing Times* no. 187 (1926): 37–41.

Padgette, Paul, ed. *The Dance Writings of Carl Van Vechten.* New York: Dance Horizons, 1974.

Page, Ruth. *Class: Notes on Dance Classes around the World, 1915–1980.* Princeton: Princeton Book Company, 1984.

Pallat, Ludwig, and Franz Hilkers, eds. *Künstlerische Körperschulung.* Breslau: F. Hirt, 1923.

Palucca, Gret. "Wie ich zu Mary Wigman kam." *Tanzgemeinschaft* 2:2 (1930): 8.

Pander, Oswald. "Mary Wigman und die neue Choreographie." *Der Kreis: Zeitschrift für künstlerische Kultur* 2:2 (1925): 1–6.

Parker, H. T. *Motion Arrested.* Edited by Olive Holmes. Middletown, Conn.: Wesleyan University Press, 1982.

Partsch-Bergsohn, Isa. "Dance Theatre from Rudolf Laban to Pina Bausch." *Dance Theatre Journal* 6:2 (Fall 1988): 37–39.

——— "Über Vertrautes hinausreichen." *Tanzdrama* 3 (1988): 14–17.

Perrottet, Suzanne. *Ein bewegtes Leben.* Edited by Giorgio J. Wolfensberger. Bern: Beutelli, 1990.

Peter, Frank-Manuel. *Valeska Gert: Tänzerin, Schauspielerin, Kabarettistin.* Berlin: Frölich und Kaufmann, 1985.

——— "Wegbereiter des modernen Tanzes: Der Tanzpublizist Fritz Böhme." *Tanzdrama* 9 (1989): 23.

Peter-Bolaender, Martina. "Den Weg zu sich selbst finden: Wigman-Technik von Gundel Eplinius." *Tanzdrama* 18 (1992): 28–30.

Pfister, Gertrud. *Frau und Sport.* Frankfurt am Main: Fischer Taschenbuch, 1980.

Pfister, Gertrud, and Hans Langenfeld. "Die Leibesübungen für das weibliche Geschlecht—Ein Mittel zur Emanzipation der Frau?" In *Geschichte der Leibesübungen,* edited by Horst Ueberhorst, vol. 3, 485–521. Berlin: Bartels und Wernitz, 1980.

"Pina Bausch." *Women and Performance* 2:1 (1984): 97–100.

Pirchan, Emil. *Harald Kreutzberg: Sein Leben und seine Tänze.* Vienna: W. Frick, 1941.

"Positionen zur Vergangenheit und Gegenwart des modernen Tanzes: Laban, Wigman, Palucca, Weidt, Rudolph, Schilling." *Arbeitshefte* no. 36. Berlin: Akademie der Künste der DDR, 1982.

Preston-Dunlop, Valerie. "Laban and the Nazis." *Dance Theatre Journal* 6:2 (July 1988): 4–7.

——— "Rudolf Laban and Kurt Jooss in Exile." In *Theatre and Film in Exile: German Artists in Britain, 1933–1945,* edited by Günter Berghaus, 167–78. Oxford, New York, Munich: Berg, 1989.

Preston-Dunlop, Valerie, and Charlotte Purkiss. "Rudolf Laban—The Making of Modern Dance." In two parts. *Dance Theatre Journal* 7:3 (Winter 1989): 11–16, 25; and 7:4 (Spring 1990): 10–13.

Preston-Dunlop, Valerie, and Susanne Lahusen, eds. *Schrifttanz: A View of German Dance in the Weimar Republic.* London: Dance Books, 1990.

Prevots, Naima. "Zurich Dada and Dance: Formative Ferment." *Dance Research Journal* 17:1 (Spring/Summer 1985): 3–8.

Price, David W. "The Politics of the Body: Pina Bausch's *Tanztheater.*" *Theatre Journal* 42:3 (October 1990): 322–31.

Prickett, Stacey. "Dance and the Workers' Struggle." *Dance Research* 8:1 (Spring 1990): 47–61.

——— "From Workers' Dance to New Dance." *Dance Research* 7:1 (Spring 1989): 47–64.

Pringsheim, Klaus. "Der Unfug der neudeutschen Tanzkunst." *Der Querschnitt* 10:9 (September 1930): 604–6.

Prinzhorn, Hans. "Grundsätzliches zum *Totenmal*, zum kultischen Stil und zum Unternehmertum des Feierns." *Der Ring* no.36 (September 1930): 623–28.

Prod'homme, Konstantin. "Die Tradition des Nicht-Herkömmlichen: Der Anteil der Musik an den Berliner Festwochen 1957." *Österreichische Musikzeitschrift* 12 (1957): 446–48.

Regitz, Hartmut, ed. *Tanz in Deutschland: Ballett seit 1945.* Berlin: Quadriga, 1984.

Rood, Arnold, ed. *Gordon Craig on Movement and Dance.* New York: Dance Horizons, 1977.

Ruyter, Nancy L. *Reformers and Visionaries: The Americanization of the Art of Dance.* New York: Dance Horizons, 1979.

Rydberg, Olaf. *Die Tänzerin Palucca.* Dresden: Carl Reissner, 1935.

Schäfer, Rolf Helmut, ed. *Yvonne Georgi.* Braunschweig: R. H. Schäfer, 1974.

Scheier, Helmut. "What Has Dance Theatre to Do with Ausdruckstanz?" *Ballett International* 10:1 (January 1987): 12–17.

Scheper, Dirk. *Oskar Schlemmer: Das Triadische Ballett und die Bauhausbühne.* Berlin: Akademie der Künste, 1988.

Scheyer, Ernst. "The Shapes of Space: The Art of Mary Wigman and Oskar Schlemmer." *Dance Perspectives* no. 41 (1970).

Schiffer, Marcellus. "Besuch bei Mary Wigman." *Die Weltbühne* 22:2 (1926): 68–69.

Schikowski, John. *Der neue Tanz.* Berlin: Volksbühnenverlag, 1924.

——— "Der neue Tanz und das Massentheater der Zukunft." *Kulturwille* 1:2 (1924): 21–22.

Schlee, Alfred. "Dancers in Germany Today." *Modern Music* 12:2 (1935): 82–85.

——— "Expressionism in the Dance." *Modern Music* 8:14 (1931): 12–16.

——— "The Modern German Dance." *Theatre Arts* 14:5 (1930): 419–29.

——— "Tänzerkongress in München." *Schrifttanz* 3:3 (November 1930): 54–55.

Schlemmer, Oskar. "Missverständnisse." *Schrifttanz* 4:2 (1931): 27–29.

Schlicher, Susanne. *Tanztheater.* Reinbek bei Hamburg: Rowohlt Taschenbuch, 1987.

Schmidt, Jochen. "At the Summit—Or Already on the Decline? German

Dance Theatre at the End of the 1980s." In *Blickpunkte II*, 6–16. Montreal: Goethe Institute, 1989.

———— "From Swan Lake to the Weed Garden: The Development of Ballet and Dance Theatre in the Federal Republic of Germany since 1967." In *Theater/Theatre, 1967–1982*, edited by Manfred Linke, 77–90. Berlin: International Theatre Institute, 1983.

Schmidt, Jochen, and Hans-Dieter Dryoff, eds. *Tanzkultur in der Bundesrepublik Deutschland*. Bonn: UNESCO, 1990.

Schuftan, Werner. "Der 3. Deutsche Tänzerkongress." *Singchor und Tanz* 47:13/14 (15 July 1930): 210–14.

Schüller, Gunhild. "Der Tanz in Wien im 20. Jahrhundert." In *Tanz, 20. Jahrhundert in Wien: Ausstellungskatalog*, edited by Josef Mayerhöfer, 15–41. Vienna: Österreichisches Theatermuseum, 1979.

Schumacher, Ewald Mathias. "Körperkultur und Tanzschulen." *Deutsches Musikjahrbuch* 1 (1923): 244–49.

Schumann, Gerhard. "Gespräche und Fragen: Mary Wigman." In *Arbeitshefte* no. 36, 36–50. Berlin: Akademie der Künste der DDR, 1982.

———— *Palucca: Porträt einer Künstlerin*. Berlin: Henschelverlag, 1972.

Schumann, Wolfgang. "As Mary Wigman Dances." Translated by Hallie Flanagan. *Theatre Guild Magazine* 8:4 (1931): 43–45.

———— "Mary Wigmans Tanzmärchen." *Der Kunstwart* 38:5 (1925): 243–45.

———— "Tanzkunst in Deutschland." *Annalen für Literatur, Kunst, Leben* 1 (1926/1927): 885–93.

Selden, Elizabeth. *The Dancer's Quest*. Berkeley and Los Angeles: University of California Press, 1935.

———— *Elements of the Free Dance*. New York: A. S. Barnes, 1930.

Servos, Norbert. "The Heritage of Freedom: Speculations about the Future of Dance Theatre." *Ballett International* 9:7/8 (July/August 1986): 50–55.

———— "Pathos and Propaganda? On the Mass Choreography of Fascism: Some Conclusions for Dance." *Ballett International* 13:1 (January 1990): 62–67.

———— *Pina Bausch Wuppertal Dance Theater, or, The Art of Training a Goldfish*. Cologne: Ballett-Bühnen-Verlag, 1984.

———— "Whether to Resist or Conform: Ausdruckstanz Then, and Now?" *Ballett International* 10:1 (1987): 18–21.

Shawn, Ted. *Every Little Movement: A Book about François Delsarte*. 1954. Reprint. New York: Dance Horizons, 1974.

———— "Germany's Contribution to the Dance." *Foreword* 18:2 (1930): 4–5.

Shelton, Suzanne. *Divine Dancer: A Biography of Ruth St. Denis*. Garden City: Doubleday, 1981.

Siegel, Marcia. "Artisans of Space." *Hudson Review* 34:1 (1981): 93–98.

———— *Days on Earth: The Dance of Doris Humphrey*. New Haven and London: Yale University Press, 1987.

———— "*The Green Table*—Sources of a Classic." *Dance Research Journal* 21 : 1 (Spring 1989): 15–21.

———— "Mary Wigman, 1886–1973: A Tribute." Interview with Hanya Holm. *Dance Magazine* 47 : 11 (November 1973): 80–81.

———— "Modern Dance before Bennington: Sorting It All Out." *Dance Research Journal* 19 : 1 (Summer 1987): 3–9.

———— *The Shapes of Change: Images of American Dance*. Boston: Houghton Mifflin, 1979.

Skoronel, Vera. "Mary Wigmans Führertum." *Tanzgemeinschaft* 2 : 2 (1930): 4–6.

———— "Mary Wigmans Kompositionsstil." *Schrifttanz* 3 : 3 (November 1930): 50.

Smith, Marian. "What Killed Giselle?" *Dance Chronicle* 13 : 1 (1990): 68–81.

Snyder, Allegra Fuller, and Annette Macdonald. *Mary Wigman, 1886–1973: "When the Fire Dances between the Two Poles."* Pennington, N.J.: Princeton Book Company, Dance Horizons Video, 1991. Videocassette.

Sommer, Sally. "Loie Fuller: From the Theater of Popular Entertainment to the Parisian Avant-Garde." Ph.D. diss., New York University, 1979.

Sommer, Sally, and Margaret Haile Harris. *Loie, the Life and Art of Loie Fuller*. New York: Putnam, 1986.

Sonner, Rudolf. "Ballett oder Ausdruckstanz?" *Die Musik* 34 : 8 (1942): 249–51.

Sorell, Walter. *Hanya Holm*. Middletown, Conn.: Wesleyan University Press, 1969.

———— *The Mary Wigman Book*. Edited and translated by Walter Sorell. Middletown, Conn.: Wesleyan University Press, 1975.

———— *Mary Wigman—Ein Vermächtnis*. Wilhelmshaven: F. Noetzel, 1986.

Spaemann, Heinrich. "Tänzerkongress." *Sozialistische Monatshefte* 34 : 9 (September 1928): 826.

———— "Wigman." *Sozialistische Monatshefte* 35 : 8 (August 1929): 757–58.

Spector, Irwin. *Rhythm and Life: The Work of Emile Jaques-Dalcroze*. Stuyvesant, N.Y.: Pendragon, 1990.

Sprengler, Joseph. "Albert Talhoff: Totenmal." *Die Literatur* 32 (1930): 716–17.

Stadler, Edmund. "Theater und Tanz in Ascona." In *Monte Verità, Berg der Wahrheit*, edited by Harald Szeeman, 126–35. Milan: Electa Editrice, 1978.

Stebbins, Genevieve. *Delsarte System of Expression*. New York: Edgar S. Werner, 1902.

Stefan-Gruenfeldt, Paul, ed. *Tanz in dieser Zeit*. Vienna: Universal Edition, 1926.

Steinbeck, Dietrich, ed. *Mary Wigmans Choreographisches Skizzenbuch*. Berlin: Edition Hentrich, 1987.

Steiner, Paul Nikolaus. *Tänzerinnen*. Munich: Delphin, 1919.

Stern, Lisbeth. "Wigman." *Sozialistische Monatshefte* 32 : 9 (1926): 267.

———— "Wigman." *Sozialistische Monatshefte* 36 : 1 (1930): 97–98.

Stewart, Virginia. "German Letter." *Dance Observer* 2:7 (October 1935): 80–81.

Stewart, Virginia, and Merle Armitage, eds. *The Modern Dance*. New York: E. Weyhe, 1935.

Stöckemann, Patricia. *Lola Rogge: Ein Leben für den Ausdruckstanz*. Wilhelmshaven: Florian Noetzel Verlag, 1991.

Suhr, Werner. "Tanzbetrachter—Tanzberater?" *Der Tanz* 10:7 (1937): 6–8.

Sulm, Peter. "Das Festspiel im Olympischen Stadion." *Der Tanz* 9:5 (1936): 15–18.

——— "Tanzbericht Berlin." *Der Tanz* 10:1 (1937): 5–7.

"Die Tagungen des Tänzerkongresses." *Der Tanz* 3:8 (August 1930): 4–12.

Talhoff, Albert. *The Call of the Dead*. Translated by M. A. Moralt. Stuttgart: Deutsche Verlags-Anstalt, 1930.

——— *So spricht Albert Talhoff*. Munich: Barth, 1958.

——— *Totenmal: Dramatisch-chorische Vision für Wort, Tanz, Licht*. Stuttgart: Deutsche Verlags-Anstalt, 1930.

"Tänze, die immer gelten: Gespräch mit Susanne Linke über ihr Dore Hoyer-Programm." *Tanzdrama* 1 (1987): 10, 14.

"Tänzer und Tanzlehrer in der deutschen Reichsstatistik." *Der Tanz* 10:6 (June 1937): 22–24.

Die tänzerische Situation unserer Zeit: Ein Querschnitt. Dresden: Carl Reissner, 1936.

Tepp, Max. *Gertrud und Ursula Falke: Tänze*. Lauenberg: Adolf Saal, 1924.

Thiess, Frank. *Der Tanz als Kunstwerk*. Munich: Delphin, 1920.

Thornton, Samuel. *Laban's Theory of Movement*. Boston: Plays, 1971.

Toepfer, Karl. "Nudity and Modernity in German Dance, 1910–1930." *Journal of the History of Sexuality* 3:1 (July 1992): 58–108.

——— "Speech and Sexual Difference in Mary Wigman's Dance Aesthetic." In *Gender and Performance*, edited by Laurence Senelick, 260–78. Hanover, N.H.: University Press of New England, 1992.

Trümpy, Berthe. "Die Anfänge der Wigman Schule." *Tanzgemeinschaft* 2:2 (1930): 8–12.

——— "Tänzerische Erziehung." *Der Tanz* 2:8 (1929): 2–3.

Villiers, Anne. "Triomphe et scandale à Berlin." *Danse et rythmes* 35 (1957): 14.

Vogt, Erich. "Tanz—Klassisch oder modern?" *Theater der Zeit* 1:2 (August 1946): 21–22.

Wallmann, Margarethe. "Mary Wigman und ihre Gruppe." *Tanzgemeinschaft* 2:2 (1930): 6–8.

Warren, Larry. *Anna Sokolow: The Rebellious Spirit*. Princeton: Princeton Book Company, 1991.

Wehle, Philippa. "Pina Bausch's Tanztheater—A Place of Difficult Encounter." *Women and Performance* 1:2 (Winter 1984): 25–36.

Weidt, Jean. *Der rote Tänzer*. Berlin: Henschelverlag, 1968.

Weidt, Jean, and Marion Reinisch. *Auf der grossen Strasse: Jean Weidts Erin-nerungen.* Berlin: Henschelverlag, 1984.

"Wer ist Albert Thalhoff?" *Völkischer Beobachter* 163 (17 July 1929).

"What Dancers Think about the German Dance." In two parts. *Dance Magazine* (May 1931): 14–15, 52; and (June 1931): 26, 57–58.

"What the Critics Say about Tanztheater." *Drama Review* 30:2 (Summer 1986): 80–84.

Wigman, Mary. "Composition in Pure Movement." *Modern Music* 8:2 (January/February 1931): 20–22.

——— *Deutsche Tanzkunst.* Dresden: Carl Reissner, 1935.

——— *Kompositionen.* Überlingen: Seebote, 1925.

——— "Das 'Land ohne Tanz.'" *Tanzgemeinschaft* 1:2 (April 1929): 12–13.

——— *The Language of Dance.* Translated by Walter Sorell. Middletown, Conn.: Wesleyan University Press, 1966.

——— "Der neue künstlerische Tanz und das Theater." *Tanzgemeinschaft* 1:1 (1929): 1–9.

——— "The New German Dance." In *The Modern Dance,* edited by Virginia Stewart and Merle Armitage, 47–63. New York: E. Weyhe, 1935.

——— "The Philosophy of Modern Dance." *Europa* 1:1 (1933). Reprinted in *Dance as a Theatre Art,* edited by Selma Jeanne Cohen, 149–53. New York: Harper and Row, 1974.

——— "Rudolf von Laban zum Geburtstag." *Schrifttanz* 2:4 (1929): 65–66.

——— "Rudolf von Labans Lehre vom Tanz." *Die neue Schaubühne* 3:5/6 (September 1921): 99–106.

——— *Die sieben Tänze des Lebens—Tanzdichtung.* Jena: Diederichs, 1921.

——— *Die Sprache des Tanzes.* Stuttgart: Ernst Battenberg, 1963.

——— "Der Tanz in seiner Beziehung zu den übrigen Künsten." *Hamburger Jahrbuch für Theater und Musik* (1947/1948): 160–73.

——— "Tanz und Gymnastik." *Der Tanz* 1:6 (April 1928): 6–7.

——— "Der Tänzer und das Theater." *Blätter des Hessischen Landestheater* 7 (1929/1930): 49–58.

——— "Tänzerische Wege und Ziele." *Die schöne Frau* 4:9 (1928/1929): 1–2.

——— "Tänzerisches Schaffen der Gegenwart." In *Tanz in dieser Zeit,* edited by Paul Stefan, 5–7. New York and Vienna: Universal Edition, 1926.

——— "Weibliche Tanzkunst." *Deutsches Musikjahrbuch* 4 (1926): 100–103.

——— "Wer kann tanzen, wer darf tanzen?" *Der Tanz* 5:11 (1932): 3–4.

——— "Wie ich zu Albert Talhoffs *Totenmal* stehe." *Der Tanz* 3:6 (1930): 3–4.

——— "Die Wigman-Schule." *Der Tanz* 13:8 (August 1940): 103–8.

Wille, Hansjürgen. *Harald Kreutzberg und Yvonne Georgi.* Leipzig: Erich Weibezahl, 1930.

Wirth, Nicholas. "Mary Wigman—Fascist." *New Theatre* 2:8 (August 1935): 5.

Wyatt, Euphemia Van Rensselaer. "Totenmal." *Catholic World* 130 (1930): 462–64.
Zivier, George. *Berlin und der Tanz*. Berlin: Haude und Spener, 1968.
——, ed. *Harmonie und Ekstase: Mary Wigman*. Berlin: Akademie der Künste, 1956.

CULTURE, POLITICS, AND THE ARTS

Akademie der Künste. *Theater im Exil, 1933–1945*. Berlin: Akademie der Künste, 1973.
Albisetti, James. *Schooling German Girls and Women*. Princeton: Princeton University Press, 1988.
Alter, Peter. *Nationalism*. London: Edward Arnold, 1989.
Anderson, Benedict. *Imagined Communities: Reflections on the Origin and Spread of Nationalism*. London: Verso, 1983.
Andritzky, Michael, and Thomas Rautenberg, eds. *"Wir sind nackt und nennen uns Du": Eine Geschichte der Freikörperkultur*. Giessen: Anabas, 1989.
Bablet, Denis. *Edward Gordon Craig*. Translated by Daphne Woodward. London: Heinemann, 1966.
Baldwin, Peter, ed. *Reworking the Past: Hitler, the Holocaust, and the Historians' Debate*. Boston: Beacon Press, 1990.
Ball, Hugo. *Flight out of Time: A Dada Diary*. New York: Viking Press, 1974.
Barron, Stephanie, et al. *"Degenerate Art": The Fate of the Avant-Garde in Nazi Germany*. Los Angeles: Los Angeles County Museum of Art, 1991.
Beacham, Richard, ed. *Adolphe Appia—Essays, Scenarios, and Designs*. Translated by Walther R. Volbach. Ann Arbor: UMI Research Press, 1989.
—— *Adolphe Appia: Theatre Artist*. Cambridge: Cambridge University Press, 1987.
Beckerman, Bernard. *Theatrical Presentation: Performer, Audience, and Act*. New York: Routledge, 1990.
Benjamin, Walter. *Understanding Brecht*. Translated by Anna Bostock. London: New Left Books, 1973.
Berghahn, V. R. *Modern Germany: Society, Economy, and Politics in the Twentieth Century*. Cambridge: Cambridge University Press, 1982.
Bergstrom, Janet, and Mary Ann Doane. "The Female Spectator: Contexts and Directions." *Camera Obscura* no. 20/21 (May/September 1989): 5–27.
Bleuel, Hans Peter. *Sex and Society in Nazi Germany*. Philadelphia and New York: J. B. Lippincott, 1973.
Bridenthal, Renate, Atina Grossmann, and Marion Kaplan, eds. *When Biology Became Destiny: Women in Weimar and Nazi Germany*. New York: Monthly Review Press, 1984.
Bronner, Stephen Eric, and Douglas Kellner, eds. *Passion and Rebellion, the Expressionist Heritage*. South Hadley, Mass.: J. F. Bergin, 1983.
Bürger, Peter. *Theory of the Avant-Garde*. Translated by Michael Shaw. Minneapolis: University of Minnesota Press, 1984.

Calandra, Denis. "Georg Kaiser's *From Morning to Midnight*: The Nature of Expressionist Performance." *Theatre Quarterly* no. 21 (1976): 45–54.

Carlson, Marvin. *The German Stage in the Nineteenth Century*. Metuchen, N.J.: Scarecrow Press, 1972.

Carter, Huntley. *The New Spirit in the European Theatre: 1914–1924*. New York: Doran, 1925.

Case, Sue-Ellen. *Feminism and Theatre*. New York: Methuen, 1988.

Clark, T. J. "Clement Greenberg's Theory of Art." *Critical Inquiry* 9 : 1 (September 1982): 139–56.

Cook, Susan. *Opera for a New Republic: The Zeitopern of Krenek, Weill, and Hindemith*. Ann Arbor: UMI Research Press, 1988.

Curjel, Hans. *Experiment Krolloper, 1927–1931*. Munich: Prestel, 1975.

Dahrendorf, Ralf. *Society and Democracy in Germany*. 1967. Reprint. Westport, Conn.: Greenwood Press, 1979.

Davies, Cecil. "The German Theatre as an Artistic and Social Institution: from the March Revolution to the Weimar Republic." In *Brecht in Perspective*, edited by Graham Bartram and Anthony Waine, 108–27. London and New York: Longman, 1982.

——— "Working Class Theatre in the Weimar Republic, 1919–1933." *Theatre Quarterly* 10 : 38 (1980): 68–96.

Davis, Tracy C. *Actresses as Working Women: Their Social Identity in Victorian Culture*. London and New York: Routledge, 1991.

——— "Questions for a Feminist Methodology in Theatre History." In *Interpreting the Theatrical Past: Essays in the Historiography of Performance*, edited by Thomas Postlewait and Bruce A. McConachie, 59–81. Iowa City: University of Iowa Press, 1989.

Deak, Istvan. *Weimar Germany's Left-Wing Intellectuals: A Political History of the Weltbühne and Its Circle*. Berkeley and Los Angeles: University of California Press, 1968.

Doane, Mary Ann. "Film and the Masquerade—Theorizing the Female Spectator." *Screen* 23 : 3/4 (September/October 1982): 74–88.

——— "Masquerade Reconsidered: Further Thoughts on the Female Spectator." *Discourse* 11 : 1 (1988/1989): 42–54.

Dolan, Jill. *The Feminist Spectator as Critic*. Ann Arbor: UMI Research Press, 1988.

Drew, David. "Musical Theatre in the Weimar Republic." *Proceedings of the Royal Musical Association* 88 (1961/1962): 89–108.

Drewniak, Boguslaw. *Das Theater im NS-Staat*. Düsseldorf: Droste, 1983.

Eichberg, Henning, et al. *Massenspiele: NS-Thingspiel, Arbeiterweihespiel und olympisches Zeremoniell*. Stuttgart–Bad Cannstatt: Fromann-Holzboog, 1977.

——— "The Nazi *Thingspiel*: Theater for the Masses in Fascism and Proletarian Culture." *New German Critique* no. 11 (1977): 133–50.

——— "'Schneller, höher, stärker': Der Umbruch in der Körperkultur um 1900 als Signal gesellschaftlichen Wandels." In *Medizin, Naturwissenschaft, Technik, und das Zweite Kaiserreich*, edited by Gunter Mann and Rolf Winau, 259–83. Göttingen: Vanderhoeck and Ruprecht, 1977.

Eisner, Lotte. *The Haunted Screen: Expressionism in the German Cinema and the Influence of Max Reinhardt*. Translated by Roger Greaves. Berkeley and Los Angeles: University of California Press, 1969.

Elam, Keir. *The Semiotics of Theatre and Drama*. London and New York: Methuen, 1980.

The Eleventh Olympic Games Berlin, 1936: Official Report. Berlin: William Limpert, 1937.

Evans, Geoffrey. "Towards a New Drama in Germany: A Survey of the Years 1933–1937." *German Life and Letters* 2 (1937/1938): 188–200.

Evans, Richard. *In Hitler's Shadow: West German Historians and the Attempt to Escape from the Nazi Past*. New York: Pantheon Books, 1989.

Flanner, Janet (Genêt). "Berlin Letter." In three parts. *New Yorker* (1 August 1936): 40–41; (15 August 1936): 35–37; and (22 August 1936): 52–55.

Fuegi, John. *Bertolt Brecht: Chaos, According to Plan*. Cambridge and New York: Cambridge University Press, 1987.

Gadberry, Glen. "The Thingspiel and Das Frankenberger Würfelspiel." *Drama Review* 24:1 (March 1980): 103–14.

Gay, Peter. *Weimar Culture*. New York: Harper and Row, 1968.

Goebbels, Joseph. *Die Tagebücher von Joseph Goebbels: Sämtliche Fragmente*. Munich: K. G. Saur, 1987.

Goldberg, RoseLee. *Performance: Live Art, 1909 to the Present*. New York: Harry N. Abrams, 1979.

Goldfarb, Alvin. "Theatrical Activities in Nazi Concentration Camps." *Performing Arts Journal* 1:2 (Fall 1976): 3–11.

Gordon, Mel. "Dada Berlin: A History of Performance, 1918–1920." *Drama Review* (1974): 114–33.

——— "German Expressionist Acting." *Drama Review* 19:3 (1975): 34–50.

——— "Lothar Schreyer and the Sturmbühne." *Drama Review* 24:1 (March 1980): 85–102.

———, ed. *Expressionist Texts*. New York: Performing Arts Journal Publications, 1987.

Graham, Cooper C. *Leni Riefenstahl and Olympia*. Metuchen, N.J.: Scarecrow Press, 1986.

Green, Harvey. *Fit for America*. New York: Pantheon, 1986.

Green, Martin. *Mountain of Truth*. Hanover, N.H.: University Press of New England, 1986.

Greenberg, Clement. *Art and Culture*. Boston: Beacon Press, 1961.

Gropius, Walter, ed. *The Theater of the Bauhaus*. Middletown, Conn.: Wesleyan University Press, 1961.

Haley, Bruce. *The Healthy Body and Victorian Culture*. Cambridge: Harvard University Press, 1978.

Hart-Davis, Duff. *Hitler's Games*. New York: Harper and Row, 1986.

Hermand, Jost, and Frank Trommler. *Die Kultur der Weimarer Republik*. Munich: Nymphenburger Verlagshandlung, 1978.

Hinz, Berthold. *Art in the Third Reich*. Translated by Robert and Rita Kimber. New York: Random House, 1979.

Hirschbach, Frank D., et al., eds. *Germany in the Twenties: The Artist as Social Critic.* Minneapolis: University of Minnesota, 1980.

Hoberman, John. *The Olympic Crisis.* New Rochelle, N.Y.: Caratzas, 1986.

Huelsenbeck, Richard. *Mit Witz, Licht, und Grütze: Aus den Spuren des Dadaismus.* Wiesbaden: Limes, 1957.

Huyssen, Andreas. *After the Great Divide: Modernism, Mass Culture, Postmodernism.* Bloomington: Indiana University Press, 1986.

Innes, C. D. *Edward Gordon Craig.* Cambridge: Cambridge University Press, 1983.

——— *Erwin Piscator's Political Theater.* Cambridge: Cambridge University Press, 1972.

Jameson, Fredric. *Aesthetics and Politics.* 1977. Reprint. London: Verso, 1980.

Jelavich, Peter. "Modernity, Civic Identity, and Metropolitan Entertainment: Vaudeville, Cabaret, and Revue in Berlin, 1900–1933." In *Berlin: Culture and Metropolis,* edited by Charles Haxthausen and Heidrun Suhr. Minneapolis: University of Minnesota Press, 1990.

——— *Munich and Theatrical Modernism.* Cambridge: Harvard University Press, 1985.

Jordan, James. "Audience Disruption in the Theatre of the Weimar Republic." *New Theatre Quarterly* 1:3 (1985): 283–91.

Kane, Martin. "Erwin Piscator's 1927 Production of *Hoppla, We're Alive.*" In *Performance and Politics in Popular Drama,* edited by D. Bradby, L. James, and B. Sharratt, 189–200. Cambridge and New York: Cambridge University Press, 1980.

Kaplan, E. Ann. "Is the Gaze Male?" In *Women and Film: Both Sides of the Camera,* 23–35. New York: Methuen, 1983.

Kern, Stephen. *Anatomy and Destiny: A Cultural History of the Human Body.* Indianapolis: Bobbs-Merrill, 1975.

——— *The Culture of Time and Space, 1880–1918.* Cambridge: Harvard University Press, 1983.

Koonz, Claudia. *Mothers in the Fatherland: Women, the Family, and Nazi Politics.* New York: St. Martin's Press, 1987.

Kowalke, Kim. *Kurt Weill in Europe.* Ann Arbor: UMI Research Press, 1979.

Kracauer, Siegfried. *From Caligari to Hitler.* Princeton: Princeton University Press, 1947.

——— "The Mass Ornament." *New German Critique* no. 5 (Spring 1975): 67–76.

Kühn, Volker. *Das Kabarett der frühen Jahre.* Berlin: Quadriga, 1984.

Laqueur, Walter. *Weimar: A Cultural History.* London: Weidenfeld and Nicolson, 1974.

"Leni Riefenstahl." Issue devoted to Leni Riefenstahl. *Film Culture* no. 56/57 (Spring 1973).

Ley-Piscator, Maria. *The Piscator Experiment: The Political Theatre.* New York: James Heinemann, 1967.

Liess, Andreas. *Carl Orff: Idee und Werk.* Zurich and Freiburg i.Br.: Atlantis, 1977.

Luhan, Mabel Dodge. *Movers and Shakers.* 1936. Reprint. Albuquerque: University of New Mexico Press, 1985.

Maier, Charles S. *The Unmasterable Past: History, Holocaust, and German National Identity.* Cambridge: Harvard University Press, 1988.

Mandell, Richard. *Nazi Olympics.* New York: Macmillan, 1971.

Maur, Karin von. *Oskar Schlemmer.* Munich: Prestel, 1979.

Meisel, Martin. *Realizations: Narrative, Pictorial, and Theatrical Arts in Nineteenth-Century England.* Princeton: Princeton University Press, 1983.

Melzer, Anabelle. *Latest Rage the Big Drum: Dada and Surrealist Performance.* Ann Arbor: UMI Research Press, 1983.

Mosse, George L. *The Crisis of German Ideology.* 1964. Reprint. New York: Schocken, 1981.

———— *Fallen Soldiers: Reshaping the Memory of the World Wars.* New York: Oxford University Press, 1990.

———— *Masses and Man: Nationalist and Fascist Perceptions of Reality.* New York: Howard Fertig, 1980.

———— "National Cemeteries and National Revival: The Cult of the Fallen Soldier in Germany." *Journal of Contemporary History* 14:1 (1979): 1–20.

———— *Nationalism and Sexuality.* New York: Howard Fertig, 1985.

———— *The Nationalization of the Masses.* New York: Howard Fertig, 1975.

———— *Nazi Culture: Intellectual, Cultural, and Social Life in the Third Reich.* New York: Grosset and Dunlap, 1968.

Müller, Henning. *Theater der Restauration: Westberliner Bühnen, Kultur und Politik im Kalten Krieg.* Berlin: Edition neue Wege, 1981.

Mulvey, Laura. "Visual Pleasure and Narrative Cinema." *Screen* 16:3 (Autumn 1975): 6–18.

Patterson, Michael. *The Revolution in German Theatre, 1900–1933.* Boston: Routledge and Kegan Paul, 1981.

Pavis, Patrice. *Languages of the Stage: Essays in the Semiology of Theatre.* New York: Performing Arts Journal Publications, 1982.

Petro, Patrice. *Joyless Streets: Women and Melodramatic Representation in Weimar Germany.* Princeton: Princeton University Press, 1989.

Piscator, Erwin. *The Political Theatre.* New York: Avon, 1963.

Raabe, Paul, ed. *The Era of German Expressionism.* Translated by J. M. Ritchie. London: Calder and Boyars, 1974.

Rentschler, Eric. "Fatal Attractions: Leni Riefenstahl's *The Blue Light.*" *October* 48 (Spring 1989): 47–68.

Roach, Joseph R. "Theatre History and the Ideology of the Aesthetic." *Theatre Journal* 41:2 (May 1989): 155–68.

Rorrison, Hugh. "Piscator's Production of *Hoppla, wir leben!*" *Theatre Quarterly* 10:37 (1980): 30–41.

Rouse, John. *Brecht and the West German Theatre.* Ann Arbor: UMI Research Press, 1989.

Rückhaberle, Dieter, ed. *Theater in der Weimarer Republik.* 2 vols. Berlin:

Kunstamt Kreuzberg und Institut für Theaterwissenschaft der Universität Köln, 1977.

Rühle, Günther. *Theater für die Republik, 1917–1933: Im Spiegel der Kritik.* Frankfurt: S. Fischer, 1967.

———— *Theater in unserer Zeit.* Frankfurt: Suhrkamp, 1976.

———— *Zeit und Theater: Vom Kaiserreich zur Republik.* 3 vols. Berlin: Propyläen, 1973.

Samuel, Richard, and R. Hinton Thomas. *Expressionism in German Life, Literature, and the Theatre (1910–1924).* Philadelphia: Albert Saifer, 1971.

Sarris, Andrew. "Fascinating Fascism Meets Leering Leftism." In *Politics and Cinema,* 107–15. New York: Columbia University Press, 1978.

Scheffauer, Herman George. *The New Vision in the German Arts.* London: Benn; New York: B. W. Heubsch, 1924.

Schmidt, Hugo Wolfram. *Carl Orff: Sein Leben und sein Werk in Wort, Bild, und Noten.* Cologne: Wienand, 1971.

Schrader, Bärbel, and Jürgen Schebera. *The "Golden" Twenties: Art and Literature in the Weimar Republic.* New York and London: Yale University Press, 1990

Segel, Harold. *Turn-of-the-Century Cabaret.* New York: Columbia University Press, 1987.

Smith, Susan Valeria Harris. *Masks in Modern Drama.* Berkeley and Los Angeles: University of California Press, 1984.

Sontag, Susan. "Fascinating Fascism." *New York Review of Books* (6 February 1975), 23–30.

Stachura, Peter D. *The German Youth Movement, 1900–1945: An Interpretive and Documentary History.* New York: St. Martin's Press, 1981.

Steinberg, Michael. *The Meaning of the Salzburg Festival: Austria as Theater and Ideology, 1890–1938.* Ithaca: Cornell University Press, 1990.

Stern, Fritz. *The Failure of Illiberalism: Essays on the Political Culture of Modern Germany.* New York: Knopf, 1971.

Styan, J. L. *Max Reinhardt.* Cambridge and New York: Cambridge University Press, 1982.

Wardetzky, Jutta. *Theaterpolitik im faschistischen Deutschland.* Berlin: Henschelverlag, 1983.

Welch, David. *Propaganda and the German Cinema: 1933–1945.* Oxford: Oxford University Press, 1983.

Willett, John. *Art and Politics in the Weimar Period.* New York: Pantheon, 1978.

———— *Brecht on Theatre.* New York: Hill and Wang, 1964.

———— *The Theatre of the Weimar Republic.* New York: Holmes and Meier, 1988.

Williams, Raymond. *The Politics of Modernism.* London: Verso, 1989.

———— *The Sociology of Culture.* New York: Schocken Books, 1982.

Williams, Simon. "The Director in the German Theater: Harmony, Spectacle, and Ensemble." *New German Critique* 29 (1983): 107–31.

Wingler, Hans M. *The Bauhaus: Weimar, Dessau, Berlin, Chicago.* Translated by Wolfgang Jabs and Basil Gilbert. Cambridge: MIT Press, 1969.

Wolff, Janet. "Reinstating Corporeality: Feminism and Body Politics." In *Feminine Sentences: Essays on Women and Culture,* 120–41. Berkeley and Los Angeles: University of California Press, 1990.

Wulf, Joseph. *Theater und Film im Dritten Reich.* Gütersloh: Sigbert Mohn, 1964.

Zortman, Bruce Harold. *Hitler's Theatre.* El Paso: Firestein Books, 1984.

Index

Absolute dance: Fritz Böhme on, 20, 68; by Dadaist dancers, 68–69; Rudolf von Delius on, 15–16, 18; *Idolatry* as, 67–68; Lincoln Kirstein on, 23; John Martin on, 21; Hedwig Müller on, 26–27. *See also Gestalt im Raum*

Adenauer, Konrad, 247

Affectos Humanos (Hoyer and Linke), 13, 43, 228, 230–31

Alf, Fé, 93, 273, 316n.3

Allan, Maud, 34, 99

Alt, Marlis, 242

American critics, 257–65, 283. *See also* Kirstein, Lincoln; Martin, John

American Dance Festival, 270. *See also* Bennington Festival

American modern dance: *Ausdruckstanz* and, 240, 261–62, 283–84; Bennington consensus on, 9–10, 256; constructed Americanness of, xiv–xv, 255–57, 261–63, 264, 281–82; Hanya Holm's role in, 261–62, 263, 264, 281; Jill Johnston on, 23–24; Lincoln Kirstein on, 22–23; leftist and humanist wings of, 9–10, 256, 263, 265–66, 267, 269–71, 275–78; Don McDonagh on, 282; John Martin on, 21–22, 260, 261–64, 284; self-reflexivity of, 25; Marcia Siegel on, 255; Mary Wigman's role in, 21–22, 23, 24, 255–56, 260, 263, 264. *See also Ausdruckstanz;* Modern dance

Anderson, Benedict, 1, 11, 28

Anthony, Mary, 282

Appia, Adolphe, 73, 74–75, 147

Archetypes. *See* Representational strategies

Arp, Hans, 71

Association of German Girls (Bund deutscher Mädel), 172

Ausdruckstanz (dance of expression): and American dance, 240, 261–62, 283–84; ballet competing with, 8, 21, 22–23, 134, 221, 222, 228–29, 240–

41, 271; Fritz Böhme's genealogy of, 20–21; fascist alliance with, xiv, 5–6, 172–73, 248–49; Horst Koegler on, 238–39, 240–41, 246–47; as modernist and avant-garde, 7–8; patronage of, 8, 132–33, 134–35, 221, 250–51; renamed German Dance, 203; and *Tanztheater*, 9, 25–26, 221–22, 244–47, 249–50, 315n.54; Mary Wigman on, 192, 193, 241. *See also Deutscher Tanz; Tanztheater*

Autobiographical persona. *See* Representational strategies

Avant-garde: and modernism, 7–8

Ave Maria (Duncan), 35, 37, 41, 293nn.51,52

Bach, Rudolf, 93, 94, 129, 136

Balanchine, George, 19, 23, 24–25, 265

Ball, Hugo, 57, 68, 69, 71

Ballet: as American dance model, 255–56, 265; Cultural Ministry mandating, 175, 193, 251, 308n.17; Greenbergian modernism of, 24–25; male gaze of, 1, 27–28, 31–32, 33, 292n.45; modern dance competing with, 8, 21, 22–23, 134, 221, 222, 228–29, 240–41, 271; parody of, 81, 118; *Tanztheater* proponents on, 247–48, 249

Ballets Russes, 22, 40

Barlach, Ernst, 5

Barron, Stephanie, xiv

Bassow, Margrit, 204, 205

Bathtubbing (Im Bade wannen, Linke), 254

Bausch, Pina, 25–26, 241, 242–43, 244–45, 246, 250

Beacham, Richard, 75, 297n.63

Beckett, Samuel, 235

Benkert, Hanns, 213

Bennington choreographers, 9–10, 256, 263, 265–66, 269–71, 275–78. *See also* American modern dance

Compositor: G & S Typesetters, Inc.
Text: 10/13 Baskerville
Display: Baskerville
Printer: Malloy Lithographing, Inc.
Binder: John H. Dekker & Sons